D0764667

A SEASON OF YOUTH

ALSO BY MICHAEL KAMMEN

COLONIAL NEW YORK: *A History* (1975)

PEOPLE OF PARADOX: *An Inquiry Concerning the Origins of American Civilization* (1972)

EMPIRE AND INTEREST: *The American Colonies and the Politics of Mercantilism* (1970)

DEPUTYES & LIBERTYES: *The Origins of Representative Government in Colonial America* (1969)

A ROPE OF SAND: *The Colonial Agents, British Politics, and the American Revolution* (1968)

(EDITOR)

"WHAT IS THE GOOD OF HISTORY?" *Selected Letters of Carl L. Becker, 1900–1945* (1973)

THE HISTORY OF THE PROVINCE OF NEW-YORK, *by William Smith, Jr.* (1972)

THE CONTRAPUNTAL CIVILIZATION: *Essays Toward a New Understanding of the American Experience* (1971)

POLITICS AND SOCIETY IN COLONIAL AMERICA: *Democracy or Deference?* (1967)

(CO-AUTHOR)

SOCIETY, FREEDOM, AND CONSCIENCE: *The American Revolution in Virginia, Massachusetts, and New York* (1976)

(CO-EDITOR)

THE GLORIOUS REVOLUTION IN AMERICA: *Documents on the Colonial Crisis of 1689* (1964)

A SEASON OF YOUTH

The American Revolution and the Historical Imagination

MICHAEL KAMMEN

OXFORD UNIVERSITY PRESS
New York

First published by Alfred A. Knopf, Inc., 1978
First issued as an Oxford University Press paperback, 1980,
by arrangement with Alfred A. Knopf, Inc.

Grateful acknowledgment is made to the following for permission to reprint previously published material:
Farrar, Straus & Giroux, Inc. and Faber and Faber Ltd:
Excerpt from "George III" from *Day by Day* by Robert Lowell.
Copyright © 1975, 1976, 1977 by Robert Lowell.
Reprinted by permission of Farrar, Straus & Giroux, Inc.
Harcourt, Brace, Jovanovich, Inc: Excerpt from *After Strange Gods*
by T. S. Eliot. Reprinted by permission of the publishers.
William Morrow & Company, Inc:
Excerpt from *Felix Frankfurter Reminisces,* edited by Harlan B. Phillips.
Copyright ©1960 by Harlan B. Phillips.
Random House, Inc: Excerpt from *Burr* by Gore Vidal.
Copyright © 1973 by Gore Vidal.

Library of Congress Cataloging in Publication Data
Kammen, Michael G. A season of youth.
Includes bibliographical references and index.
1. United States—History—Revolution—1775-1783—Influence.
2. United States—History—Revolution, 1775-1783—Art and the war.
3. United States—History—Revolution, 1775-1783—Literature and the war.
I. Title
E209.K35 1978 973.3 78-54918 ISBN 0-19-502707-8 pbk.

Printed in the United States of America

For my good friends in

THE JUNTO REDIVIVUS

Who are never altogether satisfied with any book

and are unlikely to start with this one

The whole junto will be soon known in America

for a set of wicked unprincipled debauched wretches,

from the old Deceiver down to the young Cockatrice.

—ABIGAIL ADAMS *to* JOHN ADAMS,

October 21, 1781

For my good friends in

THE [illegible]

Who are never altogether satisfied with any book

and are unlikely to start with this one

The whole game will be soon known in America [illegible]

[illegible]

[illegible]

—ABIGAIL ADAMS to JOHN ADAMS,

October 2[illegible], 178[illegible]

CONTENTS

ILLUSTRATIONS

Following page 102

PREFACE

THE TITLE I might have liked for this book was preempted forty years ago by Henry Beston, when he called one of his volumes *American Memory, Being a Mirror of the Stirring and Picturesque Past of Americans and the American Nation.* But even if Mr. Beston hadn't beaten me to the mark, and thereby caused me to settle for a more prosaic title, I would still want to say a few prefatory words about the orientation of this project. I shall not say very much, however, because the first section of Chapter One is meant to serve as an ample introduction to the book as a whole.

On July 4, 5, and 6, 1976, *The New York Times* ran a series of general interest articles on such topics as "The Spirit of '76 in the Nation" and "The Meaning of the American Revolution." The former essay found a highly ambivalent mixture of "self-doubt, hope and pride" in the populace as a whole; the latter one concluded that historians today do not agree on what the Revolution was all about. Although this lack of consensus among scholars concerns me personally, it is *not* the subject of my book; for the views of contemporary, professional historians are really not a very reliable measure of general social attitudes toward the nation's past.

We can never fully know the intricacies through which a society weaves a knowledge of its origins and development; but we are likely to learn more from the gossip of popular culture than from the gospel of academe. Here is an example of the former from Ann Landers's column, dated June 21, 1976.

> Dear Ann Landers: I am just as enthusiastic about the Bicentennial as the next person, but the lunatics who live across the street have made our neighborhood the laughing stock of the town. People come from miles around just to look.
>
> They painted their house red, white and blue. Five flagpoles in the front yard fly Old Glory from dawn till dusk. Last week they put up three huge papier mache figures: Betsy Ross sewing a flag; George Washington crossing the Delaware, and John Hancock signing the Declaration of Independence.
>
> There are two enormous neon lights on the front porch that flash off

and on all night long. The message is "Happy Birthday, U.S.A." We can't get to sleep because the lights shine in our bedroom window.

The worst is the music. A public-address system blasts the "Battle Hymn of the Republic," the National Anthem and "God Bless America" from 6:00 p.m. until midnight.

Yesterday the nut who owns the house was out mowing the grass in an Uncle Sam costume—fake beard, hat and all.

The traffic jam in front of our place was unbelievable. Our lawn is a mess. What can we do about this? —We Love America, Too, But . . .

Dear Love: You can notify the police. Mr. Superpatriot is infringing on your inalienable right to the pursuit of happiness. He is also disturbing the peace and creating a public nuisance. Get going.

One such incident is merely amusing; but an entire museum full of them can be immensely revealing if the contents are properly sorted and examined.

When Captain Cook made his incredible Pacific explorations in the later eighteenth century, he faithfully recorded what he called "Remarkable Occurences." By contrast, I have attempted to record, arrange, and explain a great variety of occurrences which, taken singly, are unremarkable. Considered as a mosaic, however, they turn out to reveal profoundly important patterns.

We want to reconstruct such mosaics because, as the social theorist Edward Shils has observed, society's impulses "to have a valued past, to be continuous with some aspect or strand of the past, to justify oneself by reference to a real or alleged connection with some vital point in the past, are all problematic. They call for analysis in their own right and as parts of the system of mechanisms of persistence through which the past lives into the present, or is even sometimes partially resurrected into the present."

Shils would have us analyze what he calls "the properties of tradition," as well as "modes and mechanisms of the traditional reproduction of beliefs."[1] I have tried to do exactly that with respect to the role of the American Revolution in national tradition. The effort has become far more complex, convoluted, and sprawling than I ever imagined it might be; and my book, in consequence, is a good deal longer than the one I conceived four years ago. The cost of such expansion has been to omit from this book a component I envisioned all along as an integral part: namely, a comparative discussion of the American Revolution in our national tradition with the role of other such revolutions and wars in their respective cultures.[2] I have the French and Russian revolutions in mind particularly, as well as the two world wars. But having done some of the digging for that component, my innocence is lost and my illusions are shattered. I now realize that such comparative analysis properly requires a book in itself, not merely a chapter in this one. Therefore, I have chosen to save the comparative dimension for a separate study, and have accordingly restrained some of the generalizations I intended to make here about the *peculiar* qualities of tradition in the United States.

A related point: I should like to think that this book might make some contribution to our sense of phasing in American culture. Periodization in the history of popular thought has been too dependent upon the more familiar chronology of political history. The several strands are intertwined, to be sure; but cultural history has impulses and rhythms of its own.[3] One of the cultural historian's major tasks should be to locate and understand them. I therefore hope that I have helped to clarify, rather than blur, some of those significant rhythms.

Why? To what ultimate end? Well, from the perspective of society at large, it is instructive simply to recall the aphorism that we live forward, but we understand backward. And from the author's personal perspective, there is much to reflect upon in remarks once made by the late Richard Hofstadter:

> As soon as the historian's span of attention becomes sufficiently enlarged to take in more than a tiny segment of the historic past, he confronts the precariousness of human effort, sees the passing not only of great states and powerful institutions but of militant faiths and, most pertinent for him, of the very historical perspectives that were identified with them. At this point he is persuaded to accept the imaginative as well as the cognitive side of his own work, to think of history as being not only the analysis but the expression of human experience . . . and he realizes more fully than before how much history is indeed akin to literature.[4]

One last issue: this book has an unusual and somewhat irregular topography. Yet I would like to believe—and in turn be able to persuade you—that its vagaries are rational; or at least, can be rationalized. Essentially, the various chapters have different textures and different sorts of thrust because they serve different purposes. So a few words here may be helpful by way of guidance. We are going to proceed from a chapter that is conceptual to one that seeks to provide a chronological framework, then to three that are expository by genre, and finally to two at the end that are the most explanatory and interpretive.

The first chapter attempts to pose a problem: a problem for American culture as well as in our historical knowledge. That problem, which has to do with the quirky role of tradition in national life, is intellectually contextual to all of the particulars that follow. Chapter Two then indicates the overall rhythms of Revolutionary perception between 1776 and the present. It suggests that the American Revolution has undergone revisions for many reasons, but mainly because the society itself has become less favorably disposed toward revolutions of any kind. The next three chapters are organized by genre—iconography, poetry and drama, historical novels—because there are interesting qualities distinctive to each genre, and also because there are discrete lessons to be learned from each one. Nevertheless, the conceptual framework of Chapter One and the conservative drift established in Chapter Two remain very much operative in the next three expository chapters.

These three, in turn, become structural pediments on which the arguments of Chapters Six and Seven are built. The three genre chapters foreshadow major lines of interpretation in the final two—particularly the "season of youth" obsession, which is examined in Chapter Six, and the compulsive quest for character, which is treated in Chapter Seven. The busy reader in a huge hurry who wants to know in a nutshell what "this book is about" might proceed directly to Chapter Six. It is the book's main "thesis" chapter, to be sure, though it will very likely seem less meaningful and persuasive without the preparatory sections that have been designed to precede it. Although Six builds especially upon the explication of historical fiction in Chapter Five, it offers an interpretation that seems to me richly symptomatic of all the genres—and therefore of American culture generally.

The final chapter touches upon dissenting visions of the Revolution, ones that are implicitly critical of those mainstream views described earlier. It also looks at very recent imaginative responses, of 1974–7; and it seeks to integrate some themes that previously have been pursued individually. Tying loose ends together would be an inelegant (but honest) way to put it. As I said, it's an irregular topography, but not without purpose. Now it is up to you (and the Junto) to decide whether it works.

HARVESTING HISTORICAL MATERIALS for this book has been a fascinating experience. Like any cultivator working in fertile but unfamiliar fields, however, I have depended heavily upon others and have accumulated a great many debts in the process. Although I cannot adequately repay them, it is very satisfying at least to acknowledge them publicly.

The book was written during 1976–7 at the Center for Advanced Study in the Behavioral Sciences, in Stanford, California—an idyllic institution once described by a perceptive priest as "a retreat house for the intellect." Through the Center I received support from the National Endowment for the Humanities, for which I am most appreciative. I am deeply grateful, also, for the assistance I received from four very special staff members at the Center: Margaret Amara and Christine Hoth, the lovely librarians; Heather Maclean, my marvelous typist; and Joan Warmbrunn, who helped with typing, tedious collating, and proofreading. Their services were indispensable.

Various people have done many things to facilitate my research as work on the book progressed. Mrs. Antoinette M. Wilkinson of Ithaca, New York, allowed me to use her personal collection of American popular fiction and children's literature. In several instances she owned copies of nineteenth-century dime novels that were unavailable anywhere else. Henry F. Bedford, Librarian at the Phillips Exeter Academy, provided me with access to a stunning cache of Kenneth Roberts's letters. Mr. and Mrs. Linwood M. Erskine, Jr., of Worcester, Massachusetts, talked with me at great length about their aunt, Esther Forbes, and showed me the reflective third-story room where she wrote *Johnny Tremain*. Paul Z. DuBois permitted me to read his fascinating biography of Paul Leicester Ford in galley proof. And my Cornell colleague, Richard Polenberg, put me onto several good leads—among them the historical art of Larry Rivers and imagery from the Revolution used by Americans who were involved as partisans in the Spanish Civil War.

During the past four years, while working on this project, I have had abundant opportunities to float *ballons d'essai*; and I benefited immensely from the thoughtful responses I received on those occasions. In January 1976, I was privileged to give the

Commonwealth Fund Lecture and Colloquium in American History at University College, the University of London. It was an exhilarating experience and I am much obliged to my host, Professor Maldwyn A. Jones; to my designated critic, Professor Marcus Cunliffe; and to Professor Ian R. Christie, who presided. On that occasion I presented portions of Chapters Five and Six, which I also offered in a somewhat different form during October 1975, as Bicentennial lecturer at the University of Utah (Salt Lake City), Utah State University (Logan), and Weber State College (Ogden). A very compressed version of those lectures has been published as an essay in *Legacies of the American Revolution* (Utah State University Press, 1978), edited by Larry R. Gerlach.

I delivered sections of Chapter Two at Pennsylvania State University (York) in May 1976, and at a conference sponsored by the Institute of American History at Stanford in July 1976. A version of those presentations has been published as an essay in *Tradition, Conflict, and Modernization: Perspectives on the American Revolution* (Academic Press, 1977), edited by Richard M. Brown and Don E. Fehrenbacher.

I offered a preliminary exploration of Chapter Three in October 1976 to the annual meeting of The American Antiquarian Society; and also at the University of California (Berkeley), Indiana University, and Tennessee State University (Nashville). That lecture has since been published in the *Proceedings of The American Antiquarian Society*, volume 86, part 2 (April 1977), 237–72. I am particularly indebted to Marcus A. McCorison, John B. Hench, Winthrop D. Jordan, Paul R. Lucas, and Robert L. Middlekauff for their courtesy on those occasions.

I was also privileged to address the 1974 annual meeting in Cooperstown of the New York State Historical Association; to give the first Carl L. Becker Memorial Lecture at the University of Northern Iowa in 1975; to present the Lyceum Lecture for 1976 at the Essex Institute in Salem, Massachusetts; and to address the Spring 1976 Honors Convocation at Lawrence University in Appleton, Wisconsin. On each of those occasions I explored materials pertaining to this book, as well as in public lectures presented to the American Civilization programs at Harvard, Notre Dame, the University of California (Santa Cruz), and Kalamazoo College in Michigan.

Still other sections of the book were tempered in lectures given at the universities of Virginia and Washington, and at Wisconsin, Tennessee, Iowa State and Colgate universities, as well as at ten colleges: Williams, Dickinson, Colby, Hiram, Hartwick, Thomas More, Mansfield State, Baruch, California State College (Sonoma), and the Grand Valley State Colleges in Allendale, Michigan. I very much appreciate the gracious hospitality that I received at all of these institutions.

Once again I have imposed upon good friends to give me their critical suggestions for improving the book. All of it was read in manuscript by Professors Bernard Bailyn, John Dizikes, Douglas S. Greenberg, John Higham, and Joseph F. Kett; and portions of it by August Meier and Laurence R. Veysey. Given the rather eclectic nature of my materials, it is no mere convention for me to absolve them of any responsibility for the flaws that remain.

Although Alfred A. Knopf is now retired from the publishing house that proudly carries his colophon, he is still for me a personal source of encouragement, a mellow curmudgeon of sound judgment, and (after fifteen years) an abiding friend. I cannot imagine when American publishing will know his like again. And once more, Jane Garrett and Carol Kammen have served invaluably as midwives: Carol to the gestation of a more coherent manuscript, Jane to the genesis and subsequent birth of this book. I can only hope that it will give neither one occasion to cite those lines from *Richard III*: "A grievous burden was thy birth to me; Tetchy and wayward was thy infancy."

MICHAEL KAMMEN

The Andrew D. White House
Cornell University
September 1977

It is not of advantage to us to indulge a sentimental attitude towards the past. For one thing, in even the very best living tradition there is always a mixture of good and bad, and much that deserves criticism. . . . What we can do is to use our minds, remembering that a tradition without intelligence is not worth having, to discover what is the best life for us not as a political abstraction, but as a particular people in a particular place; what in the past is worth preserving and what should be rejected; and what conditions within our power to bring about, would foster the society we desire.

—T. S. ELIOT, *After Strange Gods* (1933)

I must say I agree very much, about tradition and the past, with a remark by Chesterton, when he says, "Tradition means giving votes to that obscurest of classes, our ancestors. It is the democracy of the dead. Tradition refuses to surrender to the arrogant oligarchy of those who merely happen to be walking around."

—W. H. AUDEN, *The New York Times* (1971)

A SEASON OF YOUTH

CHAPTER ONE

REVOLUTION AND TRADITION IN AMERICAN CULTURE

"There is no past for us"

ONE OF THE MOST persistent problems throughout the history of American culture also happens to be one of the most neglected, and consequently, least understood. I call it the problem of tradition; and I shall devote a hefty portion of this first chapter to defining what I mean by "the problem of tradition." It really is not a very obscure matter at all, however, certainly not for anyone who has read the comments made by visitors to the United States who came from more traditional, or tradition-oriented, societies. Remarking upon the social and intellectual diversity of Americans, Alexis de Tocqueville pointed out that "there are no traditions, or common habits, to forge links between their minds."[1] So when I speak about the problem of tradition, I simply have in view the comparative lack of shared historical interest in the United States, or the weakness with which *national* tradition—as opposed to particular ethnic, or religious, or regional traditions—has been felt, perceived, and perpetuated.

Our heterogeneity was only one among a whole constellation of root causes that Tocqueville had in mind. Entrepreneurial ambition was another. "Those Americans who go out far away from the Atlantic Ocean," he wrote,

> plunging into the West, are adventurers impatient of any sort of yoke, greedy for wealth, and often outcasts from the states in which they were born. They arrive in the depths of the wilderness without knowing one

another. *There is nothing of tradition, family feeling, or example to restrain them.* Laws have little sway over them, and mores still less.[2]

Elsewhere in the book he pinpointed yet another reason: constant, unpredictable social mobility. "Among democratic peoples," he declared, "new families continually rise from nothing while others fall, and nobody's position is quite stable. *The woof of time is ever being broken and the track of past generations lost.* Those who have gone before are easily forgotten, and no one gives a thought to those who will follow."[3]

Still another cause in Tocqueville's constellation he derived from our chronological immaturity, and from the unusual capacity to record our history as it was actually being made—thereby helping to strip it of legendary qualities.

The taste for analysis comes to nations only when they are growing old, and when at last they do turn their thoughts to their cradle, the mists of time have closed round it, ignorance and pride have woven fables round it, and behind all that the truth is hidden. America is the only country in which we can watch the natural quiet growth of society and where it is possible to be exact about the influence of the point of departure on the future of a state.[4]

Many others, among Tocqueville's contemporaries as well as those who came later, reiterated these refrains. Friedrich List came from Württemberg in 1825, stayed for five years, and then asserted that "anything new is quickly introduced here, and all the latest inventions. There is no clinging to old ways, the moment an American hears the word 'invention' he pricks up his ears."[5] Michel Chevalier, who visited the United States from France in 1833, 1834, and 1835, felt that the past had never taken deep root here; and Richard Cobden, the English economist and politician who toured the country in 1835 (and once again in 1859), regarded the Americans as "a novelty-loving people."[6] A generation later, when James Bryce came to write his classic work on *The American Commonwealth* (1888), he remained just as impressed as his predecessors had been by "the monotony which comes from the absence of historical associations."

Sophisticated tourists were not alone, however, in commenting upon the relative absence or neglect of tradition here. Some Americans added their voices to the alien chorus as well. "Our attention is so completely absorbed by the present and future that very little of it remains to be bestowed upon the past," wrote one native essayist in 1840; "such grand though shadowy anticipations are forever vaguely present before our minds, that the things of the past have but little interest or value for us." Appraising "The Modern American Mood" more than half a century later, William Dean Howells put it most succinctly: "there is no past for us; there is only a future."[7]

The causes and consequences for American culture of such a persistent, prevalent outlook are immensely important, yet strangely neglected by historians. Let us begin, therefore, with causes. There is, first of all, that influential Jeffersonian attitude, most eloquently expressed in a letter written to James Madison in 1789, "that the earth belongs in usufruct to the living: that the dead have neither powers nor rights over it. . . . The earth belongs always to the living generation." I find constant echoes of that statement all through the nineteenth century: made by delegates to state constitutional conventions, by national politicians in the heat of public crises, and by social critics in their discussions of the need for reform.[8] Their rationale, by and large, was that new situations require fresh solutions. And in their view, the comparatively young United States seemed to spawn only situations without precedent. As Abraham Lincoln put it on December 1, 1862, "The dogmas of the quiet past are inadequate to the stormy present. . . . As our case is new, so we must think anew, and act anew. We must disenthrall ourselves, and then we shall save our country."[9]

Parallel to this problem-solving present-mindedness there was a network of attitudes attached to that elusive American ideology (or pattern of belief and values) known as liberalism; for liberalism, as one scholar has expressed it, "insisted on the independence of men, each from the other, and from cultural, traditional, and communal attachments."[10] As an attitudinal consequence of the Revolution, Americans overwhelmingly believed that they had been liberated from the past: alike from the incubus of Old World history and from their own colonial heritage of nonage and oppression. What seemed most important to our citizens in the half century after 1790 was "improvement" (to use their word), ostensibly in order to be useful to society; but in reality, I believe, on account of personal ambition.[11]

More altruistic Americans had a philosophic rationale of their own for repudiating the burden of the past. As Ralph Waldo Emerson wrote to his aunt in 1826, when the nation commemorated its fiftieth anniversary of Independence, "it is wrong to regard ourselves so much in a *historical* light as we do, putting Time between God and us." This would become one of Emerson's most characteristic themes over the next few decades. Among his best known essays is "Nature," which he wrote in 1836. It opens with these resounding sentences, which thousands upon thousands of Americans read with nods of approval ever after:

> Our age is retrospective. It builds the sepulchres of the fathers. It writes biographies, histories, and criticism. The foregoing generations beheld God and nature face to face; we, through their eyes. Why should not we also enjoy an original relation to the universe? Why should not we have a poetry and philosophy of insight and not of tradition, and a religion by revelation to us, and not the history of theirs?[12]

What Emerson went on to argue in that influential essay subsequently became a creed, if not a dogma, to more than a generation of his countrymen, namely, that Nature must be our foremost teacher, and personal experience our most reliable historian. Nature rendered tradition irrelevant. Consequently, in looking so single-mindedly to the future, Americans tended to agree with a contributor to the *United States Magazine and Democratic Review* who declared in 1839 that "we are entering on its untrodden space, with the truths of God in our minds, beneficent objects in our hearts, and with a clear conscience unsullied by the past."[13]

A third source of non-traditionalism had to do with our being a nation of immigrants, if I may borrow Franklin Delano Roosevelt's phrase. The members of this pluralistic society have not all experienced the same historical forces. Their ancestors came at various moments in time: some on the *Mayflower*, others prior to 1776, more still in the two generations after 1800, vastly more in the decades 1880–1914, and still others since then. Anthropologists, such as Margaret Mead and Geoffrey Gorer, have attempted to explain the American character in terms of our immigrants' *breaking* with tradition. Newcomers could not entirely forget the past upon arrival; and those who became candidates for citizenship had to learn a little something about our political system and its origins. Yet most of the millions of immigrants regarded the United States as a land of freedom, progress, and opportunity. Its destiny, therefore, and theirs, had everything to do with the future, and little (apparently) to do with the past.[14]

My fourth and perhaps most important explanation for the weakness of tradition in the United States was tersely put by James Fenimore Cooper in his *Home as Found* (1838): "We are a nation of change." Throughout the nineteenth century, most Americans prized change above stability. Tocqueville remarked upon that explicitly, and so have students of our culture ever since. "It is this constant change," David Potter observed in 1954, "paced by our economic richness, which . . . has caused each generation to reject its predecessor and to expect its successor to reject it."[15] Twenty years later, even as the United States was swept by a mood of nostalgia, and prepared for its two hundredth birthday party, Daniel J. Boorstin phrased his critique in harsher language. "American civilization," he contended, "seems to thrive not merely on the planned obsolescence of last year's products and services, but on the planned obsolescence of the whole past."[16]

These are simply some of the most fundamental reasons, then, why the sense of tradition has been rather weak in American culture: the Jeffersonian affirmation that the earth belongs to the living generation; the liberal, or "liberated" attitude after the Revolution that the American people, in particular, had been released from the burden of the past; the idealistic feeling articulated by Emerson that the individual ought to experience everything afresh, rather than vicariously through the senses of his (or her) predecessors; the fact of our being a nation of newcomers who arrived at various times for diverse reasons, therefore lacking a sense of *shared* historical experience; and finally, our expectation of, and desire for, change.

Yet we are not, needless to say, a nation entirely devoid of traditions. Indeed, the central purpose of this book is to delineate what I take to be the core, or axis, of our collective notions of nationality.[17] But in a society where inadvertent flux and technological change have been the norm, even our most essential traditions have been subject to some startling shifts, as I shall attempt to demonstrate. There is nothing inherently wrong or strange in that phenomenon. It does mean, however, that the nature of tradition as it has developed in the United States does not fit very well with the generic descriptions or definitions of tradition provided in recent years by such astute social theorists as Edward Shils, Clifford Geertz, or S. N. Eisenstadt. Shils, for example, asserts that "traditions are beliefs with a particular social structure; they are a consensus through time." Subsequently he states that

> Much of the reception of beliefs inherited from the past is to be attributed simply to the massive fact of their presence, to their widespread acceptance by other persons to an extent which hampers the imaginative generation of plausible alternative beliefs. In any given particular situation in which long recurrent beliefs are widely accepted, this kind of reception, which we shall call "consensual reception," is probably a major factor in the acceptance of beliefs and norms which have been observed in previous generations and which are recommended traditionally by the elders to their juniors. In other words, this kind of reception reinforces reception on the basis of "pastness."[18]

Shils recognizes that national traditions are neither inflexible nor immutable, and that they may sometimes "yield when their 'unfittingness' and the ineffectiveness of their recommending authorities become evident." Nevertheless, he concludes that the most fundamental traditions, "even though they undergo a radical change during a crisis period, settle back into an approximation to their previous pattern."[19]

Generalizations such as these do not apply very well to the American historical pattern, and for a variety of reasons, as we shall see in subsequent chapters. The most basic reason is that our traditions and our perceptions of them have, in fact, changed significantly over time. The role of the American Revolution in American tradition, for instance, has evolved and altered markedly since 1776.

A second reason is that in some respects tradition became a component of American culture instantly, yet artificially and rather superficially in the years after 1785 (witness the efforts of Noah Webster, Parson Weems, and David Ramsay), whereas in other key respects *enduring* traditions evolved here ever so slowly and hesitantly.

A third reason is that unlike the ancient Greeks, let us say, we have never systematically developed the art of memory as a means of imparting tradition, nor do we formally train individuals, like the West African griots, whose vocational responsibility it is to transmit ancient lore and legends just exactly as they have been received.[20] We make a modern distinction, moreover, between myth and history, which the ancients and primitive peoples did not do. The narrative story of the American Revolution is reasonably well known, for example (although there is no consensus among scholars as to its precise causes and consequences), yet the Revolution as a mythos, or part of our popular culture, is surprisingly blurry.[21]

Although tradition in America does not make a neat fit with the paradigmatic definitions of social theorists who have been interested in tradition, that discrepancy does not necessarily obviate the value of their insights. Quite the contrary; my understanding of American traditions has been enlarged and illuminated in many ways as a result of reading Professors Shils and Geertz, Deutsch and Eisenstadt. But I have reached the conclusion that in addition to having substantive traditions unlike those elsewhere—which is scarcely surprising—the very *process* of tradition works somewhat differently here in certain critical respects. Even though "American exceptionalism" and "the problem of our uniqueness" are being questioned these days, I am persuaded that the function and character of tradition in America are distinctive.[22] Much of what appears in the following chapters will, I hope, sustain my persuasion and help to explain it.

There are various ways one might trace the distinctiveness of American traditions, both in terms of substance and as a matter of process. One might look, for example, at the changing uses of tradition for different cohorts of Americans. John Winthrop's generation had the job of sifting and winnowing European traditions, while for Cotton Mather's generation half a century later, tradition served as a means of self-evaluation ("How well do I measure up by the standard of our forebears?"). To the Founding Fathers, in 1787 let us say, tradition, in the form of accumulated political experience, served as the rationale for establishing certain political institutions rather than others. Much later in the nineteenth century, especially the 1890s, some spurious forms of tradition served as vehicles of nostalgic escape and as justifications for nativism. Early in the twentieth century, George Santayana produced an elegant and effective critique of what he called "the Genteel Tradition" in literature, while Van Wyck Brooks issued a *cri de coeur* (actually a series of such appeals) calling for the establishment of a distinctive American tradition in literary history and critical evaluation.

In addition to the variability of tradition's role in America—the impermanence and changing uses of social memory might be a better description—surely one of the most pronounced aspects of our sense of the past is that it is both fragile and, at times, stubbornly farcical. I do not mean to suggest that we have a monopoly upon either quality, not by any means. But rather, that lacking a clear consensus about essential, enduring traditions, we may have a heightened consciousness of our history's occasional foolishness and perishability. Here are a few illustrative items.

• *Newsweek* describing Robert Altman's new film, *Buffalo Bill and the Indians, or Sitting Bull's History Lesson*, as "a metaphor for America's insistence on turning its historical and spiritual substance into a kind of vaudeville." (June 28, 1976, p. 77)
• Jacqueline Kennedy at the White House in 1961 installing mid-nineteenth-century wallpaper depicting battle scenes from the American Revolution, and Betty Ford ordering it removed from the family dining room in 1974 because she found it "kind of depressing."
• A complete set of the fifty-six autographs of the signers of the Declaration of Independence selling at auction in October 1975 for $120,000. The purchaser was actually a consortium whose spokesman declared: "It's a commercial venture." (The last previous set was sold in 1922 when Henry E. Huntington, the railroad tycoon, outbid Harry Houdini, the magician, at $19,750.)

Apart from the commercialization of American tradition, which is a serious problem itself, many of our citizens have been put off because certain groups have customarily claimed a kind of exclusive possession of the earlier American past. Once the Society of the Cincinnati, or the American Revolution Society, or the Seventy-Six Association, or the National Monument Society, or the Mount Vernon Ladies Association had staked their claim, other well-meaning trespassers were warned off, as it were. To latecomers and newcomers, "tradition" therefore seemed to be tainted, affected, pretentious, and, perhaps, somehow congenital. Consequently, they felt, let those self-appointed custodians of the past wallow in tradition, while we denizens of the modern world pursue progress and personal opportunity. They don't want us, but neither do we need them.

The comparative weakness of tradition in American culture also owes something to the fact that there has not been a strong or viable conservative ideology here. Although our social thought has in many real respects become ever more conservative during the past century, a liberal ideology continues to dominate the national rhetoric. Without the coherent articulation and pervasive acceptance of conservative values or beliefs, however, a sense of tradition must make its own way unassisted, which is rather more difficult.

To complicate matters still further, our two regions richest in a sense of tradition, New England and Dixie, each underwent a protracted phase (between about 1885 and 1925) in which leading spokesmen repudiated the past and cried out for liberation from the oppressive weight of tradition. Charles Francis Adams and Brooks Adams excoriated Puritanism while Henry Grady appealed for a New South to rise, like that fabled Phoenix, from the ashes of the old.[23] The repudiation of Puritanism was not confined to New England, moreover, and as that repudiation swept the nation during the 1920s, it verged upon being a rejection of New England's hegemony over the exposition of American history. Because New England was our most tradition-oriented section—a region in which the dense historiography approximates what Clifford Geertz calls "thick description"—the reaction against Puritanism became a means of repudiating the burden of the past in American life generally.[24]

By contrast to cultures rich with ritual, there has been a certain impoverishment in the rather disembodied, ceremonial, republican formlessness of tradition-related efforts in the United States. We have hung grim pictures of George Washington in every American schoolroom, celebrated Abraham Lincoln's birthday by keeping kids out of school, built a marble monument to Thomas Jefferson, kept Andrew Jackson's Hermitage just as it was, and preserved Teddy Roosevelt's birthplace as a museum.[25] These are not bad or even necessarily banal things to do; in fact, they have the potential to be socially valuable. But without substantive knowledge and historical understanding, they are not very meaningful. They represent a curious quest for authenticity and a pattern of remembrance that rarely penetrate beneath the surface of daily routine to touch national nerves affecting aspiration, motivation, and conscience.

George Templeton Strong, a perceptive young New York lawyer, put his finger on part of the problem back in 1854. By that time, he recognized, there was beginning to be a desperate lunging about on the part of some for emblems of tradition, however superficial:

We are so young a people that we feel the want of nationality, and delight in whatever asserts our national "American" existence. We have not, like England and France, centuries of achievements and calamities to look back on; we have no *record* of Americanism and we feel its want. Hence the development, in every state of the Union, of "Historical Societies" that seize on and seal up every worthless reminiscence of our colonial and revolutionary times. We crave a history, instinctively, and being without the eras that belong to older nationalities—Anglo-Saxon, Carolingian, Hohenstauffen, Ghibelline, and so forth—we dwell on the details of our little all of historic life, and venerate every trivial fact about our first settlers and colonial governors and revolutionary heroes.[26]

By the time Strong confided these thoughts to his diary—in the mid-nineteenth century—there began to be occasional voices raised in criticism against what was paraded under the guise of "tradition" in the United States. Thus Richard Frothingham, treasurer of the Middlesex Canal Company and sometime Massachusetts legislator, wrote a *History of the Siege of Boston, and the Battles of Lexington, Concord, and Bunker Hill,* published in 1849, because he felt skeptical "as to tradition" and determined to set the story straight.[27] Thus George Bancroft wrote to Moses Coit Tyler in 1887, thanking him for a copy of Tyler's new biography of Patrick Henry and commending him: "You have rejected all the trash called tradition which cannot stand the test of historic criticism."[28]

In the three generations that have passed since Bancroft acknowledged Tyler's book, there have been complaints from time to time about "all the trash called tradition"—such complaints may have reached a crescendo during 1976, the Bicentennial year. Much more influential than these complaints, however, have been those waves of nostalgia that seem to wash upon our shores at roughly generational intervals, specifically: the 1890s, the 1930s, and the 1970s. Significantly, all three of these decades have been times of grave national self-doubt accompanied by deep concern for the future. Perhaps the past, in such difficult periods, was all that our society could grasp with any assurance. Perhaps it might be said that a country's quest for its heritage intensifies in direct proportion to its apprehension about the present.[29]

Whenever Americans have felt a buoyant sense of optimism about the present and the future, they have been comparatively uninterested in their origins. So long as the society lacked a sense of antecedents, moreover, it could rely upon covenant theory and natural law for sources of legitimacy and social control. Only as custom and usage evolved did covenant theory and natural law come to seem both artificial and arbitrary. And only as crises of confidence occurred, as they did during the 1890s, 1930s, and 1970s, would the nation seize upon its past as a source of security and comfort. "Memories, as such, do not determine the living present," one psychiatrist has remarked,

> but the emotional context of the present determines which events will be recalled. It is necessary, however, to recognize the events which *endure* longer, not just those which occurred a very long time ago. The enduring events are discovered and rediscovered in many recurrent moments of existential time. They survive by evoking fresh relevance and fresh reality sense for the organic meaning of the present. Thus, because related events tend to endow each other with a common reality sense, the memory of any single occurrence may have a sense of reality entirely different from that of the episode itself.[30]

Most recently, a cluster of disparate causes has heightened public interest in national tradition. Watergate, an emblematic phrase that evokes a disturbing cache of lapses in public ethics, aroused fresh interest in our political institutions, their interrelations, and how they were intended to function. Second, our tragic involvement in Vietnam stimulated concern about the so-called Imperial Presidency and its historic equilibrium (or disequilibrium) with the Congress. Third, the dramatic decline of new immigration during and after the 1920s made it possible for an increasingly homogeneous society to feel some mutual sense of shared historical experience: the Great Depression, World War II, the fiercely partisan years of Lyndon Johnson and Richard Nixon. Fourth, American Blacks have become intensely interested in their own roots and subsequent entanglement with the "mainstream" of American history.[31] Black pride has provoked a massive effort to recover an obscure heritage, much as art preservationists might seek to salvage a classic fresco, such as Leonardo's *Last Supper*, which has been fading from view. Fifth, and finally, the growth of leisure has helped to facilitate a heightened curiosity about tradition. Our first three centuries produced, for most Americans, a work-oriented culture, a culture of busyness and non-leisure. Such a culture, infected by the work ethic, is much less likely to be concerned about the past. Ever since the 1950s, however, leisure has become a more important component of American life. With shorter work weeks and longer paid vacations, a larger number of citizens has had the affluence that enables them to visit historic monuments and restorations, as well as the time to read historical fiction or witness pageants about the past, such as Paul Green's popular and enduring outdoor dramas.

I find it fascinating in this regard that among the American Indians tradition normally served as a central component of their culture. In part this was because their lives were more leisurely, more oriented to seasonal exigencies and less subject to the time-clock of an industrial day or week. We know, for example, that the Indians of California enjoyed an unusual amount of leisure, much of which they diverted into the performance of elaborate rituals, and into the creation of myths or complex song-cycles.[32] Franz Boas, the pioneering anthropologist, made these perceptive observations as long ago as 1898 about the Indians of British Columbia:

> The coast tribes north of Fraser River are divided in totemic clans, each of which has a clan tradition. All the privileges of the clan are explained by the clan traditions, which, for this reason, are considered a most valuable property. That this is so is indicated by the jealousy with which the property right to certain traditions is guarded by the families of the coast tribes.[33]

Insofar as property rights have been cherished by Americans, however, the exclusive "ownership" of particular traditions has not been a major source of bourgeois friction. Whether or not Columbus, or Madoc the medieval Welsh prince, or some lucky Viking was the first white man to set foot in the New World is about as far as we go in that direction. Which is a pity, in a way, because the most meaningful sources of tradition can serve as important agents of social cohesion and understanding. There is an old saying among the Teton Sioux that goes to the heart of the matter: "A people without history," they claim, "is like wind upon the buffalo grass."

"On the mount of Remembrance"

INSOFAR as we have had a feeling for tradition at all, however, I am prepared to argue that the American Revolution has been at its core. The Revolution is the one component of our past that we have not, at some point or other, explicitly repudiated. For that reason it stands in stark contrast to our rejection of Puritanism in New England, or our disillusioned realism about the Cavalier myth of the South, and our most recent embarrassment about the deadly impact of the westward movement upon native Americans already inhabiting those regions. Unlike the Civil War, moreover, the Revolution has been an ongoing stimulus to cultural activity in the United States. William Dean Howells remarked in 1867 that the late "war has not only left us a burden of a tremendous national debt, but has laid upon our literature a charge under which it has hitherto staggered very lamely," a lament reiterated most recently by Daniel Aaron after he completed an exhaustive inquiry into the Civil War's literary consequences.[34]

The Revolution, by contrast, gradually became a non-controversial phenomenon to most Americans. By 1876 it had ceased to be vulnerable to political partisanship. Early in the 1830s, for example, a great brouhaha occurred in Congress over whether or not a painting of the Battle of New Orleans ought to be commissioned for the Capitol Rotunda. General Andrew Jackson had been the hero of that event (in January 1815), and President Jackson continued to be very controversial. Indeed, bitterness buzzed all around his second administration. Hence the sentiment voiced in 1834 by Henry A. Wise of Virginia concerning historical paintings that might then be commissioned: "I would be content to confine the subjects to a date prior to 1783." Many of his countrymen shared that preference for "the events of the Revolution."[35]

When W. Lloyd Warner, the pioneering sociologist, made his study a generation ago of the symbolic life of Americans, he found that the Revolutionary era was by far the most vivid and meaningful in their minds, much more so than any other phase or episode of national history.[36] Those formative events that occurred during the period 1776 to 1789 have helped to supply subsequent immigrants to this country with a common source of political culture. The Declaration of Independence, the Constitution and Bill of Rights, taken together, served as that component of American tradition to which all newcomers could give their allegiance, and which might be most gladly grafted upon other inherited traditions. An Italian immigrant in Boston had little use for John Winthrop, just as a German in Charleston had scant need for John C. Calhoun, or a Jew in Nashville for Davy Crockett. To all of these hyphenated-Americans, however, the civics lessons of their naturalization course were rooted in sacred documents and institutions shaped by the pivotal thirteen years of experience that commenced in 1776. And among indigenous Yankees also, many continued to share the outlook of Ralph Waldo Emerson, succinctly expressed in his widely read *American Scholar* address of 1837: "If there is any period one would desire to be born in, is it not the age of Revolution?"[37]

In traditional societies, as S. N. Eisenstadt has suggested,

> always some past event remained the focal point and symbol of the social, political, and cultural orders. The essence of traditionality is in the cultural acceptance of these cultural definitions of tradition as a basic criterion of social activity, as the basic referent of collective identity. . . .[38]

In the United States that "past event" became the American Revolution, though it took until the 1820s for sufficient unanimity of understanding to develop so that it might serve a substantial majority as "the basic referent of collective identity." Between 1783 and about 1820 the young republic underwent an anxious quest for cultural cohesion. Those who wrote our history during these decades were either personally inclined, or else felt socially obliged, to minimize the existence of divisiveness among earlier Americans and to maximize the distinctive coherence of our moral character as it emerged from the crucible of Revolution.[39]

Edward Shils has remarked that "traditions are sometimes sought for" by persons wanting "to 'create a past' for themselves which will legitimate them in a way which just being themselves in the present will not allow them to do."[40] That statement accurately describes a basic cultural impulse of the immediate post-Revolutionary generation. A common exhortation customarily ran as follows: "The records of the American Revolution ought to be sacredly preserved. That event we justly consider as the noblest monument of our national glory. We hope, that it will not in future time reproach the degeneracy of posterity."[41] The moment of those particular remarks happens to have been 1804; but for two decades thereafter they would be inculcated by various dedicated persons bent upon the establishment of national traditions. Thus,

• "The present is a most propitious period," wrote Benjamin Elliott to Hezekiah Niles in 1816. "The feelings and sentiments of '76 were never so prevalent as at present."[42]

• In 1823 George Ticknor praised William Tudor's new biography of James Otis because Ticknor feared that twenty years hence, "all the traditions will have perished with the old men from whose graves he has just rescued them. It . . . will, I think, do much good by promoting an inquiry into the most interesting and important periods of our history."[43]

• "We can win no laurels in a war for independence," Daniel Webster declared in 1825. "Earlier and worthier hands have gathered them all. . . . But there remains to us a great duty of defence and preservation."[44]

• That same year, in an oration delivered at Concord, Edward Everett reminded his assembled auditors of the solemn responsibility "to hand down the traditions of their day to our children; to pass the torch of liberty unquenched to those who stand next us in the line."[45]

Many contemporaries who were both earnest and willing to comply, however, found that it was no simple matter to do so. For some that was because they believed the stuff of tradition necessarily had to be venerable. One man complained in 1811 that any historical novel set in America would fail because, "should it be attempted, the theatre must be erected on the field of the revolution, an era not sufficiently remote . . . to be arrayed in the vesture of fiction." He assumed that centuries must pass before the Revolutionary period might provide the setting for a successful novel.[46]

All sorts of bizarre problems arose that reveal to us the uncertainty felt by Americans in the young republic about the proper form and content of traditions-in-the-making. From 1799 until 1816 an intermittent debate occurred over whether or not George Washington ought to be buried in the private plot at Mount Vernon, or, more properly, in an impressive public tomb. If the latter, what sort of mausoleum would be most suitable in a non-monarchical society?[47] With the awesome double deaths of Thomas Jefferson and John Adams on July 4, 1826, a popular impulse arose that for a time verged upon being a cult of ancestor worship—still another way of creating a sense of national tradition—but the impulse aroused opposition and soon lost momentum.[48]

The lesson, I believe, is very plain. In acquiring or shaping a formal, collective sense of its own past, the American people between 1776 and 1826 had few models or points of reference. The results were consequential for American cultural history: to stimulate controversy over the acceptability of particular phenomena as tradition, as well as over the proper form any given tradition ought to take; to slow down the process whereby broadly acceptable traditions emerged at all; and to stimulate the production of regional variants of the same tradition.[49]

To complicate matters still more, so many of the leading revolutionaries underwent intellectual shifts that made it possible for their disciples and devotees to seize upon the alternative, conflicting implications of their careers. Thomas Jefferson came to be claimed as both the liberal Father of Democracy and as the conservative Father of States' Rights, the advocate of strict constitutional construction and the questionable purchaser of that vast Louisiana Territory.[50] During the crisis decade of the 1850s, George Washington was hailed simultaneously by the South as one of their own, a plantation owner and slaveholder, and by the North as a nationalist and advocate of Union.[51] The reputations of Samuel Adams, Ethan Allen, Alexander Hamilton, and Patrick Henry were all subject to the same sorts of vicissitudes.[52] They managed to mean different things to different people in different times and places—a fact that would have chagrined some of them and bemused others, because all of them had been immensely concerned about their own roles in shaping national tradition, and about their positions in the eyes of "Posterity." Hence the importance of what *followed* John Adams's oft-quoted assertion that "this radical change in the principles, opinions, sentiments, and affections of the people was the real American Revolution."

> By what means this great and important alteration in the religious, moral, political, and social character of the people of thirteen colonies, all distinct, unconnected, and independent of each other, was begun, pursued, and accomplished, it is surely interesting to humanity to investigate, and perpetuate to posterity.
>
> To this end, it is greatly to be desired that young men of letters in all

the States, especially in the thirteen original States, would undertake the laborious, but certainly interesting and amusing task of searching and collecting all the records, pamphlets, newspapers, and even hand-bills, which in any way contributed to change the temper and views of the people and compose them into an independent nation.[53]

Although Adams does not say so explicitly in this well-known letter, by 1818 he had become extremely apprehensive about the matter of by whom, and in what manner, the Revolution would be understood. "I See no disposition to celebrate or remember," he told John Trumbull on New Year's Day, 1817, "or even Curiosity to enquire into the Characters, Actions or Events of the Revolution."[54] Two days later Adams informed Hezekiah Niles that he considered "the true history of the American revolution & of the establishment of our present Constitutions as lost forever."[55]

In a very real sense, Adams was right; but for reasons more complex than he could have known at that time. What happened during the decade between 1810 and 1820 is quintessentially captured in Ralph Waldo Emerson's aphorism that "time dissipates to shining ether the solid angularity of facts." During the quarter century that followed 1783, a number of historical writers had been rather optimistic about the prospect that our national origins, as Abiel Holmes put it in 1805, "can now be accurately ascertained, without recourse to such legends as have darkened and disfigured the early annals of most nations." Or, as John Lendrum asserted in 1795, "perhaps no people on the globe can trace the history of their origin and progress with so much precision."[56]

Very few among that first cohort of historians writing about the Revolution shared the Reverend Jeremy Belknap's caution and "proper allowance for the imperfection of human memory."[57] But by the second decade of the nineteenth century, we can trace the very human lapses of memory by which history is transmuted into something else—call it tradition, aberrant legend, or national mythology. "What is to become of our past revolutionary history?" Thomas Jefferson asked Joel Barlow in 1811; "Of the antidotes of truth to the misrepresentations of Marshall?" Here Jefferson was worried by the historical and partisan writings of Chief Justice John Marshall, a devout Federalist.[58] Just a few years later, however, we see Jefferson's own powers of recollection beginning to fail. In 1814, for example, he wrote a long and fascinating response to William Wirt, the biographer of Patrick Henry.

Over and over again Jefferson is obliged to confess that "I have no journals to refresh my memory"; "I do not indeed recollect it, but I have no recollection to the contrary"; "this, to be sure, is conjecture, and may rightfully be rejected by any one to whom a more plausible solution may occur"; "I do not remember the topics of Mr. Henry's argument"; "I recollect nothing"; and finally, a poignant closing paragraph in which Jefferson acknowledged his awareness of the dilemma:

> It is truly unfortunate that those engaged in public affairs so rarely make notes of transactions passing within their knowledge. Hence history becomes fable instead of fact. The great outlines may be true, but the incidents and coloring are according to the faith or fancy of the writer.[59]

Jefferson's correspondence during the last decade of his life is punctuated with this sort of lamentation, agnosticism, and confessional: "I have nothing now but an impaired memory to resort to"; "and who else I do not remember"; "records should be examined to settle this accurately"; and, "having been prevented from retaining my collection of the acts. . . ." Only on occasion does he inject such assurances as "my memory cannot deceive me," or "I am certain I remember also. . . ."[60]

When Joseph Delaplaine of Philadelphia submitted some questions in 1817 about the drafting and signing of the Declaration of Independence, Jefferson's answers were unintentionally casual and imprecise. Two years later Samuel A. Welles, who was preparing a biography of his grandfather, Samuel Adams, sought Jefferson's help; and his response, especially his memories of the Declaration's genesis, are significantly inconsistent with established facts that can be verified by contemporary evidence. Nor was Jefferson unique in this respect. John Adams also forgot significant details; and Thomas McKean, a signer, became confused in his recollections.[61] By 1823 Adams confessed to one correspondent that "my old brain boils up so many reminiscences of ancient facts and conversations which I think ought to be committed to writing, but which I am utterly incapable of doing, that they sometimes over-balance my reason."[62]

There is something sad in the spectacle, that same year, of Jefferson's concession of decline in finding fault with Adams's sense of the past. Timothy Pickering had delivered an oration at Salem on July 4, 1823, in which, on John Adams's authority, he made various assertions about the Declaration of Independence. When the oration appeared in print, Jefferson took exception and stated his criticisms in a long letter to James Madison:

> Mr. Adams's memory has led him into unquestionable error; at the age of eighty-eight, and forty-seven years after the transactions of Independence, this is not wonderful, nor should I, at the age of eighty, on the small advantage of that difference only, venture to oppose my memory to his, were it not supported by written notes, taken by myself, at the moment and on the spot.[63]

One might cite many another instance of memory's impotence. In 1835, for example, when Ralph Waldo Emerson was preparing his address to Concord on the occasion of that town's bicentennial, he read all that he could and interviewed aged survivors of the fateful fight that occurred at North Bridge on April 19, 1775. Emerson felt pity and a twinge of embarrassment when he overtaxed the memory of Thaddeus Blood for details. It was "hard to bring them up," the old man complained; and so he doubted whether the truth of what had happened would ever be known.[64] By the second quarter of the nineteenth century—when Emerson and Everett, Webster and Hawthorne, Cooper and Simms had become the transmitters of that Revolutionary experience—the American Revolution had passed from the realm of memory to that of imagination.

"Who has made any thing out of America?"

Our primary concern throughout this book is with the imaginative impact the Revolution has had upon our national culture. It seems suitable, therefore, to pause for a moment in order to clarify the nature of my approach in general, and my use of "imagination" in particular. As the preceding section hopefully made clear, I shall pay much less attention to things written and said prior to the 1820s, because in that earliest time period memory had not yet fully given way to imagination so far as the Revolution was concerned, and also because the first phase, 1776–1815, has been dealt with already in a rather thick body of literature.[65]

Second, I am going to have little to say about the professional historiography of the Revolution that has proliferated in the twentieth century, in part because that, too, has accumulated a shelf-full of studies;[66] but more importantly because my particular concern is with the Revolution's place in American popular culture. I am not altogether oblivious to the scholarly literature for there are times, to be sure, when scholars have been affected by what Alfred North Whitehead once called "the climate of opinion." But, by and large, my focus will concentrate upon the Revolution as it evolved as a central component of national culture and tradition generally. I do so because I share Michael Walzer's feeling that "the union of men can only be symbolized; it has no palpable shape or substance. The state is invisible; it must be personified before it can be seen, symbolized before it can be loved, imagined before it can be conceived."[67]

Symbolism and imagination are enormously useful in defining nationality, loyalty, and tradition; but they are also slippery to the point of being elusive. What do we really mean by them? George J. Goschen, in his inaugural speech as rector of the University of Edinburgh in 1891, addressed himself to the "Uses of Imagination," and had some perceptive things to say. Imagination, as he defined it,

> is the power of picturing absent things, of presenting to the mind's eye visions of the past or the future, of realizing the mental attitude and thoughts of another person or an alien race. This constructive imagination takes its start from facts, but it supplements them and does not contradict them.

After differentiating between creative imagination and the faculty of analysis, Goschen specifically compared historical analysis with historical imagination. The latter, he suggested,

> will endeavor mentally to restore a picture of a past age of which the colors have faded with time. It will not neglect details, for details are a great part of life. It will endeavor to restore the special character, the movement and the stir, which drier annals have failed to preserve.[68]

Northrop Frye has pointed out that "the world of literature is a world where there is no reality except that of the human imagination."[69] When we go to watch a Shakespearian tragedy, we hope to be moved by the power of imaginative exposition; and we seek the personal growth, or maturity, that comes with the acquisition of insight into human motives and behavior. G. M. Trevelyan, the evocative English historian, has written in more personal terms about the meaning of historical imagination:

I saw my first play (apart from London pantomimes) in the old Stratford theatre; it was Frank Benson in *Richard III*. Small as I was, historical imagination was already the keenest pleasure of my life. I knew the *Lays of Ancient Rome* by heart . . . and my father [George Otto Trevelyan, also a distinguished historian] was my playmate, with his entrancing talk and familiar jokes about historical scenes and persons. . . . And now, for two blissful hours in Stratford theatre, I actually lived in the past, seeing real people walking about in gorgeous Fifteenth Century clothes.[70]

Considering what Frye, Trevelyan, and others have had to say about the imaginative power and impact of theatre, it should come as no surprise that my emphasis in the chapters that follow will fall heavily upon literary sources: drama and poetry, but most of all, historical fiction. Just as anthropologists, like Lévi-Strauss, have been reaching out for closer collaboration with linguists, so too, in my opinion, historians of social thought must pay closer attention to the imaginative use of language in popular culture.[71]

My reliance, moreover, will often fall upon second-rate romances and third-rate novels: partially because I believe that they are important indexes to the popular culture, and partially because many of our finest writers have not been particularly inclined to use historical materials for the substance of their major creative efforts. I find that fact somewhat puzzling; for there is no lack of evidence to suggest acute historical awareness on their part. James Russell Lowell told Nathaniel Hawthorne that he found *The House of the Seven Gables* to be "the most valuable contribution to New England history that has been made" because it typified "that intimate relationship between the Present and the Past in the way of ancestry and descent, which historians so carefully overlook."[72]

So I shall be looking long and hard at literary artifacts that either had some influence upon American culture, or else, perhaps more commonly, seem to have embodied its value patterns and beliefs at various points in time. I shall, here and there, be looking through the lens of Murray Krieger, a literary critic who has raised this provocative query: "Are the forms through which we are to perceive a past moment in our culture a model configuration like that through which the poet asks us to perceive his dramatic episode?" For I share with Krieger the belief that inevitably, perhaps, "we allow the shaping selectivity of the hourglass to substitute for our unshaped consciousness of the fullness of time."[73]

During my first period of intense concern, the quarter century following 1820, each of the three distinct regions produced a major author deeply concerned about the recovery or establishment of national tradition: James Fenimore Cooper in New York, Nathaniel Hawthorne in Massachusetts, and William Gilmore Simms in South Carolina. Hawthorne and Simms, like so many others among their contemporaries and those who followed them as well, were much affected by Cooper's novels. *The Spy*, published in 1821, was the first historical tale to utilize the American Revolution for its very essence. *The Spy*'s tremendous success encouraged immediate imitators, and then much later, by negative reaction, what we might call "deviant" novels about the Revolution. For better or for worse, Cooper's imaginative perception of that pivotal period in our history has become the reference point for hundreds of authors ever since.

Simms was especially intrigued by Cooper's later novels because they consciously contrasted American traditions and institutions with those of Europe. A long essay by Simms about Cooper's writings, published in 1842, gave voice to a deeply felt concern of his generation, and one that is also central to the focus of this chapter:

> The writer of European romance, unquestionably, possesses greater resources in history than he who confines himself to what is purely American. Time, which hallows all that he touches, had there laid away precious stores for centuries, long before the new world was opened to the eye of European day. The antiquities of the old world are so many treasures of fiction, to attain which, the critic of the American story, must task his invention.[74]

In a series of lectures, essays, and reviews presented between 1842 and 1845, Simms articulated all of the frustrations felt by an author bent upon the imaginative uses of tradition in a society "wanting in homogeneousness at first, and but recently segregated from their several patriarchal trees." The events that shaped our nationality were too recent, too well known, and insufficiently mysterious.[75] He went on to differentiate between *tradition*, by which he meant that folklore through which the nation catches a hazy glimpse of its past, and *history*, by which he meant the "certified chronicles of the historian." He found the former vastly more interesting, needless to say, and insisted that "no nation of our magnitude—sprung from such famous stocks—having such records of the past—having such hopes of the future—with our enthusiasm of character, and with our boldness of design—can long remain without its *Genius loci!*"[76]

Nathaniel Hawthorne, by contrast, was less optimistic about our eventual capacity to generate and perpetuate authentic traditions. In several of his historical tales the point is either made that so many New England traditions are specious, or else that New Englanders simply lack historical knowlege and understanding entirely.[77] Hawthorne discovered to his dismay that a republican society is not only present- and future-oriented, but also scornful (or at best merely tolerant) of the past. He presented old Esther Dudley as a symbol of memory in Massachusetts; and then suggested that after 1776, once a new beginning had been made, the people of Boston could not look her in the eye. They were content, instead, to leave her in the Province House and neglect her there. Unhappily for Esther Dudley, however, an elderly gentleman at the Province House, called "the old tradition monger," doesn't even have a sufficient store of legends to last the evening; and an eighty-year-old erstwhile Loyalist has equal trouble conjuring up an alternative sense of the Revolutionary past.[78]

Although Hawthorne earnestly wished to preserve New England's more meaningful history from oblivion, he found it challenging and difficult to recreate the early American past in an imaginative way—never mind kindling for his mundane contemporaries a viable sense of tradition. To the elderly, who had actually imbibed historical experiences, memory and what passed for tradition had become conflated in blurry ways.[79] As for the rest, they seemed mostly to be interested in the status that accrued from money and success, or sometimes in achieving personal immortality, like Septimius Felton; but all of them, in Hawthorne's view, cared "more for the present and future than for the past."[80]

This provided a constant concern for Cooper also. As late as 1831, after a decade of success with half a dozen major novels, he informed his publisher that

> America is of all countries one of the least favorable to all sorts of works of the imagination. . . . Give me English Naval History for my subject,

and they shall see a book on Marine Romance as they never yet dreamt of. Remember how much I forego, by abstaining from the use of such materials as fleets, victories, historical characters and all the etcetera of their annals. If America is so favorable to fiction why do not people avail themselves of it? Heaven and Earth is ransacked for materials, and yet who has made any thing out of America?[81]

Well, Cooper himself had, for one. Hawthorne was covertly working on historical tales that were just then beginning to appear. Simms was preparing to bring forth a lengthy series of romances set in Revolutionary South Carolina. And a goodly number of their contemporaries—mostly men and women of lesser talent, to be sure—were also scribbling feverishly in the hope that they, too, might support themselves by the profits of their pens.

The decade of the 1820s appears as a fairly sharp point of demarcation in the shaping of national tradition. The Fourth of July celebration had fully taken hold by then as a formulaic and distinctive American occasion. During the early twenties also, the oration, which served as a solemn annual highlight on the Fourth, began to display sectional variations (that would endure for decades to come) on account of the fierce debates over the possible admission of slaveholding Missouri to the Union.[82] In 1821 George Alexander Otis completed and published an English translation of Carlo Giuseppe Botta's *History of the War of the Independence of the United States of America* (during the next quarter century it went through nine revised editions), which meant that thereafter ordinary Americans could read a full-scale European version of their national genesis—a symptomatic filtering process that helped to draw a certain haze between the Revolutionary era and citizens one full generation removed from it.[83]

In addition, we can spot a steady stream of autobiographical reminiscences by Revolutionary veterans being published in the early 1820s—important volumes because they provided a mine of anecdotes and personal material that novelists would read and exploit for decades to come.[84] Others, at the same time, advocated the necessity for individual states to possess historical self-knowledge in order to develop "pride and character." Thus the first distinct movement to establish state and local historical societies occurred between 1820 and 1828.[85]

By the later 1830s, a sufficient amount of material had been published—both fiction and non-fiction—so that the seeds of tradition had not only been implanted, but also a certain sense of discrimination among the more discerning cultivators of tradition. As George Bancroft said in commending Benjamin Trumbull (the historian of Connecticut) in 1838: "He read all sorts of records; he picked up and tested traditions."[86]

During the subsequent two decades, however, the problem of tradition in a post-Revolutionary society took some peculiar (but profoundly revealing) twists and turns. First, the historical romances and Fourth of July orations now became so stylized and hackneyed that by the mid-1840s we begin to find them being satirized on occasion. Even George Washington sometimes appeared in farcical sketches, and humorists would burlesque the worst excesses of foolish hero worship.

Second, still other writers started to feel, during the later 1840s and 1850s, that native sources of tradition had nearly been picked clean, and that what remained was on the verge of withering away.

Third, there seems to have been a self-conscious desire on the part of some leading authors at this time to democratize American history by disseminating it more broadly. Such popularizers as Joel T. Headley, John W. Barber, and Benson J. Lossing wished to make the past "accessible to our whole population . . . to scatter the seeds of knowledge broadcast amid those in the humbler walks of society."[87] The dilemma created by their egalitarian impulse, however, was that the democratization of tradition for an ever more diverse society required would-be disseminators to reduce the national heritage to its lowest common denominators. Complexities had to be smoothed over, and those subtleties of 1776 that might be incomprehensible, say, in 1856, must be eliminated. The picture books, compilations, and biographical volumes that resulted necessarily became highly derivative, and too often in the process riddled with errors as well.

Edward Shils has observed that the development or generation of totally new traditions is improbable and occurs infrequently: "New traditions emerge as modifications of existing ones."[88] What happened during the middle third of the nineteenth century is surely a case in point; for the embryonic traditions of the American Revolution that had begun to develop during the 1820s and 1830s were subsequently altered and modifed in significant ways, as we shall see in Chapter Two. The nation shifted its interest and emphasis, for example, from the Declaration of Independence to the Constitution, from the more radical principles of 1776 to the consolidation of power that occurred in 1787.

One fascinating consequence of these alterations is that the attitudes of leading American spokesmen and statesmen toward the Revolution's role in national tradition came to be fraught with ambivalence. Let us take Emerson and Lincoln as cases in point. I have already mentioned Emerson's antipathy toward the acquisition of knowledge through history, a process he regarded pejoratively because it meant that the stuff of experience would be learned about vicariously rather than directly. I have also, however, made reference to Emerson doing diligent historical research in preparation for his oration to the people of Concord on the occasion of that town's bicentennial.

Throughout Emerson's long career, he vacillated between acknowledging the determinative force of tradition, and urging Americans to shake off its yoke. He knew full well that his paternal grandfather had been killed in the War for Independence; and as a boy, Ralph was told that his own mother (when she was seven) had been dandled on George Washington's knee. At the age of eleven, young Emerson composed a poem: "Lines on Washington Written at Concord, December 24th, 1814." One year later he wrote a long "Poetical Essay" about the direction of history and American Independence.[89] The tone of "Nature," which he composed in 1836, was powerfully anti-historical; yet a year earlier he pieced together his "Historical Discourse," as a result of which he gained a new and special sort of eminence in Concord. In 1837 Emerson did his part for a local patriotic celebration by contributing some poetic lines that could be set to music as a hymn. His first stanza, of course, has achieved the most extraordinary immortality:

By the rude bridge that arched the flood,
Their flag to April's breeze unfurled,
Here, once, the embattled farmers stood,
And fired the shot heard round the world.

Yet the casualness with which that immortality began is startling. When the monument commemorating April 19, 1775, was dedicated on July 4, 1837, Emerson did not even bother to be present to read his poem or hear it sung as a hymn. He was away at the time on a social visit to Plymouth. Although the "Concord Hymn" was later published among Emerson's poems during the 1840s, it would not be cut in stone and made lapidary until 1875: the centennial anniversary of the struggle at Concord that had opened the War for Independence.[90]

On April 19, 1867, Emerson served as orator at the dedication of Soldiers' Monument in Concord. In 1873 he composed and read a poem entitled "Boston" at a ceremony held in remembrance of the Boston Tea Party. And on April 19, 1875, he delivered a short address—the last he ever composed—to the assembled thousands in Concord, a throng that included President Grant, cabinet members, various governors, famous authors, and other dignitaries. Nevertheless, in the years separating these ceremonial occasions when Emerson gave dutiful but inspirational performances, he praised progress and the future more often than he celebrated tradition and history. Although he felt a certain reluctance "to quit the remembrance of the past," as he put it, his ultimate emphasis fell upon the quest for individual development in the here and now, and communal perfection in the not too distant future.[91]

Abraham Lincoln's ambivalence about the American Revolution had more to do with political exigencies than with his intellectual proclivities. In a speech delivered in 1842, on George Washington's birthday, he found in America's past an uncomplicated explanation of her fortunate present:

> Of our political revolution of '76, we all are justly proud. It has given us a degree of political freedom, far exceeding that of any other of the nations of the earth. In it the world has found a solution of that long mooted problem, as to the capability of man to govern himself.[92]

Four years earlier, however, in an address treating "the perpetuation of our political institutions," Lincoln expressed deep concern about the growing disregard for law that he saw pervading the United States. What could be done about it? The answer, according to Lincoln, "is simple. Let every American, every lover of liberty, every well wisher to his posterity, swear by the blood of the Revolution, never to violate in the least particular, the laws of the country." Yet some paragraphs later, toward the close of this speech, the whole matter of swearing by the blood of the Revolution turns out to be less than simple because Lincoln acknowledges that the founders all had gone, and with them the living history they embodied.

I do not mean to say, that the scenes of the revolution *are now* or *ever will be* entirely forgotten; but that like every thing else, they must fade upon the memory of the world, and grow more and more dim by the lapse of time. . . . At the close of that struggle, nearly every adult male had been a participator in some of its scenes. The consequence was, that of those scenes . . . *a living history was* to be found in every family . . . a history, too, that could be read and understood alike by all, the wise and the ignorant, the learned and the unlearned. But *those* histories are gone. They can be read no more forever.[93]

Later, as the crisis of the Union developed, especially between 1856 and 1861, Lincoln found himself in the peculiar position of seeming to argue against self-determination for particular groups in specific localities. At least that was one of the charges hurled against him by opponents who did not wish to curtail the expansion of slavery. As one critic put it: "do the black republicans seek to enforce the very doctrines which caused the American revolution and a separation from the mother country? The mother country imposed upon the colonies local laws against their consent, and denied them the privilege of regulating their own domestic affairs—hence the revolution." When secession came, President Lincoln was indeed obliged to repudiate the South's right of revolution and self-determination. He did so, of course, in order to preserve the Union. "What is now combatted," he proclaimed on July 4, 1861, "is the position that secession is *consistent* with the Constitution—is *lawful*, and *peaceful*." Few persons today would dispute the correctness of Lincoln's actions in 1861. He did what had to be done. In the process, however, he had to deny what many had come to regard as a viable American tradition, the right of revolution; and in so doing, Lincoln had to find his justification in 1787 rather than 1776.[94]

These twists and turns among American attitudes provide us with confirmation, from a different angle of vision, for Edmund Morgan's contention that the American Revolution "remains at once the most significant and the most elusive episode in our national history."[95] But above all, they demonstrate the complexity of our quest to determine the national character—a quest that occurred intermittently for two generations following the end of hostilities in 1783, and to which I shall return in greater detail near the conclusion of this book.[96]

James Sullivan sounded the feelings of his fellow Americans in 1788 when he declared that "it is now full time that we should assume a national character, and opinions of our own," a sentiment echoed more notoriously by Noah Webster: "every engine should be employed to render the people of the country national; to call their attachment home to their country; and to inspire them with the pride of national character."[97]

As the nineteenth century unfurled, however, perceptions of the national character became intertwined with changing views of American tradition in general and the Revolution in particular. One year after the fiftieth anniversary of Independence had been celebrated, for example, Jared Sparks declared that "to emulate the noble deeds of ancestors, who have been instrumental in securing the freedom and happiness of their posterity, is equally the dictate of patriotism and gratitude; and the character of such ancestors is the richest inheritance, that any nation can receive."[98]

A cultural situation had arisen, however, in which their perception of tradition provided many Americans with aching pangs of self-reproach. Why? Because they felt themselves to be inferior in character and ability to their Revolutionary forebears. "The ideal of success has totally changed with the blandishments of prosperity," one critic remarked in 1855, "from the resources of character to the artifices of wealth."[99]

It is unlikely that very many citizens of the United States had then read or even heard of Edmund Burke's discussion of society, the state, and tradition.[100] It occurs in his *Reflections on the Revolution in France* (1790), where Burke asserts that the historical development of the state makes it a partnership: "As the ends of such a partnership cannot be obtained in many generations, it becomes a partnership not only between those who are living, but between those who are living, those who are dead, and those who are to be born."[101] Assessed within Burke's frame of reference, the obvious difficulty in post-Revolutionary America was manifold. Many felt that any partnership between the living and the dead was unequal because the living were so inadequate to their obligations—both to the contemporary society and to the long-term implications of that partnership. Others simply denied the existence (or the importance) of a partnership with the dead. Still others conceded the existence of such a partnership, but hoped to escape from its contractual obligation.

Amid these tangled, incompletely formed, and sometimes contradictory views of tradition in America, historical imaginations nonetheless began to unravel various versions of the Revolution's role in determining our national character.

CHAPTER TWO

REVISIONS OF THE REVOLUTION IN AN UN-REVOLUTIONARY CULTURE

ONE OF THE MOST important lessons to be learned from examining these materials is that the American Revolution, while meaningful in some way to many Americans, has not meant the same thing to successive generations of Americans. Stated so baldly, that lesson may seem rather obvious. Be that as it may, no one has yet explained why; or provided a comprehensive description of what the Revolution has meant to whom, at which times, or with what cultural consequences.[1]

Therefore, it should be useful, at this particular point, to attempt an overall periodization of the Revolution's place in national tradition—a conjectural chronology, as it were, covering the two centuries from 1776 until 1976. The periodization I offer is admittedly artificial and retrospective. It might not even be entirely recognizable to the historical participants. I am convinced, nonetheless, that it reveals some fundamental rhythms in our cultural heritage and thereby may have a certain utility. At the very least, it is intended to supply a frame of reference for the chapters that follow.

As the reader moves on, however, to chapters that look at the Revolution's impact upon art, drama, poetry, film, and especially historical fiction, he (or she) may eventually feel perplexed by the prospect of superimposing somewhat deviant schemes of periodization, depending upon which sort of cultural material one happens to examine. Plays and poems, novels and pictures, have been produced according to cycles that overlap but do not always coincide. It would be pleasing to have them all in tidy alignment; but Culture, alas, is oftentimes less neat than Nature, and certainly not so well arranged as the historian might like. In any case, each of the several sorts of materials I have examined turns out to possess an integrity of its own, an integrity that stubbornly defies symmetrical classification by lumped-together categories.

In the chapters that follow, I shall do my best to respect the integrity of these materials, even at the sacrifice of symmetry and tidiness. In this chapter, however, I offer a periodization that to some degree is independent of those cultural artifacts. It is, rather, a periodization that reflects our changing political values, and that is based upon our attitudes toward certain national holidays, commemorative occasions, public controversies, non-fiction works of popular history, biographies of Revolutionary heroes, opinions expressed in newspapers and magazines, and governmental responses to various requests for the preservation of Americana (such as "saving" Mount Vernon or Monticello).

What explanation can I offer beyond a simple declaration of "the stubborn integrity" of these diverse artifacts and their creators? There is an explanation, in fact, and it has to do, ultimately, with certain deeply rooted conflicts within our society; more particularly, with the ways in which different segments of a heterogeneous society are affected by such ambiguities, or the unequal lengths of time required for divergent segments to respond to them. What I mean, more concretely, is that tradition makes its way awkwardly and establishes itself hesitantly in a society that seeks or professes to be egalitarian. In such a society, Revolutionary origins managed or perpetuated by an élite—by Jefferson's "aristocracy of talent"—present certain problems. The society wants to admire its heroes, but not worship them. And later, when the impulse comes to humanize its heroes, which actually occurred in the 1920s, there is a danger that humanization will wash over into wanton degradation.

We need to believe that the American Revolution was made by "the people," by patriots of every class and station. And yet, whenever we face a serious national crisis, we also yearn for charismatic leadership and recognize that societies with a visible élite are more likely to produce such leadership than a blandly egalitarian nation where no man is recognized as better than another. Here is just one pertinent example of such yearning and recognition. The writer is Francis Parkman, the time is early in 1862, and the message is from an open letter he wrote to a Boston newspaper:

> Our ship is among breakers, and we look about us for a pilot. An endangered nation seeks a leader worthy of itself—the ascendant spirit which shall render its redundant energies into effective action. In a struggle less momentous it found such leaders; men who were types of the national heart and mind, and whose pre-eminence our enemies were forced in bitterness to confess. Out of three millions, America found a Washington, an Adams, a Franklin, a Jefferson, a Hamilton; out of twenty millions, she now finds none whose stature can compare with these. She is strong in multitudes, swarming with brave men, instinct with eager patriotism. But she fails in that which multitudes cannot supply, those master minds, the lack of which the vastest aggregate of mediocrity can never fill. As well an army without generals as an imperilled nation without its counsellors and guides. Where are they? Why is mediocrity in our high places, and the race of our statesmen so dwindled?

Parkman subsequently supplied an answer to his own rhetorical question: an excess of egalitarianism. "The people have demanded equality, not superiority, and they have had it;—men of the people, that is to say, men in no way raised above the ordinary level of humanity. In degrading its high offices, the nation has weakened and degraded itself."[2]

The imperatives of an egalitarian society—and one that accepted new immigrants—frequently meant that potentially rich and complex traditions would have to be reduced to their simplest common denominators. Those imperatives also meant that monuments to Revolutionary battles and heroes would normally be financed in the democratic manner, by public subscription, even though that was an agonizingly slow way to construct physical reminders of national origins. Begun in 1825, the Bunker Hill Monument was not completed until 1843; begun in 1848, the Washington Monument was not completed until 1885. At the Bunker Hill dedication, held on June 17, 1843, Daniel Webster declared that "the hopes of its projectors rested on voluntary contributions, private munificence, and the general favor of the public." He then conceded that, for quite a time, "the prospects of further progress in the undertaking were gloomy and discouraging."[3]

The ethos of egalitarianism also aroused ambivalence when segments of the society became obsessed with genealogy during the 1840s, and once again at the close of the nineteenth century. Why? Because those segments recognized, and in some cases admitted, that tracing one's ancestry back prior to 1776 was neither democratic nor even nationalistic.[4]

Comparable feelings of ambivalence arose during the 1930s. On the one hand, a proletarian push at that time called for greater attention to the lives of ordinary Americans during the Revolutionary struggle. But on the other hand, bicentennial recognition of the birth dates of Washington, Adams, and Jefferson (1732, 1735, and 1743) resulted in the appointment of special congressional committees, the construction of costly memorials, new biographies of heroic proportions, and a copy of Gilbert Stuart's grim Washington being placed in every American classroom. It scarcely seems a satisfactory solution for the arbiters of tradition to have mediated between their meritocratic and their democratic impulses by clumsily attributing "human" qualities to the Revolutionary heroes. Hence, for example, this ludicrous contention by the editor of *Washington's Birthday* that "we are swinging around toward the idea of a lovable, fallible, very human personality with humor, a hot temper, and a genuine love of pleasure."[5]

As we proceed, the reader should expect to encounter quite a number of cultural contradictions whose resolution was no more successful than envisioning George Washington as lovable, fallible, and sybaritic. We will discover the advocates of constitutional ratification in 1787–8 trying desperately to disentangle their affection for the principles of 1776 from their contempt for the Articles of Confederation—which had emerged directly from those principles of 1776. We will find figures like Jefferson being claimed by partisans on *both* sides in the crisis of 1832–3: by the South Carolina Nullifiers and by the Unionist Jacksonians. We will notice that after about 1845 the solemn ceremonial of July 4 celebrations would begin to lose its appeal *pari passu* a steady popularity for publications about the Revolution in general and the events of 1776 in particular. We will observe the Constitution and its writers' intentions being reinterpreted by sectional partisans, especially between 1858 and 1860. We will see the South, which had little interest in the Declaration of Independence during the 1840s and 1850s, suddenly invoke the Declaration in support of its "right of revolution" in 1861. And we will watch organized labor gradually shift from a very positive identification with the Declaration during the 1820s and 1830s to eventual contempt for it as a hypocritical document by the close of the nineteenth century.

My point, ultimately, is that the Revolution has not remained constant in our national tradition. It has been misunderstood and re-understood. Its reputation has undergone shifts both subtle and gross. The reasons are complex; but they have much to do with the persistence of an egalitarian ethos in a society that in fact became ever more stratified. The guardians of tradition so often were obliged to invoke certain sentiments, while pursuing policies that belied those hoary phrases of 1776, and in consequence produced cultural ambiguities of profound importance if one is to understand the dynamics of this society. Also, the appearance of cultural artifacts emblematic of the Revolution—such as novels and paintings, plays and poems—at times and in places seemingly out of phase with one another. In sum, we find those multiple, overlapping (but not quite coinciding) patterns of periodization that I mentioned earlier. We shall look at each one in some detail; first, the most general pattern—that which reflects the fluid mainstream currents of political ideology—in this chapter; and then the more particular cultural patterns in the chapters that follow.

"Nothing but the first act of the great drama is closed"

WHAT I FIND MOST interesting within the Revolutionary era itself (1776–99) is the presence of counterpoised alternatives: varied views on the meaning and proper interpretation of the Revolution. One such divergence, for example, concerned its true chronological locus. John Adams put it this way in a famous letter to Jefferson that reiterates a position Adams had taken ever since 1783: "The Revolution was in the Minds of The People, and this was effected, from 1760 to 1775, in the course of fifteen Years before a drop of blood was drawn at Lexington." Benjamin Rush had quite a different perspective, however, which he voiced at Philadelphia in 1787: "The American War is over, but this is far from being the case with the American Revolution. On the contrary, nothing but the first act of the great drama is closed."[6]

The difference between these two lines of interpretation is important because by 1787–8 the Revolution had become, first, a touchstone for those involved in drawing up the blueprint for a new national government; and second, a point of reference for polemicists engaged in debate over acceptance of the new Constitution. In Massachusetts, for example, one newspaper made this appeal for ratification late in 1787: "Consider that those immortal characters, who first planned the event of the revolution . . . have now devised a plan for supporting your freedom, and increasing your strength, your power and happiness."[7]

It is important for us to recognize that the Federalists as well as the Anti-Federalists, and not just the latter alone, drew upon Revolutionary principles to bolster or justify their positions in 1787–8. The critical point to be made is that they were inclined to stress different aspects of what had been said and done between 1763 and 1783. While the Anti-Federalists preferred to emphasize the Revolution's origins, especially colonial resistance to intervention by a remote central authority, the Federalists tended to talk much more about the war years, 1775–83, when the new republic required unified organization and direction for the maximum mobilization of national strength.

These polemics demanded greater agility on the part of the Federalists. They had to be critical of the Articles of Confederation in order to argue the logic of replacing those Articles as the instrument of government. Yet they could not escape the factual reality that the Articles had been written during the Revolution as an integral part of the process whereby Americans won their Independence. It became the Federalist strategy, therefore, to separate the Articles from other aspects of Revolutionary endeavor; and they did so by suggesting that the Articles had been inadequately drafted, and suffered accordingly, because the mid-1770s had not been a propitious time to develop the most suitable frame of government.

Political partisans quite willingly permitted other differences to show, however, in these early years. Republican (or Jeffersonian) organizations always included a public reading of the Declaration of Independence at their Fourth of July festivities, whereas the

Federalists were likely to omit that reading and replace it with prayers or hymns. The reason for that omission seems to have been a conservative discomfort with the Declaration's more radical doctrines.[8] Whatever the reasons—and they remained somewhat shrouded—the orations that resulted from both sets of gatherings are interesting because they reveal just how many enduring attitudes and precedents were established prior to 1800, many even prior to 1789. These orations narrated the history and nature of the nation's birth; identified the great heroes, George Washington most prominently; praised the advantages of our geography; glorified our accomplishments in agriculture and commerce; offered the United States as an asylum for the oppressed; emphasized the extensiveness of public education; proclaimed the egalitarian character of American society; and presumed our destiny to be part of God's handiwork.

By the 1790s, owing to the intense partisanship of domestic politics as well as controversy over the relative virtues and horrors of the French Revolution, those alternative points of view first articulated during the 1780s by Adams and Rush took on new forms that would persist for a very long time to come. One position, advocated especially by such New England Federalists as Fisher Ames and Timothy Dwight, and by Gouverneur Morris, contended that the Revolution was a unique and completed event whose implications had been entirely fulfilled by the creation of the American republic. This conservative view left little room for the Revolution as an exemplar to oppressed peoples elsewhere, or for subsequent rebellions at home (such as Daniel Shays', or the Whiskey Rebellion of 1794).[9] During the nineteenth century it would be continued by Edward Everett and Daniel Webster, and by such Federalist-Whig historians as George Gibbs. This belief that America's Revolution and political system are not exportable has been perpetuated in the twentieth century by Daniel Boorstin and Louis Hartz, among others, but along diverse lines of reasoning.[10]

The counter-position, which tended to be that of the Jeffersonian Republicans—but not singularly so—received its most succinct expression later on in a letter from Jefferson to John Adams: "The flames kindled on the 4th of July 1776 have spread over too much of the globe to be extinguished by the feeble engines of despotism. On the contrary they will consume those engines, and all who work them."[11] Proponents of this view perceived the Revolution as exportable, and therefore as being meaningful overseas. Unlike the Federalists, they also regarded social and political change at home with greater equanimity because change seemed to be an inescapable part of the legacy of 1776. For many of them the Declaration of Independence was less a historic document than a living creed.[12]

David Ramsay put it forcefully in a Fourth of July oration which he gave in 1794: "Let us forward this desirable revolution . . . that other nations, struck with the fruits of our excellent constitution, may be induced, from free choice, to model their own, on similar principles."[13] His point of view would be echoed by many a Jeffersonian newspaper during the nineteenth century; by Abraham Lincoln on several occasions; and in the twentieth century by such public figures as Henry A. Wallace and Senator Elbert Thomas.[14]

Thus two fundamentally different visions of the Revolution's meaning had very clearly developed during the last decades of the eighteenth century. By the end of John Adams's administration, partisan politics had grown so nasty that ideological opponents could not disentangle their sense of the present from their remembrance of the past. Unable to celebrate the Fourth of July together, they held separate processions, separate dinners, and heard separate orations—a situation that continued until the Federalist party died out during the second decade of the nineteenth century. One characteristic toast of the day, reported in 1799, ran as follows: "John Adams—may he like Samson slay thousands of Frenchmen, with the jawbone of Jefferson."[15]

These particular and parochial forms of bitterness would eventually fade. Soon after the War of 1812 ended, it once again became possible for communities to hold unified celebrations on the Fourth of July.[16] Other signs appeared, however, without fanfare or controversy, that were symptomatic of certain basic tendencies in the American response to tradition, and of long-term changes that would not be fully realized for almost a century. Here are just two specific illustrations of such harbingers.

• In 1781 the Continental Congress had voted to provide financial support for Ebenezer Hazard's proposed "Documentary History of the Revolution." The editor, publisher, and sometime postmaster general

(1782–9) labored diligently at his task, and collected source materials that were especially rich for the period 1776–82. In 1792 and 1794 Hazard published his two-volume *Historical Collections, Consisting of State Papers and Other Authentic Documents;* but they sold very poorly and the whole project had to be abandoned. This was not the form in which most Americans wanted to discover their Revolution. They wanted biography, which they began to get from Parson Weems in 1800, and they wanted historical fiction, which Fenimore Cooper started to provide them in 1821.

• Robert Treat Paine (1773–1811), a widely read poet of the Federalist era, was born at Taunton, Massachusetts, the second son of Robert Treat Paine, a signer of the Declaration of Independence. The son had actually been christened Thomas; but in 1801 he legally changed his name in order not to be linked or identified in any way with the notorious, radical author of *The Rights of Man* and *The Age of Reason.* By then, in 1801, this newly minted Robert Treat Paine, a self-denying Thomas, had become one of New England's strongest spokesmen for a neo-Roman cult of patriotism. His nationalistic feelings had much to do with the Revolution, even with that document his father had so proudly signed in 1776. But the principles of Tom Paine? the taint of that accursed French Revolution? and *The Rights of Man?* Heaven forbid!

By 1800, Tom Paine was to many Americans a figure in disgrace.[17] Thomas Jefferson, the author of that Declaration which Robert Treat Paine (senior) had signed, was now more controversial than ever before, vilified almost as viciously as Tom Paine the atheist. Without acceptable radical heroes and spokesmen, would it be possible for any image of a Revolution with radical aspects to survive in the national mind?

"We are among the sepulchres of our fathers"

THE DEATH OF George Washington in 1799 marked the end of an era in American Revolutionary tradition. The publication in 1800 of Mason Locke Weems's *Life of Washington* heralded another. It became a fabulous best-seller and had the most extraordinary impact. Many decades later Lorenzo Sabine, first American historian of the Loyalists, looked back upon his boyhood in the beginning of the nineteenth century. "A top, a ball, a hoop, a knife, and a fishing rod, Weems's *Life of Washington* . . . *Gulliver's Travels,* and *Robinson Crusoe,* comprised every article of property which I could call my own."[18]

Weems initiated an important component of the American tradition, and for several reasons. First, because biographies of Washington, taken together, have sold more than any other single strand of historical writing in the United States. The genre runs from Weems and John Marshall to Jared Sparks and James Kirke Paulding, from Joel Headley and Washington Irving to William E. Woodward and Rupert Hughes, right on down to Douglas Southall Freeman and James T. Flexner in our own time. Second, because so many of these biographies were really a life-and-times of the Revolutionary era. (One wag remarked that Justice Marshall's ponderous five-volume *Washington* was so boring because it had too little life and too much times.)

It is especially interesting to note that while Washington achieved instant immortality in 1800, those whom we regard today as the other Founding Fathers waited much longer to take their places securely within the Pantheon: Jefferson, perhaps, with the publication of Henry Randall's three-volume biography in 1858; Franklin, in a sense, with the first complete American edition of his *Autobiography* in 1868. Adams, Hamilton, Madison, and Jay? It is hard to say just when their niches were permanently filled and their contributions beyond cavil (though I will have more to say about this later).

Instead, men whom we now regard as figures of secondary importance were thought of as immortals during the first quarter of the nineteenth century: John Paul Jones, whose *Life and Adventures* became a popular seller in 1807; General Francis Marion, the "Swamp Fox," because of a very successful biography by Weems and Peter Horry, published in 1810; Patrick Henry on account of William Wirt's fabulous biography, first printed in 1817; James Otis and Richard Henry Lee for similar reasons during the 1820s. Those men who did *not* go on to have national and controversial careers after the Revolution became the undisputed heroic luminaries of the early nineteenth century. Only later, as their luster dimmed, did those whom we think of as being in the first rank outshine them and take their permanent places in the firmament of founders.[19]

The Revolutionary tradition during these early decades of the nineteenth century was perpetuated by several sorts of writers other than biographers, of course. There were also the narrative histories of David Ramsay, Mercy Otis Warren, and Timothy Pitkin—the first two hard at work well before 1800. Despite serious attempts in recent years to resuscitate their reputations, these works have an antique quality—often because of their retrospective yearning for the Revolution as a Golden Age, and withal a rather tedious tone. Such books certainly helped to sustain the Revolution in American tradition; but it would be difficult to say what they added to that tradition of an enduring nature.[20]

Then there were the chroniclers with those wonderfully biblical names: Abiel Holmes, Hezekiah Niles, and Jedidiah Morse. Their documentary compilations were barely arranged in any logical order, despite this delightful assertion by Holmes in the preface to his 1829 edition:

> Without [chronological] arrangement, effects would often be placed before causes; contemporary characters and events disjoined; actions, having no relation to each other, confounded; and much of the pleasure and benefit, which History ought to impart, would be lost. If history, however, without chronology, is dark and confused; chronology, without history, is dry and insipid.[21]

What is most interesting about the 1820s, perhaps, is the fact that many Americans became engaged, in various ways, upon a quest for political order, social stability, and national identity. Remaining survivors of the Revolution were now cherished—their memories and, to a lesser degree, their guidance, were sought. Daniel Webster made a lengthy visit to Monticello in 1824, for example, and had extensive conversations with Jefferson, who reminisced in detail about the Revolution. As Webster wrote subsequently to a friend:

> Mr. Jefferson is full of conversation, & as it relates, pretty much, to bygone times, it is replete with information & useful anecdote. All the great men of our Revolutionary epoch necessarily had a circle of which they were, severally, the centre. Each, therefore, has something to tell not common to all. Mr. [John] Adams & Mr. Jefferson, for example, tho' acting together, on a common theatre, at Philadelphia, were nevertheless far apart, when in Massachusetts & Virginia, & each was at home, in the midst of men, & of events, more or less different from those which surrounded the other.[22]

Jared Sparks and Martin Van Buren had made similar calls upon Jefferson during the early 1820s, just as young George Bancroft had interviewed the aged John Adams in 1818.[23] With the death of William Ellery in February of 1820, only four original signers of the Declaration still lived: William Floyd (who died in August 1821), Jefferson, Adams, and Charles Carroll (the last to go in 1832). The nation clasped these survivors to its bosom. Looking back upon those years from 1850, Edward Everett felt wistful twinges of nostalgia for "our heroic age," which had been providentially prolonged into the 1820s. "There were still lingering among us distinguished leaders of the revolutionary struggle. . . . Amidst all the hard realities of the present day, we beheld some of the bold barons of our Runnymede face to face."[24]

Days passed—in some areas, weeks—before the country realized that both Jefferson and Adams had died on the very same day, and that day actually the fiftieth anniversary of their signing the Declaration of Independence. Many Americans decided that it had pleased Providence immensely to take the two patriarchs on that date. Some felt certain that it had delighted the two deceased men as well. There were even those who believed that Jefferson and Adams had chosen to expire on July 4, 1826, and had *willed* this symbolic testimonial.[25] James Monroe managed to breathe his last on July 4, 1831; and newspaper reports of his death suggested that the fifth President seemed to realize that it was his destiny to cooperate in this divine scheme of coincidences. When the noise of celebration began at midnight on the third, according to one account, Monroe "opened his eyes enquiringly; and when the cause was communicated to him, a look of intelligence indicated that he understood what the occasion was."[26]

Americans made a special effort during these years to invite aged revolutionaries to perform special roles in the formulaic Fourth of July celebrations: fire a cannon, read the Declaration or the Bill of Rights, give a toast, or simply sit at the head of a table. Occasionally an embarrassing mistake occurred. At Indianapolis in 1822, for instance, it was discovered that one "old hero of '76" had, indeed, fought in the American Revolution—but as a Hessian soldier on the British side![27]

By then the established ritual for properly observing the Fourth had developed into a fixed pattern all over the United States. A town wit was invariably present to offer some appropriate toast, such as this one from a village cobbler at Boston in 1826: "The *Shoemakers* of the *Revolution*—they risked their little *all* upon the great *end*, and gave *short quarters* to the foe, in 'the times that tried men's soles.' "[28]

By the later 1820s, also, the Fourth of July had come to be regarded as a day with special significance in the minds of working-class people: a day for renewing the Spirit of '76, for dramatizing working-class demands, and for rewriting the Declaration to restore the rights employers "have robbed us of." It was a day for such toasts as: "The Working Men—the legitimate children of '76; their sires left them the legacy of freedom and equality. They are now of age, and are laboring to guarantee the principles of the Revolution."[29]

Why such strident claims? Because the feeling had arisen among labor circles, especially at the close of the decade, that workers were increasingly being exploited by capital; that even though the "leathern aprons" had played a major role in making the Revolution, its idealistic goals were not being enjoyed by their children and grandchildren. A young artisan argued this quite vocally at Philadelphia in 1827. Frances Wright picked up the theme in her 1829 oration on the Fourth of July, and concluded that the Declaration had been a valuable document, but that it would not serve the interests of ordinary Americans unless it was rewritten with certain guarantees added. New York's trade unions responded later in 1829 by presenting "The Working Men's Declaration of Independence" to the public. Some newspaper editorials argued, notably in 1830, that working-class people were in the same oppressed condition as the colonists had been in 1776, "beset by a mercenary foe." Some suggested that perhaps another revolution would be needed, this time against domestic tyranny and exploitation.[30]

When Harriet Martineau visited the United States in the years 1834–6, she found Americans still interested in the Declaration and its ideas. They had been for several decades; but by the mid-1830s, their fascination was in fact beginning to wane—an important phase and turning point in the history of American culture. Until the early 1790s, the Declaration had been regarded as significant simply because it justified the separation of thirteen colonies from the jurisdiction of their mother country. Thereafter, ever so gradually, more attention was paid to the philosophical preamble than to the enumeration of grievances against George III. The Declaration, consequently, came increasingly to be perceived as having a more transcendent purpose: defining the rights of free men and the goals of civil government. The publication in 1805 of Mercy Otis Warren's history of the Revolution did help to articulate and disseminate praise for the Declaration in language and along lines we now take for granted.[31]

Only in the generation after 1815, owing in part to the demise of the Federalist party, would the Declaration achieve unequivocal standing as a sacred text to which the entire society should subscribe its fealty. During the summer of 1817, *Niles Weekly Register* published an exchange of letters between John Adams and Thomas McKean that reminisced about the genesis of the document and its drafting. That caused public interest to quicken considerably. In 1818 and again the following year, popular engravings were made of the Declaration by two competitive firms—copies that enjoyed very wide sales. Bickering between the firms struck a good many sparks; and the embers were still hot in 1823 when Timothy Pickering re-fired and enlarged the conflagration with a controversial Fourth of July oration at Salem, Massachusetts. Meanwhile, John Trumbull's tableau of Jefferson's committee presenting its draft to the Continental Congress, completed in 1818, was exhibited in various cities prior to its permanent installation in 1826 at the Rotunda of the U.S. Capitol. Finally, John Quincy Adams caused an exact facsimile of the Declaration to be made in 1823, and Congress directed a thorough distribution of numerous copies in 1824.[32]

Although it is impossible to be precise about such things, it would appear that public interest in the Declaration peaked in 1826 (understandably perhaps), and then slowly crested thereafter. As early as 1818, when the subject of Latin American independence touched off a lengthy debate in Congress, there were indications of an impending conservatism in the United States—a conservatism that took the form of feeling some embarrassment at living in a nation whose recent origins were Revolutionary. Those in Congress who did not wish to recognize the former Iberian colonies, now newly free—or did not want to be hasty in doing so—denied the logic of any viable analogy between the American rebellion in 1776 and the Latin struggle for freedom that had been in progress since 1810. Our own Revolution, they insisted, had been discussed rationally, conducted moderately, and had only been advocated *reluctantly* after legitimate petitions for redress had been ignored or denied. When the congressional debates ended and the matter came to a vote in 1818, supporters of a resolution to appropriate funds for a minister to South America were defeated. Three years later, in 1821, Edward Everett asked rhetorically: "How can our industrious frugal yeomen sympathise with a people that sit on horseback to fish?"[33]

There were, then, signs of discomfort on the part of some as to the potential uses of our Revolutionary tradition at the hands of those persons with internationalist and more liberal sympathies.[34] Yet such discomfort did not mean repudiation of the American Revolution—nothing could have been more remote from their minds—only that the Revolution required a cautious interpretation. The chief custodians of that carefully nurtured understanding would be Jared Sparks and George Bancroft.

Sparks came first, and established his preeminence very soon after 1826. He appeared on the scene and played an interesting role in 1821–3 by serving as chaplain in the U.S. House of Representatives. There he met and gathered information from many persons who had known George Washington and his political circle. Sparks thereby added to the stock of Revolutionary lore accumulating in oral tradition; and, equally important perhaps, fired an enthusiasm for his life's work. "I have got a passion for revolutionary history," he wrote in 1826, "and the more I look into it the more I am convinced that no complete history of the American Revolution has been written."[35]

Sparks, a New Englander, made an extraordinary research trip through the Southern states the same year, gathering up or copying documents in public repositories and private hands. By 1828 he was receiving reports on the Revolution and letters of interpretation from elder statesmen, such as this one from James Madison in January of that year.

> It has always been my impression that a re-establishment of the colonial relations to the parent country previous to the controversy was the real object of every class of the people, till despair of obtaining it, and the exasperating effects of the war, and the manner of conducting it, prepared the minds of all for the event declared on the 4th of July, 1776.[36]

I find it very revealing, and symptomatic of a powerful tendency at work by the later 1820s, that Madison's stress should be so strongly upon the cautious *reluctance* of the revolutionaries. It contrasts markedly with his emphasis forty years before, when he proudly praised the founders for their bold vision and willful innovations. "They accomplished a Revolution which has no parallel in the annals of human society," he wrote in 1787. "They reared the fabrics of governments [the state constitutions of 1776–80] which have no model on the face of the globe."[37]

Sparks started to work on his huge George Washington editorial project in 1827. It occupied him for a decade and eventually resulted, between 1834 and 1837, in the publication of twelve volumes of letters. During this period Sparks also edited the *Diplomatic Correspondence of the American Revolution* (1829–30) in twelve volumes, and *The Works of Benjamin Franklin* (1836–40) in ten. Indeed, Sparks began to have a rather proprietary feeling about his role as paramount editor and historian of our Revolution. In 1833, when he learned that Edward Everett planned an edition of Franklin's papers, Sparks determined to beat Everett with his own rendition of Franklin's letters. And in 1840 Sparks became very upset by the prospect that his general history of the Revolution—always envisioned but never written—would be preempted by George Bancroft. So Sparks pleaded with William Hickling Prescott to divert Bancroft by enticing him to write a biography of Philip II of Spain, but to no avail.

Before we spill into the 1840s, however, this question must be answered: why regard the year 1832 as a point of demarcation in this conjectural chronology? There are several reasons. First, because the centennial of George Washington's birth, celebrated in 1832, seemed to denote a poignant and difficult historical distance from the world of the founders. That centennial was marred, moreover, by a quarrelsome, petty divisiveness that contrasted with the comparative consensus of 1826, the fiftieth anniversary of the Declaration of Independence. In 1832, for instance, a great ruction arose over whether to dig up George Washington's remains from his tomb at Mount Vernon and rebury him beneath the Rotunda of the Capitol. Among all the arguments and counter-arguments, my favorite came from Wiley Thompson, a congressman from Georgia:

> In the march of improvement, and the rapid progress of the increase of population in the United States, it is probable that our settlements will not only extend to the Rocky Mountains, but reach beyond, stretching down to the Pacific coast. But say that the foot of the Rocky Mountains

will form their western boundary—and we may reasonably suppose that this will happen at no distant period—then bring the great, the powerful West to act upon a proposition to remove the site of the Federal Government, and who can doubt that a location more central will be found and established on the banks of the Ohio? Shall the remains of our Washington be left amidst the ruins of this capitol, surrounded by the desolation of this city?

To such rhetoric Joel B. Sutherland of Pennsylvania retorted: "If our population is to reach to the Western Ocean, and the seat of Government to be removed, when we carry away the ensigns of power from this place, we will carry with us the sacred bones of Washington."[38]

Another reason why 1832 marks a watershed in the American sense of tradition, and perhaps a more important reason, is that Charles Carroll died that year—the last surviving signer of the Declaration of Independence. As the *Daily National Intelligencer* put it, Americans were "feelingly alive to the privation sustained by the Republic, in the death of the last of her fathers." Contemporaries sensed the end of an era.[39]

"Losing sight of our revolutionary landmarks in the fogs of partyism"

DURING THE THIRD, and in many respects most pivotal phase (1833–74), intergenerational perceptions and apprehensions affected the Revolutionary tradition in fundamental ways. In 1840 an anonymous polemicist cited, with invidious comparison to the present, the "stern courage of our revolutionary sires." And the most constant refrain of these decades, repeatedly invoked with reference to the Revolutionary tradition, was this one:

Fathers! have ye bled in vain?

It recurs continuously in odes and orations of the 1830s, 1840s, and 1850s, in the South as well as in the North. It raises explicitly the questions that seem to have been on so many minds: Are we worthy of our Revolutionary forebears? Are we undoing, by our divisiveness, all that they worked so hard to achieve?[40]

Those founders whose longevity made them mentors to the

Jacksonian generation had helped to raise the level of anxiety. Jefferson, for instance, wrote to John Holmes, a senator from Maine, that

> I regret that I am now to die in the belief, that the useless sacrifice of themselves by the generation of 1776, to acquire self-government and happiness to their country, is to be thrown away by the unwise and unworthy passions of their sons, and that my only consolation is to be, that I live not to weep over it.[41]

Many of the Revolutionary sons felt this psychic pressure intensely, and tried to fulfill their sense of responsibility by writing and editing books about the founders, most especially during the two decades following 1832. Hence William Jay's two-volume *Life of John Jay* (1833), or John Church Hamilton's two-volume *Life of Hamilton* (1834–41), or Charles Francis Adams's two-volume *Letters of John Adams to His Wife* (1841), or Henry C. Van Schaack's *Life of Peter Van Schaack* (1842), or William B. Reed's two-volume *Life and Correspondence of Joseph Reed* (1847). We also know that in 1832 John Quincy Adams began to work on a biography of his father.

Their motives were quite clearly stated. First, as William Jay put it in his preface, there was the imperative of filial obligation: "The generation by whom the independence of these United States was established and secured, is rapidly passing away; and before long, we shall seek in vain for a patriot of the Revolution to receive our homage." Second, as Henry Van Schaack wrote in his, there was the straightforward urge to preserve precious information: "It seemed probable that the manuscripts and information in [Peter Van Schaack's] possession would be lost to the public unless submitted by himself."

One symptomatic consequence of these acts of filial obligation was an inversion in the pattern of book dedications. Back in 1817 William Wirt had dedicated his *Patrick Henry* "to the young men in Virginia," and in 1822 Hezekiah Niles's *Principles and Acts of the Revolution* had been "dedicated to the young men of the United States." In 1837, however, when Peter Force began to publish his *American Archives*—Revolutionary source materials in volumes of staggering proportions—his dedication was to the Founding Fathers. Others in this period followed that example.

As the sectional crisis deepened, especially between the mid-1850s and the later 1860s, poignant lamentations and a sense of political inadequacy punctuated the sentences of those seeking to cope with national disunion and hoping to discover where they had gone astray. In 1855 the *North American Review* ran an essay-review on three volumes of Bancroft's *History*. Its opening paragraph is revealing. "One by one they totter and die," it said, "the remnants of that sturdy race in whose ears the drums yet beat, in whose eyes the colors stream, as they tell to the children of their children the story of the Revolution, of its battles and its trials. It becomes us to save what is fading from the memory of men." Then, on the next page, came pangs of anxiety at their unworthiness, being lesser folk: "Filial duty and scholarly research bring every day to light more and more of their inmost thoughts, and we may well ask ourselves, why the cheek tingles when we think how pure they were, how few were their faults and frailties. . . . Those who fought the great battle,—better, alas! than we could fight it!"[42] As late as 1868, politicians continued to voice variations on this theme: both because they believed in it, and because it seemed to be so resonant in the national chambers of memory and self-doubt.[43]

Fulfilling the founders' expectations, and preserving their achievements, was the most persistent theme in the decades after 1832; yet it was by no means the only strand of our Revolutionary tradition at that time. In a more positive emphasis, the Revolution came to be regarded as a major point of demarcation in the history of mankind. Robert Rantoul, Jr., a Democratic reformer from Massachusetts, put it this way in a speech at Gloucester in 1833: "The independence of the United States of America is not only a marked epoch in the course of time, but it is indeed the end from which the new order of things is to be reckoned. It is the dividing point in the history of mankind; it is the moment of the political regeneration of the world." By 1850 the Revolutionary tradition was also being used in a very conservative fashion: to resist changes, either institutional or intellectual. One handy way to express opposition to any innovation was simply to argue that it seemed inconsistent with the principles of 1776 or 1787.[44]

These attitudes, responses, and uses of the Revolution were not the singular possession of any particular section, class, or social group. They were pervasive. Half a dozen individuals, however, were most instrumental during the middle third of the nineteenth century in shaping America's sense of the Spirit of

1776. I have already mentioned two of them: Jared Sparks, whose *Life of Washington* (1839) became a best-seller, and who prepared the first academic offering in an American college on the Revolution—a course of twelve lectures at Harvard, also in 1839; and Peter Force, the indefatigable editor who gathered together his vast (though never finished) *American Archives* with the help of a handsome but intermittent congressional subsidy.

Force may have conceived of his ambitious scheme as early as 1822. By the beginning of 1830 he had started to work full time at the task of gathering all historical evidence that illuminated the American Revolution in any way. On July 18, 1831, Force and his partner, Matthew Clarke, submitted a memorial to the Secretary of State proposing to publish "A Documentary History of the American Revolution" (1764–89). Congress considered the proposal in 1832; and, after intensive lobbying by Clarke, it was passed and finally signed on March 2, 1833. Five years later, when Force's volumes began to appear, one enthusiastic reviewer even placed a *curse* upon anyone who might say or do anything unfavorable about the project![45]

The other four principals who preserved and enhanced the Revolutionary tradition at this time were Benson J. Lossing, William Gilmore Simms, Lorenzo Sabine, and George Bancroft. Lossing's *Pictorial Field Book of the Revolution,* first serialized and then published in two stout volumes (1850, 1852), may have done more than any other publication to foster popular pride in United States history during the second half of the nineteenth century. His interviews with octogenarian survivors of the War for Independence, and his hundreds of woodcuts of Revolutionary scenes and battle sites, made the birth of a nation both palpable and visual at a time when memories were growing dim, settlers were moving westward (more remote from erstwhile colonial localities), and new immigrants lacked personal ties to the cosmic events of 1765 to 1789.[46]

Simms was important for his cycle of seven novels about the Revolution in the South (1836–56); for biographies like his *Life of Francis Marion,* a best-seller in 1844; and for such patriotic poems as "The Swamp Fox" and "Battle of Eutaw Springs." I shall discuss his contribution much more fully in subsequent chapters concerning poetry and historical fiction.

Lorenzo Sabine, a Massachusetts man who lived in Maine near

the Canadian border for many years (1821–49), came to know the Tories and their descendants intimately. His *American Loyalists* (1847) remains a valuable, pioneering work; but it also stirred up a heated controversy that would continue intermittently for several decades thereafter—tangling up retrospective views of the Revolution with the bitterness of sectional strife. Sabine boasted that there had been fewer Loyalists in New England than in the South, and condemned South Carolina in particular as a hotbed of Toryism.[47]

Needless to say, William Gilmore Simms, a South Carolinian, could not allow that barb to go unchallenged;[48] and so the feud began. It raged for years—coinciding with the Civil War era. Back in 1824, Daniel Webster had been generous in his praise of cooperation between New England and the South: "indeed *they made* the Revolution," he wrote.[49] By the early 1850s that illusion of unity had gone a-glimmering. Theodore Parker's sketches of *Historic Americans,* such as Franklin, Washington, Jefferson, and Adams, were clearly shaped by Parker's role in the anti-slavery campaign of the 1850s.

The important point to bear in mind is that the ideology and rhetoric of abolitionism, most especially in New England, reverberated with Revolutionary lore. On April 12, 1852, for example, Parker delivered a stirring sermon, called "The Boston Kidnapping," before 2,000 people at the Melodeon in Boston. "Some of you, I think, keep trophies . . . won at Concord or at Lexington," he said, "powderhorns, shoe-buckles, and other things from the nineteenth of April, 1775." Then came Parker's challenge: "Where are the children of the patriots of old? . . . Adams and Hancock died without a child. Has nature grown sterile of men?"[50]

What Parker was reacting to so strongly, of course, was a popular response to the Fugitive Slave Law that to him seemed little more than pusillanimous. In urging defiance of duly constituted law, Parker's speech was symptomatic of a change that had become quite perceptible by the early 1850s: a gradual decline in the binding authority of customary patriotism, and a greater willingness on the part of disaffected persons to question some of the traditional verities. We can see it in minor ways during the 1840s, when free Negroes refused to participate in Fourth of July celebrations, which they regarded as a hypocritical sham. (They set aside July 5, instead, to mark the nation's birthday.) We can see it during the late 1840s and early 1850s in the sudden growth of interest in the roles played by Negroes and women in the patriot cause.[51] We can see it through the beginnings of critical revisionism in American historical writing after 1849, when Richard Hildreth, Richard Frothingham, Henry B. Dawson, and others became determined to cut through all the patriotic cant, and tell as well as they could discover what really happened during the Revolutionary era—even if that meant allowing just a bit of sympathy for the British side.[52]

Most of all, we can see it reflected during the final fifteen years before the American Civil War in changes that occurred in the nature of July 4 celebrations. For the first half century or so of its observance, the Fourth of July was a fairly solemn occasion accompanied by church services. This was especially true in New England; but even in other regions the ceremonies had a strong religious cast. Starting in the 1830s, however, a process of secularization begins to be visible, and it accelerates during the 1840s. The day became less solemn and more given over to festivities, firecrackers, and gorging. At Cadiz, Ohio, in 1840, "the spirited log cabin boys" consumed 2,100 pounds of bread, 1,100 pounds of ham, 15 young pigs, 500 pounds of cheese, a barbequed ox weighing 1,500 pounds, and, needless to say, "plenty of hard cider."[53]

Such excess in the consumption of food and liquor was matched by oratorical overindulgence, with the result that occasional satires of the classic Fourth of July oration began to be heard during the 1850s. This irreverence would have been unthinkable previously; now, suddenly, there were references to "rant and extravagance," to "exhuberant pride and boastful fancy," and to the "parade of vain glory, cheap and vulgar. . . ." In 1857 one cynic could comment that "our usual synonyme for bombast and mere rhetorical patriotism is a 'fourth of July oration' "; and in 1860 a complaint appeared that the traditional gala day had become "a symbol of empty pomp and rhetorical boast."[54]

What caused the decline and change in attitudes? Sheer bombast, obviously, and boredom; but also partisanship and special pleading by high-minded reformers. Anti-slavery and Negro colonization groups, temperance types, women's suffrage advocates, Sunday school and peace societies all sought to use the Fourth of

July as an occasion to promote their respective causes. Some members of the American Peace Society even denounced the American War of Independence, "the holiest war on record," to demonstrate the evils and immoralities of armed conflict. They did not doubt the existence of due cause for separation from Great Britain, but rather questioned the means that had been used to achieve independence. The point, ultimately, was to show "the effects of war upon a people confessedly as good as any on earth."[55]

Most of all, however, the growing feeling among southerners that they were being oppressed by a sectional alliance between the North and the West lessened their enthusiasm to observe the anniversary of Independence. The day had always been celebrated in Norfolk, Virginia, prior to 1850; but in that year it passed almost entirely without notice. As the Norfolk *Argus* put it, rather poignantly, "it is a question whether the South have at this day any independence to boast of."[56]

As early as 1820, during congressional debates over the possible admission of Missouri as a slave state, southerners had tried to assert that the Declaration's drafters had not literally meant that God created all men equal.[57] Twenty-five years later, when the annexation of Texas became a hot topic of congressional discussion, the American Revolution once again posed problems of partisan interpretation. Representative James Edwin Belser of Alabama, for instance, conceded that many southerners sought a place for Texas in the Union so that slavery would be extended; but the South had basically fought to defend northern interests during the Revolutionary War, he contended, and now the time had come for northerners to reciprocate. Representative Joshua Reed Giddings of Ohio declared, in turn, that he opposed annexation because the inevitable, subsequent war with Mexico would be fought by northern men while "our southern friends must remain at home to watch their slaves," just as they had done during the War of Independence![58]

During the 1850s, as southerners very slowly began to lose their control over the institutions and mechanisms of the federal government, sympathetic journalists started to compare this southern predicament with that of the colonists prior to 1776. "If our fathers had cause for disunion with England," one wrote, "tenfold now are the right and the duty which point us to a similar course."[59] When Representative Lawrence M. Keitt of South Carolina resigned from Congress in 1856 (after being censured by the House for failing to help prevent Preston Brooks from caning Charles Sumner), Keitt devoted most of his farewell speech to an aggressive defense of the southern contribution to American Independence. The South had been more patriotic and had actually been foremost in areas where the North long claimed the initiative. He pointed out, for example, that in 1765 North Carolinians had seized a British ship loaded with stamped paper, had then publicly burned the paper, and prevented the stamp master from executing his duties. "Here was an act of heroism and magnanimity greater than that of the Boston tea party or the battle of Bunker Hill." Since northerners traditionally asserted that *they* had placed the greatest number of patriotic troops in the field, Keitt smugly provided a list of 100 Massachusetts soldiers who had been declared unfit for service![60]

By 1858, and most especially during the three years that followed, northerners and southerners both invoked the principles of '76 in support of their respective causes—a competition which suggests that those principles in general and the Declaration in particular had been vulgarized for partisan purposes. To complicate matters even more, northern and western spokesmen could not even agree among themselves about the proper interpretation or application of Revolutionary events. In 1858 and 1859 Abraham Lincoln appealed to the Declaration in arguing against the extension of slavery. In September 1859, Senator Stephen A. Douglas insisted—through a widely read article which appeared in *Harper's*—that the great issue (hence the true meaning) of the American Revolution was the right of each colony to self-government. Popular sovereignty surely *must* have been the name of the game in 1776.

Lincoln responded on February 27, 1860, in his famous speech at the Cooper Union in New York City. The founders of the republic, he insisted, had regarded slavery as an absolute evil, "not to be extended but to be tolerated only because of and so far as its actual presence among us makes that toleration and protection a necessity." He indicated that the Republicans would continue to tolerate slavery where it already existed, "due to the necessity arising from its actual presence in the nation." They would not, however, abandon their belief in the immorality of slavery, or their efforts to exclude it from the territories.[61]

Despite Lincoln's moderation, and despite the accuracy of historical knowledge which he displayed, southerners felt only despair; and their perceptions of the past were adjusted accordingly.

• "No National Party can save us," wrote William Lowndes Yancey to another Alabamian in 1858; "no Sectional Party can do it. But if we could do as our fathers did, organize Committees of Safety all over the cotton States . . . we shall fire the Southern heart . . . and at the proper moment, by one organized, concerted action, we can precipitate the cotton States into a revolution."[62]

• The Charleston *Mercury* declared, on November 8, 1860, that "the tea has been thrown overboard; the revolution of 1860 has been initiated."[63]

• Alfred Iverson, from Georgia, took his stand on the Senate floor a month later: "While a State has no power, under the Constitution, conferred upon it to secede from the Federal Government or from the Union, each State has the right of revolution, which all admit."[64]

• On January 10, 1861, Jefferson Davis declared that "if the Declaration of Independence be true, (and who here gainsays it?) every community may dissolve its connection with any other community previously made."[65]

• And on July 4, 1861, the New Orleans *Daily Picayune* announced very boldly that "the Confederate States of 1861 are acting over again the history of the American Revolution of 1776."[66]

Essentially, by the middle of 1861 our Revolutionary tradition was a shambles, the victim of hypocritical abuse and exploitation for partisan purposes. Southerners who had been uncomfortable with the principles of 1776 for two decades, who had discontinued public readings of the Declaration because they were too embarrassing, now fell all over themselves to invoke the concept of self-determination. Northerners, on the other hand, who had maintained their faith in the Declaration all along, and some of whom (like William Lloyd Garrison) had damned the Constitution as a covenant with the Devil, now felt obliged to reverse themselves, invoke the Constitution, and interpret it strictly for the sake of preserving the Union. Northerners asserted that secession violated the most fundamental intent of the American Revolution, whose patriots had struggled to create the Union. Southerners, in turn, invoked their own favorite lines from the Declaration.[67]

National symbols were being snatched or discarded like cheap gewgaws; and this erratic behavior continued markedly for another fifteen years. George Fitzhugh used the *Southern Literary Messenger* to announce in 1863 that "the Revolution of '76 had nothing dramatic, nothing novel, nothing grand about it." This essay, entitled "The Revolutions of 1776 and 1861 Contrasted," seemed to please Fitzhugh so much that he reprinted it verbatim in 1867.[68]

For some while following the end of civil strife in 1865, it got to be exceedingly awkward to invoke Revolutionary rhetoric or symbolism—so misused and confused had they become. Most white southerners, for example, ceased to observe the Fourth of July during Reconstruction times. That holiday became an exclusively Negro festival in the South. The editor of the Richmond *Times* remarked on July 4, 1866, that the Founding Fathers would "find it difficult to ascertain by what strange freak of national lunacy the negro has been permitted to monopolize the Fourth of July." The *Rockingham Register* of Harrisonburg, Virginia, moaned on July 7, 1870: "Alas! for the 4th of July, 1776, is no more to *us* now than any other day in the calendar."[69]

George Bancroft's four volumes on the Revolution appeared between 1858 and 1874, years when the United States was distracted by national disunion, and perhaps the least concerned of any time in our entire history about what really might have taken place between 1764 and 1789. Nevertheless, Bancroft remained both popular and influential, in part, I suspect, because he somehow managed to be all things to all people. He argued, for instance, that the Revolution "was most radical in its character, yet achieved with such benign tranquillity that even conservatism hesitated to censure."[70]

By 1874, when the last of Bancroft's volumes on the Revolution appeared, a new phase was ready to emerge—one that started by being remarkably *un*historical in its orientation, and ended (with the century) in maudlin nostalgia for tradition as well as some strange perversions of the past.

"Uncle Sam's a Hundred"

OUR CENTENNIAL ACTIVITIES and outlook displayed less a judicious assessment of Revolutionary origins than a mawkish celebration of the present accompanied by high hopes for the future. The national mood in 1876 was ebullient, on the surface, full of self-congratulation for a century of progress. Huge ceramic urns, made for the United States by the Haviland Company at Limoges, in France, were emblazoned, respectively: "1776, THE STRUGGLE," and "1876, PROSPERITY."[71]

There were some doubts and doubters, to be sure. On July 1, 1876, for instance, an editorial appeared in the Newark *Daily Advertiser* that looked back searchingly to the jubilee year and concluded that in 1826, "patriotism was more fervent than at the present time. People lived a little closer to the fountain-head of liberty than we do now, and they had not fallen into the whirlpool of fast living which keeps the present generation on such a constant tensile strain." So there was some concern and ambivalence about the moral consequences of material progress; yet the nation had finally started to recover from a serious depression, and most eyes looked ahead rather than backward in 1876.[72] Here is a characteristic song of that year, taken from a *Centennial Songster.*

"UNCLE SAM'S A HUNDRED"

Oh, ye Powers! what a roar.
Such was never heard before—
Thundering from shore to shore:
"Uncle Sam's a hundred!"

Cannons boom and trumpets bray,
Fiddles squeak and fountains play—
'Tis his great Centennial day—
"Uncle Sam's a hundred!"

Stalwart men and puny boys,
Maids and matrons swell the noise,
Every baby lifts its voice:
"Uncle Sam's a hundred!"

Nervous folks who dote on quiet,
Though they're half distracted by it,
Can't help mixing in the riot:
"Uncle Sam's a hundred!"

Robert C. Winthrop, scion of an old and distinguished Massachusetts family, was selected to be Boston's orator on July 4, 1876; and his remarks on that occasion were typical of mainstream sentiments across the nation. He acknowledged the presence of such serious problems as crime, political corruption, and a demoralizing Civil War whose consequences were still being felt.[73] Nevertheless, he saw a rising demand for civic virtue and individual integrity, and therefore expressed the hope that by April 30, 1889, when the nation would commemorate the Centennial of Washington's inauguration as our first President, "the thick clouds which now darken our political sky may have passed away."[74]

Having disposed of all his qualms about the present and the future, Winthrop lavished praise upon "a century of self-government completed," and assured his auditors about the "progress of freedom which was to have no backward steps." If the Founding Fathers could only "look down on all which has been accomplished, they would feel that their toils and sacrifices had not been in vain." (What a stunning contrast to the lamentations and protestations of inadequacy heard so often between 1830 and 1860!)[75] After enumerating all the happy consequences of the American Revolution, and giving a catalogue of our achievements (mostly commercial and technological) since then, Winthrop began to build toward the conservative climax his middle-class listeners (and subsequent readers) wanted to hear. He insisted that there was nothing radical about the Revolution. "It was no wild breaking away from all authority. . . . It was no mad revolt against every thing like government." Rather, he told them, in all of our deliberative assemblies, such as the Continental Congress, "there was a respect for the great principles of Law and Order." He reminded those people then agitating for social change of the Declaration's assertion that "governments long established should not be changed for light and transient causes." And he closed by calling for a renewal of the spirit of subordination and obedience to law.[76]

Winthrop's oration typified the dominant point of view in one other very important respect: the desire to heal and bind up those raw sectional wounds that had been festering for more than a quarter of a century. So Winthrop, a Massachusetts man, went to extravagant and explicit lengths to give Virginia "the foremost place" in his survey of the significance of July 4, 1776. Without Virginia, he asserted, Independence certainly would have been delayed, and might have seemed hopeless. Therefore, considering those contributions, "we are ready and glad to forget every thing of alienation, every thing of contention and estrangement which has intervened." Winthrop's praise for Thomas Jefferson was as generous as Edward Everett's had been lavish back in 1826; and Winthrop even emphasized that particular moment in Jeffersonian thought most appealing to southerners—states' rights. The orator praised the Union as a safeguard of liberty, but fulsomely stressed the need for Union to be constitutional and limited, "founded on compromises and mutual concessions; a Union recognizing a large measure of State rights."[77]

Following 1876, southerners once again joined the nation in celebrating the Fourth of July. By 1880, Thomas Wentworth Higginson of Massachusetts could be invited to deliver a major address celebrating the Battle of the Cowpens. There he stood at Spartanburg, on May 11, 1881, introduced by the governor of South Carolina as a representative of Revolutionary New England; and Higginson did not disappoint his audience. He pointed out that this historic battle had been won exclusively by southerners, and then went on to assert the compelling need to heal Civil War scars. "It is useless now to distribute the award of praise or blame"—a considerable reversal of Lorenzo Sabine's war of words with William Gilmore Simms back in 1847–9. In its published version, Higginson's speech became an American classic, widely reprinted and committed to memory by schoolchildren.[78]

Following the rancor of Reconstruction, many Americans perceived the Revolution—or wanted to—as a mutually shared memory, a common core of national tradition that could banish the old bitterness. What resulted from that desire? For one thing, a falsely consensual view during the three decades following 1876. This myopic generation minimized not only sectional partisanship but economic and class conflict as well, in its understanding of the Revolutionary era.[79]

As a second result the nation tended—not entirely, but very appreciably—to shift its attention and emphasis from the Declaration (susceptible as it was to radical connotations) to the Constitution. Doing so became steadily easier, of course, perhaps even logical, once 1876 had passed and 1887 approached. Nevertheless it is noteworthy that the Declaration was on public view, yet largely ignored, between 1877 and 1894. Thereafter it was locked up in a safe, and inaccessible to the American people between 1894 and 1924.[80]

What Americans wanted during these decades was not a Revolutionary view of their origins but an evolutionary one. The seeds of such an understanding can be found as far back as 1826 in Jared Sparks's journal, and 1838 in an essay-review by George Bancroft.[81] But it blossomed in this fourth phase, helped along mightily by the currency of Social Darwinism and its foremost exponent among writers of American history, John Fiske. We know that he began to work earnestly on his multi-volume series in 1883. The next year he delivered twelve very colorful lectures about the American Revolution for the Old South Association in Boston; and every year thereafter Fiske helped to support his family by repeating these lectures, in various versions, all over the country. In 1888 his study of *The Critical Period* appeared, covering the years 1783–8. Between December 1887 and December 1890, *The Atlantic* serialized his chapters on the war years, 1776–83, which Houghton Mifflin then published in two volumes as *The American Revolution.* In 1889, meanwhile, he also brought out *The War of Independence,* a briefer book successfully designed for school adoptions.[82]

It should scarcely be surprising that a freshet of historical writing about the Constitution flowed during the 1880s. Fiske's two volumes on the background of the Grand Convention in 1787 had been preceded by James Schouler's in 1880, two by Bancroft in 1882, and one by John Bach McMaster in 1883. All of them, with their moderate to conservative views of the Revolutionary era, sold successfully; whereas Herman E. Von Holst, whose *Constitutional History of the United States* appeared in eight volumes between 1855 and 1892, was not popular. It is difficult to say why with absolute assurance. But I think it reasonable to point out that that post-Civil War generation did not want to be told that the Declaration of Independence was a distinctly Revolutionary statement, and not a legal one; and that the Constitution had been accepted only reluctantly in 1787–8 by many of the American people. When Von Holst died in 1904, an obituary in *Bookman* expressed the hope that his "disappointing" volumes would be buried with him.[83]

What seems most interesting and symptomatic of all, however, is the fact that George Ticknor Curtis's *History of the Origin, Formation, and Adoption of the Constitution of the United States,* first published in the later 1850s and then in revised form in 1889, stood for half a century following the Civil War as the standard authority on the formation of our Constitution. Why should this have been so? Because Curtis, a Massachusetts man, was anti-egalitarian and deeply concerned about the protection of property rights. His book made a particular point of defending the constitutional right to hold property in slaves. No reviewer challenged that assertion in any way, and Curtis long remained *the* historical guide to those crucial proceedings of 1787–8.[84]

By the 1880s, moreover, several other developments had emerged that would permanently affect the Revolutionary tradition in American thought. First, the decline of "romantic" narrative history—the history of Bancroft and Parkman—was accompanied by the rise of positivistic, "scientific" history, the history of John William Draper and Henry Adams, with its characteristic emphasis upon material advances and technological change. The locomotive had replaced the Conestoga wagon, for example, as our national beast of burden: a long-range transformation that to many persons seemed almost as significant as our political alteration of 1776 and constitutional evolution of 1787.

Second, although American historical writing became more nationalistic than ever, it also became less national in scope. Instead, the last decades of the nineteenth century were characterized by a growing interest in regional and local history, especially the contributions made by particular localities to the Revolutionary cause. These were years of active productivity, for example, for such historians of New England as Justin Winsor, John Gorham Palfrey, and Mellen Chamberlain.[85] The Civil War and its aftermath had made it difficult to prepare properly integrated histories on a national scale. Regional writing provided one alternative solution.

Biography provided another. It was a period when lives of the founders became almost as popular as Weems's hagiography had been in the first decades of the century; but with one crucial difference. These latter-day biographies usually took pains to de-emphasize any radical activities or tendencies.[86] Instead, the founders appeared as statesmen rather than politicians, nation-builders rather than revolutionaries. It was a conservative era, and our revolutionaries were de-revolutionized accordingly.[87]

Although George Washington remained every bit the sacred cynosure he had been, and most especially in the 1890s, two others gained proportionately more in esteem during the Gilded Age: Hamilton and Franklin. Franklin, whose guidance on "the way to wealth" was very congenial to a bourgeois society, may well have received the highest encomiums of all in this period. *The New York Times* singled him out for praise at the Centennial in 1876. Seven years later John Bach McMaster declared him to be the greatest American of the Revolutionary era; and in 1887 McMaster published a separate study of *Benjamin Franklin as a Man of Letters.*[88]

Alexander Hamilton's stock slowly began to rise during the 1860s; improved in 1876 with the publication of a two-volume biography by John T. Morse; accelerated a decade later when Henry Cabot Lodge brought out both a biography and a new edition of Hamilton's writings; and then peaked early in the twentieth century with Teddy Roosevelt's cult of strenuous statesmanship. As early as 1874, an influential essay in the *North American Review* had predicted that the future course of United States history would belong to the Hamiltonian (rather than the Jeffersonian) tradition. John Fiske admired Hamilton greatly, and gladly promoted him at every opportunity in the fifteen years following 1885.[89]

Gertrude Atherton's fictional biography, *The Conqueror,* helped bring Hamilton's reputation to its apogee in 1902. Her admiration for Hamilton had been inherited from her grandfather; and on her very first trip to New York, young Gertrude visited both Hamilton's home in Harlem and the scene of his infamous duel with Aaron Burr at Weehawken. Later she gazed upon his portrait at the Treasury Building in Washington, talked with United States senators and discovered, as she put it, that "he was one of the living characters in American history to them." To Atherton, George Washington's flawless unapproachability could not compare with Hamilton's story; for his character, "of a virtue not so flawless, touches us more nearly, not only by the romance of his early life and his tragic death, but by a certain ardor and impulsiveness, and even tenderness of soul, joined to a courage equal to that of Washington himself."[90]

This was also a period when the Revolution fully entered the mainstream of American literary history: partially because of major academic projects by Moses Coit Tyler of Cornell and Barrett Wendell of Harvard,[91] and partially because of the obsession with Revolutionary America in juvenile fiction of the decades 1886 to 1906. Everett Tomlinson and James Otis Kaler are no longer household words in this country; but at least two generations of Americans grew up on books like *Washington's Young Aids* and *The Boys of Old Monmouth* by Tomlinson, or *Boston Boys of 1775* and *The Minute Boys of New York City* by Kaler.[92]

People made pilgrimages in those years to battle sites and other shrines of the Revolution, then published their accounts of these patriotic adventures in books that began in this manner: " 'What a spot this is, boys and girls!' Uncle Tom Dunlap exclaimed, with an impressive sweep of the hand. 'The atmosphere is fairly charged with patriotism; the air throbs with memories.' "[93]

And finally, to cap it all off, the very last years of this fourth phase witnessed an obsession with transplanting Revolutionary heroes to more suitable graves than their original burials had been able to provide. It may have begun in 1882, when Jefferson's oldest living grandchild petitioned Congress to construct a pantheon in Washington, D.C., and move his remains there. Nothing came of her request; but it nearly led to a controversy every bit as noisy as the one over reburying George Washington back in 1832. Then, in 1905, John Paul Jones's body was dug up from the Protestant cemetery outside Paris and eventually reburied at the Naval Academy in Annapolis. In 1909, Pierre L'Enfant was removed from the Digges family plot in Prince Georges County, Maryland, and reinterred at Arlington National Cemetery. Other examples might be cited; but the net effect should be clear. By the early 1900s the American Revolution in national tradition had been trivialized—and to a large degree, de-revolutionized.[94]

"Patriots off their pedestals"

THE MOST CURIOUS facet of this next phase is that the main flow of public opinion in the United States moved from confident nationalism before World War I to cynical disillusionment afterwards; but then shifted slowly back to ardent patriotism during the later 1930s and World War II, based upon a reaffirmation of democracy. The more radical undercurrent was scarcely less fluid. By the beginning of the twentieth century, liberals and labor leaders had become somewhat disenchanted with the American Revolution. They believed that it had only been of benefit to the upper classes. James Oneal asserted in 1909 that "the Declaration of Independence, though it does not mention a single distinct working class grievance, by its eloquent phrases deluded large numbers of the poor classes into the belief that a new era was dawning for them." Algie M. Simons developed the very same theme for his *Class Struggles in American History*, the series of essays he wrote for a popular Socialist weekly. When the Socialist party of America celebrated the Fourth of July in these years, it stated explicitly that it was *not* paying tribute to either the Revolution in general or the Declaration in particular.[95]

At the very beginning of this century, however, the dominant public voice in writing about the Revolution belonged to a Philadelphia lawyer and amateur scholar who did not even start to write colonial history until the age of forty. Then Sydney George Fisher (1856–1927) became determined to strip away the nonsense and nostalgia attributed to American origins by nineteenth-century writers. So he produced a steady flow of books and essays that gathered momentum in a mildly revisionist direction. *The True Benjamin Franklin* (1899) sought to remove the myths and humanize Poor Richard. *The True History of the American Revolution* (1903) was overtly hostile toward George Bancroft, Richard Hildreth, and John Fiske. *The Struggle for American Independence* (1908), Fisher's major work, took two volumes to insist upon the inadequacy of all previous books on the Revolution. And in 1912 he presented to the American Philosophical Society a major paper concerning "The Legendary and Myth-making Process in Histories of the American Revolution."[96]

In retrospect, however, Fisher seems significant not as the progenitor of a new approach or interpretation of the Revolution, but rather as the last gasp of a dying breed. From David Ramsay until Sydney George Fisher, serious scholarship had not been incompatible with popular appeal to a broad readership. Ramsay and Sparks, Bancroft and Lossing, Fiske and Fisher, all worked close to the primary materials. Their analyses may sometimes seem naïve or even misguided today; but they made a genuine effort to ground their writings deeply in the sources. Nevertheless, they also had a very wide appeal to laymen and enjoyed large sales.

After about 1910, however, "scholars" and "popularizers" began to diverge as discrete categories. The latter wrote well, but depended upon superficial information. The former probed our Revolutionary roots more deeply than ever before, but their writings were more narrowly monographic, their prose commonly dull or mediocre; and their audiences shrank accordingly. Claude Van Tyne, George Louis Beer, Carl Becker, Charles McLean Andrews, Arthur Schlesinger, Sr., Charles McIlwain, and J. Franklin Jameson all had very important new insights concerning the Revolution. Between 1905 and 1931 they poured out volumes of first-class history; yet their appeal lay almost entirely within the academy, and their influence upon national tradition was minimal. Only Becker (at times), Charles A. Beard, and Claude G. Bowers seemed able to bridge that growing gap between the respectable and the readable; and Beard's legacy in writing about the Revolution may have been primarily to pave the way for those heady debunkers of the 1920s.[97]

Beard's role in altering and shaping our consciousness of the American Revolution is as slippery as it was palpable in the three decades following 1913. He was far more interested in the period from 1786 until 1815 than he was in the years 1763 to 1785. He concerned himself to a much greater degree with the Constitution and the subsequent dialogue between Jeffersonians and Hamiltonians than with the circumstances of late colonial America and the political culture of rebellion. He utilized that dialogue from the Federal era, moreover, to bolster his later polemical positions about the proper posture for United States foreign policy in the 1930s and '40s. He believed, for example, that the Hamiltonian tradition had led us to the wrong kind of nationalism: namely, commercial imperialism. The Jeffersonian tradition, on the other hand, would be a positive inspiration for our foreign policy: the need to maximize national independence and economic self-sufficiency as well as to minimize foreign intrigues and entanglements. These ideals, as Beard put it in 1934, were part of a tradition in which "the old possibility of a distinct national life and character" might continue to be "a living and vital force."[98]

To complicate matters even more, there are sticky ambiguities and significant shifts in Beard's thought. Although critical of the Hamiltonian tradition, as I have indicated, he found himself in 1943 deriving support for his views on United States foreign policy from Hamilton's *Federalist Papers,* especially Number 75. In 1913–15 Beard was far more critical of the Founding Fathers, generally, than he would be twenty-five years later.[99] Moreover, he liked to think of himself as a Jeffersonian agrarian; yet he regarded Jefferson's wistful goal of an agrarian democracy as naïve, and was realistic about the inevitability of an urbanized civilization in the United States. And with the passage of time Beard conceded more importance to non-economic factors, while emphasizing class conflict less and less.[100]

Beard's impact upon members of the general public, however, was much less ambiguous—indeed, rather straightforward. They identified him quite simply with the explanation of the American Revolution offered in his widely used text, *The Rise of American Civilization* (co-authored with his wife): "American business and agricultural enterprise was growing, swelling, beating against the frontiers of English imperial control at every point." Beard called the colonial assemblies and British officials "the political knights errant in a great economic struggle that was to shake a continent."[101]

By the mid-1930s, the Beards' interpretation had deeply influenced the writing of college texts in American history and government; but they were not the only progenitors of this point of view. Arthur M. Schlesinger, Sr., had expounded it in his huge 1918 study of the colonial merchants prior to 1776, and then generalized it in a widely read essay on "The American Revolution," which was published a year later and reprinted in his *New Viewpoints in American History* (1922). James Truslow Adams, who reached a much wider audience than Schlesinger, transmitted the same emphasis (though in a more convoluted form) through a book on *Revolutionary New England, 1691–1776* published in 1923. Adams, who was very much a partisan of our "business civilization," acknowledged that the interests and ideals of the colonial merchant community were fundamentally different from those of the radicals.

Louis M. Hacker, however, took the Beardian tack without modification in a Marxist essay, "The First American Revolution," which appeared in 1935. In this frequently anthologized piece, and in subsequent writings of the late 1930s, Hacker depicted Anglo-American economic conflicts in the starkest possible form, insisting that the Revolution had nothing to do with political power or constitutional concepts. Rather, it had everything to do with colonial manufacturing, undeveloped land and furs, sugar, tea, wine, and currency.[102]

Meanwhile, as I have suggested, the influence of Beard's early critical studies of the Constitution and the Jeffersonian era may have been at least as great upon the so-called debunkers of the 1920s. And how they debunked! D. H. Lawrence brought out his *Studies in Classic American Literature* in 1922, William Carlos Williams his *In the American Grain* in 1925. William E. Woodward published *George Washington—The Image and the Man* in 1926, and Rupert Hughes his *George Washington—The Human Being and the Hero* between 1926 and 1930 in three volumes. Along with many of their contemporaries, these authors produced iconoclastic books that titillated by knocking erstwhile idols off their pedestals, shaking loose George Washington's false teeth in the process. Still others began to reconsider the very essence of democratic theory; and when they found it wanting, as Ezra Pound did, decided to use the Revolutionary era as a medium for their ire. The "New Hamiltonians," as Merrill Peterson has called them, continued to flourish during these years.[103]

By the mid- and later 1930s, however, Jefferson's stock was rising while Hamilton's was slipping. Carl Van Doren could resuscitate Franklin as the self-made exemplar of a democratic society;[104] and Esther Forbes selected an artisan of humble origins around whom to spin her charming story of American Independence, *Paul Revere and the World He Lived In* (1942).

There is nothing quite like the threat of totalitarianism to make us reaffirm democracy. Imperfect though democracy may be, we have yet to find a superior system—as Henry Adams once reluctantly conceded, it is "the only direction society can take that is worth taking"—and by the early 1940s its roots in our Revolutionary heritage would receive considerable emphasis from born-again patriots.[105]

"Nothing missing except the Revolution itself"

In looking at the literature of the last thirty years, I am most conscious of a pervasive stress upon the beneficial role of élites, charismatic leadership, and realism about human nature in Revolutionary America. The democratic dogmas of World War II now seemed quaintly innocent. Starry-eyed optimism had to be replaced by wide-eyed cynicism. Consequently, there would be greater emphasis upon the constructive nation-making of 1787 than upon the destructive break with Britain in 1776.

Among the popular writers, we find a pronounced shift toward the center and even the right. Howard Fast broke with the Communist party during the 1950s. Although he continued to write novels about the Revolution, his former Marxist edge was gone. His human sympathies remained strong, to be sure, but *April Morning* (1961) and *The Hessian* (1971) are more nearly psychological novels than didactic dramas of class conflict and exploitation.[106]

John Dos Passos, whose leftist sympathies had remained strong throughout the 1930s and World War II, thereafter found a new meaning for freedom in Jeffersonian individualism. In a series of non-fiction works published between 1954 and 1966, Dos Passos quite candidly admired the Founding Fathers for their capacity as a ruling élite. John Diggins has recently observed that Dos Passos discovered in the founders "legitimate moral authority that could be entrusted with power."[107]

Others were equally fascinated by the quality of leadership an élite could produce. Hence Douglas Southall Freeman's massive *Washington* (1948–57) in seven volumes, and James Flexner's more modest *Washington* (1965–72) in four; Dumas Malone's *Jefferson and His Time* (1948–78), or Catherine Drinker Bowen's *John Adams and the American Revolution* (1950). Theorists of revolution, meanwhile, could find little that was truly Revolutionary in our achievement of Independence. "Even if one resists this temptation to equate revolution with a struggle for liberation," wrote Hannah Arendt, "instead of identifying revolution with the foundation of freedom, there remains the additional, and in our context more serious, difficulty that there is very little in form or content of the new revolutionary constitutions which was even new, let alone revolutionary."[108]

Within the academy, meanwhile, a subtle kind of shift occurred. To call it a "conservative" shift, as some have, is misleading, for the word has too many inappropriate connotations, and a number of the professional historians involved were themselves political liberals on matters of reform, race, McCarthyism, and the Great Society programs. They arrived at their conclusions, moreover, by different routes and for varied reasons. Nonetheless, the net effect after several decades was to minimize the innovations and radical dimensions of 1776. As William Nelson stated in 1965: "In reading much of the current literature on the Revolution, one has sometimes the feeling that there is nothing missing from it except the Revolution itself."[109]

Leonard Labaree wrote with sympathy about the "Nature of American Loyalism"; and Cecelia Kenyon praised the Founding Fathers for their realism as practical politicians (1951). She admired them for being more tough-minded than Tom Paine about the imperfections of democracy.[110] In *The Genius of American Politics* (1953), Daniel Boorstin sought to depict the revolutionaries as cautious legalists; and Robert E. Brown's revisionist *Middle-Class Democracy and the Revolution in Massachusetts, 1691–1780* (1955) persuaded many scholars to pursue the idea that no "internal" revolution had been necessary—merely a formal separation from Great Britain.

Charles Sydnor and John Roche both praised the Founding Fathers for bringing to power a "democratic élite," while Martin Diamond admired them for being cautious and realistic about the pitfalls of democracy. He considered the Declaration of Independence a recklessly populistic document, devoid of guidance on the proper shape of democratic institutions.

> Our Founding Fathers more skeptically, sensibly, and soberly, were concerned how to make this new government *decent even though democratic.* All the American revolutionaries, whether they were partisans of the theory that democratic republics had to be small or agrarian or only loosely confederated in order to remain free, or whether they retained the traditional idea that democracy had to be counterbalanced by nobility or wealth, or whether they subscribed to the large-republic theory implicit in the new Constitution—all the American revolutionaries knew that democracy was a problem in need of constant solution, in constant need of

moderation, in constant need of institutions and measures to mitigate its defects and guard against its dangers."[111]

Finally, it is more than fortuitous that a founder hitherto neglected gained recognition in these years as an intellectual giant. James Madison emerged after World War II as the most carefully studied of American political theorists. A kind of cult figure on many campuses, he came to be regarded as the most profound, original, and far-seeing among all his peers. *Federalist* Number 10, I am sure, was more closely scrutinized in the 1950s and 1960s than either the Declaration of Independence or the Bill of Rights. Madison's apparent sophistication with interest group analysis, his realism about the nature of man as a political animal, and his profound understanding of the role of public opinion—all received lavish praise. Madison the modern pluralist, the student of governmental mechanisms, and the nationalist, had important messages for the American scene during the decades following 1945.[112]

THERE IS discernible movement and change within each of these six periods—often a pronounced shift in attitudes—yet each phase nevertheless had a certain cohesion. The first (1776–99) involved a divided search for the Revolution's proper meaning and implications. The second (1800–32) saw the passing of the founders and thereby the end of oral verification, as memory gave way to the wiles and imperatives of imagination. In the third (1833–74), the Revolution came to be understood in the light of those issues that precipitated the Civil War; and despite a desire to fulfill the founders' goals in order to save the Revolution from oblivion, memories of it did begin to fade in the 1860s.

The fourth phase (1875–1906) began with a somewhat apprehensive celebration of progress and the present, but ended in manipulation of the past as a fantasy world. When our own century opened, the Revolution had been effectively de-revolutionized. Between 1907 and 1944 we moved from nationalism to cynicism and then back to patriotism; so the Revolution's role in American tradition underwent adjustments accordingly. From 1945 until quite recently, historians have tended to minimize the Declaration, maximize the achievements of the Grand Convention held at

Philadelphia in 1787, and, most of all, emphasize the role of élites, interest groups, public opinion, and other political agencies whose importance was only implicitly or imperfectly recognized back in the eighteenth century.[113]

During phase I, the Revolution's future place in American tradition was uncertain, and it remained ambivalent in phase II. By the later 1820s, however, the balance began to tip visibly toward a more conservative view. John Randolph expressed contempt for anyone who might perceive a resemblance between our own Revolution and those contemporary movements for independence in Latin America. When John Trumbull, the great artist-historian of the American Revolution, published his *Autobiography* in 1841, he remarked that "the calm splendor of our own Revolution, comparatively rational and beneficial as it had been, was eclipsed in the meteoric glare and horrible blaze of glory of republican France."[114]

The balance had not been tipped entirely, however, or irrevocably so. In 1851 Horatio Greenough, the sculptor, informed William Cullen Bryant (who had written popular poems about the Revolution) that

> I wish to erect a monument which shall record on the same spot—the treason of Arnold—the capture and death of André and the fate of Capt'n N. Hale. I believe this idea may take a form exceedingly significant of our system, highly expressive of our democratic ethics—& a caution to egotistical intrigue.[115]

Nevertheless, the conservative view of our Revolution as being unique, comparatively bloodless, completed and entirely fulfilled by 1789 grew steadily stronger during the second half of the nineteenth century. Although the Revolution remained central to our sense of nationality, *pari passu* it also became trivialized. Subtly, steadily, the American Revolution became primarily a War for Independence and a backward-looking struggle simply to preserve the rights of Englishmen.[116] The special virtue of our minutemen, apparently, was that they respected Magna Carta and the Petition of Right more vigorously than George III or Lord North.

So the story stood in national tradition as late as 1975. In 1976 and 1977 the pendulum of interpretation may be just beginning to swing back, at least partially. Current work being done by Gordon

Wood, Eric Foner, and Alfred Young, to name only a few, suggests a new emphasis upon profound changes that began in the 1770s, as well as a radical legacy that endured beyond 1800, a legacy Wood has called "the democratization of mind in the American Revolution."[117]

Other thoughtful and influential writers continue to regard the Revolution as a socio-political process in fairly conservative terms. They emphasize that property qualifications for voting continued long after the Revolution, that the traditional logic of political élitism remained a powerful force, that a vigorous commitment to the protection of private property was perpetuated, and that slavery became more deeply entrenched than ever in "freedom-loving" states like Virginia. From this perspective the limited goals of the American revolutionaries are more striking than the vision some had of a society committed to equality and justice.[118]

What we find in this perspective, really, is a reaffirmation of Tocqueville's view that American society was likely to become less and less revolutionary with the passage of time. "Not only do men in democracies feel no natural inclination for revolutions," he wrote, "but they are afraid of them. Any revolution is more or less a threat to property. Most inhabitants of a democracy have property. And not only have they got property, but they live in the conditions in which men attach most value to property."[119]

Are we any closer to understanding the American Revolution than Tocqueville was? Does the passage of time help to clarify, or does it only obscure our vision? Historians cannot even agree on a proper response to such issues. In his presidential address to the American Historical Association in 1925, Charles M. Andrews confidently declared that "each generation of scholars is certain to contribute to historical knowledge and so to approach nearer than its predecessor to an understanding of the past." Well, that is one point of view; and it is, I believe, a widely shared one. But here is another that is the diametrical opposite, and one that has its strong advocates as well. The spokesman is Page Smith, writing in 1964.

> The "perspective" provided by the historian's distance in time from the particular events with which he is concerned does not insure better understanding. . . . A re-examination of the attitudes of successive generations of historians toward the causes of the American Revolution

[indicates] that the best interpretation of the causes of the Revolution was made in the decade following the treaty of peace in 1783 and that thereafter, as we moved further in time from the dramatic events of the Revolution and brought to bear on the problem all the vast resources of modern scholarship, we moved further and further from the truth about our Revolutionary beginnings.[120]

Which of these well-known historians is right? To my way of thinking, both points of view have some validity and value; and yet, both of them are ultimately wrong. Contrary to Page Smith's declaration, our knowledge and understanding of the Revolution are in fact far more subtle than that of the Jeffersonian generation. They had all sorts of remarkable insights, to be sure; but we have others unknown to them, and we are in a position to integrate these insights in ways that they could not. Contrary to Charles M. Andrews, however, is the depressing fact that some generations seem to have been further from the truth than their predecessors, rather than closer. The writings of the 1840s, 1890s, and 1920s, for example, come to mind immediately.

My point is that the momentum of our Revolutionary understanding does not push unequivocally in either direction. It does not necessarily get better and better; but neither does it relentlessly decline from the days of David Ramsay. Its rhythms pulsate in more complex ways than that; and they emanate from the varied role the Revolution has played in American social thought. The American Revolution has been an important component of our political culture. As that culture has been subjected to the winds of change, so too has the Revolution's place in our historical imagination.

CHAPTER THREE

REVOLUTIONARY ICONOGRAPHY IN NATIONAL TRADITION

PERHAPS IT WAS inevitable that certain well-worn works of art would suffer from overexposure during 1976, the Bicentennial year. That it happened is unfortunate, nonetheless, because *The Declaration of Independence* by Trumbull, *The Congress Voting Independence* by Pine and Savage, and *The Spirit of '76* by Willard are really not so trivial that they deserve to become clichés. Neither are they so outstanding, however, that we should constantly exhibit or reproduce them, and in the process neglect a fair number of equally interesting pieces of historical art that also take some facet of the American Revolution as their theme.

We are quite familiar, for example, with John Trumbull's huge historical canvases in the Rotunda of the United States Capitol: *The Declaration of Independence* (done in 1818), *The Surrender of Lord Cornwallis at Yorktown* (1820), *The Surrender of General Burgoyne at Saratoga* (1821), and *The Resignation of General Washington* (1824). But how many of us can visualize the five frescoes completed for the Capitol between 1858 and 1871 by Constantino Brumidi? These lunettes depict the Boston Massacre, the Battle of Lexington, the Death of General Wooster, Washington at Valley Forge, and the Storming of Stony Point. Or who can bring to mind the bronze doors of the House and Senate Wings, designed by the excellent sculptor Thomas Crawford during the later 1850s and executed by William H. Rinehart between 1863 and 1867? Each door is divided into ten panels. The top two are decorative; but the eight principal panels depict scenes and events from the Revolutionary era, 1775–93. They are, as it happens, very elegantly done.[1]

The problem of recognizing and interpreting our historical art is an important one for several reasons. First, because there is much validity in a striking observation by the late Dutch historian, J. H. Huizinga, that "historical understanding is like a vision, or rather like an evocation of images."[2] Second, because we need to appreciate the impact these iconographic materials have had upon our cultural life. In 1823, for example, James Fenimore Cooper visited the Military Academy at West Point, where he happened to see the stunning portrait of Jefferson done a year before by Thomas Sully (see figure 1). Cooper was not himself of the Jeffersonian persuasion. Nevertheless, as he gazed upon Sully's canvas, his admiration for both the painter and his subject were significantly altered. "You will smile," Cooper remarked,

> when I tell you its effects on myself. There was a dignity, a repose, I will go further, and say a loveliness, about this painting, that I never have seen in any other portrait. . . . In short I saw nothing but Jefferson, standing before me, not in red breeches and slovenly attire, but a gentleman, appearing in all republican simplicity, with a grace and ease on the canvas, that to me seemed unrivalled. It has really shaken my opinion of Jefferson as a man, if not as a politician; and when his image occurs to me now, it is in the simple robes of Sully, sans red breeches, or even without any of the repulsive accompaniments of a political "sans culotte."[3]

Thirty-two years later, during Nathaniel Hawthorne's English stay, he visited the elegant London home of Russell Sturgis, a financial partner of the Barings and a friend of Thackeray, the novelist. Sturgis owned a "beautiful full length picture of Washington" by Gilbert Stuart, and Hawthorne remarked in his notebook that "I was proud to see that noblest face and figure here in England; the picture of a man beside whom (considered merely as a physical man) an English nobleman would look like common beef or clay."[4]

I could quote numerous other examples of writers, politicians, or the populace-at-large being powerfully affected by some pictorial rendition of Revolutionary times; but, at this point, let us consider a third reason for believing that these works of art deserve our scrutiny: namely, because the artists themselves had an emotional or psychic investment in them—an investment that provides us with important clues to the Revolution's role in our national tradition. In 1831, for instance, Horatio Greenough wrote to Fenimore Cooper from Florence, in Italy, explaining his design of a national monument for Washington, D.C. On each of the sides he envisioned

> four points of the history of the Rev—Oppression—Remonstrance—Resistance—Independence. These I should represent in the form of historic bas reliefs—The whole I would surmount with a statue of Washington in the act of resigning his authority as General in Chief.[5]

For all of the reasons I have cited, therefore, the role of Revolutionary iconography in national tradition requires our most serious attention. Yet little has been written on this subject by cultural historians. There are a few good biographies of artists, some attractive catalogues from exhibitions, and several iconographic studies of individuals, such as Washington, Adams, and Franklin. But that is about it. My mission in this chapter, then, is three-fold. First, simply to sketch out the broad chronological pattern: Who painted what, when, and why? Second, to offer a thesis, based chiefly upon the recent proliferation of Bicentennial exhibitions, about the changing symbolism of the Revolutionary era and the young republic. (Inherent in that changing symbolism, I believe, are some fundamental attributes of the American mind as it developed between the age of Washington and the age of Jackson.) And third, to suggest that Revolutionary monuments and art have been intimately linked with aspirations for and perceptions of national character in the United States.

"Historical understanding is like an evocation of images"

During the two centuries that have elapsed since 1776, we have passed through at least half a dozen overlapping phases in which the American Revolution has been illustrated, immortalized, romance-itized, allegorized, sentimentalized, and mythologized.

Just as soon as the first shots were fired, Yankee tinsmiths and silversmiths engraved their primitive renditions of what had happened at Lexington, Concord, and the Battle of Bunker Hill.

Some years ago Clarence Brigham put together a very handsome book of *Paul Revere's Engravings*; but we ought to have a companion volume as well on Revere's contemporaries, such as Amos Doolittle, Bernard Romans, and Cornelius Tiebout.[6] Between 1775 and about 1800 they offered pictorial accounts—sometimes factually representational and sometimes allegorically melodramatic—of military encounters and other events, like Washington's triumphant reception at Trenton in 1789, or his first inauguration at Federal Hall. Often they worked from a painting, by Ralph Earl perhaps, or from a drawing by Peter Lacour. Their work tended to be crude and, in the most basic sense, hortatory.[7]

Overlapping them in time, but vastly surpassing them in quality, came a cluster of better known artists who were more formally trained and who took much greater pains to ensure that their Revolutionary illustrations would be historically accurate while still fulfilling the imperatives of aesthetic and patriotic appeal. Working during the half century from about 1785 to 1835, they sought to be documentary in their exposition in order to record notable and dramatic events of the Revolution (see, for example, figure 2). John Trumbull of Connecticut is the best known of this group, and justifiably so. Between 1786 and 1789, 1817 and 1826, and once again briefly in the 1830s, he recorded illustrious scenes—some of which he had witnessed personally during his active service as an aide to Generals Gates and Washington during the war. I am convinced that Trumbull's efforts were intended to be documentary in a way quite analogous to those of Jared Sparks and Peter Force. It is ironic that his paintings now seem to us so stylized in search of inspirational patriotism; for Trumbull felt that he was sacrificing grandeur for historical factuality. And by the artistic canons of his day, he was.

His contemporaries, of course, most especially prominent participants, were eager to know which events he planned to record, and in what manner. Thus Lafayette wrote to Trumbull in 1799:

> The pictures I have seen are York town, and Gibraltar. I knew you had The Declaration of Independence, Saratoga, and Princetown; Bunker's Hill also. Did you not intend to make Monmouth? I much wish it, because in that battle, where Gen. Greene commanded the right wing, Lord Stirling the left, while I had the second line, and where Gen. Washington was surrounded by his family, I would get several portraits very precious to me. . . . What are the other performances which compleat the collec-

tion? Wherever my definitive home is fixed, your works shall be the first, or, according to circumstances, the only Ornament of my dwelling.[8]

For the most part, Trumbull managed to please his contemporaries. Thomas Jefferson and Abigail Adams were lavish in their praise for his work. When those huge Revolutionary scenes were installed at the Capitol Rotunda in 1826–7, however, some shrill voices rose in criticism. John Randolph of Roanoke, for example, picked a nickname for Trumbull's *Declaration of Independence*. He called it "the Shin-piece," because he said that he had never before seen so many legs displayed in one picture.[9]

Such critical dissonance may partially be attributed to the overemphasis upon commemorative art and oratory that accumulated during the second half of John Quincy Adams's presidency and Jackson's first administration. In 1830, for example, Washington Allston refused a congressional commission to paint Revolutionary scenes for the Rotunda. As a partisan of Andrew Jackson, Allston did not want to get involved in the fracas over whether or not the Battle of New Orleans should be depicted. The anti-Jackson forces opposed it; and they got very noisy indeed about the issue.[10]

For about two decades following 1826, artistic interest shifted away from the Revolution. It is significant that after Trumbull's four canvases were installed at the Capitol, the remaining niches remained unadorned. Trumbull hoped in vain for a congressional commission to complete his so-called Hall of the Revolution in a unified way. Not until the 1840s were the four remaining spaces filled in the Rotunda, and then by historical scenes not from the Revolution, but rather from the careers of Columbus, De Soto, Pocahontas, and the Pilgrims.[11]

Yet the 1830s were by no means barren of Revolutionary art. Jacob Eichholtz did his charming composition called *An Incident of the Revolution* in 1831. Asher B. Durand painted *The Capture of Major André* in 1833 (see figure 3) and *The Murder of Jane McCrea* in 1839.[12] It is noteworthy, however, that most of these artists (and presumably their patrons) were far more interested in romantic landscapes than they were in historical pictures. For every one of the latter that they did, they turned out dozens (indeed, hundreds) of the former. After 1827, even Trumbull occupied himself mainly with biblical topics.

The theme of Congress voting Independence reached a kind of

peak in popularity during the early 1820s. Edward Savage completed Robert Pine's rendering of that subject by 1817; and Trumbull finished his for the Rotunda by 1818. Two years later Trumbull entrusted the difficult job of engraving this picture to young Asher B. Durand, then only twenty-four years old. By 1823 copies were selling swiftly to an eager public.[13]

During the 1830s, 1840s, and 1850s, however, when artists chose the Revolution as a subject for their work, the Declaration of Independence seemingly ceased to interest them. They turned instead to comparatively obscure events and themes, such as General Charles Lee pumping water for a kitchen maid; or McCulloch's leap into Wheeling Creek, Virginia, in 1777; or General Francis Marion in his swamp encampment inviting a British officer to share his meal—the latter known to South Carolinians as the "sweet potato picture" because that is apparently what Marion offered the famished redcoat.[14] John Blake White, who lived most of his life in Charleston, had quite a penchant for such pictures; and in the United States Capitol building, if you look hard enough near the Senate Gallery, you will find not only the *Battle of Fort Moultrie,* but also *Sergeants Jasper and Newton Rescuing American Prisoners from the British,* and *Mrs. Motte Directing Generals Marion and Lee to Burn Her Mansion to Dislodge the British.*[15] The valorous feats of Sergeants Jasper, Newton, and other non-commissioned officers serving under Francis Marion became well known in the early nineteenth century on account of the Weems and Horry "biography" of Marion. It enjoyed wide popularity.

Others found themes a bit more general and less obscure, such as *The Battle of Cowpens* by William T. Ranney, or James Hamilton's romantic *Capture of the Serapis by John Paul Jones* (see figure 4), or *Pulling Down the Statue of King George III, Bowling Green, New York City, July 9, 1776,* by Johannes Adam Simon Oertel.[16] The grand theme, however—and the most persistent once the Declaration of Independence waned in popularity after 1826—was George Washington crossing the Delaware River on Christmas night in 1776. But the tremendous appeal of this event did not suddenly begin in 1851 when Emanuel Leutze first displayed his extravaganza at the Capitol (thereby fulfilling a boyhood dream). That event only accentuated the attractiveness of this motif, and eventually made it a cliché—albeit sometimes a controversial one—in American iconography.[17]

Back in 1819, Thomas Sully had painted *Washington's Passage of the Delaware* for the state of South Carolina and then made a copy of it in the mid-1820s. Inspired by an engraving of Sully's canvas, Edward Hicks (of "Peaceable Kingdom" fame) painted at least six versions, which he usually called *Washington Crossed Here* (see figure 5). Two of them are supposed to have hung during the 1830s at either end of a covered bridge that spanned the Delaware River at Washington's Crossing.[18] (A perfectly charming sampler, by the way, made in 1842 by Julia Imhoff, is entitled "George Washington Crossing the Delaware," even though it shows the talented general astride his trusty horse. If the Son of God could walk on water, then perhaps in American folklore there's no reason why the Father of his Country couldn't ride on water.)[19]

Emanuel Leutze, meanwhile, was preparing himself for a successful career as an historical painter. He was born in Germany in 1816; but his family came to Philadelphia in 1825, where he lived for sixteen years. In 1841 he returned to Düsseldorf to complete his training as an artist. At first he experimented with the life of Columbus as a subject for patriotic pictures. But by the later 1840s Leutze was earnestly planning his great work and making preliminary sketches. He actually completed one version in Düsseldorf during 1850; when it was damaged by fire, he prepared another and sold it to a firm prior to its premier exhibition at Washington, D.C., in July 1851. Twenty-one feet wide and twelve feet high, it received an extraordinarily enthusiastic response (see figure 6). John William De Forest, the novelist, insisted that Leutze's *Washington Crossing the Delaware* was "the grandest & noblest modern picture that I have ever seen." Subsequently it became the great attraction at New York's Metropolitan Fair of 1864.[20]

Its influence upon other historical artists was both immense and immediate. William T. Ranney, for example, a genre and portrait painter from Connecticut, did an unabashedly derivative scene entitled *Marion Crossing the Peedee* (1851), with a ludicrous number of men, horses, and dogs jammed upon two rather small barges (see figure 7). It was promptly engraved by Charles Kennedy Burt, and then enjoyed wide circulation.[21] Paul Girardet did a well-liked engraving of Leutze's *Crossing* in 1853; and a few years later Currier and Ives followed with their famous colored lithograph.[22] Between 1856 and 1871 George Caleb Bingham worked intermittently upon his own version of *Washington Crossing the Delaware*, a rather handsome though crowded composition that is arranged quite differently from Leutze's.[23] Variations upon this theme continued to be done all through the later nineteenth century by anonymous vernacular painters (see figure 8), including even renditions embroidered on silk.[24] The first act of a play produced in 1858 ended with a "Tableau of Washington Crossing the Delaware"; and Joaquin Miller composed a popular poem entitled "Washington on the Delaware."[25]

George Washington has always, of course, been the most popular subject for portraits, busts, and commemorative designs.[26] But directly following Leutze's phenomenal success in 1851, historical painters began to envision Washington in every imaginable moment of Revolutionary endeavor: *Washington at Princeton* (see figure 9); or *George Washington in Prayer at Valley Forge*; or *Valley Forge in the Autumn*; *Valley Forge in the Winter*; *Washington's Residence in Germantown*; and so on.[27] Leutze himself then pursued *Washington at Dorchester Heights* (1853), *Washington Rallying the Troops at Monmouth* (1854), *Washington at the Battle of Monongahela* (1858), and *Washington at Princeton* (1859).

Between 1853 and 1912, most of the major equestrian statues of Washington were executed: by Henry Kirke Brown at Union Square in Manhattan, for example; by Thomas Ball for the Boston Public Garden; and by Henry Marvin Shrady for the Williamsburg Bridge Plaza in Brooklyn, New York. As Wendell Garrett has shown, the centennial of Washington's inauguration in 1889 elicited even more patriotism and filial piety than occurred in 1876, and Americans expressed "a growing interest in the iconography, and in some cases the relics, of the first president and the other founding fathers."[28]

As public sculpture came into its own, however, especially during the final quarter of the nineteenth century, that documentary emphasis of Trumbull's generation faded from view. Particular individuals participating in identifiable historical situations were gradually replaced by non-specific people as archetypes of courage, valor, and quiet determination.[29] What, we might ask, were the two most influential (and most familiar) icons of 1875 and 1876? One was *The Minute Man of Concord* by Daniel Chester French, unveiled and dedicated at the North Bridge by President Grant and his chilled entourage on April 19, 1875.[30] The other is simply entitled *The Spirit of '76*, by Archibald M. Willard: the grizzled veteran drummer, bandaged fifer, and inspired drummer boy—three abreast with that very same "air of sturdy defiance" as French's elevated Minute Man (see figure 10). Originally called *Yankee Doodle* and exhibited in the Annex at the Philadelphia Exhibition of 1876, Willard's picture became the most memorable "art object" generated by the Centennial. Chromolithographs and engravings of it sold widely; the painting went on a national tour from 1877 until 1879, and then came to rest at the Corcoran Gallery in Washington, D.C. Like Hicks's *Washington Crossed Here,* Willard made a number of versions, with the result that several historical societies now vie for the distinction of owning the "original."[31]

By 1876 the American Revolution had entirely lost its historical reality. It had been allegorized on banners, cast in bronze, and baked upon the bulging sides of massive ceremonial urns. Meanwhile, yet another shift occurred. From Trumbull's time until Leutze's, from the mid-1780s until the 1850s, the American Revolution in historical art had included much more than just the War for Independence. Battles had been painted, to be sure; but when they were, they usually depicted the death of a noble leader, such as Joseph Warren on Bunker Hill or General Montgomery at Quebec (see figure 11). The artist's purpose was not to glorify militarism but rather to display and explicate the American character. As Abigail Adams put it when she first saw *The Death of General Warren at the Battle of Bunker's Hill,* by Trumbull:

> Looking at it my whole frame contracted, my blood shivered, and I felt a faintness at my heart. He is the first painter who has undertaken to immortalize by his pencil those great actions, that gave birth to our nation. . . . At the same time, he teaches mankind that it is not rank nor titles, but character alone, which interests posterity.[32]

When Trumbull received his congressional commission in 1817, he selected two military events and two civil events. Significantly, the military events actually represented the conclusion of hostilities at Saratoga and at Yorktown. In Trumbull's mind these were primarily political and moral occasions rather than military ones. Trumbull considered the Declaration of Independence to be his most important subject, whereas battles as such seem to have been distinctly secondary.[33]

In addition to Trumbull's portrayal of Washington in the act of resigning his command, there is also Horatio Greenough's famous sculpture of Washington "renouncing the sword." During the first half of the nineteenth century, Washington was depicted in his presidential role at least as often, if not more so, than in his role as Revolutionary general; and more frequently in civilian clothes than in uniform.[34] This trend would have pleased "the Father of His Country." Jean Antoine Houdon visited the United States in 1785 to make a preliminary likeness of Washington for a statue commissioned by the state of Virginia. Houdon arrived at Mount Vernon, took a life mask, modeled a bust, and then took the necessary measurements for a full-length statue. As a consequence of their conversations, Houdon chose to represent him as the military hero returning to civilian life. Completed in 1788 and installed at Richmond in 1796, this statue became the prototype for most would-be sculptors of Washington during the first half of the nineteenth century: Greenough, Powers, Causici, Capellano, and Ball, for example.[35]

In Edward Everett's widely read *Oration* of 1826, he insisted that the ultimate meaning of the Revolution was neither "the military success nor the political event," but rather "the foundation of the systems of government, which have happily been established in our beloved country." When Daniel Webster spoke at the dedication of the Bunker Hill Monument in 1843, he declared that "it is not as a mere military encounter of hostile armies that the battle of Bunker Hill presents its principal claim to attention." By nightfall on June 17, 1775, "the event of Independence was no longer doubtful."[36]

By the later nineteenth century, however, we no longer hear very much about political independence and republican government. We see little of the sorts of scenes drawn earlier by Sully, Savage, Eichholtz, and Hicks. The American Revolution viewed as a moral and governmental event gives way to a bloody war, plain and simple. There is a very real sense in which the Revolution came to be reduced to battles, regiments, and colorful uniforms—and thereby got trivialized. Early in the 1860s, for instance, Reuben Law Reed, a granite worker and house painter, rendered a colorful canvas called *Washington and Lafayette at the Battle of Yorktown* (see figure 12). Aerial bombs burst as men march into battle. Perhaps it is essentially the Civil War dressed up in eighteenth-century costume. We cannot be sure; but this naïve folk painting serves as a harbinger and sets the tone for Revolutionary iconography during the next half century.[37]

The genesis of that shift, however, antedates the formal opening of Civil War hostilities at Fort Sumter in 1861. In terms of literary evidence, we can see it coming in the escalation of violence and rhetoric over "Bleeding Kansas" following 1854. Fourth of July orators in Charleston, South Carolina, began to envision the inevitability of secession. Southerners generally believed that the North was being swept by a "wild torrent of fanaticism."[38] And in the North itself military history became ever more popular: biographies of Revolutionary war heroes as well as histories of all previous American wars.[39]

In the context of iconographic evidence we can see the shift beginning in William T. Ranney's *Recruiting for the Continental Army* (ca. 1857–9), an oil on canvas at the Munson-Williams-Proctor Museum in Utica, New York. We watch the trend developing in Peter Frederick Rothermel's *State House on the Day of the Battle of Germantown* (ca. 1870), an oil painting at the Pennsylvania Academy of the Fine Arts that shows captured and wounded rebels being treated at Independence Hall on October 4, 1777. And we find it continuing in Edward Howland Blashfield's *Suspense, the Boston People Watch from the Housetops the Firing at Bunker Hill* (ca. 1879–80), now owned by the Home Insurance Company of New York, in which action is suggested more by the expressions on spectators' faces than by direct representation.

During the last two decades of the nineteenth century, the American mood was martial. In 1884 John Fiske gave a series of twelve lectures on military campaigns of the Revolution. His Boston audiences loved them; so he repeated the sequence for the Old South Association, several times more in private parlors during the afternoons, and yet again in an evening course open to the public.[40] Henry P. Johnston's *Campaign of 1776 Around New York* had sold well since its publication in 1878. Thomas Dunn English, an editor, politician, and playwright, prospered from the publication of his *Boy's Book of Battle Lyrics* in 1885. David Schenck did well with *North Carolina, 1780–1781* in 1889, as did William S. Stryker with *The Battles of Trenton and Princeton* in 1898.

The typical paintings now would be *Molly Pitcher at the Battle of Monmouth* by Gilbert Gaul (ca. 1892—see figure 13); or Charles M.

Lefferts's battle scenes, mostly done between 1900 and 1918; or John Ward Dunsmore's *Washington Examining the Plans of the Battle of Long Island.*[41] And a whole series of military heroes were immortalized in bronze statuary during the final quarter of the nineteenth century: Ethan Allen, the conqueror of Fort Ticonderoga (at Washington, D.C.); General Nathanael Greene (also at Washington); Nathan Hale (at City Hall Park in New York); and Lafayette by Paul Wayland Bartlett (at the Louvre in Paris). Even commemorative dishes depicting Revolutionary battles became very voguish at the turn of the century.[42]

Quite a different sort of art underwent a parallel transformation during the late nineteenth century: the art of illustrating books, which in our context primarily means historical fiction about the American Revolution. Just as soon as James Fenimore Cooper established his reputation as an exciting author of romances, artists of both considerable *and* mediocre quality enlisted their talents in rendering the most vivid narrative passages as dramatic scenes. Asher B. Durand, for instance, did a canvas called *Last Interview Between Washington and Harvey Birch,* and William Dunlap painted incidents of family crisis from *The Spy* (see figure 14).[43] Thomas Sully and Jacob Eichholtz both depicted episodes from *The Pilot,* such as the wreck of the *Ariel,* the dungeon scene, and the desperate plight of Long Tom Coffin. Felix Darley, James Hamilton, and Robert W. Weir illustrated various novels by Cooper as well as by James Kirke Paulding. And in 1861 Susan Fenimore Cooper compiled a popular anthology of her father's historical fiction with profuse illustrations made on steel and wood from original drawings.[44]

The point I wish to stress once again is that these illustrations made in the four decades after 1821 commonly took non-military events as their subjects: man against nature, moments of surprise and personal confrontation, family tensions and strong human emotions. Insofar as they helped to popularize that peculiarly American genre, the romance, one might say that they served to "romance-itize" the Revolution. They were not documentary pictures in search of semi-photographic accuracy, but rather renditions of what *might* have happened. For that reason they served to add distance and haze between the American public and Revolutionary realities. They prepared the way, not only for allegorizing the Revolution between 1875 and 1900, but also for its sentimentalizing by a special breed of book and magazine illustrators who came of age vocationally between about 1880 and 1905.[45]

What Harry A. Ogden and Frederick Coffay Yohn and Howard Pyle and Stanley M. Arthurs and N. C. Wyeth all shared in common was a fascination with historical legends and adventure rather than with revolution as such, with battles rather than politics, with attacks and retreats rather than moral development (see figure 15). They rendered the Revolution as a simplification of its complex essence. Soldiers and weapons were their specialization; or, as a recent exhibition of N. C. Wyeth works at the Brandywine River Museum was entitled, "Romance and Adventure." It is worth remembering that when Pyle and Wyeth weren't illustrating Cooper, or James Boyd's *Drums*, or *Poems of American Patriotism*, they were illustrating *Robin Hood*, and *Treasure Island*, and *The Boy's King Arthur*. Unfortunately they had but one basic style and one approach to their work, with the result that those who gaze upon their art just might get a sinking sensation that the American Revolution was performed according to a scenario written by Robert Louis Stevenson. When Wyeth was not illustrating the Revolution as a saga of piracy, poesy, and mystery, he was executing stirring posters for *The Delineator*, posters entitled "Fourth of July" and "The Minute Men," which at once allegorized and sentimentalized the American Revolution into a rather maudlin melodrama.[46]

The Brandywine School has not ceased to be active or influential since the early twentieth century; but interest by its members in the American Revolution has dwindled almost entirely. Andrew Wyeth's 1962 painting, called *British at Brandywine*, stands almost alone as a latter-day exemplar, and it is enigmatic—some sort of optical illusion with toy soldiers.[47] What developed instead, especially during the 1930s, was that Revolutionary folklore came to be mythologized as well as gently satirized—simultaneously by Grant Wood and by some of the artists on W.P.A. relief rolls doing murals for public buildings.

When Wood returned to Iowa in 1929, he embarked upon a quest for redefinition of the American tradition in art, a quest that managed to combine regional chauvinsim with personal inconoclasm. His *Midnight Ride of Paul Revere* (1931) and *Parson Weems Fable* (1939) are whimsical, charming, and difficult to interpret precisely because Wood was so ambivalent about our historical heritage (see figure 16). He loved America and wanted to proclaim her cultural independence from Europe; yet he despised the tub-thumping, blind patriotism of the D.A.R.—for which he made himself altogether despicable in the eyes of the Daughters and Daughter-lovers.[48]

The composer Charles Ives of Danbury, Connecticut, was a contemporary of Grant Wood—a spiritual as well as chronological contemporary. In several respects Ives sought to marry American tradition with music in much the same way that Wood did in his vernacular art. As one European critic wrote in 1932, when his music first gained recognition,

> Ives is a musical painter, if one may use such an expression, an impressionist; he is, however, not without moments of naïve realism. His art is at times coarse and clumsy, but in him there is genuine strength and inventiveness, thematically as well as rhythmically, in no way taking fashion or authority into consideration. Ives' suite *The Fourth of July* (the American national holiday) is based on national motifs; in this regard Ives is, perhaps, the only one among the composers of North America whose work is profoundly national.[49]

In addition to *The Fourth of July,* which had its world premier at Paris in 1932, Ives also composed *Concord Sonata,* and *Washington's Birthday* (which had its first major public performance in 1931), and *Putnam's Camp,* written in 1912 to be the second movement of his First Orchestral Set, called *Three Places in New England.* During the winter of 1778–9, General Israel Putnam and his Continental soldiers had camped at Redding, Connecticut, near Danbury. "Long rows of stone camp fire-places still remain to stir a child's imagination," Ives wrote. "The hardships which the soldiers endured and the agitation of a few hot-heads to break camp and march to the Hartford Assembly for relief, is a part of Redding history." That camp had been made into a memorial park, and Ives composed *Putnam's Camp* while he was having a house built a few miles away from it. He developed the work from two of his earlier, experimental compositions: the *Country Band March* and the *March 1776.* The latter had been an overture for an opera he intended to write, based upon his uncle Lyman Brewster's blank-verse play called *Major John André.*[50]

Meanwhile, the Treasury Department came to the relief of impoverished painters by paying them to do mural designs for federal buildings. And during the mid-1930s a remarkable number of these artists selected Revolutionary scenes, such as *Shays' Rebellion* by Umberto Romano, in the post office lobby at Springfield, Massachusetts; or *The First Provincial Convention in North Carolina* in the courthouse at New Bern; or *Benedict Arnold Commanding the First Naval Battle on Lake Champlain* by Stephen Belaski, at the post office in Rutland, Vermont; or *Molly Pitcher* in the post office at Freehold, New Jersey. These are not, needless to say, great art; and they owe certain stylistic debts to the Brandywine brushes of Pyle and Wyeth. Nonetheless they transcend the naïve, undiluted patriotism of 1900, and link national legend with personal sympathy for political rebellion and social protest.[51]

There hasn't been much Revolutionary iconography since World War II. After being documented, illustrated, romanceitized, allegorized, sentimentalized, and mythologized, what was left to be done? Basically, American art went off in other directions—*very* other.[52]

What did remain to be done, of course, was criticize: criticize national sham and shame, or parody the discrepancy between American rhetoric and sordid realities. Therefore, in the age of Watergate, our Bicentennial art became *George* [*Washington*] *and Mona* [*Lisa*] *in the Baths of Coloma*, a glazed ceramic by Robert Arneson; or *Young General George*, using polymer on canvas by Roy DeForest; or *The Spirit of '76*, acrylic on canvas by Peter Saul (see figure 17). In 1975 the Allan Frumkin Gallery planned a Bicentennial Exhibition for the big year and invited various artists to create works especially for it. As their efforts arrived and were unpacked, it became manifestly clear that all of them took a humorous (if not jaundiced) view of Revolutionary iconography. What the artists apparently *do* take seriously, however, is their own talent. *A Bicentennial Bedroom*, by Shari Urquhart, sells for $1,800. *Celebrating the Bicentennial: Big Tits and Money*, by Richard Notkin, cost $1,500 (and was snapped up quickly by an eager collector). Peter Saul's update of Archibald Willard's classic cost a cool $12,000. (When last I checked, it had not yet been bought.)[53]

Even so, the most significant aspect of American Revolution iconography during the Bicentennial was not to be found in the Frumkin Gallery at all, though that show really was good fun. It was to be found in the exhibitions—about a dozen major ones across the country—mounted by museums, university galleries, and historical societies. And what seemed to fill the place of artistic statements about the Revolution was the creative display of aesthetic and historically significant objects from the Revolutionary era itself. In going to see those shows, and in studying their catalogues closely, I was able to put together some otherwise elusive clues to the role of Revolutionary iconography in our national tradition at a determinative stage—clues that might only have emerged from the special sort of juxtaposition characteristic of the exhibitions.

"It is impossible to point out an important change in the political organization of a people, a change by which it has been rendered more or less favorable to liberty, without discovering a correspondent effect on their prosperity"

THERE WERE, as I have indicated, about a dozen of these major exhibitions; and they seem to group themselves into four natural categories. First, those that were most political in orientation and concentrated upon the liberation of a colonial society quite ready to undertake the process of becoming a nation. Here I include "In the Minds and Hearts of the People" at the National Portrait Gallery in 1974; " 'The Dye Is Now Cast.' The Road to American Independence, 1774–1776," at the same gallery a year later; "To Set a Country Free" at the Library of Congress in 1975; and "A Rising People: The Founding of the United States, 1765 to 1789," jointly sponsored by three major institutions at Philadelphia in 1976.[54]

The second category might be described as rather more personal in that it focused upon particular participants in the Revolutionary society. I have in mind "Paul Revere's Boston: 1735–1818" at Boston's Museum of Fine Arts in 1975; "The World of Franklin and Jefferson, 1706–1826," which toured Paris, Warsaw, and London in 1975, then came to this country in 1976; and "The Black Presence in the Era of the American Revolution, 1770–1800" at the National Portrait Gallery in 1973.[55]

A third category stressed the struggle for *cultural* independence during the Revolutionary era. These shows concentrated upon aesthetic and cultural values, especially in the decorative arts; and here one thinks of "American Art: 1750–1800, Towards Independence" at the Yale University Art Gallery; "The Eye of Thomas Jefferson" at the National Gallery in Washington; and a wonderful but rather neglected show, "The Pennsylvania German Influence" at the Historical Society of York County in York, Pennsylvania—all three put on in 1976.[56]

A fourth category consists of displays that looked at what the Revolution wrought: the art, taste, and cultural aspirations of a new republic. I am thinking of "William Bingham: America—A Good Investment," at the Roberson Center in Binghamton, New York, during 1975; or "The Early Republic: Consolidation of Revolutionary Goals," at the Worcester Art Museum in 1976; or "Remember the Ladies. Women in America, 1750–1815," which opened at Plymouth, Massachusetts, in 1976, and subsequently moved on to several other museums and galleries; or "Lewis and Clark's America: A Voyage of Discovery" at the Seattle Art Museum in 1976.

Finally, one might add a fifth (and rather marginal) category of shows inspired by the Bicentennial but not directly concerned with the Revolution and its iconography. I have in mind "A Bicentennial Treasury: American Masterpieces from the Metropolitan," at New York City in the summer of 1976; or "200 Years of American Sculpture," at the Whitney Museum in New York; or "America 1976," a large exhibition of landscape paintings which started at the Corcoran Gallery of Art in Washington as the first stop of a national tour that continued until 1978; or "The Handwrought Object, 1776–1976" at the Johnson Museum of Cornell University in Ithaca, New York.

Could there possibly be any persistent themes or characteristic qualities in these remarkable performances of curatorial creativity? One hesitates to reduce them to some artificial common denominator because, despite a degree of repetition and overlap, they were very diverse. Indeed, there are even a few contradictions to be noticed: first, the Yale show emphasized our continuing artistic dependence upon Europe, while the Worcester exhibit stressed the emergence of an indigenous decorative style; second, so many of the shows relied heavily upon portraits, which in the nature of things highlight individuals and their personal achievements, whereas the texts of the catalogues tend to glorify The

People as some sort of collective entity ("the minds and hearts of the people," "a rising people," and "We, the People");[57] and third, there is a contrast between the professed egalitarianism of various prefaces and visual designs, on the one hand, and the inevitable élitism of many of the artifacts on the other. Much of what we gaze upon unavoidably reflects the *high* culture of Anglo-colonial and early republican society. Yet Merrill Rueppel's preface asserts that "Paul Revere was a common man, a working craftsman," while Charles and Ray Eames, designers of "The World of Franklin and Jefferson," set aside an entire wall for portraits of anonymous people by anonymous painters of the Revolutionary period. The point is supposed to be that these are Mr. and Mrs. Sam Citizen, neither urban aristocrats nor rough frontiersmen—just folks, like you and me.

Even so, despite these provocative dualisms, there is a certain coherence to the exhibitions; and that cohesion cuts through all the encrusted layers of sentimentalization, allegorization, romance-itization, immortalization, and documentation, thereby returning us to confront directly the trial-and-error reality of Revolutionary America. One of the most fascinating aspects of these materials, for example, is that so many of them are preliminary sketches for paintings, or preparatory architectural plans, or drafts of letters and public documents. We get a sense of imperfection, of accommodation, and compromise. Alongside the gorgeous glaze of polished mahogany and restored canvas, we also see manuscript revisions on printed documents, the watering down of Jeffersonian idealism in the draft Declaration of 1776, and Franklin's marginalia on the Federal Constitution of 1787. Their quest for clarity of meaning, their adaptations as well as their inflexibilities, and their desire for felicitous expression all come sharply into view.[58]

Most of the exhibitions are developmental in their orientation. Revere's Boston, 1735 *to* 1818; American Art . . . *Towards* Independence; a *Rising* People; the *Consolidation* of Revolutionary Goals; and, as William Howard Adams puts it in his Introduction to *The Eye of Thomas Jefferson*: "the *development* of that eye and the mind and imagination behind it is the subject of this exhibition."[59]

Nevertheless, despite the stress upon development, discontinuities and stubborn patterns of persistence are not ignored out of deference to national chauvinism and platitudes of progress.

Walter Muir Whitehill reminds us that the neo-classical style continued to dominate in the decorative arts; that the brilliant furniture-makers John and Thomas Seymour settled in Boston from Britain as late as 1794. Several catalogues reveal the intellectual importance to Americans of making the Grand Tour—both before and after the American Revolution. When Thomas Jefferson, that dedicated republican, returned from France in 1789, he apparently brought back no less than eighty crates of Louis XVI furniture. Monarchical furniture, indeed, for Monticello.[60] The practicality and the idealism alike of these revolutionaries comes through loud and clear. As Charles Eames has remarked, with reference to Franklin and Jefferson, they were "two practical men, deeply involved in the 18th-century's utopian thought, trying to make it work on the edge of the wilderness."[61]

It was inevitable, I suppose, that we would encounter a certain number of familiar objects and quotations, some of them almost clichés by now; but what is so delightful is that we encounter unfamiliar artifacts and phrases as well—some of which are simply lapidary:

• The four courageous slaves who signed a petition to the Massachusetts General Court in April 1773, and asserted that "We expect great things from men who have made such a noble stand against the designs of their *fellow-men* to enslave them."[62]

• Or the interpolation by Julian P. Boyd of John Jay's observation that it would take "Time to make Sovereigns of Subjects."[63]

• And William Howard Adams's use of an exquisite quotation from Jefferson about "the important truths that knowledge is power, that knowledge is safety, and that knowledge is happiness."[64]

Several of the authors and editors of these catalogues assert that pictures and artifacts are "historic documents in themselves," which is true enough. Nevertheless, their texts do not consistently analyze the objects as cultural symbols that really do have a story to tell us. Merrill Rueppel makes the perfectly valid point that "only rarely have many of the objects been seen in public together. They are now assembled to recapture old relationships." Yet some of the most critical relationships remain inert because our attention is not called to them, and so their interconnectedness remains unexplored. In the pages that follow, I shall try to remedy that; or at least make a start in the right direction.

It would not be particularly profound of me to point out that eagles fly all through the halls of these exhibitions, and perch on every other page of their catalogues. There are eagles engraved on shields, inlaid on game tables and candlestands, clamped on top of banjo clocks, stamped on spoons, and punched on porringers. They fly out of the *Columbian Magazine*, alight on ceremonial Indian armbands and peace medals, get embroidered on coverlets (looking like plucked chickens in the process), eventually land on top of books, branches, mirrors, a magnificent bombé desk and bookcase, and even, in about 1800, on the trade card of Paul Revere and Son, promoting their bell and cannon foundry in North Boston.[65] Congress adopted the eagle design for our national seal on June 20, 1782, and it began to appear instantaneously on objects as elaborate as John Cogswell's spectacular chest-on-chest, which is documented as having been made in Boston that very same year.[66]

Admittedly, we would expect there to be a lot of eagles swooping around in republican America—Benjamin Franklin's strictures to the contrary notwithstanding. The eagle symbolized our freedom, ebullience, capacity to soar ever higher, and so forth. It is an aggressive and very masculine emblem, except, as I said, when rendered poorly on a coverlet to look like a starkly vulnerable capon.[67]

The whole business gets a bit more complicated, however, when you leaf through these exhibition catalogues a second and third time, and begin to notice that the eagles are often not alone, not perched upon some isolated, godforsaken aerie, but usually are hovering around a chick—and in this instance I don't mean a freshly hatched hen or eaglet, I mean a demure young woman named Liberty. You might even say that Liberty and that ubiquitous eagle hang around together. No one takes much note of it in these catalogues, perhaps because you wouldn't want your Lady Liberty flitting around with a fish-eating bird. Or maybe you don't object to their amity, but you wouldn't want your Liberty to be too intimate with one. Whatever the reason, there they are.[68]

Yale's spectacular catalogue shows eagles inlaid in wood on the front and back covers; on the spacious double title page, Liberty strides rather confidently between the divided cornice of a chest-on-chest. Ladies and eagles get a lot more frisky than that, however. In the Worcester Art Museum's catalogue, for example, there is a stipple engraving by Edward Savage, dated 1796, in which the eagle is about to swill some beverage from a goblet delicately upheld in Liberty's hand (see figure 18). Later on we find that in 1804 one Mary Green executed the very same picture prettily at home in needlework.[69] It was quite a popular theme. Between 1799 and 1807 various gold pieces were minted with Liberty's lovely head on one side and a rampant eagle on the other. In about 1815 an anonymous artist drew a piquant design (in watercolor on paper) called "Liberty and Independence. Ever Glorious Memory. United States America 1776." There's the blushing Miss Liberty, of course, supporting a liberty pole topped by the characteristic cap, plus a flag with you know what kind of a bird dominating the field of blue right above her head (see figure 19).[70]

Similarly, the Mattatuck Museum in Waterbury, Connecticut, has a creamware pitcher made in about 1815, also, with a side panel showing Liberty upholding her pole and cap while the spread-eagle dominates an American flag in the sky. Finally, in Statuary Hall at the United States Capitol, a large plaster figure of Liberty made by Enrico Causici (1817–19) has a vigorous eagle perched by her right hand, and yet another with wings outstretched not far beneath her feet (see figure 20).[71]

These delineations of Liberty with her eagle friend are interesting for various reasons. They suggest that the intricate ideological relationship between Power and Liberty, which Bernard Bailyn has discussed for the period prior to 1776, does not lapse from the American mind after 1783—only that the relationship perceived between Power and Liberty shifts from one of antipathy to one of mutual support.[72] My essential concern here, however, is not with Liberty and Power, but rather with Liberty and Prosperity. My basic contention, moreover, is that the idea of Liberty obsessed the American mind from the opening of the Revolutionary crisis until about the close of James Madison's presidency. Insofar as any heterogeneous society can keep an abstraction clearly in view for very long, Liberty was the one for Mr. Jefferson's generation—perhaps because it seemed to some of them a palpable thing rather than a mere abstraction.

By the 1820s, however, a new one had already begun to supplant it. Not all at once, but gradually. And the new notion, which they later came to call "Peace and Plenty," also had its iconographic symbols. We can see them budding in the later pages of some of these catalogues; and if we watch closely enough, we can even pinpoint the transition—the pivotal period when different cultural symbols come briefly into balance, and after which the older ones begin to recede while the newer ones become dominant. The pivotal moment for this shift from Liberty to Prosperity occurs in the last few years of the eighteenth century and the first decade of the nineteenth.

Before we explore the particulars of that shift, a few words are in order about the origins of these symbols and phrases. None of them was newly minted in the young republic. One can find their occasional precursors in the culture of Georgian England and colonial America: a picture of Britannia (executed in 1761), for example, in which *Libertas* holds something like a liberty cap in one hand and a cornucopia in the other; or an advertisement to induce colonization from Ulster to North America (in 1771), which promised "Freedom, Peace, and Plenty"; and Adam Smith writing in *The Wealth of Nations* (1776) that "plenty of good land to manage their own affairs their own way, seem to be the two great causes of the prosperity of all new colonies."[73]

In England, these images were neither recurrent nor especially resonant. They appear infrequently in British literature and iconography; and when they do, it is incidental to an understanding of the dominant values in Georgian political culture. In the new republic, however, the perpetuation of Liberty and Prosperity, or Peace and Plenty, became part of a fresh configuration of explicitly articulated values involving agrarian simplicity, civic virtue, and a homogeneous national character.[74]

The Jeffersonian generation had to reconcile its desire for prosperity with the imperatives of republican simplicity, its sense of moral superiority with the dictates of egalitarian rhetoric. The ways in which those men and women sought to do so help us to differentiate between the mere occurrence of certain symbols in, say, 1761, and their vastly augmented cultural significance in an ideologically altered setting. Let us first examine the substance of this shift; then attempt to locate it with some exactness; and finally, explain its importance.

Look in *Paul Revere's Boston* (p. 110), for example, at the *Perspective View of the Blockade of Boston Harbour*, a watercolor done by Christian Remick in about 1768 (see figure 21). Above the premier port of the English colonies a banner flutters, and it reads "Magna

Carta." Now look in *The World of Franklin and Jefferson* (p. 27) at the view of New Orleans harbor in 1803 by John L. Boqueto de Woiserie (see figure 22). Over the budding Gulf port, full of hope for its commercial prospects, our rampant eagle holds a banner that reads: "Under My Wings, Every Thing Prospers."[75]

From "Magna Carta" to "Every Thing Prospers" in thirty-five years;[76] can we achieve any greater chronological precision than that? Yes, I think we can. Let's look next at two creamware pitchers (or "jugs," as the experts like to call them) that can be dated with some specificity. The first one was made during John Adams's presidency. We know that because he is honored as such in the print on one side of the jug (see figure 23). But the obverse is more interesting for our purposes. There we find a design with Liberty and the eagle, both of them quite familiar by now, and scarcely a surprise in the late 1790s. Liberty, however, happens to be clutching a cornucopia full of fruits and flowers; and the motto below the bird reads: "Peace, Plenty and Independence." So here are the two sets of symbols in approximate equilibrium. The date must be about 1798.[77]

There is also another pitcher, this one from Jefferson's presidency. We know that because it says so on the side with his likeness. But once again it is the *other* side that supplies us with the link we seek. The fifteen states are represented by as many stars, braided together to form an elliptical panel, within which there is a poem:

O Liberty thou Goddess
heav'nly bright,
Profuse of bliss,
and pregnant with delight,
Eternal pleasures
in thy presence reign
and smiling plenty leads
thy wanton train.[78]

Thus, the decade after 1796 comprises the watershed between a Revolutionary culture whose attitudinal axis was the concept of Liberty and a republican culture whose aspirational axis was the expectation of Prosperity—eventually expanded, after about 1825, to "Peace & Plenty."[79] And just as Liberty had its cluster of iconographic symbols—Miss Liberty, the pole and cap, the eagle, and the printing press—so, too, did Prosperity have its cluster of images. They include the cornucopia, bowls of luscious fruit (especially bulging bunches of grapes), ripe grain being harvested, and most of all, the plough.[80]

The plough as a symbol starts to show up in about 1785. It is the focal point of an attractive logo on the title page of *An Address, from the Philadelphia Society for Promoting Agriculture* (see figure 24). The next year a plough appeared in a handsome little engraving made for volume I of the *Columbian Magazine* (see figure 25), with this legend underneath: "Venerate the Plough."[81] In 1793 Joseph Richardson, a Philadelphia silversmith, engraved an Indian peace medal. Behind George Washington and a chieftain smoking the peace pipe, there is a farmer with two oxen drawing the venerated plough (see figure 26).[82]

The plough served as a perfect symbol of peace and prosperity: not merely because this was ideally a nation of yeomen farmers, nor solely on account of the vast wilderness just waiting to be brought under cultivation, but also because a biblical Protestant nation knew perfectly well that ploughshares were what swords were supposed to be beaten into. After the long and wearisome war, in other words, what other single symbol could have served them so well?[83]

In 1819 Jethro Wood patented the cast-iron plough; and that same year agricultural journalism really began in New York when Solomon Southwick launched *The Plough Boy* in Albany. The first Yankee character-type really to take hold in the American theatre was Jonathan Ploughboy, introduced around 1825 in Samuel Woodworth's play *The Forest Rose, or American Farmers.*[84] By 1830 most farmers had learned that iron ploughs turn over deeper furrows. A decade later Ezra Cornell was selling them in Maine and in Georgia. Can there be any doubt, then, that the primitive painting in figure 27 accurately catches one important facet of the American mind at mid-century? The artist is unknown, but the inscription speaks volumes: "He That Tilleth His Land Shall Be Satisfied."[85]

Although the iconographic transition from Liberty to Prosperity was fully realized by the 1840s, Americans had not entirely forgotten the meaning of their Revolution.[86] Indeed, they fixed upon a fairly obvious and satisfying way to link the plough (and thereby republican Virtue) with the birth of freedom in 1775.

Henry David Thoreau recalled, in *A Week on the Concord and Merrimack Rivers* (1849), that many of the patriotic heroes "were ploughing when the news of the massacre at Lexington arrived, and straightaway left their ploughs in the furrow, and repaired to the scene of action."[87] In 1850 an essayist recalled that after fighting in the French and Indian War, Israel Putnam "returned to the plough, and was in the act of guiding it, when he heard the news of the battle of Lexington. Like Cincinnatus of old, he left it in the furrow, and repaired at once to Cambridge." Not surprisingly, then, Congress commissioned Constantino Brumidi in 1855 to prepare two frescoes for the Capitol. (You can see them in the House Appropriations Committee Room.) One is named *Calling of Cincinnatus from the Plow;* and the other *Calling of Putnam from the Plow to the Revolution* (see figures 28–30).[88]

During the next two decades, this symbolic link between patriotism and the plough became an established bond in American iconography. Henry Wise, for instance, explained the true meaning of Houdon's statue of Washington to a Fourth of July audience in 1856. The figure, he pointed out, "stands on the mother earth, the plough share placed on the left by his foot. These signify the idea of 'Country.' " The Minute Man that Daniel Chester French would sculpt in 1874 for Concord's Centennial celebration brought the whole motif to explicit perfection. The Minute Man is shown at that precise moment when he is leaving his plough and taking up a gun in order to defend the country. French knew that the yeoman farmer's arms must look as though they could handle that old, rugged plough with ease.[89]

"Our ideas of his character, and of our own character"

CONSIDERING THE POINTS I have been trying to emphasize, it is altogether appropriate that Jefferson and Franklin were the two dominant figures in those dozen or so Bicentennial exhibitions: Franklin, whose artifact was the printing press;[90] and Jefferson, whose achievement it was during the early 1790s to improve the moldboard plough, which he regarded as "the most useful of the instruments known to man."[91] As he wrote to Charles Willson

Peale in 1813: "The plough is to the farmer what the wand is to the sorcerer. Its effect is really like sorcery."[92]

Jefferson and Franklin were coupled, so to speak, in the big Eames exhibit sponsored by the American Revolution Bicentennial Administration, the Metropolitan Museum of Art, and the IBM Corporation. Jefferson cerebrated visibly in his own vast one-man show at the National Gallery; and, in a more restrained way, at "The Early Republic" exhibition of the Worcester Art Museum. Sophisticates at home in the unpolished New World, Franklin and Jefferson wore the guise of simplicity when in Europe, and adapted from its culture whatever seemed attractive and appropriate for a self-consciously republican culture.[93]

More to the point, however, although each one played a major role in the achievement of our liberty, they both anticipated that shift in psychic orientation from Liberty to Prosperity which was our central theme in the preceding section. As early as March 1780, Franklin informed George Washington from Passy that "I must soon quit the Scene, but you may live to see our Country flourish, as it will amazingly and rapidly after the War is over." Writing just a year or two later in his *Notes on the State of Virginia,* Jefferson anticipated that, in America, "utopia" would be defined in terms of prosperity.[94] He developed this theme more fully on March 4, 1801, in his first inaugural address. There he spoke about "a rising nation, spread over a wise and fruitful land, traversing all the seas with the rich productions of their industry." And he concluded his inaugural by beseeching "that Infinite Power which rules the destinies of the universe" to give the American people "peace and prosperity."[95] Nothing could shake his faith that Prosperity was our national destiny—for better and for worse—not even the European depredations that precipitated the War of 1812. "When these shall be over," he wrote to John Adams,

> it will be the impressment of our seamen or something else; and so we have gone on, and so we shall go on, puzzled and prospering beyond example in the history of man. And I believe we shall continue to grow, to multiply and prosper until we exhibit an association, powerful, wise and happy, beyond what has yet been seen by men.[96]

There is a poignant problem, of course, because Jefferson's vision of the well-rewarded yeoman farmer, walking behind his plough and oxen, was being undermined even before the image had achieved its full iconographic impact. Land may well have been our greatest resource during the first half of the nineteenth century, but the yeoman farmer, his wife, and their hired hand did not prosper nearly so much as the land speculator and his agents. Nor was the virtuous farmer so influential or important as the big speculator in real estate. (In this regard, the most representative object in all of these exhibitions may very well be the surveyor's chain, made early in the nineteenth century and displayed at the William Bingham show in Binghamton.)[97]

Nevertheless, while Jefferson foresaw American abundance and regarded its powerful impact as being inevitable, he never lost sight of Liberty, rather than Prosperity, as our most precious blessing; and he did much to ensure that iconographic symbols would endure to remind Americans that Liberty must be cherished. John Trumbull visited with Jefferson at Paris in 1785, and together they discussed the artist's projected series of history paintings. Trumbull recalls in his autobiography that he began his major canvas, *The Declaration of Independence*, after getting information and advice from Jefferson.[98] When Charles Bulfinch made the Grand Tour in 1785, he too came under Jefferson's influence; and Bulfinch brought back the principles of neo-classicism in architecture, suitably modified for Boston and later for designing the Capitol in Washington, D.C.[99]

In purchasing the vast Louisiana Territory, Jefferson believed that he could increase our security as well as our prosperity. But when obliged to defend his decision, he spoke less of security and prosperity than of extending "an Empire for Liberty." That incredible Purchase would add yet another dimension—a western one—to American iconography: because of the Lewis and Clark expedition, which is superbly recalled in the Seattle show;[100] by means of the wonderful Indian portraits made by Charles-Balthazar-Julien Févret de Saint-Mémin;[101] and, eventually, in the art of George Catlin, Seth Eastman, and George Caleb Bingham. By their day, the 1840s, "Peace & Plenty" had supplanted "Liberty" as the dominant watchword of our national culture. The iconography had altered accordingly, and the subtle nuances of that important transformation are, to me, the most fascinating aspect of those truly splendid Bicentennial exhibitions.[102]

Within a decade, moreover, Liberty encountered still another

1. *Thomas Sully,*
Thomas Jefferson (*1822*).

2. *John Vanderlyn,*
The Death of Jane McCrea (*1803-5*).

3. *Asher B. Durand,* The Capture of Major André *(1833-4).*

4. *James Hamilton,* Capture of the Serapis by John Paul Jones *(1854).*

5. *Edward Hicks,* Washington Crossed Here *(1830s?).*

6. *Emanuel Leutze,* Washington Crossing the Delaware (*1851*).

7. *William T. Ranney,* Marion Crossing the Peedee (*1851*).

8. Washington Crossing the Delaware, *artist unknown (late nineteenth century).*

9. *M. M. Sanford,* Washington at Princeton (*ca. 1850*).

12. *Reuben Law Reed,*
Washington and Lafayette
at the Battle of Yorktown
(*ca. 1860*).

10. *Archibald M. Willard,*
The Spirit of '76 (*1876*).

11. *William Mercer,*
Battle of Princeton (*ca. 1786-90*).

Courtesy of the Abby Aldrich Rockefeller Folk Art Collection, Williamsburg, Va.

13. *Gilbert Gaul*, Molly Pitcher at the Battle of Monmouth (*ca. 1892*).

14. *William Dunlap*, Scene from "The Spy" (*1823*).

15. *Howard Pyle,* The Battle of Bunker Hill (*1898*).

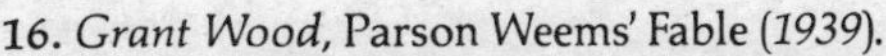

16. *Grant Wood,* Parson Weems' Fable (*1939*).

Courtesy Amon Carter Museum, Fort Worth, Texas.

17. *Peter Saul,* The Spirit of '76 (*1976*).

18. *Edward Savage,* Liberty as Goddess of Youth (*1796*).

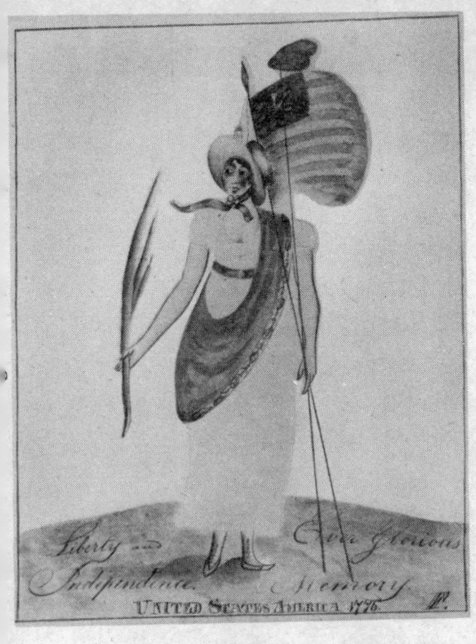

19. Miss Liberty (*ca. 1815*).

20. *Enrico Causici*, Liberty and the Eagle (*1817-19*).

21. *Christian Remick*, Perspective View of the Blockade of Boston Harbour (*ca. 1768*).

22. *John L. Boqueto de Woiserie,* View of New Orleans in 1803 (*1803*).

23. Creamware Pitcher (*ca. 1798*).

24. *Logo from the title page of* An Address.

25. *From the* Columbian Magazine, *I* (*1786*).

26. *Joseph Richardson, Jr.,* Indian Peace Medal (*1793*).

27. He That Tilleth His Land Shall Be Satisfied (*ca. 1850*), *artist unknown.*

29 *Constantino Brumidi*, Calling of Cincinnatus from the Plow (*1855*).

28. General Putnam Leaving His Plow for the Defense of His Country, *artist unknown*.

30. *Constantino Brumidi,* Calling of Putnam from the Plow to the Revolution (*1855*).

31. *Joseph Pickett,* Washington Under the Council Tree (*1914-18?*).

32. *Peter Saul,* George Washington Crossing the Delaware *(1975)*.

misfortune—a misfortune symptomatic of various setbacks she had suffered ever since the early nineteenth century. In 1856 Thomas Crawford received his last congressional commission: to create an allegorical statue suitable for placement atop the Capitol dome. This project required seven years, and eventually had to be cast in bronze posthumously by another sculptor, Clark Mills. Crawford's original intention, Liberty wearing the Revolutionary liberty cap, was unacceptable to Jefferson Davis, President Buchanan's Secretary of War. Why? Because it might be construed as symbolizing an endorsement of freedom for the slaves. Crawford obligingly substituted an Indian headdress for the liberty cap, and called his 19-foot figure "Armed Freedom."[103]

Thomas Jefferson's vision of "an Empire for Liberty" in which the religion and customs of all people would be respected—"thereby converting dangerous enemies into valuable friends"—had been subtly subverted. By 1860 there were baffled spokesmen in every section wondering what had gone wrong. A North Carolina newspaper declared that

> as a nation, we possess all the elements of greatness and power. Peace smiles upon us from all quarters of the globe; a material prosperity, unparalleled in the annals of the world, surrounds us; our territory embraces almost the entire continent; we enjoy wide-spread intelligence, and universal plenty.[104]

Yet something had gone wrong; something seemed wildly out of order if thoughtful men and women were willing to exchange all these blessings for the questionable benefits of a southern confederacy. Martial solutions to contemporary problems made it all but inevitable that martial interpretations would be placed upon historical problems. Thomas Crawford's "Armed Freedom" proved to be prophetic. And before the nineteenth century ended, Henry Cabot Lodge explained the true meaning of the Revolutionary era: the emergence of "an armed democracy."[105]

In a very real sense, Houdon's Washington returning to civilian life (1796) and Greenough's Washington the lawgiver (1841) were supplanted in the American mind by Washington as a "man on horseback." When the new equestrian statue of Washington was placed at the Boston Public Garden in 1869, genteel Bostonians trilled their praise and delight.[106] When William Trego painted *Washington Reviewing His Ragged Army at Valley Forge* (1883), he kept the authoritative general on horseback. So did Daniel Chester French in doing his heroic statue for the Place d'Iéna at Paris in 1899. Even Joseph Pickett's charming primitive, *Washington Under the Council Tree* (1914–18), presents the general in an unlikely mounted position to plan the Battle of Trenton (see figure 31). And the trend continues to our own time.[107]

The varied ways in which Washington has been presented comprise an important barometer of national aspirations and self-knowledge. In 1829, when James Fenimore Cooper learned that Horatio Greenough had begun a monumental sculpture of Washington, he encouraged him with enthusiasm:

> I am glad you have undertaken a Washington. Go on boldly with the work. Make the figure as severe and simple as possible, for these two qualities contain the essence of the imaginative with such a man. It will also suit our ideas of his character, and of our own character. Aim rather at the natural than the classical, taking care always to preserve the dignity of the man and his station.[108]

We cannot overestimate the impact of Washington iconography throughout the nineteenth century; and even, perhaps, as late as his bicentennial in 1932. Ordinary Americans were deeply affected by such simple pictures as *Washington Welcomed* (ca. 1820), *Washington and Friends After a Day's Hunt in Virginia* (1868), and *Washington's Triumphal Entry into New York in 1783* (ca. 1880).[109] But so were sophisticated Americans like Ralph Waldo Emerson. In July of 1852 he contemplated a portrait of Washington that hung in his own dining room:

> I cannot keep my eyes off of it. It has a certain Appalachian strength, as if it were truly the first-fruits of America, and expressed the Country. The heavy, leaden eyes turn on you, as the eyes of an ox in a pasture. And the mouth has a gravity and depth of quiet, as if this MAN had absorbed all the serenity of America, and left none for his restless, rickety, hysterical countrymen. Noble, aristocratic head, with all kinds of elevation in it, that come out by turns. Such majestical ironies, as he hears the day's politics, at table.[110]

These were reflections confided to his commonplace journal; and it was Emerson, remember, who once uttered the cynical crack that "every hero becomes a bore at last."

Just as George Washington epitomized the *ne plus ultra* in American national character—a perfect model for emulation—so too the capture of Major André became one of the most popular incidents delineated in nineteenth-century art about the Revolution. At the end of Chapter Two we noticed its impact upon the historical imagination of Horatio Greenough; and we know that in 1851, when Greenough visited the Trumbull Gallery in New Haven, he became fascinated by the self-portrait that André had sketched on the very day of his execution. Although it lacked artistic value, Greenough remarked that "it has a historic and personal interest of a high order."[111] Thus Jacob Eichholtz painted *The Capture of Major André* in 1809. Thomas Sully produced a picture with the same title that was widely exhibited in 1812, then subsequently engraved. And in 1833 Asher B. Durand did his version of the same theme—a picture so popular that for more than a decade vernacular painters made homely copies, yet still could not fully supply the demand.[112]

What can explain the extraordinary appeal of this peculiar episode? There are many factors; and we shall wait to examine most of them in the context of historical poetry and drama a chapter hence. For now, let us be content with this immensely important yet hitherto neglected explanation by James Fenimore Cooper, to be found in his *Notions of the Americans*, first published in 1828.

The fate of André became an object of the keenest solicitude to both armies. From the commencement of the struggle, to the last hour of its continuance, the American authorities had acted with a moderation and dignity that gave it a character far more noble than that of a rebellion. In no one instance had the war been permitted, on their part, to assume the appearance of a struggle for personal aggrandizement. It was men battling for the known rights of human nature. . . . Major André was the servant of a powerful and liberal government, that was known never to reward niggardly, and the war in which he served, was waged to aggrandize its power, and not to assert any of the natural rights of man. With doubtful incentives, and for the attainment of such an object, did this accomplished young soldier condescend to prostitute his high acquirements, and to tamper with treason. . . . Whatever might have been the original error of André, in accepting a duty of so doubtful a nature, there is but one opinion of his subsequent conduct. It was highly noble and manly. The delicacy of the court, and his own frankness, were alike admirable. Though admonished to say nothing that might commit himself, he disdained subterfuge, or even concealment. . . . There were in England (naturally enough perhaps) many who affected to believe this execution had sullied the fair character of Washington. But these miserable moralists and their opinions have passed away; and while they are consigned to oblivion together, the fame they thought to have impeached is brightening, as each day proves how difficult it is to imitate virtues so rare. Among impartial and intelligent men, this very act of dignity and firmness, tempered as it was by so much humanity, adds to the weight of his imposing character.[113]

André's capture by "the incorruptible Paulding, Williams and Vanvert" helped to sustain the society's faith in "an armed democracy" of patriotic citizens. Admiration for the gallant André as prisoner, however, provided a pretext for diminished Anglophobia during the later nineteenth century, not to mention reconciliation in the twentieth. And most complicated of all, close attention to André enabled the United States to celebrate an incident that turned out well for them, yet because it involved an unsuccessful attempt at betrayal, really required no monument. For Americans were exceedingly uneasy about historical monuments in what was supposed to be an egalitarian and non-traditional society.

The problem with monuments, of course, was that they seemed so Old Worldly, so aristocratic, so un-republican.[114] And they were expensive, besides, especially at a time when the Treasury had limited resources and most commemorative devices had to be paid for by public subscription. In an era of fiscal restraint, hard choices had to be made. In 1817, for example, some advocates proposed the erection of an "American Repository" to house the sculptured and painted portraits of United States Presidents and military heroes. The idea was abandoned, however, because all available funds were needed to push on with completion of the Capitol building itself.[115]

Our earliest experience with monumental statuary, moreover, was not entirely satisfactory—in part because the visibly European hands involved did not produce satisfactory results. In fact, the results seemed flatly un-American. One of the earliest statues of Washington, for example, had been commissioned by North Carolina for placement in the state capitol rotunda at Raleigh. The great Italian sculptor, Canova, got the commission; and he completed it between 1817 and 1821, but with unhappy effects. It was one of Canova's last works, and far from his best. He had copied Washington's face from a very poor plaster bust made by Cerrachi, another Italian. The figure is heroic in size, and dressed in Roman armor. Washington holds a tablet at one knee on which he is inscribing a message to the people of the United States—entirely in Italian![116]

That statue was ruined by fire in 1831. A year later, the centennial of Washington's birth, Congress awarded its first major commission to an American sculptor. It ordered a grand statue of our founding President to be designed for placement in the U.S. Capitol Rotunda. Fenimore Cooper and Washington Allston helped Greenough to get that commission; but the lawmakers felt pleased with their decision because all previous renditions of Washington had been executed by European artists. Greenough was studying in Italy, however, and worked on this project in Florence under the spiritual influence of Greek, Roman, and Florentine masters. The conception he decided upon derived from a lost antique masterpiece, the Phidian *Zeus*, as reconstructed and published by Quatremere de Quincy in 1814.[117]

A fiasco ensued. The statue reached the United States in 1841, and had its unveiling at the Rotunda in May 1842. Ralph Waldo Emerson called Greenough "the American Phidias"; but everyone else was outraged. Critics dubbed it "George Jupiter Washington." It didn't look right in the Rotunda because of inadequate lighting. A tumult of indignation arose. Philip Hone declared that "it looks like a great Herculean, warrior-like *Venus of the Bath* . . . undressed, with a huge napkin lying in his lap and covering his lower extremities, and he, preparing to perform his ablutions, is in the act of consigning his sword to the care of the attendant."[118]

The legislators soon had Greenough's Greco-Roman Washington put out on the Capitol grounds, where the pigeons could deface it with impunity. Eventually, the Smithsonian claimed it—a happy ending, of sorts. And Greenough got the last word in, a decade later, with this observation: "Monuments to really great men are opportunities on which to hang the proofs of the development of art. The great need them not. We need them."[119]

Others, however, were less ambivalent or hostile in their feelings about Revolutionary monuments, even those endowed with an active historical imagination. Young George Templeton Strong visited Boston in 1836. On May 8, following church services and Sunday dinner, he took a long walk and climbed to Bunker Hill. "The ground being elevated," he wrote, "the whole scene of action lies before you like a map, and it is easy to fancy the aspect it must have presented on the morning of the action. The monument in the middle of the entrenchments will be a superb thing, when it is finished."[120]

It is all very tricky and elusive, these relationships between art and tradition in a republican society. How does one define democratic monuments? Monuments may be metaphors for social values; but the meaning of metaphors is not always self-evident. How praise the character of our leaders without enshrining an élite? How humanize the Revolutionary heroes without stripping them of that necessary aura of dignity? And how encourage the selfless love of country—so admired in a Warren or a Hale—amid a bourgeois land of opportunity where men were burning with personal ambition? Not even our patriotic painters were immune to bourgeois values and jealousies. Most of them conceded, at one time or another, that they painted subjects that would sell, and in a format that would provide, in Trumbull's words, "more adequate compensation for my labor."

The author of a public discourse delivered at Richmond seems to have penetrated to the heart of the matter in 1856:

> When we pause before these historical paintings which adorn the great hall of our national capitol, it is well that the eye can take in at a glance the surrender at Yorktown, and the Declaration of Independence; for that crowning triumph of American valor, around which exultant patriotism will ever love to linger, derives all its lustre from the earlier and grander victory of peace.

The orator explained that he intended to discuss the essayists and politicians who defended the colonial cause in the decade after 1765 and thereby precipitated Independence. Then came his ultimate rationale—the one I find so pervasive in American thought, most especially between 1800 and 1860:

> It is essential to the unity and elevation of our national character, that from time to time we should review those epochs which constitute as it were the grand climacterics of our history, and passing judgment upon the passions and principles they have in turns developed, incorporate with our moral and intellectual life, all of the imperishable truth and sentiment to which they have given birth.[121]

That preoccupation with the American Revolution as an inspiration for the definition and development of national character will come to the fore repeatedly as we turn to examine poetry, drama, and above all, historical fiction. It is utterly central to a proper understanding of the American mind, and most especially to the Americans' belief in the uniqueness of their culture. As one essayist remarked of the Revolution: "that event we justly consider as the noblest monument of our national glory." Hence the importance of "sacredly" preserving its records. Hence their hope that the patriotic heroism of 1776 "will not in future time reproach the degeneracy of posterity."[122]

CHAPTER FOUR

RESHAPING THE PAST TO PERSUADE THE PRESENT

"Among a democratic people poetry will not feed on legends"

William Gilmore Simms remarked in 1842 that "a national history, preserved by a national poet, becomes, in fact, a national religion."[1] Much as he might have hoped that that concatenation of events would occur in these United States, it never came to pass. Many of the poems written about the American Revolution, it is true, have a strong religious cast.[2] Shadows of divinity filter through quite a few of them, and thereby give our patriotic poetry a certain distinctive character as compared, for example, with most art, history, biography, or fiction about the Revolutionary era—all of which tend to be considerably more secular. Simms, however, had in mind the particular case of Scotland and Robert Burns, for whom we simply have no counterpart. No major American poet has devoted himself so single-mindedly to the *historical* stuff of our national experience, or been so beloved; and the poets of lesser talent who did (or tried) remain deservedly unread. To steal a phrase from one of them, they have been ignored "down the winds of memory."[3]

Writing at just about the same time that Simms did, Alexis de Tocqueville provides us with a piece of the explanation. "Among a democratic people," he suggested,

> poetry will not feed on legends or on traditions and memories of old days. . . . Human destiny, man himself, not tied to time or place, but

face to face with nature and with God, with his passions, his doubts, his unexpected good fortune, and his incomprehensible miseries, will for these peoples be the chief and almost the sole subject of poetry.[4]

Although most of our major poets at one point or another wrote something about the Revolution—William Cullen Bryant and Longfellow, James Russell Lowell and Lanier, John Greenleaf Whittier and Whitman all did—few of them wrote very much about it. Their intent was usually aimed elsewhere, as we shall soon discover. In 1832, for instance, Whittier published a long poem entitled "Moll Pitcher" that has nothing at all to do with that Revolutionary heroine. As he told Mrs. Sigourney on February 2, 1832: "I have indeed thrown together a poem of some length, the title of which ('Moll Pitcher') has very little connection with the subject." Whittier went on to reveal that what pressed most urgently upon his mind that winter was the contemporary crisis in national politics. He had also just begun to write "a work of fiction, which shall have for its object the reconciliation of the North and the South,—being simply an endeavor to do away with some of the prejudices which have produced enmity between the Southron and the Yankee."[5]

On a few occasions American poets have consciously tried to bring national traditions, and especially the preservation of tradition, to public attention. The examples of Oliver Wendell Holmes and Ezra Pound come quickly to mind:

• Holmes wrote "Old Ironsides" at the age of twenty-one. Having read that the frigate *Constitution* was about to be destroyed, he impetuously dashed off the poem in pencil on a scrap of paper; and the Boston *Daily Advertiser* printed it on September 16, 1830, next to a column containing an elaborate announcement of the celebration, to occur a day later, of Boston's bicentennial. This poem caught the public fancy, spread through the national press, and was even reprinted on handbills distributed in the streets of Washington, D.C. The *Constitution* was saved in consequence.

• Between 1934 and 1940, Pound published his Cantos about Thomas Jefferson, John and John Quincy Adams. "Are you ready," Pound wrote to John Crowe Ransom, "for a revival of American culture considering it as something specifically grown from the nucleus of the American Founders, present in the Adams, Jefferson correspondence?"[6] Hence his ten extensive Cantos on the career and thought of John Adams. Pound pointed out that neither Adams nor Jefferson "would have thought of literature as something having nothing to do with life, the nation, the organization of government." And he asserted, ultimately, that "a total culture such as that of Adams and Jefferson does not dodge such investigation."[7]

Despite these uncommon illustrations, however, our men and women of letters have not done especially well by the American Revolution. The reasons are complex, and will be examined in the context of poetry and drama in the pages that follow.

Why poetry and drama in the same chapter? One reason is because so many authors wrote both. (Many of the plays are written in blank verse, and some are even in rhyming iambic tetrameter.) Hugh Henry Brackenridge (1748–1816), Madison's classmate at Princeton, wrote such patriotic plays as *The Battle of Bunker's Hill* (in 1776) and *The Death of General Montgomery* (in 1777), as well as poems like "Off from Boston." So did John Williamson Palmer, Epes Sargent, Nathaniel Parker Willis, and Thomas Dunn English. In 1826 George Pope Morris (1802–64) did a drama called *Briar Cliff*, based upon incidents of the Revolution, which enjoyed a long run and made a good deal of money. Morris also wrote such poems as the "Song of Marion's Men," "Seventy-Six," "A Hero of the Revolution," and "The Land of Washington."[8] When Sidney Lanier (1842–81) completed his cantata, *The Centennial Meditation of Columbia, 1776–1876*, he then began the long Centennial ode entitled "Psalm of the West." A passionate assertion of the time-wrought triumph of freedom in the United States, and conceived as a symphonic poem, it was first published in the July 1876 issue of *Lippincott's Magazine*.[9]

The second reason for examining historical poetry and drama in tandem is that there is a certain sequential rhythm in their appearance. Both have been produced intermittently in the centuries since 1776; but poetry about the American Revolution may be said to have flourished to a greater degree in the period 1776–1876, while historical drama has come into its own, and been somewhat less derivative (from novels) as well as more influential in the twentieth century. In part that is because poetry had a long and honored heritage by 1776, whereas many Americans disapproved of the theatre—indeed, found it morally reprehensible—as late as the 1850s. In part, also, that is because poetry seems to have greater appeal to an educated élite, whereas drama may be more suitable for a mass society. As American culture became more egalitarian in the twentieth century, drama and film rose in importance, while poetry declined in its proportionate appeal.

Both historical poetry and drama, of course, are forms of imaginative literature, which means that the author of either form enjoys a fair amount of artistic freedom and undertakes certain creative obligations. To undertake historical poetry, however, or historical drama, nevertheless entails some diminution of aesthetic freedom, and an expansion of responsibility (to both the present and the past), as well as (oftentimes) an encounter with ideological complications. Theodore Roosevelt remarked upon one part of this snare in his 1912 presidential address to the American Historical Association, entitled "History as Literature":

> It is a shallow criticism to assert that imagination tends to inaccuracy. Only a distorted imagination tends to inaccuracy. Vast and fundamental truths can be discerned and interpreted only by one whose imagination is as lofty as the soul of a Hebrew prophet.[10]

Just how distorted or accurate, undiscerning or prophetic have our poets and dramatists been in their attempts to recapture our Revolutionary past?

"The American Revolution might afford subjects to employ the poet"

Because my central concern is with the Revolution's role in national tradition, I shall say very little here about that earliest production of poetry-by-participants. I mean the likes of Francis Hopkinson (1737–91), Jonathan Mitchell Sewall (1748–1808), David Humphreys (1752–1818), and Philip Freneau (1752–1832). They have been written about extensively; and their perceptions of the patriots, who obviously fought for Liberty, and the British, who were mostly brutal tyrants, are not especially complicated. Even more important, the haze of distance, the myth-making process, and the Revolution's entanglement with subsequent events were only starting to materialize in the period from 1776 until about 1818. I do not mean to suggest for a moment that "The Battle of the Kegs" (1778), or the "Burning of Fairfield" (1779), or "To the Memory of the Brave Americans Who Fell at Eutaw"

(1781) are unimportant as artifacts in American cultural history; but their importance has already been established and assessed by others. Such poetry was frequently regarded by contemporaries as partisan propaganda, and it seems to me, in any case, separable from the more particular kind of inquiry I have undertaken here.[11]

In December 1818, an anonymous essay appeared in the *North American Review.* Entitled "National Poetry," it made an important appeal which I shall have occasion to refer to more than once. It began by complaining about the lack of historical understanding in American culture. "None can be blind to the invaluable uses or the dignity of history. Yet how few among the more numerous ranks of the community derive from it any thing to influence their feelings or inform their understandings?" Then the author moved into the most pointed part of his polemic:

> It can hardly be doubted, that the American Revolution might afford subjects to employ the poet, with success and glory, limited only by his talents. The materials it would furnish are infinite, its characters innumerable. . . . All ranks of the community took part in it; every station of life was reached by its agitations. The hopes and fears of the remote cultivator and *woodsman,* no less than the busy townsman, the concerns of lovers, their plans for connubial welfare, the prouder calculations of men of property and station, all were at the mercy of the times. Above all, the crisis was brought upon them by their resolute adherence to principles esteemed just.[12]

There are other dimensions we might add; and, in fact, the author did have still more to say, as we shall see. But that comprehensive statement could still stand as a challenge to American poets today. Its promise has not yet been fulfilled. Let us raise these questions, therefore, in ascending order of importance: What is most familiar in American poetry about the Revolution? What is most predictable? And then, what is most unusual? First, the familiar.

It should not be surprising to anyone that quite a few of the emphases already encountered in Chapters Two and Three also turn up in our poetry. As with iconography, for example, there is a shifting emphasis from Liberty to "Peace & Plenty" during and after the Revolutionary era. Leaving the plough in 1775 to defend freedom, and returning to the fields in 1783 to achieve prosperity, are central themes. As Wallace Rice put it at the close of the nineteenth century in "The Minute-Men of Northboro' ":

The Minute-Men of Northboro' let rust the standing plough,
The seed may wait, the fertile ground upsmiling to the spring.

The hands that here release the plough have taken up a strife
That shall not end until all earth has heard the battle-cry.

In thankfulness they speed their bolt against the British Crown;
And take the plough again in Peace, their warrior's duty done.[13]

As with iconography, also, poets in the period 1875–1915 become obsessed with battles. For them, as for their contemporary painters and illustrators, the American Revolution gets reduced to little more than a wearisome war for independence—and a bloody one at that. So Thomas Dunn English (1819–1902) wrote "Assunpink and Princeton," "The Battle of Monmouth," "Arnold at Stillwater," and "To the Battle of Cowpens." John Williamson Palmer (1825–1906) produced "The Maryland Battalion." Clinton Scollard (1860–1932) turned out "The Boasting of Sir Peter Parker," "Ballad of 'Old Glory,' " "Saint Leger," and "Wayne at Stony Point." And Arthur Guiterman (1871–1943) gave us "Haarlem Heights" and "The Storming of Stony Point."[14]

As Gilbert Gaul's painting of *Molly Pitcher at the Battle of Monmouth* (ca. 1892) might have suggested, that heroic woman became something of a favorite in American verse of the later nineteenth century. Her message, according to Kate Brownlee Sherwood (1841–1914), was in

Telling the king in his stubborn pride
Women like men to their homes are true.[15]

Molly achieved immortality, of course, because she could load and fire a cannon just as well as her fallen husband had.[16] But other poems sang proudly of women who used their feminine wiles to deceive the British. "The Ballad of Sweet P," by Virginia Woodward Cloud, is all about Penelope Penwick, a patriot lass who enchanted the British officers at a dance on Christmas night, 1776, while Washington and his men achieved an important element of surprise by crossing the icy Delaware.[17] "The Little Black-Eyed Rebel," by Will Carleton (1845–1912), is all about young Mary Redmond, who lived in Philadelphia during the British occupation. She secretly delivered letters written home to loved ones by husbands and fathers fighting in the Continental army.[18]

Many of these poems concerned the tragic separation of lovers, such as the inaccurately titled "Janet McRea" by George P. Morris; or else the persistence of domesticity and romance despite the ravages of wartime, such as "Aaron Burr's Wooing" by Edmund Clarence Stedman (1833–1908). On several occasions, apparently, Burr managed to cross fifteen miles of the "Neutral Ground" in Westchester County, New York, in order to court the lovely Widow Prevost. (He married her after the war.)[19]

Such poems were entirely in keeping with the injunctions of the 1818 essay, however, for the author of "National Poetry" had declared that,

> though the elements of poetry are chiefly strong passions and great interests, and consist not with feeble emotions, yet are the tender affections essential in its composition. . . . Even those who were engaged in the most arduous operations, the civil and military heroes of the times, were involved in the various fortunes, and often romantic adventures of heart-formed connexions.

In fact, there was supposed to be something peculiarly American, apparently, about this attachment to family; for the British brutes needed raw sex, and not necessarily from loved ones, whereas the Americans, although indifferent to mere pleasures of the flesh, never lost their ties to home. "Unlike the European military," you see, "who, on entering their armies and fleets . . . separate themselves from all domestic interest and feelings, the American soldiery retained in the fort and field every concern and sympathy of the fireside and neighbourhood."[20]

There are many other themes now familiar to us to be found in these poems. One concerned the poignant passing of Revolutionary veterans during the 1820s and 1830s. As Philip Freneau put it in 1822 when he revisited "The Military Ground" near Newburgh, New York,

> *The Hills remain!—but scarce a man remains*
> *Of all, who once paraded on these lands.*[21]

Or as Oliver Wendell Holmes wondered fifteen years later in "Lexington," would the children recall their parents' sacrifices and preserve their achievements?[22]

There is also the theme of sectional reconciliation during the 1870s following Reconstruction. In "How We Became a Nation," Harriet Prescott Spofford (1835–1921) stressed the contributions of all the states in winning Independence.[23] "Under the Old Elm" by James Russell Lowell, an important poem read in Cambridge on the one hundredth anniversary of George Washington's taking command of the American army (July 3, 1775), lavishes praise upon Virginia, who "gave us this imperial man," and then asks rhetorically:

What shall we give her back but love and praise
As in the dear old unestrangëd days
Before the inevitable wrong began?[24]

And in 1889 John Greenleaf Whittier composed "The Vow of Washington" for the centennial of his first inauguration. Whittier had misgivings about the quality of this poem, and wanted to recall it after it had been mailed off. The nation responded very favorably, however, especially to these lines:

A century's suns o'er thee have risen and set,
And, God be praised, we are one nation yet.[25]

The debunking tendencies of the 1920s and the early 1930s, which one author then referred to as "patriots off their pedestals," had its poetic embodiment also, though it mostly took the form of humanization rather than hostile repudiation. We can see it in *A Book of Americans* (1933) by Rosemary and Stephen Vincent Benét, and in "Death and General Putnam" by Arthur Guiterman.[26]

There is throughout all these poems a distinct biographical orientation, as one might expect, with John Paul Jones and Francis Marion among the strongest nineteenth-century favorites.[27] But the most popular of all, for significant reasons, were George Washington, Benedict Arnold, and his accomplice, Major André. Why such polar extremes? Because of the Americans' continuing concern, as already noted at the close of Chapters One and Three, with *character.* Washington, of course, epitomized integrity, courage, civic and military duty, leadership, and loyalty. Therefore, the proper remembrance and emulation of his character comprised our best effort to approximate the Spirit of '76. So the man and his humanity,[28] the dedication of his monument in 1848, and the completion of his monument in 1885 (not to mention his annual birthday), all became the stimuli for patriotic poems.[29] Although there is no dearth of poor ones, I can happily report that Washington inspired some of the better efforts, such as "Under the Old Elm" by Lowell.[30]

By contrast Benedict Arnold, despite his acknowledged military talents, displayed some of the worst character traits and thereby served as the ultimate illustration of moral reprobation in American history. Here is the concluding stanza of "Arnold at Stillwater" by Thomas Dunn English:

Oh, that a soldier so glorious, ever victorious in fight,
Passed from a daylight of honour into the terrible night!—
Fell as the mighty archangel, ere the earth glowed in space, fell—
Fell from the patriot's heaven down to the loyalist's hell![31]

Major André, on the other hand, won the grudging admiration of Americans on account of his stoic acceptance of fate, personal courage, and soldier's code of honor. Washington rejected André's request to be shot rather than ignobly hanged; and somehow, that has tugged at the heartstrings of Americans ever since. André's gaiety and warmth, his youth and good looks, have given him a positive character in our folklore—not to mention twinges of guilt or regret.[32]

The Boston Tea Party, Lexington and Bunker Hill, Yorktown: it is scarcely surprising that these events have been fairly commonplace in American patriotic poetry. Or that the enormous appeal of "Paul Revere's Ride" should have elicited as much emulation as it has. Those rousing verses first appeared in *The Atlantic Monthly* at the beginning of the Civil War, and then Longfellow incorporated them into his *Tales of a Wayside Inn*, published on November 25, 1863.[33] Thereafter the subject of brave riders became all the vogue in national verse.[34] Helen F. Moore, meanwhile, got flustered by the unfair neglect of Revere's comrade, William Dawes:

T's all very well for the children to hear
Of the midnight ride of Paul Revere;
But why should my name be quite forgot,
Who rode as boldly and well, God wot?
Why should I ask? The reason is clear—
My name was Dawes and his Revere.[35]

Elbridge S. Brooks wrote "Rodney's Ride" (which occurred in 1776) and Wallace Bruce brought out "Parson Allen's Ride" (it happened in August 1777).[36]

Similarly, following the immense success enjoyed by Leutze

with *Washington Crossing the Delaware* in 1851, that event became a cliché of Gilded Age poetry.[37] Partially, of course, these are simply instances of writers and artists responding to the cultural marketplace. If a product sells, there is likely to be more than one manufacturer. But there is another explanation, too: so many of these people knew one another intimately, corresponded, and even lived together at times in informal communities.[38] They were not always on the same wavelength, but they often were; and they most certainly responded to many of the same social, political, and cultural stimuli. William Gilmore Simms, for example, wrote to his friend William Cullen Bryant on May 13, 1843:

> I have been on a visit to the upper part of Charleston District—the parish of St. John's &c—the old battlefield of Eutaw—the Eutaw Springs &c. The former might have inspired you. The latter would have delighted you. . . . The very scene for a poet—for dreams of peace & purity & love. I also mused upon the grave of Marion . . . if you come next year, I will make the time you spend with us, a drama full of fine scenes & pleasant incidents.[39]

Within a decade, of course, Carolinians and New Englanders were less likely to be in tune with one another than Simms and Bryant had been in 1843, although Bryant himself remained a special case—beloved everywhere as the national poet. "The Song of Marion's Men," which he first published in 1831, celebrated their exploits. The poem consequently came to be known by every proud and educated southerner. When Bryant visited Charleston following the Civil War, one prominent citizen told him that "Marion's Men" had been "sung in many a Southern bivouac, and warmed the soldier's heart at many a confederate camp-fire."[40]

The timing of its initial publication in 1831, however, and the relationship in general between Revolutionary War poetry and Civil War realities, are critically important to a proper understanding of the material being considered in this chapter. After seeing so many familiar and predictable themes in these poems, we come to the question: What is unusual about them? Or, put differently, are there any aspects of their pattern that are peculiar or different from the general public memory (which we looked at in Chapter Two), or the story of Revolutionary iconography (seen in Chapter Three), or in the nature of historical novels about the Revolution (coming next in Chapter Five)? The answer is Yes, and to get at it properly we must first notice the intermittent flow of these poems.

The periodic nature of their appearance—and this is especially true of the better and more influential poems—is the most closely bunched and spasmodic phasing of all the cultural artifacts I have had occasion to examine. Following that appeal for "National Poetry" back in 1818—presumably poems to be based upon the Revolutionary experience—very little appeared over the next thirteen years, despite all the interest generated by pictures, novels, orations, memoirs, and other Revolution-rooted phenomena. Then, suddenly, 1831 and 1832 blossomed as busy years for patriotic poetry. In addition to "The Song of Marion's Men" by Bryant, Oliver Wendell Holmes published "The Last Leaf" in 1831, about an aged survivor of the Boston Tea Party; and Fitz-Greene Halleck (1790–1867) brought out "The Field of the Grounded Arms," which some critics praised extravagantly as "the finest poem of the age."[41] It wasn't; but along with Bryant's and Holmes's efforts, it enjoyed a great vogue. It concerns the first major American victory of the war and the British surrender at Saratoga in October 1777. Sympathetic to the British army ("disarmed but not dishonored"), Halleck makes them seem gallant to the reader, so that when he comes to praise the patriot side, their purposes and courage appear even more glorious. It is, after all, a greater triumph to defeat a gallant foe than a despicable one.

During the later 1840s, coinciding with the years of our Mexican War, there was another flurry of widely noticed poetry about the Revolution: Whittier's "Yorktown," for example, and "Carmen Bellicosum" by Guy Humphreys McMaster (1829–87).[42] In the early 1860s yet another burst occurred, the most important examples being "Paul Revere's Ride," by Longfellow, and an enormous poem by Thomas Buchanan Read (1822–72) entitled "The Wagoner of the Alleghanies. A Poem of the Days of Seventy-Six."[43]

The years 1875 to 1876 occasioned the next and biggest wave, perhaps predictably; but if so, why wasn't there also at that time a proliferation of historical novels about the American Revolution? Whatever the causes may have been (and I will have more to say about the appearance of historical fiction in the next two chapters), Ralph Waldo Emerson read his "Boston" on December 16, 1873, the centennial of the Boston Tea Party. Whittier wrote

"Lexington" in 1875. James Russell Lowell composed his "Ode Read at the One Hundredth Anniversary of the Fight at Concord Bridge. 19th April, 1875":

> *Here English law and English thought*
> *'Gainst the self-will of England fought.*[44]

And the Centennial year turned out to be the biggest of all: Lowell delivered "An Ode for the Fourth of July, 1876"; Whittier composed his "Centennial Hymn"; George Henry Calvert published *A Nation's Birth and Other National Poems;* John White Chadwick (1840–1904), a Unitarian clergyman from Marblehead, Massachusetts, brought forth *A Book of Poems.* And Sidney Lanier, who had written "Martha Washington" for the occasion of February 22, 1875, both wrote his *Centennial Meditation* cantata and worked on "Psalm of the West" the following year.[45]

Now, if one seeks to account for these rather spasmodic spurts of poetry about the American Revolution—notably in 1831–2, 1847–9, 1862–3, and 1875–6—several sorts of stimuli become apparent. One, of course, is simply proud patriotism. Another emerges from the imperatives of memorial occasions. We might refer to such poetic products as nostalgic nationalism. Hence Ralph Waldo Emerson's famous "Hymn," commissioned to be sung at the completion of Concord's monument to the events of April 19, 1775. Hence "The Battle of King's Mountain" by Paul Hamilton Hayne, written for the centennial celebration of that battle on October 7, 1880.[46] Hence "Crispus Attucks" by John Boyle O'Reilly, prepared for the dedication ceremony of Crispus Attucks's monument on Boston Common, November 14, 1888.[47]

The third stimulus we can identify is perhaps the most important: anxiety induced by national crises, particularly political crises. I have pointed out that when Whittier wrote "Moll Pitcher" in 1831, he was actually preoccupied with the Nullification Crisis precipitated several years earlier by South Carolina.[48] The same is true of William Cullen Bryant, who ordinarily did not write historical poetry, but produced a rash of it in 1831. The specter of sectionalism worried him immensely, and he composed such poems as "The Song of Marion's Men," "Seventy-Six," and "The Green Mountain Boys" in order to appeal to national sentiments. That also explains his unusual participation in April 1839 at the New-York Historical Society when that organization celebrated the fiftieth anniversary of George Washington's inauguration. Bryant did not like to do this sort of "occasional" writing; but he felt a genuine sense of political obligation, and produced a poem in four stanzas that was widely published in national newspapers.[49]

The point to be made, and made emphatically, is that many of the most important and memorable poems that have been written about the American Revolution are really not about the Revolution at all; or, to put it more precisely, they were not written with the Revolution primarily in view. "Paul Revere's Ride," for example, is a vigorous patriotic ballad; it did much to stimulate the martial spirit of northerners; and, appearing as it did at the beginning of the Civil War, the message of its final stanza was perfectly plain:

For, borne on the night-wind of the Past,
Through all our history, to the last,
In the hour of darkness and peril and need,
The people will waken and listen to hear
The hurrying hoof-beats of that steed,
And the midnight message of Paul Revere.[50]

John Greenleaf Whittier's "Yorktown" is an important poem, which called attention to an unresolved ethical issue of the American Revolution: the shame of slavery. Whittier begins with the historical fact of British surrender.

Now all is hushed: the gleaming lines
Stand moveless as the neighbouring pines;
While through them, sullen, grim, and slow,
The conquered hosts of England go.

But very soon he moves on to his real concern—and reason for writing this poem.

But who are they, who, cowering, wait
Within the shattered fortress gate?
Dark tillers of Virginia's soil,
Classed with the battle's common spoil,
With household stuffs, and fowl, and swine,
With Indian weed and planters' wine,
With stolen beeves, and foraged corn,—
Are they not men, Virginian born?

Then the point is driven home:

> *Your world-wide honour stained with shame,—*
> *Your freedom's self a hollow name!*[51]

Whittier was a pacifist as well as an abolitionist. When he wrote "Lexington, 1775" he had two purposes in view. First, to suggest that the minutemen were really peace-loving rather than aggressive warriors: "No Berserk thirst of blood had they/ No battle-joy was theirs, who set/ Against the alien bayonet." And second, to suggest that the echo of their struggle continued to be heard by men and women who longed for a golden age of brotherhood.[52]

Like Whittier, Ralph Waldo Emerson had been deeply troubled by slavery; and his "Boston," first read on December 16, 1873, is generally concerned with freedom for a self-governing people, but particularly with emancipation. The authorial voice throughout is God's. Two-thirds of the way along He declares,

> *I break your bonds and masterships,*
> *And I unchain the slave:*
> *Free be his heart and hand henceforth*
> *As wind and wandering wave.*[53]

Paul Hamilton Hayne, on the other hand, a southerner who has been called "the last literary cavalier," wrote a dialect ballad based upon an incident from 1780 in Peter Horry's *Life of Marion.* The poem is called "The Hanging of Black Cudjo," and it is quite starkly a statement against Negro emancipation. The devoted slave declares:

> *"I stays wid you, (sez I again,) I meck de nigger wuck,*
> *I wuck myself, and may be, Boss, we'll bring back de ole luck;*
> *But don't you pizen me no more wid talk ob 'freedom sweet,'*
> *But sabe dat gab to stuff de years of de next fool you meet!"*[54]

Another poem by Hayne entitled "Charleston Retaken" supposedly refers to the events of December 1782 when British troops departed. In reality it has in view the end of Reconstruction and the sense of devastation that follows a bitter war:

> *No sportive flocks in the pasture,*
> *No aftermath on the lea;*
> *No laughs of the slaves at labors*
> *No chant of birds on the tree.*

Hayne takes great pride in having "dogged" the enemy "Forever from our South!" The Britons referred to, of course, are actually Yankees thinly disguised. And the poem closes with hope-by-analogy: if the "keen shock of terror" from British occupation could recede, so, too, would the waste of federal domination.[55]

In addition to the political double-entendres that pervade these poems, it must also be borne in mind that many of them are as much concerned with Nature as they are about the Revolution. In this, however, they are entirely in the spirit of "National Poetry," that 1818 benchmark exhortation. "If we take any glory in our country's being beautiful and sublime and picturesque," the essays's author had said, "we must approve the work which reminds us of its scenery by making it the theatre of splendid feats and heartmoving incidents."[56] Thus in "The Song of Marion's Men" by Bryant,

Our fortress is the good greenwood,
Our tent the cypress tree;
We know the forest round us,
As seamen know the sea.
We know its walls of thorny vines,
Its glades of reedy grass,
Its safe and silent islands
Within the dark morass.[57]

In "The Green Mountain Boys," also by Bryant, Ethan Allen and his men startle sleeping birds by marching through the pristine forest to Ticonderoga. A better day would clearly be at hand soon when man and Nature will be more in tune, when there is no longer the "hail of iron and rain of blood / To sweep and waste the land."[58]

That stress upon Nature, and the somewhat sullied but still pristine quality of American landscape in Revolutionary times, anticipates an important theme which emerged with special clarity at the time of our Centennial: namely, that an archaic colonial past died in 1775 followed by a brand-new birth. James Russell Lowell touched upon this in his "Ode Read at the One Hundredth Anniversary of the Fight at Concord Bridge": "When Buttrick gave the word / That awful idol of the unchallenged Past / . . . Fell crashing."[59] He developed it more fully in two other poems, one being the "Ode for July 4, 1876," in which he expressed admiration for the boldness of those a century before "who first off-cast"

Their moorings from the habitable Past
And ventured chartless on the sea
Of storm-engendering Liberty.[60]

The other is a little known and much shorter poem called "Lines Suggested by the Graves of Two English Soldiers on Concord Battle-ground." Of the British regulars he wrote that "they came three thousand miles, and died / To keep the Past upon its Throne." Of the American farmers, " 'Twas for the future that they fought."[61]

I find the patriotic poetry of 1876, in many respects, more revealing and symptomatic than all the other verse written about the Revolution. In Lowell's case his odes are higher in literary quality than most; he is insightful about his native land; and, in my belief, his views are representative of many persons in the mainstream of American culture at that time. He found the United States somewhat lacking in a sense of tradition, especially by comparison with Old World antiquities. He believed, nevertheless, that his nation had its own sort of monuments:

Not such as stand decrepitly resigned
To ruin-mark the path of dead events
That left no seed of better days behind.

Instead, Lowell insisted, "she builds not on the ground, but in the mind," and then launched into a list of felicitous phenomena in America: agriculture, industry, self-government, "happy homesteads hid in orchard trees" whose residents lived at peace. In identifying these monuments to progress and prosperity, Lowell echoed the Centennial Oration of Robert C. Winthrop, also given in Boston on July 4, 1876.[62]

"The Centennial Hymn" by Whittier, which in many ways is my favorite among these poems, is somewhat unusual in that it can be read today without embarrassment. He thanks the founders' God for national unity and freedom, as well as for all of the century's accomplishments. But he follows this with an honest admission that "withal, we crave

The austere virtues strong to save,
The honour proof to place or gold,
The manhood never bought nor sold!

And then, having requested the revival of austerity and integrity, he adds peace and justice, concluding:

Let the new cycle shame the old![63]

After the commemorative occasions of 1875–81 had passed, patriotic poetry did not cease to be written altogether. But it did begin a very gradual decline that would not be entirely perceptible until after the Spanish-American War and World War I had withered that distinctive form of nationalism that thrived upon "The Baptism of the Flag," or *Ballads of Valor and Victory*, or *Let the Flag Wave.*[64]

Poetry about the American Revolution flourished, primarily, during the half century following 1830. When the romanticism of Bryant, Longfellow, and Emerson declined, so did this particular genre of national expression. Fitz-Greene Halleck had visited Mount Vernon in 1817, and then wrote in a private letter: " 'Tis a pilgrimage which, as an American, I paid with feelings of devotion and of reverence." We know that Halleck, like so many of his contemporaries, loved the spread-eagle excitement in New York City on the Fourth of July; and those feelings found inspirational form in his 1831 poem called "The Field of the Grounded Arms."[65]

When Longfellow joined the Harvard faculty and settled permanently at Cambridge in 1836, he moved into the historic Craigie House, which once had been George Washington's headquarters during the rehearsal for rebellion in 1775–6. The patriotic associations of that handsome home were not lost upon Longfellow. His contemporary, Epes Sargent (1813–80), journalist, poet, dramatist, and biographer, wrote "The Death of Warren," a poem about Bunker Hill, to illustrate the theme that it is truly sweet to die for one's country; and that is also the motif of "Nathan Hale," penned by Francis Miles Finch in 1853.[66]

The mid-nineteenth-century American version of patriotic poetry was somewhat milder than the German "storm and stress" variety. Ours combined romanticism with didactic nationalism—the purpose being both to justify aggressive adventures, like the Mexican War, and also to teach the meaning of Americanism to such newcomers as the Irish, German, and other new immigrants of the 1840s and 1850s. Although historians have written much about the emergence of Manifest Destiny and American nationalism during the 1840s, I do not believe that adequate attention has been paid to the intense patriotism of the following decade. Toward the close of James P. Holcombe's *Discourse* in 1856, he asked rhetorically: "What is truly grand and inspirational?" His answer: "The ancestral voices of liberty, which breaking from her memorial tombs of patriotism, gather in resounding echoes along all the lines of future history."[67]

I find these attitudes reiterated constantly in the private letters of Benson J. Lossing during these years; and significantly, the decline of patriotism becomes a poignant theme of his correspondence in the subsequent decade. "Now is the time to hold up the example of Washington and to urge the people to follow it," wrote one friend in 1861. "As you say, patriotism seems to be lost in party spirit."[68] Hence that strong patriotic impulse in the poetry of Thomas Buchanan Read, written during the period 1855 to 1862 and culminating in "The Wagoner of the Alleghanies." Hence "The Marching Song of Stark's Men," by Edward Everett Hale (1822–1909);[69] and, far more influential, Hale's famous story, "The Man Without a Country," first published by *The Atlantic Monthly* in December 1863. The immediate purpose of that tale was to influence an impending election; but its long-term intention was to rekindle patriotism. Hale himself was a Unitarian minister and prolific author in Boston; his father was a nephew of the Revolutionary Nathan Hale, his mother a sister of Edward Everett, the patriotic orator.

Bryant died in 1878, Lanier in 1881, Longfellow and Emerson a month apart in 1882, Lowell in 1891, Whittier the next year, Holmes in 1894, and the aged Hale in 1909. As I have said, patriotic poetry did not entirely die with them; but it most certainly went into decline, and with it that particular genre of verse about the Revolution.[70] Thomas Jefferson enjoyed a certain vogue in American poems of the 1930s and early 1940s; but the emphasis in most of them fell upon "Jefferson at Monticello," to use the title of F. C. Rosenberger's composition.[71] They concerned Jefferson's mind—"so temperate, so remote, so sure of phrase"[72]—much more than his activities as a revolutionary. Not that there is anything reprehensible about writing of Jefferson's marvelous mind. I cannot think of a more worthy topic from the entire breadth of American biography. But the mode and message of mid-nineteenth-century romantic nationalism, predicated upon the Revolutionary achievement, was now essentially an archaic thing of the past.[73]

What, in the last analysis, might be said about the embodiment of that mode in historical poetry? One must be careful to claim neither too much nor too little. An assertion made by Jacob Burckhardt, for example—"History finds in poetry not only one of its most important, but also one of its purest and finest sources"—claims far too much, at least with reference to the materials we have been examining.[74] Many of these poems are scarcely about the American Revolution at all; the author's ostensible subject so often was not his actual objective.

In an interview that took place late in the Bicentennial year, Robert Penn Warren indicated that he always tries to develop his poems from some ethical issue. "My poems start with a feeling," he remarked. "Everything starts from an observed fact of life and then the search begins for the *issue*—the ethical or dramatic issue—in the fact."[75] In saying so Penn Warren comes closer than Burckhardt to catching the essence of our best poems about the Revolution. Whittier, Emerson, Lowell, and Bryant usually began with an ethical or a dramatic issue, such as the irony of cries for political freedom coming from patriots who held other human beings in bondage. Only recently have our most insightful historians called attention to such ethical issues in the Revolutionary era.[76] A handful of American poets did during the period 1831 to 1876; but precious few have done so since.[77]

Critics of Ezra Pound's historical Cantos have objected that he jumbles the past by juxtaposing unconnected episodes, or by silently joining fragments from different historical documents.[78] It is true that he does so; but his ultimate purpose was political and moral instruction. Pound did not intend to edit an anthology of the founders' writings, but rather to comment in poetic form upon some ethical issues of American politics.[79] In seeking to do so he was, willy-nilly, being more faithful than most imaginative American writers have been to an important injunction stated in that 1818 essay on national poetry: "for the purposes of moral instruction, as well as entertainment, things real may, without offence, be modified and take their form from the hand of an author not strictly historical; and it is best to leave this to the poet."[80]

"The Revolution is singularly lacking in dramatic properties"

When we turn to drama, a degree of disintegration occurs in the quality of our material; for the American theatre has not been especially fortunate in its renditions of the Revolutionary experience. Indeed, I would go further and assert that, overall, plays (and films) have been just about the poorest of all our works of art inspired by the American Revolution. The reasons are somewhat instructive and therefore deserve at least limited exploration.

The first and most general point to be made is that much the greatest proportion of American plays have been devoid of historical content altogether. Our dramatists, by and large, have not dealt seriously with aspects of national tradition, and their works are notably lacking in meaningful perceptions of the past. As one leading authority has written, "history passed through the theatre pictorially, as a pageant, but not with any sense of value for itself alone."[81] Ever since the early nineteenth century, theatre has been the most democratic form of live public entertainment in the United States. As such, its success depended upon the responses of people in *all* segments of society. As David Grimsted observed, "the will of the audience was immediately influential"; and by the Jacksonian era it became clear that melodrama held the greatest appeal for the greatest number.[82]

Although history and melodrama are not necessarily incompatible, neither do they nuzzle up to one another very easily. For whatever cultural reasons, the combination has not been especially appealing to American theatre-goers. Maxwell Anderson's *Valley Forge* (1934) sought to blend the Revolution with romance. It enjoyed greater popularity than most such efforts; yet one drama critic reported overhearing this characteristic remark by a man walking down the aisle between acts: "I do not like this—I am not interested in the material."[83]

The second point to be made, therefore, is that many of the historical plays that were written have never even been performed. As John Gassner observed in a review of *The Patriots* (1943), by Sidney Kingsley: "Both Jefferson and Hamilton have been subjects of a variety of unproduced plays, and it is not easy to create a biographical drama with them as a subject."[84] Of the plays that were actually performed, moreover, many were never published, or were published only privately in editions of very limited circulation. Paul Leicester Ford, for example, produced *Janice Meredith,* a novel of the Revolution, in 1899. Because of its great popularity, Ford and Edward E. Rose adapted a stage version that opened in New York the next year and enjoyed a good run. Ford wrote many other dramas as original plays, however, and most of them were never professionally performed or published. Insofar as they exist at all, it is in Ford's original manuscript version.[85]

The third point to be made, quite simply, is that a large number of the plays were decidedly inferior adaptations of successful historical novels. The stage, one critic remarked in 1882, "has turned novels which were dramatic into plays which excite the ridicule of the critics who praised the novels."[86] *The Spy,* by James Fenimore Cooper, first appeared in 1821 and began its New York stage run in March 1822. *The Pilot* first appeared in 1823 and had been made into a "burletta" by 1825. George Lippard's highly sentimental novel, *Blanche of Brandywine* (1846), was given a stage adaptation in 1858 by J. G. Burnett. Costume directions for the cast start with "Washington—made up after Stuart's celebrated picture"; and some of the scenes are ridiculously melodramatic. At one point in Act III George Washington, who is alone in the woods, gives a soliloquy on the perilous American situation, and then drops to his knees in prayer. Whereupon the English General Howe, who had fortuitously lost his way, happens along and offers Washington a title of nobility if he will just cease fighting and end the rebellion. The Father of his Country gives a petulant, predictable response, at which Howe blithely goes away![87]

The plays, quite obviously, are poorly imitative of other cultural forms that were both more imaginative and more persuasive. (Because the next two chapters deal with historical fiction based upon the Revolution, I shall devote little attention here to theatricals derived from those novels.) Only in touching upon the concern with patriotism, death, and personal character do the early plays anticipate or develop simultaneously a theme also central to the poetry, iconography, and fiction. *The Death of General Montgomery* by Hugh Henry Brackenridge (1777), and *Bunker-Hill; or, The Death of General Warren* by John Burk (1808), parallel that emphasis in John Trumbull's history paintings upon the nobility of sacrificing one's life for a worthy cause: the defense of homeland.[88]

As with poetry-by-participants, which I have skimmed over for reasons explained early in this chapter, so too the plays-by-participants are not an integral part of our concern here. They have already received attention from literary historians; they predate the Revolution's full embodiment in national tradition; and because their stimulus was so flagrantly political, they are less valuable in our context as culturally complex, imaginative documents. Norman Philbrick goes too far in ignoring their ideological significance when he insists that "these pamphlet plays are first of all the raw stuff of propaganda." But he is correct in asserting that their purpose was "to promote persuasion toward the American or the British cause."[89] The early plays tend to be unwieldy in structure, burdened by allegorical overlay, and gross in characterization (to the point of ridiculous caricature).

The early playwrights themselves perceived a problem in writing contemporaneously to (or so soon after) the events that were their subject matter. During the autumn of 1780, for example, soon after Major André's capture and execution, Philip Freneau started to write a drama called *The Spy,* featuring André, Arnold, Sir Henry Clinton, and Nathanael Greene. He was unable to complete it, however, and it was not published in his lifetime.[90] In the preface to *André* (1798), William Dunlap explained that he had begun the composition of this play almost ten years earlier. For various reasons he felt discouraged about completing it, among them "a prevailing opinion that recent events are unfit subjects for tragedy." Dunlap then launched into a fascinating disquisition on the difficulties of doing historical drama properly:

> In exhibiting a stage representation of a real transaction, the particulars of which are fresh in the minds of many of the audience, an author has this peculiar difficulty to struggle with, that those who know the events expect to see them *all* recorded; and any deviation from what they remember to be fact, appears to them as a fault in the poet; they are disappointed, their expectations are not fulfilled, and the writer is more or less condemned, not considering the difference between the poet and the historian, or not knowing that what is intended to be exhibited is a free poetical picture, not an exact historical portrait.[91]

It should come as no surprise, therefore, that the best and most interesting American playwrights during the nineteenth century did not deal with historical themes. Instead, there were some flurries of mediocre writing, usually in the wake of successful biographies or novels. Thus in the 1820s we find a cluster of strangely titled plays: *Marion, or the Hero of Lake George* (1821), *A Tale of Lexington* (1822), *King's Bridge Cottage* (1826), and *Paul Jones, or the Pilot of the German Ocean* (1828). During the later 1840s, when George Washington once again became a cynosure of popular attention,[92] quite a few productions in which he figured were put on. The completion of Jared Sparks's edition of Washington's correspondence helped to make that burst possible, but still more important stimuli were the militarism engendered at that time by the Mexican War, and the sectional tensions caused by slavery as a moral dilemma. More than any other figure in the national pantheon, Washington could serve as a symbol of national union, and of the yearning for unity.[93]

During the later 1850s yet another brief vogue occurred, illustrated by such plays as *Horse-Shoe Robinson; or, The Battle of King's Mountain* (1856–7), *The Golden Eagle; or, The Privateer of 1776* (1857), *The Miller of New Jersey; or, The Prison Hulk* (1858), and *Putnam, the Iron Son of '76* (a revival in 1859). The last mentioned, written earlier by Nathaniel H. Bannister, was fairly typical of the genre at that time: patriotic, martial, sentimental, and highly pictorial. The author's directions for his opening "Vision Scene" are wonderfully ludicrous:

> Slow music. Three quarters dark. Ethereal firmament, filled with silver stars. . . . Eagle flying in the air, to ascend, looking down upon a lion couchant, on trap . . . to descend. The goddesses discovered in various groups, bearing blue wands with silver stars. God of War . . . on small Roman chariot, to descend. Goddess of Liberty on trap . . . in small Roman chariot, to descend.
>
> After chorus:
>
> "We will be free, we will be free,"
>
> Music changes. Eagle ascends and lion descends. Goddesses dance around, waving wands. Goddess of Liberty and Mars point to clouds. Clouds ascend . . . and draw off . . . and (lights up) the Signers of the Declaration of Independence discovered, Ben Franklin at the head of table.[94]

After the Civil War a brief flurry of revivals occurred in 1867, notably *Love in '76* and *Moll Pitcher;* and in 1875–6 there were, predictably, about a dozen productions concerning the Revolution—not one of them either consequential or memorable. *Alexander Hamilton, or the Strategists* (1876), by T. H. Sayre, primarily concerns Major André, oddly enough, emphasizing his gallant character.[95]

What is most striking about the whole lot of nineteenth-century plays concerning the American Revolution—apart from their consistent mediocrity—is that the intrigue between Benedict Arnold and Major André clearly attracted the most attention;[96] and the tragic death of Nathan Hale, a patriot spy, may well have been the second most popular theme.[97] Why? The answer is manifold, but we already have most of its elements in view.

First of all, the American obsession with character was paramount; and character meant either integrity or the utter lack of it. Along with Washington, who figures prominently in almost all of these plays, Hale, Arnold, and André provided the ultimate examples of patriotic virtue and base villainy.

Second, the problem of allegiance and the theme of treason were powerfully resonant in a society so long torn by sectional crisis. Arnold and André were, after all, engaged in a conspiracy; and Richard Hofstadter as well as David Brion Davis have shown us just how vulnerable Americans have been to threats of subversion.[98] Thus George Henry Calvert published *Arnold and André* in 1864 because, as he wrote in the preface, Arnold's treason seemed "a suitable theme in a time of greater treason" (x, xv).

Third, the compactness of this episode, which occurred in the autumn of 1780, lent itself especially well to the imperative of dramatic unity required by the classic definition of tragedy. As William Gilmore Simms put it,

> For a moment—for a moment only—the fate of this great nation swings doubtfully in the balance! The catastrophe follows!—none more sudden,—none more complete in the whole wide world of scenic exhibition. The fall of a great man!—not by death, for death is no foe to the fame that is already sure in past performance!—not by the jealous rival, or the dark assassin;—but by the rapid spreading of the single plague-spot—the inherent baseness in his own soul. And such a fall![99]

Fourth, the authors and their audiences were all the more fascinated by Arnold's fall from grace because he had demonstrated so much ability and heroism between the winter of 1775–6 and the time of his betrayal.[100] E. G. Holland wrote *The Highland Treason,* he explained, in order to explore "the philosophical and moral significance of the revolution." He perceived Arnold as "the ablest warrior of the Revolution," and felt attracted to the subject because "the deep plotting of his intellect and the revengeful treachery of his aims, borders more strongly than . . . any other local event, on the purely tragical element."[101]

Fifth, and last, they just loved lurid spy stories.[102] On May 2, 1843, young George Templeton Strong attended a meeting of the New-York Historical Society. His diary entry for that day mocked the proceedings on account of their triviality: "A letter was read from Crosby enclosing an 'interesting Revolutionary relic'—breathless expectation—namely a button cut from the coat of a spy—I forget on which side—during the most momentous struggle."[103]

Although it is easy to understand why nineteenth-century Americans found Arnold and André so intriguing, it is more difficult to explain why they saw so little dramatic potential in other aspects of the Revolution. One wants to be charitable, and avoid the conclusion that they lacked sufficient knowledge of the Revolution to perceive its diverse possibilities. Whatever the answer, an essayist in 1882 seems representative of prevailing opinion:

> The Revolution, as we used to call it, is singularly lacking in dramatic properties. We are misled by the title . . . and it is observable that careful historical writers almost uniformly speak of the War for Independence. . . . The American Revolution set the seal to a foregone conclusion. . . . The very nature of the conflict interfered with strong dramatic situations,—situations that is, which seem to hold soluble elements of national life for a moment, and suffer them to become indestructible before our eyes. There are romantic incidents, but the only group of events during the war which offers any opportunity for an historical drama is that relating to Arnold's treachery and André's execution. In those events there would be a chance to lift the figure of Washington into dramatic prominence.[104]

The essayist then ended on an upbeat note, expressing the hope that "we may witness an increased consciousness of national being through the presentation of history in dramatic form. . . . It may well be that the reader of Hawthorne and Irving will yet have the pleasure of seeing the historic life of America epitomized on the stage in dramatic action."[105]

Unhappily, he did not see his hope fulfilled in the decades after

1882, nor has it been realized in the twentieth century. Between 1877 and 1890, just one new play about the Revolution appeared: *The Minute Men of 1774–1775*, by James A. Herne. It opened at Philadelphia in April 1886. It was not a popular success; and the editor of its only published version concedes that "the plot is conventional, and the historical background is not convincingly worked into the dramatic movement."[106] The Dunlap Society reprinted limited editions of *André* in 1888 and John Burk's wretched *Bunker-Hill; or, The Death of General Warren* (1797) in 1891—both with introductions by Brander Matthews, both designed for the bibliophile rather than for the stage.[107] This latter phenomenon only served to reinforce a tendency lamented in that same perceptive essay of 1882: "The drama has been so far divorced from literature that we have been taught to make a distinction between plays to be acted and plays to be read."[108]

During the 1890s, and especially at the turn of the century, interest in historical drama briefly revived. Several best-selling novels about the Revolution, such as *Janice Meredith* (1899), were converted into successful stage productions. Clyde Fitch's *Nathan Hale* was performed at Chicago in 1898, and his *Major André* at New York in 1903. Audiences loved both because they were extravagantly theatrical. As Fitch wrote to an actress friend: " 'Hale' *was* a very great success, both artistically and financially. . . . There were 27 calls the first night and your little pal made a *long* speech." The critics, however, hated both; and rightly so. The characterizations of historical figures like George Washington were abysmal; and the perception of Revolutionary events, banal.[109]

The only memorable and significant contribution in these years would be written by an arrogant Irishman, George Bernard Shaw. Considered one of his finest plays, in fact, *The Devil's Disciple* was first produced in 1897, and published in 1901.[110] Dick Dudgeon, General Burgoyne, and company have, of course, enjoyed a brilliant career on the American stage ever since, including several inevitable revivals for the Bicentennial. Shaw has surely shaped our image of New England in the winter of 1777. *The Devil's Disciple* does not emanate from the American theatrical tradition, however, so that we can claim little more than the sheer enjoyment of it. There may be a touch of irony, moreover, in an attempt at Niagara-on-the-Lake (the most recent major production) to cleanse the play of Shaw's iconoclasm and substitute sentimental melodrama instead—just the sort of antiquated theatre Shaw detested!"[111]

Be that as it may, we have seen scant improvement in American historical drama during the twentieth century. Even counting revised versions of the same play individually, there have only been some 150 plays written about the American Revolution in the century since 1876—and well over one-third of them were prepared in 1931–2 for the big bicentennial celebration of George Washington's birth. (The D.A.R. sponsored a grandiose playwriting contest for the occasion.)[112] Their quality, overall, is horrendous; and many have remained unpublished in manuscript form. Wild distortions of reality and chronology abound—far exceeding anything ever envisioned under the cover of "poetic license":

• George Washington reading the Declaration of Independence to the people assembled outside "Independence Hall" on July 4, 1776. (He never even signed the Declaration, because he was in New York City at the time in command of the Continental army.)

• That mysterious meeting of Washington with General Howe in the woods—an utter absurdity.

• Having Nathan Hale die at Valley Forge in the winter of 1777–8 (instead of September 1776, in New York).

• The treachery of Benedict Arnold (autumn 1780) occurring before the vile winter at Valley Forge.

• Washington crossing the Delaware well before the Declaration of Independence had been signed.

• Requiring Washington to utter such immortal lines as "Bah! Booh! Bah!" (to General Charles Lee at Monmouth).

• And the ludicrous creation of a sister for Benedict Arnold, betrothed to Major André, but later discovered by George Washington to be the very same "lowland beauty" for whom he had written love poems as a hot-blooded youth in tidewater Virginia!

One of the worst offenders, incidentally, also happens to have been one of the most popular American plays about the Revolution, *Valley Forge* by Maxwell Anderson (1934). It is bad enough to bring Mary Philipse to Valley Forge as a romantic interest for Washington that winter—it did not and could not have happened—but it is even more dangerous to strain, as Anderson does, in order to attribute unlikely sources of motivation. And Anderson added nothing new or insightful to the conventional narrative.[113] Joseph Wood Krutch nailed him properly in a brief review:

> It remains . . . primarily "theatre" of an easy, fluid, entertaining sort so old as to seem almost new. Mr. Anderson, indeed, might almost have learned the general outlines of his technique from any romantic drama of our fathers' time, for he uses the same touches of comic relief, the same passages of purple sentiment placed at strategic points, the same surefire appeal of ragged loyalty, and the same soul-satisfying little wrangle between pompous dignity and the impulsive backwoodsman which have delighted the ears of every generation since Dunlap founded the American drama.[114]

During World War II the major, and, it is fair to say, rather predictable production, came off rather well—a good deal better, at least, than *Valley Forge*. In 1939 Sidney Kingsley began to develop a play which, by 1941, he called *Jefferson*. When it opened in New York on January 29, 1943, the title had been changed to *The Patriots*. Focused upon Jefferson and Hamilton in the years 1790–1801, especially their conflicting theories of government, it offered a ringing reaffirmation of Jeffersonian democracy.[115] A special performance to honor the bicentennial of Jefferson's birth took place in April 1943, at the Coolidge Auditorium in the Library of Congress. When a congressman asked Kingsley how he happened to write the play, the playwright (then serving as a sergeant in the U.S. army) gave a revealing and symptomatic response:

> Four years ago, when this study was first begun, I knew very little about Jefferson or the other great men of our early history. I had just come back from Europe. I had seen democracy vilified and spat upon. I determined to find out the meaning of democracy for myself—to find it out from the men who made it, who pledged—and frequently paid—their fortunes and their lives to preserve it. *The Patriots* was the result of this attempt to cleave through post-World War No. 1 skepticism on the one hand and Fourth of July fustian on the other, to rediscover in all its purity the American faith.[116]

Audiences loved it; and for once the critics shared their positive response. *The Patriots* received the annual Drama Critics' Award as the best American play of the year. George Jean Nathan explained quite candidly that it

> represents almost everything for which I normally have no critical appetite. . . . Yet so honest is it at bottom, so unostentatious in its deeper dramatic current . . . and so genuinely stirring in its overtones and after-image that it amounts in sum not only to the most critically acceptable full-length offering of the season but to one of the most skillful historical-biographical plays our American theatre has shown.[117]

The National Theatre Conference scheduled productions of it in college and community playhouses all across the country, as a contribution to the war effort.

Jeffersonian democracy retained its rhetorical appeal in the postwar years, most notably in the dramatic productions of Paul Green, a staunch American nationalist and populist from North Carolina.[118] Green has been credited with developing a new theatrical art form in the years after 1937: the outdoor "symphonic drama." His skills and his success have both been considerable, but his seminal importance has perhaps been overemphasized.[119] A brief digression should explain why.

In 1918, Percy MacKaye wrote *Washington, the Man Who Made Us: A Ballad Play.* First published a year later, it underwent successful productions in two different versions: one a conventional theatre staging, another called the "Festival Version," which came with directions for open-air performance as community drama. The accompanying ballads, together with their music, were available by mail request; for, as the author explained, "without the sound of those age-old tunes in his ear (tunes still sung in the southern Appalachian mountains), the reader of this ballad-play will lack a charm which these pages cannot supply." It is a good play, in fact, and enjoyed considerable vogue during the 1920s.[120]

The George Washington Bicentennial Commission and the D.A.R. actively encouraged new plays about Washington for his two hundredth birthday observance in 1932. Some of the productions that resulted were intended to be pageants, such as *George Washington of Young America* (1931) by Esther Willard Bates, and *George Washington, a Pageant* (1932) by Henry W. Lee. *The Great American,* by Percy J. Burrell, was presented on the grounds of the Washington Monument in June of 1932.[121] Its emphasis was clearly upon music, dance, and costumes—which makes it a harbinger of Paul Green's better known symphonic dramas of the past four decades.

Green has, however, made a distinctive contribution: in part ideological, in part historical, and in part theatrical. Overall, it now adds up to the most ambitious attempt thus far to review the nation's past by dramatic devices. His symphonic dramas thrive upon their stunning natural settings in such diverse locations as Berea, Kentucky; New Philadelphia, Ohio; St. Augustine, Florida; Palo Duro Canyon, Texas; and of course Williamsburg, Virginia. Offering *The Lost Colony* at Roanoke Island, on the very spot where Sir Walter Raleigh planted a settlement, appeals to the American love of authenticity. Even more important, Green's anti-communism (he is for individualism, against collectivism) had especially potent appeal during the Cold War decades after 1945. His fundamental Christian commitment had particular resonance in the South, where most of his plays are performed.[122]

Above all, he seeks and finds reassurance in the past, and then manages to convey that sense of comfort to the millions of Americans who have seen the spectacles he orchestrates. "Thus it will be," he explains, "that from a backward look and a backward listening we can turn squarely to the future and face that future more reassured." Because Green believes in the historical process of American democracy, he has great faith in the heroic figures who developed it. Consequently, we should "seek to interpret and reinterpret, to dramatize and redramatize" their lives.[123]

His most successful work is also the most pertinent to our inquiry here. *The Common Glory: A Symphonic Drama of American History* opened in 1947 and was published in book form a year later. It has been running ever since on the banks of Lake Matoaka in Williamsburg—a great success in terms of both attendance and box office income. The story spans six critical years in the life of Thomas Jefferson, 1775 to 1781, "and is concerned mainly with his efforts to further the creation of democratic government in these United States."[124] In order to highlight the contrast between two political systems and divergent life styles, the drama is set in London as well as Virginia, and there are Loyalist sympathizers as well as Whigs. As for the title, Green has explained the meaning of his choice: "To me it means there is a common glory in our

American way of life, to be earned and shared by all of us, high and low, as we work to make our democratic ideal prevail."[125]

The cohesive amalgam for Green's personal blend of music, spectacle (battlefield scenes and warships on the James River), history, and ideology was imaginative fancy: his own and his remarkable ability to arouse it in diverse audiences. In the author's note to *The Common Glory,* Green explains that in symphonic drama "its methodology and technique are finally sufficient for all requirements and challenges of the imagination. It is the imagination we now lack—the imagination unbound!"[126]

If Green is able to bring elusive figures like Jefferson to life, he is even more successful in the imaginative creation of fictional characters who interact with the prominent historical personages. In *The Common Glory,* for example, Hugh Taylor is a tenant farmer only recently freed from indentured servitude, and Cephus Sicklemore, a drunkard and a chicken thief, represents the socially disinherited. These people add dimensions of humanity and reality to the play. They help to reveal the Revolution's anguish for every segment of society, and thereby deepen its suggested impact in shaping American democracy. Hence the drama's enormous appeal. As with *The Patriots,* critics loved it just as much as the curious tourists who pay to watch. Brooks Atkinson wrote in an enthusiastic review that *The Common Glory* is "a religious rite, without being pompous or sanctimonious, it serves the American tradition."[127]

Owing in part to the prominence he achieved in 1947–8, the National Capital Sesquicentennial Commission selected Green to prepare a symphonic drama for presentation in Washington to celebrate the establishment of our federal government there in 1800. He built the play around George Washington, and entitled it *Faith of Our Fathers.* It appeared during the summers of 1950 and 1951, but closed after those two seasons because of inadequate audiences and political obstacles. Green has placed particular blame upon the nepotism and patronage demands of "pie-counter habitués who had been foisted on our payroll by the yea-saying congressmen and politicians." Despite the commercial failure, Green recalls that "Washington's crossing of the Delaware got a hand every night." The Battle of Lexington, however, created such an incredible racket that householders who lived near the Carter Barron Amphitheater in Rock Creek Park flooded Washington newspapers with irate letters, and even resorted to legal injunctions.[128] *Faith of Our Fathers* is one of the few completed works by Paul Green that remains unpublished to this day.

For almost a quarter century after 1950, the Revolution virtually disappeared from the American stage. Paul Foster's *Tom Paine* (1967) elicited little interest until college drama departments began scratching about in search of production possibilities for the Bicentennial year.[129] William Gibson's *American Primitive. The Words of John & Abigail Adams Put into a Sequence for the Theater* was first performed in 1969, presented in revised form two years later, and published in 1972. But it, too, attracted not much attention until the mid-1970s when historical play readings acquired a certain chic in some circles. Its neglect stemmed in part from Gibson's unusual technique, which he remarks upon in a brief prefatory note. "Obviously the text is not a 'play'—it is eyewitness history, it is self-portraits by two of our parents, it is our birth certificate—and its nature lends itself to varied means of presentation."

Its neglect also stemmed from the fact that, like Foster's *Tom Paine,* it is essentially a counter-culture document: a statement of disappointment with the Vietnam war and a reaffirmation of the fellowship of man. Gibson chose as his epigram for the book version these words by John Adams: "I am ashamed of the age I live in." And near the end of the drama, Adams declares that "we ought to swim, though, against the wind and the tide as long as we can, to amend—humanity—" (p. 113).

That leaves *1776,* the Broadway musical which opened in 1969, won a Tony award, and became a film in 1972, as the only major and popular production between *The Common Glory* by Paul Green and the Bicentennial flurry of 1975–6.[130] The book version ends with a lengthy "Historical Note by the Authors." They ask the rhetorical question, "Is it true? Did it really happen that way?" Their answer is a resounding "Yes." Whereupon these words follow:

> Certainly a few changes have been made in order to fulfill basic dramatic tenets. To quote a European dramatist friend of ours, "God writes lousy theater." In other words, reality is seldom artistic, orderly, or dramatically satisfying; life rarely provides a sound second act, and its climaxes usually have not been adequately prepared for.[131]

One begins to get the sad feeling that perhaps good drama and meaningful history—history that combines insight with integrity—are simply incompatible. Though that may be accurate as a descriptive statement of the American case, it is decidedly not inevitable. The examples of Shaw and Schiller, Racine and Corneille, Büchner and Brecht, Goethe and Strindberg stand as powerful refutations.[132]

Above all, there are the ten magnificent history plays by William Shakespeare—based upon English chronicles—most notably *Richard II* and *Richard III*, *Henry IV*, *Henry V*, and *Henry VI*. It is inadequate to respond by saying that there can only be one Shakespeare; for Shakespeare's success in dramatizing England's early modern history had a great deal to do with the nature of his audience and what he could presuppose about the quality of their historical understanding. We have learned from the late Professor Lily Campbell that Elizabethan society saw a very practical utility in history as a guide to politics. Plays about the national past were regarded as immensely important, particularly when the Elizabethans became engaged in partisan debates over historical precedents, as they commonly did. It would have been impossible for Shakespeare, Marlowe, and Chapman to write those wonderful history plays—and equally impossible for audiences to watch them—without being aware of the plays' accepted application as mirrors for contemporary affairs. We now know that Shakespeare shared his age's high regard for the practical virtues of history. We know that he was thoroughly familiar with the principles and methods of historiography current in Tudor England; and finally, we know that he consciously applied them in the writing of his own historical dramas.[133]

It is precisely that mutual understanding of the intimate relation between past and present that I find missing in most of American historical drama. By and large our playwrights have been historically illiterate: they have known comparatively little about the national narrative, and even less about modes of historical thought.[134] Consequently they have not served the American Revolution, or their society, well. They have not heeded those terse lines by T. S. Eliot, found in "Burnt Norton," that

Time present and time past
Are both perhaps present in time future,
And time future contained in time past.

Appendix: The American Revolution on Film

MOST OF THE MOVING PICTURES that have been made about the American Revolution are based upon historical novels, which will be discussed in the next two chapters. Since the films are so derivative, and because no reel of many older ones has survived at all, and because in some instances the producers will not permit current distribution for viewing, I have not attempted a systematic discussion and analysis of these films.

They are obviously pertinent cultural artifacts, nonetheless; some of them have been viewed by many more people than those who read the original novel. So I have felt obliged at least to list some of the major efforts with their dates of production. I am indebted to Professor Bruce R. Powers, director of the Film Repertory Center at Niagara University, for his help in gathering this list. There is a cursory and unsatisfactory discussion by Lawrence L. Murray, "Feature Films and the American Revolution: A Bicentennial Reappraisal," in *Film and History* (September 1975), 1–6.

1 *Paul Revere's Ride* (Thomas A. Edison, 1904?).
2 *1776; or the Hessian Renegades* (Biograph Co., 1909).
3 *Man Without a Country* (Thanhouser, 1917), starring H. E. Herbert.
4 *Cardigan* (American Releasing Corp., 1922), starring William Collier, Jr., and Betty Carpenter.
5 *America* (United Artists, 1924), starring Lionel Barrymore.
6 *Janice Meredith* (Cosmopolitan, 1925), starring Marion Davies. Following the film's success, Grosset and Dunlap issued a "Marion Davies Edition" of the novel, illustrated with scenes from the movie.
7 *Old Ironsides* (Paramount, 1926), starring Esther Ralston and Wallace Beery.
8 *Alexander Hamilton* (Warner Brothers, 1931), starring George Arliss.
9 *The Last of the Mohicans* (United Artists, 1936), starring Randolph Scott.
10 *Drums Along the Mohawk* (20th Century-Fox, 1939), starring Henry Fonda and Claudette Colbert.
11 *Northwest Passage* (MGM, 1940), starring Spencer Tracy.
12 *The Howards of Virginia* (Columbia, 1940), starring Cary Grant and Martha Scott.

13 *The Unconquered* (Paramount, 1947), starring Gary Cooper and Paulette Goddard.
14 *The Scarlet Coat* (MGM, 1955), starring Cornell Wilde and George Sanders.
15 *John Paul Jones* (Warner Brothers, 1957), starring Robert Stack.
16 *Johnny Tremain* (Walt Disney, 1957), starring Sebastian Cabot.
17 *The Devil's Disciple* (United Artists, 1959), starring Burt Lancaster, Sir Laurence Olivier, and Eva LeGallienne.
18 *1776* (Columbia, 1972), starring Howard da Silva.
19 *Benedict Arnold* (Hawk Serpent Productions, 1975), a long documentary directed by Walter Gutman. In July 1975, Mr. Gutman responded to my inquiry about the film as follows: "I have always had a vague affection for Arnold, who was certainly one of the most dramatic characters of our history." For reviews see *The New York Daily News,* May 13, 1975; *The New York Times,* May 16, 1975.

Between 1910 and 1914, Thomas A. Edison formed Edison's Stock Players and made a series of "Kinetoscope" films about the American Revolution, including *The Minuteman, The Midnight Ride of Paul Revere, How Washington Crossed the Delaware,* and others that treated Nathan Hale, the Battle of Bunker Hill, and the Boston Tea Party. In 1975 the West Orange, New Jersey, Bicentennial Commission and the National Park Service (which maintains the Edison National Historic Site) reproduced nine of these antique films for distribution to schools as part of the Bicentennial celebration. The films combine romance and adventure, gallantry and patriotism. (See *The New York Times,* July 1, 1975.)

CHAPTER FIVE

A RESPONSIVE REVOLUTION IN HISTORICAL ROMANCE

"Fiction *may some day lend its charms to amplify and consecrate* facts"

HISTORICAL NOVELS have undoubtedly been the single most important source of information about, and awareness of, the American Revolution. "The great public," Samuel Eliot Morison once remarked, "when it reads history at all, takes it in the painless form of the historical novel or, at best, biography."[1] That has definitely been true of popular perceptions of this nation's birth; for the accumulated literature is now voluminous, varied, vigorously (albeit intermittently) influential, and culturally revealing.

Most of these novels, or "romances" as they were commonly called in the nineteenth century,[2] are rather banal. Many of them are, in fact, stultifyingly mediocre. The more serious ones can be rather good, however, and it just might be pertinent to add that their authors happen to have had a thorough knowledge of Shakespeare's history plays. James Fenimore Cooper's novels are filled with epigrams taken from *Henry IV, Henry V*, and *Henry VI*; as is *The Rebels* by Lydia Maria Child.[3] Shakespeare was William Gilmore Simms's favorite reading, and he clearly had the Bard's plays (dealing with the War of the Roses) very much in mind when he wrote his eight Revolutionary romances. Shakespearian quotations abound in them.[4]

The more insightful or self-aware novelists sought to preserve the proper and particular meaning of Independence as they perceived it. Hence Simms's declaration that "I summon to my aid the muse of local History—the traditions of our own home—the chronicles of our own section," and his proud boast that his romances had "suggested clews to the historian—they struck and laid bare to other workers, the veins of tradition which everywhere enriched our territory."[5]

Many of these authors encountered difficulty, however, because they felt that conventional historical writing tended to immortalize "great events, and deals only with those illustrious characters and actions, which have an immediate or remote influence on the fate of nations." What about ordinary folk and the anguish they suffered, the obscure sacrifices they made? As James Kirke Paulding put it: "The sufferings of the individual are lost in the mass of national distress, or only remembered in traditions which grow more obscure at every succeeding generation, and come at last to be considered either fabulous or doubtful."[6]

Recreating the lives of "ordinary" Americans was not the only challenge. The novelists also wished to recapture their state of mind as individuals, and the climate of opinion as well. Yet as Sarah Josepha Hale put it in 1829, "there was at that time [the Revolution] agitation in the minds of men which words can never describe." Living "in these days of peace and prosperity," she wistfully explained, "you young people have no experience, and can hardly form an idea of the trials we had endured."[7]

Consequently the novelists felt justified—more than that, felt compelled in many cases—to dramatize the origins of American nationality. In 1867 Simms referred to the process they pursued as "Memory, calling imagination to her aid"; but it had taken quite some time for the process to be established and accepted.[8] John Pendleton Kennedy expressed one point of view in 1835—and a widely shared one, at that—in his preface to *Horse-Shoe Robinson: A Tale of the Tory Ascendancy:*

> An opinion has heretofore prevailed that the Revolution was too recent an affair for our story-telling craft to lay hands upon it. But this objection, ever since the fiftieth anniversary, has been nullified by common consent,—that being deemed the fair poetical limit which converts tradition into truth, and takes away all right of contradiction from a surviving actor in the scene.[9]

It is self-serving, of course, for the novelist to speak of time transmuting tradition into historical truth. Those of us with more mundane minds may be disposed to believe that the process ordinarily runs in just the opposite direction. In reality, I suppose, each is possible in its own way. At any rate, the authors of non-fiction accounts—and even more vocally, prominent participants in the Revolution—shared a point of view different from Kennedy's. Back in 1784, Jeremy Belknap had boasted of having a special advantage in writing American history. "The historians of other countries almost universally are destitute," he explained, "their first eras being either disguised by fiction and romance, or involved in impenetrable obscurity."[10]

Within three decades of Belknap's writing that, we notice politicians with some personal stake in the Revolution being "properly narrated" expressing the apprehension that historical truth might seem stranger than fiction; or might even sound like fiction; or worst of all, might actually come to be fictionalized—and thereby distorted. "The history of the government of this country," wrote John Randolph of Roanoke in 1813, "if faithfully written, would sound like romance in the ears of succeeding generations, and be utterly discredited by them."[11] The most explicit statement of concern, however, came from the pen of John Adams in 1815. "Who shall write the history of the American Revolution? Who can write it? Who will ever be able to write it?" he asked Thomas Jefferson. "Some future Miss Porter, may hereafter, make as shining a romance, of what passed in Congress, while in Conclave, as her *Scottish Chiefs*."[12]

What on earth was old John Adams so nervous about? Is this just another instance of that crankiness for which he has long since become notorious? No, more than that was involved, because there seemed to be a great deal at stake in the way of personal reputation and national self-knowledge. Miss Porter was an Englishwoman, a contemporary of Sir Walter Scott, and she wrote historical romances that enjoyed a very considerable vogue. Her *Scottish Chiefs*, first published in 1810, may have been every bit as popular in the young republic as it was in Britain. Four years later Scott brought out *Waverley*; and the popular historical novel as we still know it today was well established.[13] Hence John Adams's deep anxiety in 1815 that American counterparts of Sir Walter Scott and Miss Porter might put the Continental Congress, and George Washington, and Thomas Jefferson, and even himself into a potboiler of some sort before scrupulous scholars could come along to set the story straight.

In this instance Adams had company, lots of company. Most of his contemporaries, in fact, especially among the active participants in our struggle for Independence, shared these fears and expressed them vocally.[14] There is a very real sense in which they had good reason to be concerned, because the authors of historical romances did, in fact, establish their version first. In 1826, on the occasion of the fiftieth anniversary of the Declaration of Independence, Jared Sparks complained that no complete history of the Revolution had yet appeared.[15] Ever since 1821, however, when James Fenimore Cooper published *The Spy* to instantaneous acclaim, the Revolution had become a great vogue to readers voracious for fiction concerned with native subjects.

It would remain in vogue for a quarter century to come; and I shall discuss the phasing of these novels in the following section, for their periodization provides an important index to the rhythms of American culture. What must be asserted here, though, is that their readership and influence were both considerable. The former expanded gradually to embrace all segments of American society, including (by the mid-nineteenth century) working-class men and women. Many of the novels, moreover, enjoyed a kind of double impact; for the practice developed of serializing them first in popular monthly journals—usually stretched out over a period of one year—and then subsequently producing them in book form.

It is important to recognize that the impact of these novels has tended to be synchronic rather than diachronic: that is, they normally enjoyed an enormous but ephemeral popularity, and then mostly lapsed into obscurity. Few of them have been elevated into the canon of great American literature. They do not rank with *The House of Seven Gables,* or *Moby Dick,* or *The Great Gatsby,* or *The Sound and the Fury*. But they did sell—some of them phenomenally—and they were read. Hence my belief that John William DeForest was being iconoclastic but half-wrong in 1868 when he remarked that

> there come to us from the deserts of the past certain voices which "syllable men's names"—names that seem to sound like "Paulding," "Brown," "Kennedy"—and we catch nothing further. These are ghosts, and they wrote about ghosts, and the ghosts have vanished utterly. Another of these shadowy mediums . . . is W. Gilmore Simms, of whom the best and

the worst thing to be said is this—that he is nearly as good as Cooper, and deserves fame nearly as much.[16]

Insofar as DeForest was simply passing judgment on the quality of their productions, he was entitled to his opinions; and many a literary critic since 1868 has shared them. But I think that he underestimated the persistence of those historical ghosts, for they have returned from time to time to engage American culture, most notably during the 1890s, the later 1930s and the 1940s. The influence of Cooper, moreover, has been considerable. Most of our historical novelists have looked nervously over their literary shoulders to take their bearings by his shadowy presence. Sometimes they simply imitated him, or borrowed devices from him. At other times they expressed absolute contempt. But again and again they perceived him as the alpha of their common genre, and so defined their own endeavors against the standards he had set.[17] In 1900 and 1901, after publishing a fabulously successful Revolutionary romance of his own called *Janice Meredith* (1899), Paul Leicester Ford began to prepare a new edition of Cooper's novels; and he insisted upon the irrefutable point that Cooper had developed character types—such as the noble Indian, the resourceful frontiersman, and the contented slave—that powerfully influenced subsequent writers.[18]

We should acknowledge at the outset that American historical novelists have not been in agreement among themselves about the nature of their craft. Some share Anthony Burgess's view that "the historical novelist is, in fact, a historian to whom a talent for imaginative fiction has been fastened. He is not a novelist with an occasional taste for history." But many others do not. Hervey Allen, the author of *Anthony Adverse* (1933) and a trilogy concerning Revolutionary America (1943–8), put it this way:

> Critical confusion results from the supposition on the part of either the writer or the reader, or both, that the historical novel is a kind of mule-like animal begotten by the ass of fiction of the brood mare of fact, and hence a sterile monster. . . . The historical novel is simply a door through which the novelist leads his readers into other times than their own. But it is not a door to a storehouse of records and specimens of the past. The novelist's door is the portal of a theater. Once the reader passes it, what he sees going on is not the actual past, but a drama arranged by the author *about* the past.[19]

It is still more difficult to find a common ground between historical novelists and historians, and I have come to believe that a steady divergence between the two has developed ever since the 1820s. Although Cooper liked to quote from Henry Fielding the remark that "I am a true historian, a describer of society as it exists, and of men as they are," he acknowledged that

> the privileges of the Historian and of the writer of Romances are very different, and it behooves them equally to respect each other's rights. The latter is permitted to garnish a probable fiction, while he is sternly prohibited from dwelling on improbable truths; but it is the duty of the former to record facts as they have occurred, without a reference to consequences, resting his reputation on a firm foundation of realities, and vindicating his integrity by his authorities.[20]

At the end of the nineteenth century we find novelists accusing historians of neglect. Referring to General Sullivan's march through the Iroquois country in 1779, for instance, one writer of romances asked: "Why is the whole subject so slurred over or ignored by the average historian?"[21] And Robert W. Chambers, who wrote a series of five very popular novels about the Revolution, observed in the preface to one of them that "Romance alone can justify a theme inspired by truth; for Romance is more vital than history, which, after all, is but the fleshless skeleton of Romance."[22]

By Kenneth Roberts's day, a full generation later, the novelists' criticism of historians had become substantive as well as aesthetic and dramatic. Late in 1935, while hard at work on *Northwest Passage*, Roberts explained to a friend the evolution of his inquiries that had already resulted in *Arundel* (1930) and *Rabble in Arms* (1933).

> As soon as I got the broad picture of what had happened, it dawned on me that nobody had ever written it—nobody: not even historians. Nobody had pieced the mosaic together and got a picture that made sense. You could find out what happened when Arnold's troops marched to Quebec, but you couldn't get the relation of the march to the war, or to the country, or to the people. You couldn't find out what the people were like who made the march, or why they were where they were, or why things happened the way they did. . . . It took me two years of the hardest sort of study to understand the 1776–77 campaigns in their entirety. All you've got to do is read the histories yourself and see what you get out of them. Read Nickerson, and how much do you understand about the re-

lation of Valcour to the rest of it? Read Mahan on Valcour, and how much do you understand about the retreat from Canada? Read the retreat from Canada, and how much do you understand about the miraculous recovery at Saratoga? Read all of them together, and how much do you understand about the part the Indians played in the campaign? If it's properly presented, I believe the experiences of the Northern Army are almost without parallel in the history of War; but out of what history can you get an understanding of it? Not out of one damned history. Or out of ten. And if that isn't a show-up of our historians, I don't know what is.[23]

Within a decade, novelists were even using the doctrine of relativism to argue for the superior desirability of their handiwork. Here is Hervey Allen's explanation in 1944:

It is in this capacity to produce an illusion of reliving the past that the chief justification for the historical novel exists. Since no one, neither historian nor novelist, can reproduce the real past, one may infer that, if supremely well done, the historical novel, by presenting the past dramatically, actually gives the reader a more vivid, adequate, and significant apprehension of past epochs than does the historian, who conveys facts about them.[24]

Historians, in turn, took somewhat longer to develop a jaundiced view of their fiction-writing counterparts. As late as 1904, when S. Weir Mitchell produced a popular pottage of fact and fancy entitled *The Youth of Washington*, so respectable a scholar as Worthington C. Ford could tell readers of the *American Historical Review* that the book "may be judged as history or as fiction, according to the taste of the reader, and possesses high merit in either aspect."[25]

Since then historians have become more harsh in their assessments of historical fiction, and some rather unseemly shouting matches have erupted, for example, between Kenneth Roberts on the one hand, and Allan Nevins and Henry Steele Commager on the other—culminating in Roberts calling Nevins "a jealous little piss-pot" and "the complete prick." Nevins reviewed *Northwest Passage* unfavorably in *The New York Herald Tribune*, and thereby outraged Roberts. The latter explained to a friend that when Nevins undertook to review historical fiction, "he was removing himself from his own side of the bed. He ought to be put back on his own side of the bed where he belongs." Nevins, he continued, "is a liar, a poseur and a stuffed shirt, and we've got him dead to rights. That so-called review of his was the product of a pinheaded soubrette in the field of letters, and he deserves a slap on the jaw for it."[26]

From the perspective of professional historians, on the other hand, there has been a fairly steady development ever since about 1890: namely, a sensible tendency to differentiate between the proper use of imagination in writing history as against its use in historical fiction. Three sequential statements may help to highlight this trend.

• If historical fiction has a real and important place in literature, its task, nevertheless, is an extremely difficult one; for, in addition to the accurate scholarship of the historian and the constructive power of the novelist, it demands the highest exercise of the historical imagination—the capacity to place one's self in the mental attitude of persons wholly different in training and environment. —WILLIAM FRANCIS ALLEN (1890)[27]

• An historian or biographer is under restrictions unknown to a novelist. He has no right to override facts by his own imagination. If he is writing on a remote or obscure subject about which few facts are available, his imagination may legitimately weave them into a pattern. But to be honest he must make clear what is fact and what is hypothesis. The quality of imagination, if properly restrained by the conditions of historical discipline, is of great assistance in enabling one to discover problems to be solved, to grasp the significance of facts, to form hypotheses, to discern causes in their first beginnings, and, above all, to relate the past creatively to the present. —SAMUEL ELIOT MORISON (1946)[28]

• The literary imagination is more closely allied to myth than to history. But this is far from saying that it is of no use at all to the historian. . . . In breathing life into a historical figure, novelists and playwrights may well get things wrong and are not likely to alter professional verdicts. But the power of their imagination may force historians to look freshly at the frieze and to perceive historical figures not as abstractions but as human beings in all their idiosyncrasy and uniqueness. . . . The artistic vision may thus reinvigorate that fundamental historical exercise, the imaginative leap into the past. . . . In this manner the literary imagination may fertilize the historical mind and serve to stretch and enrich historical understanding. —ARTHUR M. SCHLESINGER, JR. (1974)[29]

So we have had some clarification, at least from the historians, on the relative role of imagination in history and historical fiction. By contrast, we have had from the literary critics who ponder these matters little more than a series of provocative queries, such as, "Why should we worry so about fiction, *as if* it made any difference to us in our reality?" and, "Are the forms through which we are to perceive a past moment in our culture a model configuration like that through which the poet asks us to perceive his dramatic episode?"[30]

There are no definitive answers as yet, needless to say. I would not even call the questions exhaustive, for that matter. What does matter for our purposes, though, are the novels themselves; for regardless of their uneven quality, their overall configuration is highly revealing of some vitally important impulses in American culture. Before moving on to the essential character of those impulses, however, we must take our bearings with regard to matters of chronology and periodization.

"It shall go hard with us if we do not soon bring to light every remnant of tradition that the war has left!"

FROM TIME TO TIME in American literary history, exhortations have appeared that either called for historical fiction, or else assessed its current problems and cultural implications. As a rule these essays do not so much anticipate the appearance of such novels as appear in the midst of their publication. Consequently, we may crudely use them to delineate the periodicity of our Revolutionary romances. We will find these essays, for example, during the mid-1820s to 1830s; from the later 1890s into the early twentieth century; and then once again in the years 1936–44.[31] It is no accident that those very years represent the three peaks in popularity for historical fiction about the American Revolution. The chronology is a bit more complex than that, however, and worth closer examination.

With the publication of Scott's *Ivanhoe* in 1819, the historical novel became an obviously potent and lucrative literary force.[32] Cooper brought out *The Spy* in 1821, and followed with *The Pilot* in 1823, *Lionel Lincoln* in 1825, and *The Last of the Mohicans* a year later. After pursuing other literary tacks during the 1830s, he published

Wyandotté in 1843 and *Satanstoe* two years after that. Cooper established the Revolutionary romance as an American genre, and enjoyed a broad readership as well as much emulation. In 1824, for instance, a professorial appointment at the University of Virginia was offered to George Tucker. He explained his dilemma to Joseph C. Cabell:

> The proposal is, in my present situation, a tempting one and I feel myself a good deal puzzled how to act. . . . I have for more than a year conceived the project & indulged the hope that I might pursue the business of authorship as a profitable calling. I have (but this is a secret) actually charged the public favor in a novel just published in New York, and should it meet with anything like the success which has attended Cooper, I should think my prospects of profit much greater than any professorship could hold out. He has made about $5000 by each of his novels—and the Valley of Shenandoah, my new work, was written in two months. The situation to which you invite me, would about put a stop to my efforts as an author, or would confine them in a channel in which I have already found that little reputation is to be acquired & no money. . . . The offer is one that I know not how to accept or reject—I will write you further on the subject.[33]

Whether or not Tucker ever accepted—he finally did, in fact—matters less in this context than his desire to emulate Cooper's success; for Tucker was scarcely singular in his goals, nor was he the only aspirant to produce so hastily. In 1823 John Neal published two lengthy romances of the Revolution. He needed twenty-nine days to write *Seventy-Six*, and a week longer than that to complete *Randolph*. More than 100 novels set in the Revolutionary period had appeared by 1850, and still more continued to be published during the next decade.[34] Nonetheless, the first heyday of American historical fiction may be defined as having flourished during the quarter century following 1821. All of the serious and influential efforts of this phase had appeared by then, and would prompt Hawthorne to remark in 1846 that "the themes suggested by [William Gilmore Simms] viewed as he views them, would produce nothing but historical novels, cast in the same worn out mold that has been in use these thirty years, and which it is time to break up and fling away."[35]

History books of all sorts were popular during the 1820s.[36] A wave of sentimentalism swept the nation during the 1830s, and novelists rode the crest of that wave with exploitative skill. Some of them even devised ambitious schemes that were impossible of execution. Just as John Trumbull, the patriot-artist, had initially intended to paint (and then publish engravings of) thirteen subjects that would provide a chronology of Revolutionary high points, Cooper planned to write thirteen novels about the Revolution—one set in each of the colonies. *Lionel Lincoln; or, The Leaguer of Boston* (1825) initiated that series, but its lack of commercial success caused Cooper to reconsider; and his subsequent Revolutionary romances were confined to New York—the scene he knew best.[37]

Insofar as Revolutionary romances continued to appear in the decades after 1846, they reflected two significant cultural shifts. Many of them, to begin with, were only nominally about the Revolution itself. In the North, a novel like *The Rebels; or, Boston Before the Revolution,* by Lydia Maria Child, had feminism and abolitionism as its primary emphasis, with secondary attention to current problems of snobbery, social pretense, humility, and honesty.

In the South we find that Simms's Revolutionary tales published during the 1850s are most seriously aimed at defending the "peculiar institution." He declared that *The Sword and the Distaff,* printed in 1852, "is probably as good an answer to Mrs. Stowe as has been published."[38] Two years later, in *Woodcraft,* Simms comes directly to the point. On page eight a patriotic lady from South Carolina reminds a British officer to make sure that "certain negroes be restored to me, my property, which are now within the garrison—their names are in this paper, and a description of them individually, by which they may each be identified." Lest any reader might somehow miss the point—at a time when the Fugitive Slave Act was so controversial in national politics—Simms makes it explicit a page later. "Well, madam, allowing all this, it appears to me that what is expected of us, is the delivery, to the rebel commissioners, of all the negroes claimed as fugitives—" Since the chauvinistic reader would presumably sympathize with the Whiggish woman, Simms wanted her insistent request to seem equally irresistible.

Between 1835, when Simms published *The Partisan,* and 1856, when he brought out *Eutaw,* he moved from nationalism to staunch sectionalism. His Revolutionary romances are set almost entirely in South Carolina during the period 1780–1, between the

British capture of Charleston and the Battle of Eutaw Springs. He treated the Revolution increasingly as a civil war, to the point where he seems almost to anticipate the outbreak of hostilities in 1861. Eventually, perhaps inevitably, Britain's abuse of her colonies becomes a prototype for northern mistreatment of the southland. As Simms wrote to a friend in 1858, "this was the History of our share in the Revolution. It *was* forced upon the North, by absolute home trespasses of the British."[39]

In addition to these not-so-subtle southern reactions to abolitionist tracts, there was yet a second significant reason why Revolutionary romances continued to appear in the decades after 1846. We might simply call it the democratization of a genre. Those historical novels published from 1821 until the mid-1840s were essentially aimed at the middle class. They tended to be fairly long, quite convoluted, and socially respectable in content. During the later 1840s, however, a peculiar phenomenon burst upon the literary scene: George Lippard, by name, a patriotic and highly moralistic advocate of "the great mass of humanity."[40]

Based in Philadelphia, young Lippard churned out a series of sensational thrillers set in that area during Revolutionary days. They bore such titles as *Herbert Tracy; or, The Legend of the Black Rangers. A Romance of the Battlefield of Germantown* (1844), which was dedicated to Cooper; *Blanche of Brandywine; or, September the Eleventh, 1777. A Romance of the Revolution* (1846), dedicated to Henry Clay; *The Rose of Wissahikon; or, The Fourth of July, 1776. A Romance Embracing the Secret History of the Declaration of Independence* (1847); and *Paul Ardenheim, the Monk of Wissahikon. A Romance of the American Revolution, 1776* (1848). Working-class people read these novels and responded to them with gusto. By the time of Lippard's death in 1854 at the age of thirty-two, he had done much to establish a mass market for pulp historical fiction. The likes of William Gilmore Simms might make fun of Lippard as a "spasmodic litterateur,"[41] but this strange young man—a post-Christian, proto-Marxian, Christian mystic—did much to transform the literary landscape. In the process he also became a major source of popular misinformation about the American Revolution.

Historical fiction waned in popularity during the 1850s,[42] but enjoyed limited circulation during the 1860s and 1870s in the form of "penny dreadfuls" and dime novels. The publishing house of Beadle and Adams managed to reach a mass market with books on all sorts of subjects. The American Revolution was not its favorite; but from time to time books about George Washington or fierce military clashes would sell well, most especially tales in which, at some point, Washington crossed the Delaware. They bore such titles as *The Scout's Prize; or, The Old Dutch Blunderbuss. A Tale of 1776* (1864); *Captain Molly; or, The Fight at Trenton, Christmas, 1776. A Story of the Revolution* (1865); *Quaker Saul, the Idiot Spy; or, Luliona, the Seminole. A Tale of Men and Deeds of '76* (1869); *Double-Death; or, The Spy Queen of Wyoming. A Romance of the Revolution* (1872); and *Delaware Dick, the Young Ranger Spy; or, Brother Against Brother* (1878).[43]

A major producer of these slim books, which circulated widely, was one Nathaniel Colchester Iron, an obscure New York writer who seems to have flourished between the years 1860 and 1867. A typical performance was *The Maid of Esopus; or, The Trials and Triumphs of the Revolution,* published on May 1, 1861, by Beadle and Company as no. 22 in its series of dime novels. Set in the area of Kingston, New York, during 1777, its cast includes Marcus Goodheart, a lieutenant from a British regiment who eventually returns to England and marries the fair Flora; Guy Wanderer, a spy for the British; Adam Morton, the patriot hero; Silas Fearnought, an indomitable Revolutionary patriarch in Kingston; and his daughter, Isabelle Fearnought, the heroine, who is described in this manner: "Isabelle clasped her hands in agony, and cast her beauteous eyes up to the heavens to see if mercy sat upon its fleecy clouds." When Isabelle speaks she utters such immortal lines as:

"*Oh, torture unendurable,*" or
"*Oh, you know not what daggers you have planted in my heart,*" or
"*I saw an Indian peep from yonder tree.*"[44]

The book is outrageously melodramatic and sentimental, of course. Its philosophy of history is baldly conveyed in these two sentences: "Every thing recurs in the passage of time. The history of the present is but a narration of the past and an anticipation of the coming age." Its social message seems to be that like must only marry like: white Americans must marry white Americans, Indians must marry Indians, and Britons must marry Britons—that is, until later generations, when it is all right for descendants of Marcus and Flora Goodheart to marry the offspring of Adam and Isabelle Morton. Racial mixing is inconceivable, however, at least if everyone is to live happily ever after, which, after all, is the ultimate goal.[45]

From the early 1850s to the mid-1890s, however, most Americans, especially in the rapidly expanding middle class, got their historical knowledge from non-fiction publications, whether Benson J. Lossing's, George Bancroft's, or Francis Parkman's. Between about 1895 and 1909, Revolutionary romances enjoyed a period of intense popularity once again. They dominated the fiction market, produced some of the hottest best-sellers in all of American literary history, and were accompanied by a juvenile phalanx aimed at exploitation of the quickly growing market for children's literature. The dominant names in this phase were S. Weir Mitchell, Robert W. Chambers, Winston Churchill, and Paul Leicester Ford; but there were many others.

Inspired by their success, incidentally, Stephen Crane wrote an essay entitled "The Battle of Bunker Hill," which appeared in 1899 as the first in his series on *Great Battles of the World*.[46] Despite his customary linkage with the new emphasis upon literary realism, Crane's attention seems to have been caught by the historical vogue of the late 1890s. At the time of his tragic death at the age of twenty-nine, he had in fact begun to work on a Revolutionary novel of his own. He asked members of his family for pertinent books and papers, decided to join the New Jersey Historical Society, and wrote himself a little memorandum while still in England: "Write letters to all the men whom I think could help me. This list to include Henry Cabot Lodge, the librarian of Princeton Col., the president of the N.J. branch of the sons of the American rev. etc. Here in England collect the best histories of that time and also learn what British regiments served in America, also what officers who served published memoirs."[47]

In August 1899, Crane communicated with the New Jersey Historical Society in search of information;[48] and at about that time he also wrote for himself a working paper called "Plans for Story" that has survived. It is sufficiently revealing and symptomatic to be worth reprinting here in its entirety:

Possible opening chapter, Time 1775—scene an Inn at Elizabeth N.J. People talking over the situation. Their attitude. Strong Tory element. Patriots bitter. Loud words. Their denunciation by old Stephen Crane. For theme see Geo. Bernard Shaw's Napoleon, as quoted in N.Y. *World*.

As American infantry use the sixth N.J. regiment of the line, Col. Wm Crane. Use him as chief character, making young Jonathan Crane a minor string. Emphasise Hessians strongly. Look up dates, appearance and conduct of French troops. Make picture of marching British army as it passed Stephen Crane's house when he lay dying. Battle of Monmouth probably central dramatic scene. Find out if Lord Chatham's speeches were known in colonies soon after deliverance. Read Fenimore Cooper's "Spy." Pay no great heed to the dress of the people or to their manner of speech. Ask Will about the vegetation in the northern part of N.J., the names of the familiar trees and shrubs. Might have young Howard Crane off to sea with John Paul Jones and let him turn up in last few chapters as a sort of a benign influence. Study carefully the mood of the N.J. people with the idea that they were not very keen upon rebellion, showing great influence of Crane family in carrying the revolution through. Make some people wag their heads, declaring what a desperate business it will be and make some others treat it lightly saying it will be over in a few weeks. Make no distinction of diction save a use of what might be called biblical phraseology. Stephen Crane rather old, venerable, grey haired, imposing, calm. (Find out age at this time.) Make William Crane handsome, alert, slight but strong, a bit of a dandy, anxious for the conflict, in love with a girl in the neighborhood, natural leader, admired and respected by the farmers. Mention incident in which some Englishman—a magistrate or a magnate of some kind—offended him. Make Jonathan simple-minded, honest lad who gains his devotion to truth and honor mainly through his father's influence. Read D^{r}. Weir Mitchell's last book. In describing battle of Monmouth discard the Mollie Pitcher story as being absurd and trivial. Point out in some way that Americans were excessively willing to meet the British in pitch battles whereas that was not their best policy at all. Their policy was to make guerilla warfare; vide the Cubans against Spain and the Philo's against Americans. On second thoughts this was because of the stability of the American home. It was house; not a hut and if the inhabitants fled from it to the hills or wood they left behind them considerable material property. Introduce Henry Fleming's grand-father as first farmer.[49]

Although Crane's death in 1900 put an end to this project, his emphases and chosen time period were both indicative of what the Revolution had been reduced to in fiction. Most Revolutionary romances were now set in the period 1775–81, with some rather cursory attention sometimes given to explaining why a breach with England had occurred in the first place. In consequence, the War for Independence became tantamount to the American Revolution in its entirety, with the crisis years

(1763–74) foreshortened and the aftermath (1782–9) ignored in favor of resolving all romantic complications as happily and expeditiously as possible. During this second period of intense popularity for Revolutionary romances, the Revolution came to be regarded more as a military event than a political one,[50] which thereby helped to obviate any need to deal with social radicalism, the ideology inherent in the Declaration of Independence, the rights of man, and related issues that might have seemed awkward at that time.

Many of the novelists in this phase had themselves experienced the Civil War—John William DeForest and William O. Stoddard, for instance—just as many of the novelists in our next phase—like Kenneth Roberts, Edward Ellsberg, Frank O. Hough, James Boyd, and Hervey Allen—had served in World War I. Even so, Revolutionary novelists of the period 1933–48 were somewhat less preoccupied with warfare than their predecessors had been. There are several reasons. First, the fact that there were more women novelists in the 1930s and 1940s, and that their preoccupations tended to be less martial. Second, with a rising interest in determining the national character, many writers were concerned that Americans should not appear too militaristic. And third, disillusionment over our munitions makers getting rich during World War I caused a certain cynicism and fresh emphasis upon America's customary pacifism and altruism.[51]

Historical fiction about the Revolution was dominated in the years 1933–48 by Kenneth Roberts, Howard Fast, Frank O. Hough, F. Van Wyck Mason, Esther Forbes, and Inglis Fletcher. In 1948 Carl Sandburg published *Remembrance Rock,* a massive historical epic—really a trilogy concerned with colonization at Plymouth, the Revolution, and the Civil War era. The critical and public response to it was disappointing, however, and at that point this third major burst of Revolutionary novels came to an end.[52] A trickle continued through the 1950s and 1960s, to be sure—examples by Bruce Lancaster, John Brick, and Joseph Hopkins come to mind—but essentially the genre had run its course until 1974, when Gore Vidal's *Burr* and the coming Bicentennial touched off yet a fourth phase of rather minor proportions and consequence.[53]

Thus we have had an intermittent appearance of Revolutionary novels ever since 1821, most notably in the period 1821–46, even more intensively in the years 1895–1909 and 1933–48, and somewhat less so since 1974. The spasmodic aspect of their appearance can be useful to the cultural historian, for we are particularly interested in continuities and discontinuities in the attitudinal patterns of a society. In the next two sections of this chapter, I intend to examine the two most revealing lines of *dis*continuity: namely, the authors' reasons for choosing to write about the American Revolution in particular; and ways in which the novels mirror changes in the Anglo-American relationship. In the fifth and final section I shall discuss some themes common to the genre irrespective of chronological appearance. And then, in Chapter Six, I shall concentrate upon defining and explaining the dominant theme that has permeated the vast majority of these novels, regardless of period.

"A sober desire for history—the unwritten, the unconsidered, but veracious history"

WHY HAVE NOVELISTS chosen to write about the American Revolution? The primary answer to that question shifts with each of our three periods, and thereby supplies us with a look at one important line of cultural discontinuity. The stimulus in the period 1821–46 is reasonably well known, and can be summed up most simply in the phrase "literary nationalism." Sydney Smith had pricked American pride in 1820 by asking contemptuously in the *Edinburgh Review:* "In the four quarters of the globe, who reads an American book? or goes to an American play? or looks at an American picture or statue?"[54] Inevitably, perhaps, the first generation of professional authors became determined to demonstrate that there could be American books worth reading, and that their subject matter would be indigenous. Cooper disliked being called the "American Walter Scott," and in 1831 he explained his motives in writing historical fiction: "Her [the reference is to "my own country"] mental independence is my object."[55]

Cooper's contemporaries heartily held these feelings too, many of them even more strongly than Cooper himself. James Kirke Paulding pointed out to a friend in 1834 that it has always been one of my first objects, to which a great portion of my life has been devoted, to incite and encourage the genius of this country, and, most especially, to draw its attention and its efforts toward our own history, traditions, scenery, and manners, instead of foraging in the barren and exhausted fields of the Old World. I have lived to see this object in a great measure accomplished, and one of the most gratifying of all my reflexions is, that possibly I may have had some little agency in bringing it about.[56]

It is impossible to overestimate the strength of these feelings and their cultural consequences. In 1835 a novelist remarked of one character, Isabella Linwood, that in 1779 "her pride was touched. For the first time an American feeling shot athwart her mind."[57] In 1840, William Gilmore Simms spelled out the same message in a public letter for a southern journal:

A people who receive their literature exclusively from a foreign land, are in fact, if not in form, essentially governed from abroad . . . and that, as it is through our own minds, only, that we can be free, so, when these are surrendered to the tutelage of others, we are, to all intents and purposes, a nation in bondage.[58]

In this same statement, Simms also asserted that "a native literature is essential to national patriotism—to the independence of the national mind." By saying so he pinpointed one of the most salient qualities in these novels, namely, their recurrent emphasis upon patriotism (and its obverse, treason). Few sins seemed more heinous than false patriotism; and few acts could fail to be justified if they were committed in the cause of genuine patriotism. "That Providence destines this country to some great and glorious fate I must believe," George Washington says to Harvey Birch in 1781, "while I witness the patriotism that pervades the bosoms of her lowest citizens."[59]

Love of country caused virtually all of these authors to stress its uniqueness and peculiar virtues. Thus Robert Montgomery Bird struck a most unusual, maverick (almost startling) note in 1835 when he offered the following remarks in his preface to *The Hawks of Hawk-Hollow*, a romance that chronicles the decline of a prominent Pennsylvania family on account of disloyalty to the patriot cause.

The story, such as it is, is rather a domestic tale, treating of incidents and characters common to the whole world, than one of which these components can be considered *peculiarly* American. This is, perhaps, unfortunate,—the tendency of the public taste seeming to require of American authors that they should confine themselves to what is, in subject, event, and character, indigenous to their own hemisphere; although such a requisition would end in reducing their materials to such a stock as might be carried about in a nutshell. America is a part of the great world, and, like other parts, has little (that is, suited to the purposes of fiction) which it can call exclusively its own: and how far that little has been already *used up*, any one may tell, who is conversant with our domestic literature. (pp. v–vi)

When we look ahead to the period 1895–1909, we discover that the authors' principal motives have changed. As a bumptious people acquired some measure of self-confidence, Cooper's erstwhile wish to see his countrymen achieve "mental independence" had long since receded; and literary nationalism came to be supplanted by quite a different, if not more important, stimulus: in a word, nostalgia. You can catch it, for instance, in the fact that so many novels from the turn of the century take the symptomatic form of spurious "memoirs." *Richard Carvel* is offered to us as Daniel Clapsaddle Carvel's reminiscence of his grandfather, symbolically dated December 21, 1876. *Hugh Wynne, Free Quaker* is supposed to be "a memoir meant for my descendants"; and the narrator of *Maid of the Mohawk*, "reminded that my span of life is drawing toward its close," seeks to "go back through the halls of memory and open up the past."[60] Phoney authenticity is our first symptom.

The sources of this nostalgia, both in the writers and in their readers, are not at all hard to find. First, they sought to recapture the physical details of an age slipping rapidly beyond the blur of hazy reminiscence. When Cooper and Simms wrote, the quality of life was not very much changed from what it had been in Revolutionary times. Overland travel still meant a carriage or venture on horseback. People still made their butter and various essentials at home. By the 1890s, however, technology had altered the routine pace and pattern of existence. Men and women were more likely to take a train than a carriage, and were more likely to purchase their butter at the neighborhood grocery. In part, therefore, nostalgia required (and received) the recreation of physical minutiae in loving detail. The reading public that adored *Janice Meredith* immersed itself in trivia and trivets—what one author would call *The Quest of the Quaint.*[61]

We know that many of the novelists themselves shared in this mood of nostalgia. Sarah Orne Jewett, for example, confided to a friend her aspirations in writing *The Tory Lover* (1901), set in Berwick, Maine, and in England. Jewett had meant to do what she could "about keeping some of the old Berwick flowers in bloom, and some of the names and places alive in memory, for with many changes in the old town they might be soon forgotten." With his enormous royalties from *Richard Carvel,* Winston Churchill bought land in New Hampshire and built a grand house suggesting "an old time colonial estate," in which hewn timbers, given "the appearance of great age," were left exposed to view.[62]

From the perspective of the reading public, these historical novels offered a jolly kind of costume party—what Churchill wistfully referred to in *Richard Carvel* as "the picture of the past" (p. 106). An exuberant sense of expansiveness accompanied the Spanish-American War, and the national imagination—or at least the Anglo-Saxon part of it, which had the dominant say—sought out its past, delighted in it, even reveled in it. As the heroine remarks in one of the most popular romances from this period, "I like reading about brave, heroic men and beautiful women, and war and love."[63]

Later in that same novel, *Alice of Old Vincennes,* Alice makes an even more symptomatic confession: "I don't enjoy reading about low, vile people and hopeless unfortunates."[64] We should remember that a genealogical craze swept the nation during the 1890s, hence the heroes and heroines in the novels of this period so often have to solve a problem of mysterious parentage—but always with a wondrous outcome.[65] Hence, too, the nods of approval that must have come from so many readers when they reached the declarative line in *The Tory Lover:* "There is something in descent" (p. 23).

This romantic readership sought escape from the painful realities of industrialized America, from the class conflict that threatened to shred the very fabric of society—most especially during the depression years of 1893–6.[66] Then, too, there were all those immigrants: strange-looking, strange-sounding folk who printed newspapers in their own languages and wore the costumes of their native lands on feast days and other moments dedicated to the preservation of special ethnic identities. They seemed "un-American," and perhaps even "un-Americanizable." Thus, in my view, the unveiled anti-Semitism we see in books like *Richard Carvel* and *Janice Meredith*.[67] Consequently those "true" Americans who could link their ancestry to colonial times, or wished that they could, sought solace in the Revolution, the Founding Fathers, and a simpler, more homogeneous America that was comparatively free (they thought) of class conflict, social protest, and industrial violence. "The political faith of our forefathers," Churchill declared, "was made to fit a more or less homogeneous body of people."[68]

Wistful nostalgia, then, was the paramount motive as well as primary motif in late-nineteenth-century historical fiction. As Thompson exclaimed in *Alice of Old Vincennes*, "led by that wonderful guide, Imagination, we step back a century" (p. 11). When we move on to the 1930s and 1940s, however, neither literary nationalism nor nostalgia is any longer the key element. They have not disappeared entirely, but both become far less important than a new rationale: the assessment of our national character, and especially its origins in formative times. Imaginative authors now stress the development of those qualities that will one day make the nation great: courage, individualism, endurance, self-reliance, pioneering hardihood, and most particularly leadership. We get long paeans to leadership in Roberts's *Northwest Passage*, for instance, and little homilies like this one, from John Paul Jones, in James Boyd's *Drums:* "Jest ye remember this: to lead men in a fight, the great thing is this—to show them the way yourself and yet to keep your wits and eyes about ye and observe how matters stand" (p. 362).[69]

Then, too, we get the notion of American nationality being a compound of ethnic ingredients—the whole much greater than the sum of its parts. Winston Churchill's emphasis upon homogeneity becomes turned entirely inside out now. So in *Drums Along the Mohawk* we find key characters of English, Dutch, Irish, Scots-Irish, and Palatine German origin, each one acting according to the characterological imperatives of his or her native stock. Or in *Raleigh's Eden*, by Inglis Fletcher, there are French Huguenots, Highland and Lowland Scots, Dutch, English, Moravians, Welsh Quakers, even a Moorish architect who designs Governor Tryon's fabulous palace at New Bern, and an unspecified Oriental who sells his wares at the wharves in Edenton.[70] In James Boyd's *Drums*, when that famous encounter between the *Bonhomme Richard* and the *Serapis* occurs, we find that the crew of the *Bonhomme Richard* is a kind of all-American team. In the heat of battle we are informed that a tall Vermonter mutters gloomily, a stocky Pennsylvania Dutchman nods his head with cheerful vigor, and a red-haired Georgian oozes laconic common sense. But each one does his part.[71]

There is a related phenomenon at work in these novels, but one which at least some of the authors seem to have been somewhat ambivalent about: and that is a greater sympathetic emphasis than ever before upon the lives of ordinary people. This is true of Edmonds and Fletcher, who have already been mentioned, but far more of Esther Forbes in *Johnny Tremain* (1943), say, or Edward Stanley in *Thomas Forty* (1947), or even of Kenneth Roberts in *Oliver Wiswell*—both in his treatment of the Leighton family and of the back-country Loyalists in South Carolina. A higher proportion of the historical novels written between 1933 and 1948 are set somewhere on the frontier. As Carl Sandburg insists in *Remembrance Rock:* "The hog-drover understands the theory of natural rights without reading John Locke."[72]

The most essential point being made about these ordinary people involves their independence and freedom—a freedom believed scarcely possible anywhere else in the eighteenth-century world. As Bruce Lancaster said about his purpose in writing *The Guns of Burgoyne* (1939), "I wanted to show free men—the free men of the colonies—and it seemed to me that the best way to do that was to let them be discovered by a man who never had been free, who had, when he came here, no conception of freedom."[73]

And yet, although the *menu peuple* are often treated with sympathy and understanding by these authors, there is also an underlying strand of skepticism toward them. At times it becomes quite overt. They are frequently referred to as "rabble," and pejoratively as the "rag-tag and bob-tail democracy." Even Johnny Fraser of North Carolina (the young hero of *Drums*), although disillusioned in London by English fatuousness and decadence, observes that "maybe the government here is not as good as the American loyalists think it is, but it's better than an American Revolutionary mob."[74] A number of these novelists, and a goodly part of their audience, I believe, were élitists whose mood during the later 1920s and throughout the 1930s was hostile to the expansion of democracy. There are clear signs that the kind of democracy they preferred was a deferential one; or at least, that democratic government worked best in a quasi-democratic society where status had its perquisites and the élite provided real leadership.[75]

Ultimately the novelists shared no clear consensus on questions of class conflict and social mobility. Most of them revealed at least some interest in such matters, but came down on different sides. Whereas Kenneth Roberts could be acerbic in his contempt for the hoi polloi, Inglis Fletcher indicated the futility of being too preoccupied with class distinctions, and of misusing political labels. "Why can't a yeoman or a freeholder voice his wrongs without being called a rebel," asks the heroine of *Raleigh's Eden*, "will you tell me?" Fletcher's emphasis is upon the logical alliance among all free men and women with an affinity for the land; and eventually she suggests that persons of every status should unite in support of a truly patriotic cause. "In North Carolina the torch of revolution was held aloft by all classes."[76]

The patriotic cause they really had in mind, of course, was World War II; and on that matter, also, agreement emerged slowly. Disillusionment with World War I found its way into many of the Revolutionary novels written in the following decades. The fiction is filled with anti-war statements: the foolishness of war as a means of settling disputes, the way that certain entrepreneurs seem to profiteer from wartime needs, and the tendency of politicians to blunder under the pressure of crisis conditions.

• "All of a nation's woes . . . have their rise in men's inability to recognize the truth, or their unwillingness to tell the truth—the truth as to why wars are fought, and how they are bungled and protracted, while those who fight them lose their lives and fortunes."

—ROBERTS, *Rabble in Arms* (1933), p. 577[77]

• "I thought of all the wars of which I'd read, and clearly saw at last that not one of them—not one—had brought one solitary benefit that couldn't have been attained by peaceful means if only those who fought had been content to wait—had been wise enough to make the concessions that all human beings must make if they're to live in amity."

—ROBERTS, *Oliver Wiswell* (1940), p. 354[78]

• "I know more now than I can understand. The more I know the deeper twists the bitterness. I trust no one, not even myself. Tories and rebels, they both lie and lie how noble they are, how sacred their causes. On both sides false and cunning trickeries, crazy hate and defiance. Both sides wanted this war. Now they have it. Your Sam Adams wanted it. You followed him wanting it. Now you've both got it."

—SANDBURG, *Remembrance Rock* (1948), p. 516[79]

In the last analysis, however, there turns out to be such a thing as the "just cause." When it occurs, one must support it to the hilt and not hang back. An individual truly committed to the defense of freedom will do so, as will a people whose national character is properly virtuous. Hence Inglis Fletcher's condemnation (in 1940) of conciliation. "I don't trust men who evade a definite stand," one participant remarks.[80] Hence Carl Sandburg's conversation about idealists who hold deathless dreams: "There are men thankful they can live in a time when great dreams take hold of men." And later: "Love of country is a holiness that comes and goes and those too sure of it better beware. It exists as a wonder."[81]

Patriotism in Revolutionary fiction had now come full cycle, from the ardent affirmation of *The Spy* in 1821, to the jaundiced cynicism of novels during the 1930s,[82] and then the reaffirmations of the 1940s. After World War II, a gradual reaction developed in opposition to the notion of national character. Critics attacked the concept and linked it with racism and the worst aberrations of nationalism.[83] When novels about the American Revolution surfaced once again in the mid-1970s, they would have little to do with explicit discussions of national character—ours or that of anyone else. A tradition of long standing had been broken, with important cultural consequences.[84]

"Bringing the British lion and Yankee eagle together"

CULTURAL DISCONTINUITY can also be discerned in the novelists' treatment of Anglo-American relations. Overall there is a steady flow from Anglophobia toward Anglophilia, which will hardly come as a surprise to anyone. The ways in which this trend develops, however—its peculiar manifestations—are instructive. We must be careful, moreover, not to exaggerate either the totality of anti-British feeling in Cooper's day, or the extent of rapprochement by the time of World War II. In both *The Spy* and *The Pioneers*, for instance, Cooper suggests the happy alliance of English and American families joining by intermarriage in the generation following the Revolution.[85] In *The Pilot* he seems to grope, on occasion, toward understanding the ambiguities of conflicting allegiance: "It is possible to feel a double tie," one character concedes (pp. 130–1). Although the long-term shift I have in view is a pronounced one, then, it is hardly absolute.[86]

During the period 1821 to 1846, anti-British feeling vastly outweighed any sort of residual or restored empathy for the former mother country. It had, after all, been a bitter war for American Independence from Britain. More recently, moreover, the War of 1812 had occurred, in which the British won no endearment by burning the Executive Mansion in Washington. And in 1823 the Monroe Doctrine was proclaimed because of a desire in the United States—most passionately felt by John Quincy Adams—to keep the western hemisphere free from Old World influence. Then the Canadian boundary question heated up in 1837–40, aggravating old sores and opening new ones. The result, essentially, was that public opinion tended to be anti-British, that both sides in American party politics expressed their hostility accordingly, and that such writers as Washington Irving and James Kirke Paulding cut their literary teeth, so to speak, by biting John Bull in various and sundry fleshy places.[87]

In *The Pilot,* for instance, we are told by John Paul Jones that he first left Britain "because I found in it nothing but oppression and injustice" (p. 134). Subsequently he explains to a shipmate:

> It is true, I wear your republican livery, and call the Americans my brothers; but it is because you combat in behalf of human nature. Were your cause less holy, I would not shed the meanest drop that flows in English veins, to serve it. . . . Is there no merit in teaching these proud islanders that the arm of liberty can pluck them from the very empire of their corruption and oppression? (p. 195)

Two years later, in *Lionel Lincoln,* Cooper enjoys some ironic inversions by calling the British grenadiers at Boston "rioters," implying that they, rather than the colonists, were in fact guilty of unlawful behavior and therefore responsible for all the disorder in 1775. Before he is done, the grenadiers have become a bloodthirsty, sadistic mob (pp. 327, 330–1). In 1826 George P. Morris may have put his finger (or his pen) on a major cause of American Anglophobia at this time: their prickly reaction to perceived condescension. As one Musgrave exclaims: "America! There's nothing here but mosquitoes, bats, savages, equality, sour crout, 'liberty' and bumble bees!"[88]

A great deal of residual hostility remained right through the 1840s and 1850s. We can see it in the writings of Joel T. Headley, and in American anger at the liberties taken by William Makepeace Thackeray in his novel *The Virginians* (1857–9), most especially regarding the sacred character of George Washington.[89] But a slow thaw had nonetheless begun. By the time he published *Katharine Walton* in 1851, William Gilmore Simms was ready to acknowledge virtues in England's form of government, church, and legal system. Four years later, Nathaniel Hawthorne recorded these sentiments after visiting Westminster Abbey:

> I had a glimpse of Major André's monument, which is a pretty little show of miniature-sculpture. . . . How glad I am that England has such a church, its walls incrusted with the fame of her dead worthies, ever since she was a nation. . . . An American has a right to be proud of Westminster Abbey; for most of the men, who sleep in it, are our great men, as well as theirs.[90]

And one year later, in 1856, Emerson published his *English Traits*, an empathetic volume.

Civil War diplomacy caused serious problems to develop anew; but the 1870s brought fresh efforts at cordiality. The anticipated arbitration of Anglo-American differences provided for in the 1871 Treaty of Washington resulted in unprecedented English observances of the Fourth of July in 1872, not to mention toasts to Queen Victoria by American diplomats.[91] In March of 1875, while John Greenleaf Whittier was working on "Lexington, 1775," a commemorative poem, he explained to a friend that he had "added two verses, mainly for the sake of bringing the British lion and Yankee eagle together."[92]

During the Centennial celebrations of 1876, American newspapers stressed our Anglo-Saxon origins and reported the goodwill expressed for the occasion by speakers in England. Robert C. Winthrop's oration in Boston overflowed with effusive praise for British ideals and institutions. He suggested that bygones could be bygones because Britannia had "long ago learned that such a rebellion as ours was really in her own interest, and for her own ultimate welfare; begun, continued, and ended, as it was, in vindication of the liberties of Englishmen."[93]

Even so, some economic and political problems remained right through the last quarter of the nineteenth century. Our serious depression of 1873–6 called attention to Britain's commercial hegemony. Many Americans resented having a persistent imbalance of payments, resented the role of British investors in western lands and Britain's insistence upon strict maintenance of the gold standard. Diplomatic ties became quite strained during the period 1885–9.[94] Hence these dilemmas were reflected in a certain ambivalence about Anglo-American relations in such Revolutionary novels as Harold Frederic's *In the Valley*, published in 1890.[95]

A residue of avid Anglophobia remained especially strong in parts of the Middle West and in coastal Massachusetts. Samuel Eliot Morison's delectable reminiscence of his childhood during the 1890s informs us that

> one of my boyhood friends from New York, a girl who married a Bostonian, told me that the one thing that struck her on coming here was that Boston was still fighting the War of Independence. The traditions of the American Revolution were central to my upbringing; memorials and landmarks of it were all about us. Popular extracurricular reading was Charles Carleton Coffin's *Boys of '76*—Philip Weld told me that I must read it, or fight him! I was proud of Faneuil Hall and the Adamses, highly approved the Cleveland-Olney diplomatic sock-in-the-jaw to Lord Salisbury, firmly believed America to be the best country and Boston the finest city on earth; and that the United States Navy, having "licked England twice," could do so again, if necessary. It was only *after* growing up that I began to entertain feelings of kindness and admiration toward our mother country.[96]

But for most Americans a turning point occurred between 1894 and 1898. First, agitation for annexation of Canada to the United States dissipated after 1893. Second, Great Britain got out of a territory claimed by Venezuela, which we desperately wished her to do. Then Britain stood aside when we became involved in Cuba, and after that helped to neutralize the rest of Europe while we picked upon pathetic Spain for a "splendid little war." The result was a perceptible shift in which Anglophobia gave way to lukewarm affection, and eventually to détente and alliance.[97] That shift was mirrored explicitly in most of the historical fiction about Revolutionary America that became *à la mode* after 1897. Here are the very last lines of *Richard Carvel*, for example:

> Ere I had regained my health, the war for Independence was won. I pray God that time may soften the bitterness it caused, and heal the breach in that noble race whose motto is Freedom. That the Stars and Stripes and the Union Jack may one day float together to cleanse this world of tyranny![98]

Authors now took pains to point out that many English statesmen, such as Lord Chatham, had been pro-American, not to mention most ordinary Britons. And after the war, "England was no longer an angry, contemptuous enemy, tyrannous and exacting, and determined to withhold the right of liberty from her own growing colonies. All those sad, familiar prejudices faded away."[99] Paul Leicester Ford informed the English public that one of his purposes in writing *Janice Meredith* had been to demonstrate that the losing side in the Revolution had heroes and merits too. His novel was, in fact, well received in England: *The Spectator* called it (on December 23, 1899) an "excellent, if somewhat exuberant romance of the American Revolution."[100] In two American plays about the Revolution that appeared in 1900 and 1901, emphasis rested upon the British perspective from occupied Philadelphia. The best dramatization of the surrender at Yorktown is called *An English Gentleman* (1911), written by John Lawrence Lambe, a British playwright. Its title comes from the curtain line, when a young lady says of George Washington: "God made him . . . an English gentleman."[101]

Mild ambivalence about Britain continued through the 1920s, however, mostly fostered by the partisanship of virtually every history textbook in the United States. Encouraged by the Hearst press, the Knights of Columbus, and demagogues like Mayor "Big Bill" Thompson—who vowed that if King George V ever so much as set foot in Chicago, "I'll crack him in the snoot"—school boards would refuse to adopt any textbook with the slightest taint of support for Great Britain in the American Revolution. The purpose of textbooks was to inculcate absolute patriotism, plain and simple.[102]

An unusual episode occurred at the end of World War I that ought to be mentioned in this context, an episode that helped to prepare the way for a more fully favorable treatment of Britain and the British during our third phase of historical fiction. In 1917 a film entitled *The Spirit of '76* had been made in the United States. It concerned the Revolution, and depicted certain well-known events, such as Patrick Henry's most famous speech, Paul Revere's ride, and the Wyoming Valley (Pennsylvania) massacre, among other scenes. A federal judge, however, directed that the movie be seized. His reason was that America had just entered World War I as England's ally; and, under the terms of a recently passed Espionage Act, in the court's opinion this film was "calculated reasonably so to excite or inflame the passions of our people or some of them as that they will be deterred from giving that full measure of co-operation, sympathy, assistance, and sacrifice which is due to Great Britain, as an ally of ours," and "to make us a little bit slack in our loyalty to Great Britain in this great catastrophe."[103] The producer went to prison, believe it or not, for three years; and the movie was destroyed. The court case itself surely has the most wonderful title in all of our constitutional history: *United States* v. *The Spirit of '76.*[104]

At any rate, by the mid- and later 1930s Great Britain had a very positive image in most of the United States. After 1939, of course, the Anglo-American alliance became stronger than ever before, and those realities required some major readjustments by the authors of novels about American Independence. It seemed so much less appropriate than before to cast as the customary villains George III, Lord North, Charles Townshend, and all their political henchmen in Parliament; and so an alteration did, in fact, occur. We hear very little about them, all of a sudden, and the Revolution becomes less of an imperial conflict and even more of a civil war within the colonies. The villains are now likely to be indigenous Loyalists; or certain apolitical dolts, the so-called neutrals, who lacked the native wit to see on which side the future of a great republic lay; or else nasty and brutish Indians, like Joseph Brant, who supposedly ran around the countryside massacring innocent patriots. Moreover, if one wanted "bad guys" from Europe, one didn't need to blame nice Englishmen because there were always those "ox-eyed" Hessians—bloodthirsty, mindless, mercenary robots—obvious forerunners of Hitler and his twentieth-century Huns.[105] And if one was still determined to pin the rap on George III, then one carefully pointed out that he really wasn't English anyway, but a Hanoverian German with totalitarian tendencies who hired Hessian storm troopers to do his bidding.[106]

After 1939, novels about the American Revolution made quite a serious effort to present the colonial *as well as* some sense of the British viewpoint. We find warm praise for Lord Cornwallis's character coming from the most ardent American Whigs; and we meet kindly British fusiliers who even befriend patriot orphans.[107] The point is now made much more emphatically than in 1895 to 1909 that "there are two Englands," as a Sandburg character explains to his son. "The England of Pitt and the people he speaks for—and the England of a mad King and his ignorant, arrogant and selfish ministers." No rational American had actually wanted separation, anyway, not even the most avid patriot. Mary Warden explained the situation to Sara Rutledge, a Loyalist, late in 1775:

> What they really want is not to break with England, Sara. Don't you realize how long it has been since Lexington? They are still trying to convince the British Ministry that if they make concessions, there will be no revolt. The leaders are trying by every means to get redress of their grievances without an actual break with the Mother Country.[108]

What is also intriguing about this period is that particular people who logically should have written fiction about the Revolution did not, apparently because psychologically they *could* not; whereas certain sorts of people who traditionally had not been associated with the genre now got involved.[109] It became possible, perhaps even acceptable, for Englishmen to do so; and in 1940 Robert Graves—poet, mythographer, and polymath—produced *Sergeant Lamb's America*, a bizarre narrative adaptation of Lamb's "campaign experiences in the American War of 1775–83." That book was sufficiently successful that Graves followed it with a sequel, called *Proceed, Sergeant Lamb*. He highlights the war's unpopularity in Britain by 1779, and the accompanying desire for conciliation: "a speedy accommodation of our present unnatural differences." We are reminded that "men of all races are equally brave," and that atrocities were committed by partisans on both sides. In November 1781, after Yorktown, an American and an Irish veteran become friends, reminisce, and exchange hospitality. Just in case any dull reader had somehow managed to miss the point, Lamb lays it out baldly at the end:

In the long run I believe it to have been for the best that the two nations were thus at last separate, in fact as well as by a fiction. It may even come about some day that, remembering the ancient ties of affection and language that, despite all, yet bind the two nations, the Americans will join in armed alliance with us against the French or other relentless foes who threaten our common liberties.[110]

Meanwhile, someone like Howard Swiggett ought to have written historical fiction about the Revolution. He had, after all, written about it at great length in non-fiction, and he was one of the most popular American novelists of the day.[111] Yet none of his fiction touches the Revolutionary era, and I think I know why. From 1940 until 1945 Mr. Swiggett served in New York as deputy director general of the British Ministry of Supply Mission, for which he eventually received the O.B.E. He was a strong Anglophile, and my suspicion is that he, and others like him in this period, did not want to cope with the problem of writing imaginative literature about a time when the United States and Britain were enemies. There simply were too many complexities in setting up the "good guys" and the "bad guys," not to mention the dramatic imperative of eliciting sufficient hatred of the enemy.[112]

In our own phase, which really means ever since 1973–4, historical fiction about the Revolutionary era has taken a curious but fairly predictable inward twist. The authors are barely interested in the Anglo-American relationship at all. Instead, the new novels are mainly psychological studies that seek to probe the interior of a mind, a family, or a community. They are more interested in what it feels like to fight—fear, hunger, pain, exhaustion—than they are in exploring public aspects of the American Revolution. Insofar as they do the latter at all, we hear echoes (hardly surprising) of the Vietnam war and Watergate.[113]

"The more pregnant echoes of the past"

In each of the periods we have been examining for purposes of contrast and perceiving discontinuity—1821–46, 1895–1909, 1933–48—historical fiction seems to have come along at a moment of cultural indirection, and, at least initially, served a very real social purpose. All of these periods were, in some significant sense, critical or transitional times in American life. Precisely because they were so, national values needed to be defined or redefined: Can we be faithful to the vision of our founders, and will their legacy endure (1821–46)? Is the political structure they willed us flexible enough to accommodate unanticipated social diversity and class conflict (1895–1909)? And do we have the national character necessary to endure a devastating, prolonged depression from within[114] and totalitarianism from without (1933–48)?

Before each of these three phases of historical fiction had run its course, needless to say, other more memorable breakthroughs took place in American literature. The significant innovations invariably make the Revolutionary romances seem even more archaic and irrelevant than they actually were. How do our three phases make contact, then, with the deeper impulses of American thought? To what extent do they overlap and help to stimulate certain contemporaneous and deservedly more famous episodes in American literary history? I have in mind, of course, the emergence of Transcendentalism in the later 1830s, Naturalism at the start of the twentieth century, and Modernism in the late 1930s and 1940s. There are, I believe, some antiphonal relationships between, let us say, Cooper and Emerson, or between S. Weir Mitchell and Theodore Dreiser, or Kenneth Roberts and William Faulkner. No one would deny the greater merit of Emerson, Dreiser, and Faulkner; but I hope that we will also acknowledge the cultural significance of their contemporary counterparts. Cooper, Mitchell, and Roberts are not great novelists, though at their best they are very good indeed. What does seem beyond dispute, however, is their weathervane veracity.

With that in mind, I must round out this chapter by giving some attention to matters of continuity, merit, and themes common to the genre (irrespective of period). All of the next chapter will be devoted to an extended discussion of the overwhelmingly dominant and singular message that shapes most of these novels. But there are some lesser yet nonetheless persistent themes that are at least worth brief mention. There is also a need to address the question of merit: How good and how bad are they? Did John Adams and the other aging survivors have due cause for that anxiety expressed back in 1815 to Thomas Jefferson?

The inescapable answer to this query is that our novels are rather like the little girl with the little curl in that familiar nursery rhyme: when they are good, they are very, very good; but when they are bad, they are horrid. It would serve no useful purpose to expound upon their banalities at length. Some of them really do end with: "They lived happily ever after, or at least somewhat beyond three score and ten, and left behind them a good name and numerous descendants." A few hit rock bottom by adding a sentence like this one: "They lived in a stately white mansion on a hill overlooking a vast tobacco plantation, where hundreds of negro slaves worked and sang by day and frolicked by night."[115] There are factual absurdities (such as Adam Rutledge owning 2,700 plantation slaves in 1765), gross exaggerations (suggesting that North Carolina was the most radical colony in 1770), and odd inconsistencies (in one novel Lafayette is tall, in another he is short).

But what of their virtues? These are, in fact, considerable. Although based upon limited research and considerable intuition, the novels seem repeatedly to have anticipated some of the best insights and emphases of professional historians. Until the 1970s, for instance, the Loyalists were a neglected lot in early American historiography; whereas the novelists have long been interested in Loyalists and their relations with the Whigs.[116] Likewise the role of Indians and the frontier in Revolutionary America. That subject has only begun to get its due from professionals during the past fifteen years; but it has been an important matter to the novelists ever since the 1820s.[117]

Carl L. Becker stimulated his colleagues in history for half a century by posing the provocative thesis that from 1765 until 1776 two issues agitated colonial politics: "The first was the question of home rule; the second was the question, if we may so put it, of who should rule at home."[118] Yet the notion of the Revolution as a civil war, an internal power struggle, and as a class conflict emerges quite clearly in Cooper's *The Spy,* Simms's *The Partisan,* Kennedy's *Horse-Shoe Robinson,* especially in Frederic's *In the Valley,* and in many other romances written during the nineteenth century.[119] The best of our novelists were not oblivious to those famous lines from *King Lear:*

> *Love cools, friendship falls off, brothers divide.*
> *In cities, mutinies; in countries, discord; in palaces, treason;*
> *And the bond cracked 'twixt son and father.*

In the decade following 1965, Professor Bernard Bailyn of Harvard University had an immense impact upon Revolutionary scholarship by offering what seemed to be a fresh ideological interpretation. He has stressed certain psychological transformations that took place in the Whig mind between 1750 and 1776, especially that inversion whereby the colonial sense of social and cultural inferiority gave way to a belief in their moral superiority over their English cousins. Bailyn also sketched out features of the Tory mentality—its concern for rank, hierarchy, deference, order, obedience, and so forth.[120]

Yet James Fenimore Cooper, and the best of his successors, have been embellishing those very lines of interpretation for 150 years.

• "Behold, my dear Cecelia, the natural consequences of this rebellion! It scatters discord in their ranks, and, by its damnable levelling principles, destroys all distinction of rank among themselves; even these rash boys know not where obedience is due." —COOPER, *The Pilot* (1823), p. 316[121]

• "A new light had broken upon her, and she began to see old subjects in a fresh aspect. . . . She for the first time perceived the folly of measuring American society by a European standard."

—SEDGWICK, *The Linwoods* (1835), I, p. 210

• "Irresistibly there came into my mind the grand and simple characters of our own public men in America, and it made me shudder to think that, while they strove honestly for our rights, this was the type which opposed them. Motives of personal spite and of personal gain were laid bare, and even the barter and sale of offices of trust took place before my very eyes. . . . They drew their chairs closer, some wearing that smile of superiority which to us is the Englishman's most maddening trait."

—CHURCHILL, *Richard Carvel* (1899), pp. 296–7[122]

The transformation of provincial consciousness may have seemed a new angle of vision to professional historians after 1965, but it had been a familiar one in Revolutionary romances for a very long time. I could cite any number of additional instances. Frederic's *In the Valley* (1890) anticipates Professor Kenney's sound explanation of Dutch Anglophobia in the Hudson River Valley during 1775–6 and the years following.[123] In *The Old Continental* (1846), James Kirke Paulding anticipates the late Professor Crary's discovery that James Rivington, the presumed Tory printer, actually must have been a double agent ultimately loyal to George Washington.[124] And *The Duke of Stockbridge. A Romance of Shays' Rebellion* (1879), by Edward Bellamy, anticipates Professor Lockridge's influential hypothesis concerning the heightened scarcity of land in New England by the Revolutionary era.[125] Precisely because land does seem to be in short supply, many of the heroes in these novels dream of going westward after the Revolution in order to resettle and enjoy the autonomy that abundant acreage would provide. This is true of Perez Hamlin in *The Duke of Stockbridge,* a New England novel; of Thomas Forty in the New York-based novel that bears his name; and of Adam Rutledge in *Raleigh's Eden,* a southern story set in North Carolina and Virginia.

Another theme common to the genre as a whole involves the myriad ways in which love and politics intersect. Frequently a well-intentioned hero who starts out with Loyalist tendencies will eventually be converted to the patriot cause by an attractive, intelligent, and politically savvy woman. This is the case with Lieutenant Wallingford and Mary Hamilton in *The Tory Lover,* as well as with Adam Rutledge and Mary Warden in *Raleigh's Eden.* Then there is the recurrent situation of women who made unfortunate first marriages to Loyalists, but subsequently have much more satisfactory marriages to Whigs, which happens in Frederic's *In the Valley* and in *Queens Gift* by Inglis Fletcher (1952). Finally, for those who savor ironic symbolism stirred in with tragedy, we have this stock device. Patriot husband and wife conceive a child in the autumn of 1775; the father is killed in battle during the late spring of 1776; but a son is born just a few days or weeks before July 4th, 1776. The child will grow up with the new nation, of course, and thereby perpetuate the vital bloodline of patriotism.[126]

Yet another recurrent theme involves the problem of parentage. Over and over again our heroes and heroines are orphaned at a very early age, like Richard Carvel and Johnny Tremain. William Gilmore Simms's main characters are often orphans, or else have no mothers.[127] The same is true in Cooper's novels: Cora and Alice, the sisters in *Last of the Mohicans,* have no mother. Nor does Andrew Merry in *The Pilot.* Nor does Harvey Birch in *The Spy*—"I had none but a father to mourn my loss"—nor most of the other young men and women, for that matter. Here is a bit of dialogue from *The Spy:*

"Peace, my brother, and listen," continued Isabella, rousing herself with an effort that was final; "here is the innocent, the justifiable cause. We are both motherless; but that aunt—that mild, plain-hearted, observing aunt, has given you the victory. *Oh! how much she loses, who loses a female guardian to her youth.* (p. 305)

Breaking the bonds with Mother England is part of the authors' intended symbolism—weaning colonial children from matronly Britannia. But also, when the mother dies quite young in these novels she invariably leaves behind some strange problem about her origins, and more particularly, a serious question about her relationship to the hero's father. Johnny Tremain's mother had a mysterious marriage to a Frenchman. The mothers of Hugh Wynne and Philip Kent (in John Jakes, *The Bastard,* 1974) are French. We are thereby reminded, presumably, that French assistance—financial aid and naval cooperation—was needed to make possible the birth of a nation.

Most of our novelists of the Revolution have tried to strike a balance between the imperatives of social respectability and those of democracy. They must give adequate attention, on the one hand, to proper lineage, native heritage, social stability, and virtue; but on the other hand stress egalitarianism, the absence of snobbery, and compassion for the unfortunate. Thus John Esten Cooke wanted his Virginia cavaliers to have just the right combination of aristocratic breeding and democratic outlook; and George Washington emerges as the perfect exemplar of this distinctively American blend.[128] Harold Frederic has his narrator, Douw Mauverensen, a young colonial of Dutch descent, explain the matter explicitly. Douw has finally figured out the bizarre personality of Philip Cross, his Tory enemy.

His talk about my being well born helped me now to understand his character better than I had before been able to do. I began to realize the existence in England—in Europe generally, I dare say— of a kind of man strange to our American ideas, a being within whom long tradition and sedulous training had created two distinct men—one affable, honorable, generous, likeable, among his equals; the other cold, selfish, haughty, and harsh to his inferiors. It struck me now that there had always been two Philips, and that I had been shown only the rude and hateful one because my station had not seemed to entitle me to consort with the other. . . . In his own country he would doubtless have made a tolerable husband, a fair landlord, a worthy gentleman in the eyes of the only class of people whose consideration he cared for. But over here, in the new land, all the conditions had been against him. He had drawn down upon himself and all those about him overwhelming calamity, simply because he had felt himself under the cursed obligation to act like a "gentleman," as he called it.[129]

Precisely because there were various kinds of cross-cutting social cleavage—British and American, Loyalist and Whig, merchant and farmer, gentry and tenants—many authors liked to use the "neutral ground" of Westchester as their setting. Doing so, they believed, intensified the aura of tradition. From Kingsbridge to the Highlands along the Hudson River, as Paulding explained, was "a sort of 'debateable land,' like the English and Scottish borders before the union of the two kingdoms. It was occupied by neither party, and it might almost be said there was neither law or gospel there."[130]

A neutral ground also facilitated the passage of spies back and forth; and as we have seen, the business of spying and treason fascinated American readers. Tales of Benedict Arnold and Major André had enormous appeal, and therefore had to be transplanted or else replicated in other settings for other sections. Thus in *Horse-Shoe Robinson* (1835), Arthur Butler is accused and stands trial in 1780 for the very same offense with which André was charged; but it all happens in the Carolinas, and Butler is actually a patriot. In 1903 William O. Stoddard gave Virginians their version, called *The Spy of Yorktown: A Story of Arnold and Washington in the Last Year of the War of Independence.* And in *Raleigh's Eden* we eventually learn what we have suspected all along: that William Warden is really a British spy. He is hanged by the patriots in 1780, just like André; and lest there be any doubt that this is a southern version of the classic drama, Cornwallis tells Mary Warden that "he was as great a hero as John André, if the truth of his work were known."[131]

Where there are spies, there will be prisoners; and, as it happens, most of these novels have a hero or a heroine or a villain (or all three) who undergoes an awful experience of captivity.[132] Sometimes it happens on one of the infamous prison ships, those floating hulks so rife with hunger and disease.[133] Sometimes it happens in England, as with Roger Wallingford in *The Tory Lover* and Robert Rogers in *Northwest Passage*. Most often it seems to happen in New York City so that the hero will have a hideous encounter with William Cunningham, the sadistic Provost Marshal who was placed in charge of prisoners, a vicious Irishman described in *The Linwoods* as "the most formidable of the bulldog race of jailers."[134]

These captivity situations serve many different sorts of purposes, the most important of which relates to the central argument of Chapter Six and follows shortly. A lesser function, but a persistent dramatic device nonetheless, is that imprisonment of the hero sets up a situation where some weak or helpless person must go before a powerful foe in order to plead the cause of a hapless friend or lover. In *Lionel Lincoln,* therefore, Cecil Dynevor must appear in George Washington's camp to plead for permission to see Lionel, her arrested fiancé. In *Horse-Shoe Robinson* Mildred Lindsay must go before Cornwallis to beg that no harm befall her fiancé, Arthur Butler. And in the most successful recent Revolutionary novel for children, *My Brother Sam Is Dead,* young Tim Meeker begs General Israel Putnam to spare the life of his older brother Sam.[135]

There are, then, any number of devices—structural, aesthetic, and historical devices—that are used repetitively by these novelists, such as relying heavily for narrative purposes upon some character who kept a journal or diary during the American Revolution.[136] The net result, especially when we get to the period 1933–48, is a rather tired condition that has been well described by one literary critic:

> that art must imitate art rather than life: that poems must, in the end, conform to earlier fictions, to the dominant imaginative structure that absorbs all fictions to itself, instead of keeping its eye on the object of imitation out there in the world, beyond all poems.[137]

Thus *Thomas Forty* (1947) has too many points of resemblance to *Johnny Tremain* (1943).[138] Thus Langdon Towne's relationship to young Ann Potter in *Northwest Passage* (1937) seems to provide a model for Julian Day and Tibby Mawes in *Dawn's Early Light* (1943). The artistic Towne's disciple role in relation to Robert Rogers appears to be emulated in *Burr,* where Charlie Schuyler eventually has to redefine his relationship with Aaron Burr. And the 1775 tar-and-feather scene in *Remembrance Rock* (1948) is derivative from "My Kinsman, Major Molineux," by Nathaniel Hawthorne (1832).[139]

Although the novels of James Fenimore Cooper may seem somewhat hackneyed and tired to us today, Cooper was actually the true pioneer. He is, to some degree, a victim of the very success his genre has enjoyed. A problem exists for the imaginative writer, which is well described in a phrase by Edward Shils: "There is at the very root," he has written, "a war between originality and tradition." What made Cooper and Kenneth Roberts and Esther Forbes so popular, among others, was their capacity as historical novelists to fuse originality with traditionality. They made the former work within the framework of the latter; and they enjoyed phenomenal success as a result.[140]

One last point: if the novelists seem to echo one another, their themes also reinforce many of the general tendencies we watched at work in earlier chapters. Robert Montgomery Bird, for example, announces on page one, sentence one, of *The Hawks of Hawk-Hollow* that "America is especially the land of change"; and then, on the very last page, he concludes by relating that to the weakness of tradition in the United States:

> Our inquiries after the fate of the less important personages of our tradition have been very satisfactory in results. Americans are a race of Utilitarians, all busied in the acquisition of profitable knowledge, and just as ready, if not as anxious, to forget all lore of an useless character. The little anecdotes of a district last but for a generation; the fathers tell them to the children, but the children find something better to think about, and so forget them.

One of the most popular historical novelists of the past generation, Conrad Richter, reiterated that assertion in 1950: "Change has been apparently the one constant factor in American life and character."[141]

There are all kinds of connections that link these novelists fairly closely to their counterparts in poetry and art. In 1827, for instance, William Cullen Bryant mailed to the editor of the *United States Review* a volume of Simms's poems and *Paul Jones: A Romance* by Allan Cunningham.[142] The incident that gave rise to that famous "sweet potato picture" of Francis Marion and the British officer also finds its way into the fiction.[143]

Ever since the heyday of Howard Pyle and N. C. Wyeth eighty years ago, there have been some interesting relationships between our artists and writers. N. C. Wyeth illustrated modern editions of Cooper's novels, plus three volumes of American patriotic poetry, several works of historical non-fiction, the dust jackets for such Kenneth Roberts novels as *Arundel* (1930) and *Rabble in Arms* (1933); he also provided romantic pictures for James Boyd's *Drums*. The cultural impact of this commercial involvement should not be underestimated. In December 1927, two years after *Drums*, which is set in Revolutionary North Carolina, had been published, Wyeth came to see Edenton. The historical memories and associations that arose prompted him to write to Boyd:

My dear Boyd,

Some tower in the brilliant moonlight has just rung out the hour of two. I have tried to sleep but the crowded hours of the day are racing through my mind at such a pace that sufficient composure for slumber seems out of the question. Perchance this letter will invite sleep—if not to me mayhap to you.

For the last two hours, lying by the open window, I have listened to the night sounds of this little town and have contrasted them with those Johnny Fraser heard so often, and by doing so have enjoyed revealments which, for moments at a time, became very poignant and very moving.

At this instant a dog is barking somewhere on the edge of the city; there is also the faint muffled staccato of a small power-boat out on the sound. Occasionally, the sudden angry grind of a Ford, new-starting in the cold, shatters the quiet. But the silence following becomes the more pregnant of the echoes of the past.

I am actually not many feet from the cubic areas occupied by the boy Johnny and his dad in their candlelit room at Hornblowers. My window faces the harbor and I too can look upon "dim shapes of fences, walks, houses—" some of them identical with only the changes of roof coverings. Dimly bulking against the glow of the moon on the water I can see the angular shapes of three warehouses. There they stand as Johnny Fraser saw them!

This afternoon was spent wandering in and about these relics of 1770. My heart went out to them, because you, Boyd, have made them live for me. The oak timbers, whose adze-marked surfaces are still crisp on their protected sides and smoothed to gentle undulations where the sun and rain of years have touched them, thrilled me like music. . . .

Approaching Edenton on the ferry the waterfront became monstrously enlarged for a few moments by a mirage—a "loom," as the Maine fisherman would call it. It affected me queerly. It was as though the little port had stood up from a seated position, open-eyed, to view with alarm the impertinent coming of another man to reveal her past when one had already accomplished the job. That no other one of the twenty passengers in the boat made a comment on this phenomenon, I am convinced that it was a personal affair!

Well, I am going to try some sleep, but not before I express my warmest thanks to you and Mrs. Boyd for your kindnesses. You have given me a wonderful start in the new adventure *Drums*—and I do hope I succeed.[144]

Being haunted by a historical imagination can be infectious, it seems—at least, once upon a time it was.

CHAPTER SIX

THE AMERICAN REVOLUTION AS NATIONAL *RITE DE PASSAGE*

"A people, like an individual, must needs pass through a season of youth in its progressive development"

TOWARD THE CLOSE of the preceding chapter, I suggested that certain recurrent themes—such as mysterious parentage or brutal imprisonment for the main figures in these novels—formed part of a complex and meaningful pattern in Revolutionary fiction. The capture and prolonged captivity of Arthur Butler, for example, supply a central focus for *Horse-Shoe Robinson.* When Mildred Lindsay, Butler's betrothed, "set forth in that emergency upon her pilgrimage of duty," we are watching part of a ritual process unfold.[1] What is the nature of that process? Why is it so critically important that we understand it? And what are its implications for an enlarged understanding of American thought and culture? To answer those questions, we must explore at some length the single most pervasive emphasis to emerge from all these historical novels.

There has, indeed, been a dominant angle of vision that persists irrespective of period. It is as remarkably single-minded as it is complex; yet this peculiar perspective is also elusive to explain, in part because it has become so formulaic. I find it easier to illustrate than to define or explicate. Therefore, I want to begin by offering one example from each of our phases. With these instances in mind, we should be in a better position to proceed with analysis and explanation.

My first illustration comes from *The Dutchman's Fireside* (1831) by James Kirke Paulding, the story of Sybrandt Westbrook, who is introduced to us as "a bashful young gentleman." The time is a few years prior to the Revolution, and because Sybrandt seems to be too bookish and lacking in aggressive self-confidence, he is sent to spend some time with William Johnson, Superintendent of Indian Affairs, in the northern part of Britain's continental empire.

> Every day when the weather permitted, and indeed often when a dandy sportsman would have shrunk from the war of the elements, they pursued the manly, exciting sport of hunting. The image of war, most especially in this empire of savages and beasts of prey—this course of life gradually awakened the sleeping energies of Sybrandt's nature that had been so long dozing under the scholastic rubbish of the good Dominie Stettinius. . . . He acquired an active vigor of body, together with a quickness of perception and keen attention to what was passing before him, that by degrees encroached deeply on his habit of indolent abstraction. He caught from the stranger something of his fearless, independent carriage, lofty bearing, and impatience of idleness or inaction. In short, he acquired a confidence in himself, a self-possession, and self-respect, such as he had never felt before, and which freed him from the leaden fetters of that awkward restraint which had hitherto been the bane of his life.[2]

My second illustration comes from *Hugh Wynne, Free Quaker* (1897) by S. Weir Mitchell, a story set in Philadelphia. Young Hugh, the hero, was born in January 1753, the son of a Welsh Quaker father who turns out to be a "passive Tory," and a French Quaker mother. The tale opens in 1765 when Hugh is twelve years old, and ends in February 1783 shortly before the proclamation of peace, when Hugh marries his beloved Darthea in an Episcopalian ceremony. Thereafter, of course, the patriot couple lives happily ever after "in the great stone house at Merion." In August of 1773 we get from Hugh, then aged twenty, this soliloquy:

> I reflected, with a certain surprise, at the frequent discovery, of late, on how much older I seemed to be. It was a time which quickly matured the thoughtful, and I was beginning to shake off, in some degree, the lifelong shackles of limitation as to conduct, dress, and minor morals, imposed upon me by my home surroundings. In a word, being older than my years, I began to think for myself. . . . I had learned, too, in my aunt's house, the ways and manners of a larger world, and, if I had yielded to its temptations, I had at least profited by the bitter lesson. I was on the verge of manhood.[3]

My third illustration comes from Carl Sandburg's *Remembrance Rock* (1948). The second portion of this huge trilogy, called "The Arch Begins," opens in 1775 around Boston, and then moves with the war to New York, Philadelphia, and Valley Forge, where a young patriot named Robert Winshore dies of double amputation resulting from frostbite. His brother, John Locke Winshore, had married Ann Elwood on May 26, 1776, and then been killed a week later while carrying a message to George Washington at New York. In February of 1777, however, Ann gives birth to their child, John Locke Winshore, Jr., a babe symbolic of the infant nation.[4] Back in the winter of 1774–5, we hear a dialogue between the father of these two martyrs, a Massachusetts printer named Ordway Winshore, and his son John (who is called affectionately by his middle name, Locke).

> The father knew he couldn't really laugh off more questions that kept coming up from under the others. First he had fathered his boy and after the boy was born he had done considerable mothering. For years the boy had talked free with him about nearly everything, even the first hairs of puberty when the father had laughed, "You're a man now, Locke, though not yet man-size," and then sober counsels where they talked about the vast mystic caverns and labyrinths of sex. . . . Now the boy was man-size. It was his wish to leave Philadelphia six months ago and come to New York and see how life went when he was no longer "tied" to his father, as Locke had said, adding, "I don't mean you have tied me to you, I've had plenty of freedom but I want to see what'll happen when I'm away from you."[5]

My illustration for the most recent phase of historical fiction comes from *My Brother Sam Is Dead* (1974) by James Lincoln Collier and Christopher Collier, the most commercially successful children's book about the Revolution to be published in the Bicentennial years. Set in western Connecticut, near Danbury and Redding between April 1775 and 1777, it involves two brothers, Sam and Tim Meeker. Their father, a tavern-keeper, hopes to remain neutral in the war; he comes into conflict with Sam, a sixteen-year-old in 1775 who is determined to fight in the Continental cause. Father and son have vitriolic, recurrent arguments over whether Sam is a man yet, or still a boy. And then, in the winter of 1776–7, young Tim undergoes a rapid process of self-recognition.

> Ever since I had got the wagon home by myself I hadn't felt like a boy anymore. You don't think that things really happen overnight, but this one did. Of course I was dead tired when I went to bed that night, and Mother let me sleep late in the morning. And when I woke up I was different. I noticed it first at breakfast. . . . I didn't wait for Mother to tell me what to do: I brought the subject up myself. . . . About halfway through breakfast I began to realize that I had changed. I wasn't acting my usual self, I was acting more like a grownup. You couldn't say that I was really an adult, but I wasn't a child anymore, that was certain.[6]

What are we to make of these passages, and of literally hundreds more just like them? What they mean, almost to the point of numbing monotony, is that imaginative writers have consistently perceived the American Revolution as a national *rite de passage,* and have relentlessly projected that vision to an ever-widening readership. We must indicate very precisely what is intended by that, however, and with what implications. First of all, *I* am not perceiving the Revolution as a *rite de passage* (although in certain limited respects I can regard it that way). Rather, I must insist that that has been its favorite and quintessential meaning in American popular culture.

Second, we must clarify the usage and nuances of *rite de passage* in this context, for that phrase has a conceptual history in the subdisciplines of cultural and symbolic anthropology. It was introduced in 1909 by Arnold Van Gennep (1873–1957), a Belgian ethnographer who published *Les Rites de Passage* in French. His primary concern was with self-conscious rituals in primitive societies: ways in which adults formally incorporate adolescents and young adults into the community of mature men and women. That sort of ceremonial *rite de passage* does not provide us with a pertinent analogy here; but subsequent anthropologists have embellished and explicated the concept Van Gennep introduced, and have done so in ways that help to illuminate the cultural artifacts we have been examining.

Alfred M. Tozzer, for example, suggested in 1925 that rites of passage are undertaken in conjunction with birth, adolescence, marriage, and death, which are not merely phases in the individual life cycle, but often produce crises of one magnitude or another. Nevertheless, Tozzer's discussion continued to stress the individual's progress rather than the society's rationale for having such rituals; and he continued to think in terms of planned, formulaic ceremonials.[7] During the mid-1960s, however, as Victor W. Turner began to move from social and cultural anthropology into symbolic anthropology, he adapted and refined Van Gennep's analytical tool in a direction useful to us. He tells us:

> Van Gennep himself defined *rites de passage* as "rites which accompany every change of place, state, social position and age." To point up the contrast between "state" and "transition," I employ "state" to include all his other terms. It is a more inclusive concept than "status" or "office," and refers to any type of stable or recurrent condition that is culturally recognized. Van Gennep has shown that all rites of passage or "transition" are marked by three phases: separation, margin (or *limen,* signifying "threshold" in Latin), and aggregation. The first phase (of separation) comprises symbolic behavior signifying the detachment of the individual or group either from an earlier fixed point in the social structure, from a set of cultural conditions (a "state"), or from both. During the intervening "liminal" period, the characteristics of the ritual subject (the "passenger") are ambiguous; he passes through a cultural realm that has few or none of the attributes of the past or coming state. In the third phase (reaggregation or reincorporation), the passage is consummated. The ritual subject, individual or corporate, is in a relatively stable state once more and, by virtue of this, has rights and obligations vis-à-vis others of a clearly defined and "structural" type.[8]

Turner's emphasis upon the element of cultural recognition is useful to us because it opens up for consideration the ways in which groups other than so-called primitive societies may recognize and ritualize critical aspects of their development. Certain political transitions retrospectively acquire new symbolic meaning, so that the fate of an individual may become a metaphor for the destiny of a tribe, a community, or even a nation. Turner has elaborated in social theory what an American essayist, David Hatch Barlow, declared back in 1851, namely, that "a people, like an individual, must needs pass through a season of youth in its progressive development, and . . . during this season the individual partakes of the youthfulness of the community to which he belongs."[9]

David Barlow may or may not have been consciously reiterating Tocqueville's observation that "nations, like men, in their youth almost always give indications of the main features of their destiny." Barlow may or may not have read an essay on "National Ballads" that appeared two years earlier in the *Southern Literary*

Messenger, in which the author had observed that "there is, perhaps, no similitude more trite and familiar,—certainly there is none more striking and true, than that which likens the origin and progress of nations to the growth and development of children."[10] Whatever the case, Barlow was simply stating as a generalization an assumption that the historical novelists had been asserting ever since Cooper put these words into the mouth of Dr. Sitgreaves, a surgeon serving the Continental army: "I say nothing of oppression; the child was of age, and was entitled to the privileges of majority." By "the child," needless to say, he meant the American colonies on the eve of Independence.[11]

In order to dispel any lingering shred of doubt about the *explicit* intentions of these novelists in every period and at all levels of social articulation, let us now look at five brief quotations that demonstrate how the heroes and heroines were intended as personalized figures for the emerging nation as a whole: one quotation taken from each of our four major phases, and a fifth from a dime novel written between periods one and two for a working-class audience.

- Of course, the whole of the open space was more or less disfigured by stumps, dead and girdled trees, charred stubs, log-heaps, brush, and all the other unseemly accompaniments of the first eight or ten years of the existence of a new settlement. This period in the history of a country, may be likened to the hobbledehoy condition in ourselves, when we have lost the graces of childhood, without having attained the finished forms of men.[12]
- We want to govern ourselves, and to dispense with your authority in England. All boys, when they come to manhood, seek to direct their own affairs, and are generally competent to the task. So a colony, when it finds the parent State querulous and avaricious, and grasping at all the profits of the copartnership, is apt to be discontented and inclined to dissolve the union.[13]
- "Our country is like a boy hardly come to manhood yet, who is at every moment afraid that he will not be taken for a man of forty years," said Mr. Franklin, smiling. "We have all the faults of youth, but, thank God, the faults of a young country are better than the faults of an old one. It is the young heart that takes the forward step. The day comes when England will love us all the better for what we are doing, but it provokes the mother country now, and grieves the child. If I read their hearts aright, there have been those who thought the mother most deeply hurt, and the child most angry."[14]

Now, in the crisis, what good was he to this land of pines, of long mountain men, of tight-lipped, straight-eyed women—he struck his hand down on the sod—this land of his! He was no more than half a man; he tried to bend his locked elbow on his knee; a sparkling flame shot to his armpit, the elbow would not budge. He let his arm drop with a bitter grin; no more than half a man. Yet why should he complain? What else had he ever been? Did he rate himself a hero or even a man because blind chance had put him to sea on a Continental raider? The man was he who had gone in with open eyes, who through famine, defeat, and nakedness had stuck it out or, permitted to stick it out, now lay safely shrouded, enriching the land which gave him birth. Let him look at himself as he had been—a youth so large in his own conceit, his silly head so easily turned by specious show, that he could wholly fail to gauge his country's worth. . . .[15]

• Indeed, he thought as he neared Philadelphia, if America as a whole dared to seek what Sam Adams openly desired—total independency—she would be, in a sense, what he had been from the beginning: a bastard child thrust into a dangerous world alone and unprotected; a bastard child exposed to countless risks the more timid and secure would never experience, a bastard child forced, on occasion, to kill other human beings in order to survive—[16]

Repetition may well be boring, but it is nonetheless an essential element in the creation, establishment, and perpetuation of national traditions. "The function of repetition," as Lévi-Strauss has reminded us, "is to render the structure of the myth apparent."[17] There is more to this particular myth, however, than merely "a burning interest in the question of equal manhood."[18] There is an entire network of associated assumptions about our coming of age in the 1770s and 1780s; and some of the components in that network deserve specific mention.

First, there is the question of how children get their knowledge of public affairs and acquire the rudiments of a political ideology. Richard Carvel tells us that it is an almost "impossible task on the memory to trace those influences by which a lad is led to form his life's opinions, and for my part I hold that such things are bred into the bone, and that events only serve to strengthen them." Subsequently, however, we discover that young Richard has learned about early American history and libertarian politics from Mr. Swain, a good and dedicated Whig in Annapolis who quietly led the Sons of Liberty.[19] There is also a related problem: when do teen-age boys become old enough to be trusted with serious political secrets? When will Richard Carvel and Johnny Tremain and Adam Cooper (in *April Morning* by Howard Fast) be sufficiently mature and trustworthy to listen in at confidential meetings of the committees of correspondence? Being permitted to attend their first meeting, needless to say, is a significant signpost in each one's coming of age.

Second, there is the slow process of achieving true political awareness and understanding. In part because of his Quaker background, and in part because of his Tory father, Hugh Wynne remains a non-combatant for quite some time. But his point of commitment comes in the autumn of 1777 when he declares, " 'I will go,' and in a moment I had made one of those decisive resolutions which, once made, seem to control me, and to permit no future change of plan." So Hugh joins the Continental army. Young Johnny Fraser, the hero of *Drums,* is similarly racked by political indecision for a very long time; but finally, before it is too late, he tells John Paul Jones in a quiet voice, "I want to get into this war."[20] Richard Carvel and Thomas Forty do not take nearly so long to make their allegiances firm; yet they, too, must undergo a hesitant political growth.

Third, there is the very important symbolic process of leaving home in order to support a cause, for, as anthropologists have explained, rites of passage provide a formal means by which changes of status, condition, and location may be recognized.[21] On September 30, 1777, Hugh Wynne reflects that "I was about to leave home, perhaps forever, but I never in my life went to bed with a more satisfied heart." In an important story by Sarah Josepha Hale, however, we get the whole process step by step, and with greater agonizing. An aged veteran who tells the tale was twenty years old in 1777 when his narrative occurred. Two years earlier, as "news of the Lexington battle arrived, I was eager to be a soldier—but my father objected. 'No, my son,' he said, 'you are not yet arrived at your full strength, and the country requires the assistance of men.' " In a subsequent crisis, he is told: "My son, you may go. The crisis demands the sacrifice of all selfish and private feelings on the part of Americans—You shall go." At that point, the aged hero recalls, he had some anguished second thoughts, for "there was something in this preparation for wounds and death, that could not but be somewhat appalling to one who had always lived in the security and shelter of home."

Thereafter, he admits, "I never felt that fear, that utter despondency, that misgiving of spirit, which I endured when taking my leave of home."[22]

Often, of course, the hero leaves home because his family is bitterly divided over questions of ideology and allegiance; and that, too, becomes a metaphorical means of discussing the Revolution in terms of *rites de passage.* In one of Kenneth Roberts's prison scenes, we have this symptomatic little dialogue. "One of the prisoners spat the word 'parricide' at him. Evelyn looked puzzled. 'Parricide? Parricide? You mean I'm in rebellion against my parents, intending to be their assassin?' "[23] Over and over again we encounter confrontations between father and son, between brothers, and among cousins; for as a character explains in an 1831 short story, "I have often regretted this unnatural war . . . to see children of the same family engaged in a cruel and bloody conflict."[24]

In some instances, of course, a divided family exemplifies the divided empire; but much more common is the intergenerational conflict between father and son within the colonies, or a young man and his prospective father-in-law.[25] I would argue, in fact, that mature adults are rarely portrayed in these novels as complex people with legitimate political, social, and even romantic problems of their own. More often than not they are presented only one-dimensionally as parents, as stick-figures for their three-dimensional children to react against. The fact that Benjamin Franklin was an elder statesman during the Revolution presents a bit of a problem, therefore, but not an insuperable one. "Age is wont to be narrow and to depend upon certainties of the past," we read, "while youth has its easily gathered hopes and quick intuitions. Mr. Franklin is both characters at once,—as sanguine as he is experienced."[26]

If these novels are so heavily concerned with coming of age and with family conflict, what about young women? Has it been part of this dominant motif that the American Revolution was a *rite de passage* for females as well? Well, that has been true on occasion. Miss Eliza Leslie, for example, published in 1833 a popular piece entitled *Russel and Sidney; or, The Young Revolutionists.* The heroine is Sidney Campion, whose mother died in 1775 when Sidney was sixteen. She lives with her father near the Brandywine River along the Maryland-Delaware border, and we are told that "even the retiring timidity that characterises the female youth of America, was at this time tinctured with an enthusiasm corresponding to that of their fathers and brothers." Later on, when the English Captain Effingham falls in love with Sidney and proposes to her, she rejects him curtly: "Nothing can alter my resolution never to be the wife of an enemy to my country."[27]

Alice Roussillon, who turns twenty in the year 1775, "had been accustomed to . . . sudden changes of conditions; but this was the first time that she had ever joined actively in a public movement of importance." We learn that "a great change was coming into her idyllic life"; and at the end, when she is "on the verge of a new life," her foster father gives her a little lecture. "You can't always be a wilful, headstrong little girl, running everywhere and doing just as you please. You have grown to be a woman in stature—you must be one in fact."[28] Tibby Mawes, the plucky heroine of *Dawn's Early Light,* is eleven in 1775 and therefore just old enough to marry Julian Day when the war ends late in 1781. Her coming of age is emotionally central to that novel; and similarly, we learn in *The Rebels* that Peggy Ashford McLean (in 1777) "had passed out of girlhood forever." Peggy also, by the way, marries Philip Kent immediately following the end of hostilities at Yorktown.[29]

Often as not, even where the author is a woman, the heroine's coming of age is eclipsed by the hero's. Sidney Campion, for example, has a younger brother named Russel. Although he is only sixteen in 1777, he loathes being called a "boy." "I wish you would never again reproach me with being a boy," he says to Sidney. "Cannot I load and fire as well as any man?" Soon enough his opportunity comes to fight the British, and he assists Maxwell's riflemen, a group of irregulars, at the Battle of Brandywine. When Russel offers his services to a sentinel in Washington's army, however, he is rejected with an abrupt dismissal: "If we were to take all the boys that offer, we should soon have the camp full of them." Subsequently, "our juvenile hero," as the author refers to him, demonstrates his manliness by wounding Captain Effingham; and in 1779 Russel gets his commission, a symbolic recognition of his achieving manhood at the age of eighteen.[30]

When we look at our second phase, the years from about 1895 until 1909, female rites of passage are utterly obscured by the dominant emphasis upon achieving manhood and masculinity. Youthful fist-fights abound—between twelve-year-old Richard

Carvel and Philip, his foppish, royalist cousin; between Douw Mauverensen and the future Tory, Philip Cross—and even virtuous young Whigs are inclined to enjoy card playing, horse racing, betting, and drinking.[31] It's all part of being "red-blooded," and it is unmistakably linked to the American cult of manliness that became so popular during the 1890s and right after the turn of the century. Analogies between individuals and the nation pervaded the climate of opinion; for as one advocate of manliness wrote in 1909, "nations, like individuals, struggle through hardship to supremacy, grow weak through idleness, are overcome by a more virile nation, and lose their power or even die."[32]

The successful development of an extensive juvenile literature during the three decades 1885–1915 served to reinforce this resonant theme of *rite de passage.* Much is made in these books of Lafayette's being a "boy general." One author called his popular volume, *With Washington at Valley Forge,* "the story of a boy's exciting part in the incidents of that memorable winter of 1777–78. . . . But the object has been to interest the reader in the boy hero; and, after the experiences herein related, Hadley Morris can scarce longer be called a boy; for experience makes us old, not years." Lest the reader find it curious that Hadley Morris, "though but a boy, obtained a lieutenant's commission," the author takes pains to demonstrate that, in historical reality, it was the sort of struggle in which youngsters could distinguish themselves.

> Nor was it so strange at that time that a mere boy should be an officer in the American army. There were many boys at Valley Forge that spring of '78 whose names were destined to be enrolled upon America's record of honor. There was that boy of less than twenty, called James Monroe. Who was there then to prophesy that one day his "doctrine" should keep America unpolluted from the grasp of European politics? There were two other youths there—still mere boys—whose names were destined to be linked sorrowfully together in later life—Aaron Burr and Alexander Hamilton. General Lafayette himself was scarcely of age, and the future Chief Justice of the United States, John Marshall, bore a musket in the Third Virginia, and suffered with the patience of a high-minded youth at Valley Forge.[33]

Everett Tomlinson was singlehandedly responsible for a great many books during this period; and you will notice in two of the most successful among them, *The Boys of Old Monmouth* (1898) and

A Jersey Boy in the Revolution (1899), that they record heroic trials and adventures of an orphan, Tom Coward, who is an apprentice (or "bound-boy," as they were called).[34] This whole genre of historical novels, by the way, abounds with orphans. Richard Carvel was one; consequently, he must assume major responsibilities at an early age. Charles James Fox, whom Richard meets and admires in London, had a doting father who properly prepared him to be socially and politically precocious. But Richard's father was killed in the French and Indian War; and to make matters worse, Richard's tutor is dissolute, dishonest, and a rake. Who, then, would help prepare Richard to take his place in the world? The American Whig would obviously have to be self-reliant, self-taught, almost self-generating.[35]

Alice Roussillon knows virtually nothing about her identity—neither the names of her parents nor where she was born. She had been an Indian captive until the age of twelve. Yet somewhere back in the mysterious past, her dying mother had entrusted the child to M. Roussillon, who promised her that Alice would remain a Protestant.[36] Thomas Forty is also presented to us as an orphan, the bastard son of an Irish serving girl. And *Dawn's Early Light* is chock-full of orphans and illegitimate children. Kit and Tibby Mawes begin the book in the latter category, and in 1781, when their mother dies at war's end, become orphans as well. Tibby eventually marries Julian Day, whose mother died in childbirth. Julian arrives at Yorktown in 1774, age twenty-one, his father having just died at sea on the trans-Atlantic crossing. St. John Sprague, an important supporting character in the same novel, was orphaned as a child in England; and when his Uncle Colin (a planter-lawyer on the James River) died in 1771, Sprague came over to settle the estate, then moved to Williamsburg with his Aunt Anabel. His sixteen-year-old sister, Darthea, joins them in 1772.[37]

It should come as no surprise that the metaphor of a disrupted family also dominated history books written for school use. The Anglo-American relationship was usually presented in a very personalized form—often as the story of a harsh mother (or stepmother) and her courageous son. As J. Merton England has suggested, it is not the Oedipus myth, but that of Orestes modified. "Orestes spares his mother, Clytemnestra, but renounces her and her sinful city. He goes off to live in the wilderness alone. But ultimately he returns to friendly relations with his mother and her metropolis."[38]

"Complex processes of symbolic transformation mediate the distance between cultural or social upheavals on the one hand and theoretical developments on the other"[39]

WE NOW MUST raise two related questions about this notion of the American Revolution as national *rite de passage*: Where did our historical novelists pick up such an extended metaphor in the first place; and then, given its potent appeal, what purpose has it served—what function does it fulfill—in the society's self-image?

As for where they got it, they did not simply make it up—natural and easy though that might have been. By the end of the colonial period, in 1775, the American mind already had rich precedents for regarding private quests as part of a communal experience. They also had some acquaintance with social experience presented symbolically in terms of an individual's mission. In Puritan writings of New England, for example, the Atlantic crossing became a figure for spiritual voyaging. (In the more secular nineteenth-century novels, crossing an ocean or a major river frequently became a metaphor for the Revolutionary *rite de passage*.)[40] To early historians of New England, the Atlantic crossing was perceived as a tribal response to a divine call. There are any number of religious *rites de passage* described in the *Magnalia Christi Americana,* for Cotton Mather was preoccupied with the progression of souls into a state of grace. As one scholar has written: "It was their quest for self-realization through introspection and self-examination that truly concerned him."[41]

A shift occurred during the course of the eighteenth century, however, because by 1775 self-realization came less through introspection than through action: Sam Adams manipulating, Paul Revere galloping, Dr. Joseph Warren leading, and even Benedict Arnold marching to Quebec. The people with real problems, apparently, were those despicable neutrals who chose inaction. But regardless of one's political persuasion, parent-child imagery was commonly used once the drama of Independence opened. We find Samuel Seabury, a Loyalist, answering Alexander Hamilton late in 1774:

Do you think, Sir, that Great Britain is like an old, wrinkled, withered, worn-out hag, whom every jackanapes that truants along the streets may insult with impunity? You will find her a vigorous matron, just approaching a green old age; and with spirit and strength sufficient to chastise her undutiful and rebellious children. . . . I would make many more concessions to a parent than were justly due to him, rather than engage with him in a duel. But we are rushing into a war with our parent state without offering the least concession.[42]

In 1775 we see Richard Wells declaring that "the day of independent manhood is at hand," and a year later, in *Common Sense,* Tom Paine asked the rhetorical question that soon came to be on so many tongues: "Is it the interest of a man to be a boy all his life?"

These polemical writers were in turn picking up a metaphor that had been in occasional use during the developmental decades of the colonial period. Back in 1712, for instance, Governor Hunter of New York had explained to the Secretary of State at home that "in the Infancy of the Colonies the Crown was lavish of priviledges as necessary for their nurseing, but a full grown boy makes commonly but Indifferent use of that Indulgence requisite toward a Child."[43] David Hume would embellish these sentiments half a century later; and soon after the Revolution, in 1787, a British author published anonymously a picaresque novel about a hapless Massachusetts farm boy who became a fugitive from the war. All of these occasional sentiments enjoyed some circulation, and are echoed in the Revolutionary romances that blossomed after 1821.[44]

Equally important, perhaps even more so, were the autobiographies of aged veterans printed during the 1820s and 1830s. Lowly soldiers as well as famous officers published memoirs and were the subjects of popular biographies,[45] and one often finds in them a retrospective view of the Revolution as being both a personal and a communal coming of age. Here are a few typical passages from one of them, published in 1830:

I declare to you, that helpless as we were in comparison with such a force, and young as I was for such encounters, the moment I saw what the danger was, I felt at once relieved, and, nothing doubting that an engagement must take place, I longed for it to begin. . . .

One of my comrades, who saw me fallen, returned with the news to my parents. They heard no more concerning me, but had no doubt that I was slain. They mourned for me as lost, and a rude stone was erected near the graves of my family, in the burying-ground, to record the fate of the one who was not permitted to sleep with his fathers. . . .[46]

Now, as our little whaleboat bounded over the waves, I felt bold, joyous, and triumphant. I thought then that there were moments in a life of changes, which atone for the heaviness of many of its hours. . . .

Never was there such a confusion in our village. The young were eloquent in their amazement, and the old put on their spectacles to see the strange being who had thus returned as from the dead. The house was crowded with visitors till far into the night, when the minister dismissed them by calling on my father and mother to join him in an offering of praise, "for this son which was dead and is alive again, which was lost and is found."[47]

The Adventures of Ebenezer Fox in the Revolutionary War, published in 1838 and reprinted in 1847, was still better known. Born in 1763, Fox became an apprentice in 1770 and worked five years in the service of a farmer. In looking back he equated his personal dissatisfaction with that of the colonies.

Boys are apt to complain of their lot, especially when deprived of the indulgences of home. . . . I had for some time been dissatisfied with my situation, and was desirous of some change. I had made frequent complaints of a grievous nature to my father; but he paid no attention to them, supposing that I had no just cause for them, and that they arose merely from a spirit of discontent which would soon subside. . . . Expressions of exasperated feeling against the government of Great Britain, which had for a long time been indulged and pretty freely expressed, were now continually heard from the mouths of all classes. . . . It is perfectly natural that the spirit of insubordination, that prevailed, should spread among the younger members of the community. . . . I, and other boys situated similarly to myself, thought we had wrongs to be redressed; rights to be maintained; and, as no one appeared disposed to act the part of a redresser, it was our duty and our privilege to assert our own rights. We made a direct application of the doctrines we daily heard, in relation to the oppression of the mother country, to our own circumstances; and thought that we were more oppressed than our fathers were. I thought that I was doing myself great injustice by remaining in bondage, when I ought to go free; and that the time was come, when I should liberate myself from the thraldom of others, and set up a government of my own.[48]

What follows is formulaic in terms of developing a set pattern for political socialization and coming of age. In 1775 Fox seeks a friend and finds one in an older boy (like Rab Silsbee in *Johnny Tremain*), and he draws a contrast between the cautious outlook of older people and the gutsy recklessness of younger ones. Next, at age twelve we get a miniature version of the prodigal's return; and then, late in 1775, he enters into a four-year apprenticeship, which ends in 1779 when he is almost sixteen. In September of that year he joins the militia as a substitute for his employer; and in 1780 he goes to sea—lured by a recruiting officer who entices apprentices with bad masters to desert them in favor of the navy. He is captured, however, and remains a prisoner on the infamous *Jersey*, a vile British prison ship. Following a fifty-three-page description of his captivity, Fox is eventually released; and in 1783 he is reunited with his family once again. He had been away for three years, refers to himself as "the poor wandering boy," returns to Mr. Bosson's service, and remains with him until the age of twenty-one, when he sets up his own business and lives happily ever after—or at least until 1843 when he dies at the ripe old age of eighty.[49]

It is all there. Rites of passage serve to demarcate transitions between the so-called fixed or stable stages of the life cycle. The notion of a stage of being, or "state," may apply to an individual or to an entire community at a given time. And, as Victor Turner suggests, "a transition has different cultural properties from those of a state." It is more than fortuitous, by the way, that Fox should suggest during the 1830s that the Revolution encouraged youthful autonomy at the expense of parental authority. Many Americans of the Jacksonian era wanted to clarify their relationship to the Founding Fathers. What that involved, more particularly, was the need to strike a proper balance between respect for the founders, on the one hand, and to create a new, autonomous identity for themselves on the other. This is what Cooper's *Satanstoe* was all about: "the true character of the rising generation in the colony of New York."[50]

Once this leitmotif had been established, it continued to surface in every period. Chapter 20 in *Janice Meredith* (1899) is entitled "The Logic of Honoured Parents and Dutiful Children." Robert Rogers is built up to monumental proportions in the first half of *Northwest Passage* (1937), so that his disintegration during the second half will occasion disillusionment in young Langdon Towne. That disillusionment sets Langdon psychologically free, and permits him to achieve his own very different identity as an artist—and eventually, therefore, to achieve his own maturity.[51] Such a transition is duplicated in the relationship between Aaron Burr and Charles Schuyler in Gore Vidal's *Burr*. Both of these immensely successful novels are concerned with the psychological burdens one generation confers upon another—most especially when the younger generation has been in awe of its mentors.

The historical realities that constitute the backdrop for our Revolutionary romances were not simply psychological realities. They seem to have been concretely demographic as well. There is reason to believe that, at least in New England, parental control over marriageable sons and daughters diminished after the mid-eighteenth century. There is also evidence that historical young men (as distinct from fictional ones) chafed under parental power during the 1770s and sought to accelerate the process whereby economic autonomy could be achieved. In various material respects, the war years helped them to accomplish this goal; and therefore many would later look back upon 1775–81 as a transitional phase in the maturation of American society.[52]

Several scholars have quite properly remarked that the concept of family served as "the very *lingua franca* of the Revolution," for it "linked individual psychology to political action in historical reality."[53] When historical fiction came to be written a generation afterwards, it seemed perfectly natural to use family politics as a symptomatic metaphor. Quite early in *Lionel Lincoln* (1825), an old man declares that he has "noted the increase of the town as the parent notes the increasing stature of his child." Not long thereafter, the authorial voice explains that "from 1763 to the period of our tale, all the younger part of the population of the provinces had grown into manhood, but they were no longer imbued with that profound respect for the mother country which had been transmitted from their ancestors." The cause and the consequences were both entirely clear: "A youth who casts off the trammels of his guardians is not apt to doubt his ability to govern himself. England has held these colonies so long in leading-strings, that she forgets her offspring is able to go alone."[54]

Dr. Samuel Johnson once remarked, referring to the relationship between fiction and reality, that "imitations produce pain or pleasure, not because they are mistaken for realities, but because they bring realities to mind."[55] Accordingly, we would be well advised to bear in mind that apprenticeship as a social institution—as a customary means of compulsory recruitment for the labor force—was already in decline during the final decades of the colonial period. We would also be wise to recall that in the years after 1815 it became common for some Americans to refer to Indians as their "red children," thereby invoking a paternalistic role for white authorities.[56]

Which brings us to the critical question of whether the American Revolution was in reality a *rite de passage*. Or, putting the matter more modestly, to what degree did the Revolution actually function as a coming of age? We must step back in order to seek some perspective, reminding ourselves as we do so of the contrast between the relative orderliness of traditional art and the actual disorder of life. So many of these novels tend to present the Revolution as a neatly wrapped package with no loose ends. How far, then, has the general public been pulled toward a simplistic presentation of our national origins?

"When this New World awoke to man's estate"

ONE MUST BEGIN by admitting that there is a very large grain of truth to this tale we have been told so often. The historical prototype of Kennedy's "Horse-Shoe" Robinson was in fact born in 1759 in Virginia. In 1776, at the age of seventeen, he enlisted in the Continental army, performed some heroics during the war, grew up with the country, and died in 1838 at the age of seventy-nine.[57] Just as young Douw Mauverensen serves as an aide to General Schuyler in Harold Frederic's *In the Valley*, and later to General Herkimer of the militia as well, so young Alexander Hamilton (born in 1757) served as an aide to George Washington; Aaron Burr (born in 1756) served Washington in 1776 and General Israel

Putnam subsequently; Rufus King (born in 1755) served as an aide to General John Glover; Morgan Lewis (born in 1754) served as an aide to General Horatio Gates; and Robert Troup (born in 1757) also served in 1777 as an aide to Gates. In almost every instance, a surrogate father and son relationship developed. The older man's wise tutelage would never be forgotten.[58]

The real-life case of Robert Troup is especially interesting. He was, in fact, orphaned at age ten, graduated from King's College (later Columbia) in 1774, joined the Continental army a year later (despite the opposition of his Loyalist relations), was captured at the Battle of Long Island, and remained a British prisoner from August 26 until December 10, 1776. During his captivity aboard *The Mentor,* Troup suffered great discomfort. Relatives visited him on the ship and urged him to renounce his foolish allegiance to the patriot cause. But the stalwart young man refused. In 1777, following his release in a prisoner exchange, Troup served under Gates through the Battle of Saratoga. In May 1777, when Troup was still only twenty, Gates sent him on a two-week journey alone through New York and New England in search of fresh supplies for the patriot forces. He succeeded, and upon his return to Albany Troup received the responsibility of transporting some thirty cannons, plus ammunition and supplies, from Albany to Fort George. In 1780, realizing that his commitment to the Whig cause meant an irrevocable breach with remaining members of his family, Troup confessed to James Duane: "The anxiety I feel at the melancholy Prospect of being separated, during Life, from all my nearest Relatives."[59]

As cultural anthropologists have explained, rites of separation are commonly followed after an appropriate interval by rites of incorporation that denote the individual's return from a trip or an ordeal in an altered condition of consciousness. Our novelists have often been explicit about the symbolic importance of a transformed individual's new beginning;[60] and there are, indeed, well-documented instances of such personal development among very ordinary soldiers and sailors during the War for Independence.[61] A case that subsequently acquired considerable importance in American folklore is that of Andrew Jackson, whose father died two months before Andrew's birth in 1767, and whose mother died in 1781, leaving him an orphan. That very same year

Jackson was badly wounded, captured by the British, imprisoned for several months, caught smallpox and suffered high fevers. Jackson's youth became legendary in his own lifetime, and I suspect that his experiences helped to make many a Revolutionary novel seem more historical as well as plausible to the reading public.[62]

Plausibility is one thing, however, and persistent popularity quite another. Why, we must ask, has this extended metaphor of the Revolution as *rite de passage* been so meaningful? Does it fulfill some special function in the national ideology? The answer is Yes, and it helps us to address the troublesome issue of uniqueness; for the literary genre we have been examining surely has no monopoly on heroes and heroines who come of age. Each of us can think of examples elsewhere in our own literature as well as in those of other societies, particularly the *Bildungsroman*—the educational novel in which we learn of a young person's growth in self-awareness. To my view, however, such books as *The Sorrows of Young Werther* seek out the universality of a particularly poignant aspect of human experience. Moreover, they establish tensions between the young person and his society and then build much of their drama upon those tensions. The individual and society are customarily positioned at cross-purposes.[63]

One might also raise these related queries. Hasn't the coming-of-age motif been highly visible in modern war novels? Isn't *The Red Badge of Courage* (1895) usually regarded as a tale of initiation? Isn't it true that by enduring the trials of warfare such beardless youths are preparing for adulthood? Yes, but modern war novels are also decidedly different. Why?

- Because they so often make the point that it is young men who fight their nations' wars, which in turn are precipitated by the collective failures of the generation in power. In other words, immature soldiers must indemnify with their bodies and their lives the sins of their fathers. The generation in power has caused crises that can only be resolved with bloodshed. By contrast, that is normally not the *rite de passage* rationale in our Revolutionary romances.

- Because they generally make the point that going to war is a primary *and irreversible* kind of passage from home into the great world beyond. In our romances, by contrast, the hero is often reintegrated into his family and community.

• Because so often these modern forms of war fiction are really what W. M. Frohock has called "novels of erosion," i.e., that the experience of initiation commonly ends disastrously for the quester. Take the characteristic example of James Jones's *From Here to Eternity* (1951). For the hero, Robert E. Lee Prewitt, preparation for manhood is impossible because he has self-destructive tendencies. Every action moves him inexorably toward death. Like so many other heroes in the modern war novel, Prewitt's initiation turns out to be a passage toward alienation, disintegration, and fatality. By contrast, as we have seen, that has not been true of mainstream fiction about the American Revolution. The reason is very simply because the Revolution itself is regarded as an integrative and creative event, rather than a constrictive or destructive one.

• Because the modern *Bildungsroman* usually reaches a climactic moment of realization in which self-recognition is the crucial component. In the Revolutionary romances, by contrast, self-knowledge is much less important than acknowledgment by society of the individual's maturation. The individual's *rite de passage* is a paradigm of the larger society's coming of age. So often in twentieth-century war novels, moreover, the point is made emphatically that the human predicament universally may have passed beyond the point of no return. They plot the dehumanization of mankind as a ubiquitous phenomenon.[64]

In the novels we have been examining, the authors are not at all interested in the universality of human experience. Their heroes' *rites de passage* are meant to analogize God's chosen children coming of age, and in the process becoming a people. By understanding the aspiring colonial adolescent, we are supposed to acquire an empathetic knowledge of the single most critical moment in our own national history. Far from being a *Bildungsroman, Johnny Tremain* is offered as a personalization of Revolutionary Boston and its inevitable destiny; and the success of Esther Forbes's tale has been phenomenal. Since its publication in 1943, *Johnny Tremain* has sold more than two million copies, has been made into a full-length film (by Walt Disney), and adapted for television as well.[65] Its plot, quite simply, is an epitome of the American Revolution as *rite de passage.* I need not recite all the details here; but the book, which won the John Newbery Medal as "the most distinguished contribution to American literature for children in the year of its publication," and has had at least equal appeal for adults, encapsulates the dominant view of our Revolution in American popular culture.

Johnny was born in 1759, and is nearly fourteen when the book opens in 1772. We are given constant anticipations of what will happen when Johnny is "man-grown." His transformation really starts when he burns his hand severely with molten silver. Looking into the bedroom where he convalesced, he reflects that "in a way he had died in that room; at least something had happened and the bright little silversmith's apprentice was no more. He stood here again at the threshold, but now he was somebody else."[66]

Johnny's time of troubles and his symbolic rebirth coincide exactly with that of the colonies. The winter of 1773–4 is pivotal. As the pretty Cilla says to Johnny: "This is the end. The end of one thing—the beginning of something else . . . there is going to be a war—civil war."[67] Later on, in 1775, a woman asks Johnny his age. When he tells her "sixteen," she replies, "And what's that—a boy or a man?" He laughs. "A boy in time of peace and a man in time of war." At the end Miss Forbes refers more and more to manhood, not merely Johnny's achieving it, but his passing through a crisis of confidence about courage, manliness, and even the acceptance of death in a just cause. The book's last words, "A man can stand up," provide a residual refrain throughout.[68]

The fact that Johnny discovers his parentage and true identity in 1775, at the age of sixteen, is quite obviously symbolic though not nearly so heavy-handed as my flat statement of it might sound. Likewise the fact that his tragic injury forces him to rethink his calling. And likewise the fact that all these personal troubles of 1772–5 have served to prepare him for Lexington, Concord, Independence, and a brave new world beyond that. He has undergone the psychic experience required to transform a boorish, socially inferior adolescent provincial into a militant, morally superior young American.[69]

A book like *Johnny Tremain* is so central to an understanding of the national ideology, and is so symptomatic of its place in the popular culture, because it powerfully reinforces what C. Vann Woodward has recently called "the myth of America as the land of youth." Or, as Oscar Wilde once remarked, "the youth of America is their oldest tradition. It has been going on for three hundred years."[70] That tradition has been expressed more explicitly at certain moments in time than at others—the Young America movement of the 1840s comes immediately to mind, for instance—yet overall our citizens have been more inclined to admire Hebe, the goddess of youth, than to summon Clio, the muse of history.[71] It marked a significant shift, I suspect, when an essayist declared in 1864 that "the nation in its childhood needed a paternal Washington; but now it has arrived at manhood, and it requires, not a great leader, but a magistrate willing himself to be led."[72]

We have been aware for quite some time that the Revolutionary generation played frequent variations on John Locke's theme that a maturing young man ought not to obey his father if his father should "treat him still as a boy." But what is equally striking, perhaps even more so, is how that theme was reechoed in various ways for two centuries thereafter. Lévi-Strauss has observed that a "myth grows spiral-wise until the intellectual impulse which has produced it is exhausted."[73] In the United States, however, the myth has outlived its original intellectual impulse precisely because the myth has become an integral part of our national ideology.

Although the *rite de passage* theme predominates in our mainstream Revolutionary romances, as we have seen, that theme has also been powerfully reinforced by non-fiction statements in American political rhetoric.

• Thus Edward Everett in 1826: "When the rising state has passed the period of adolescence, the only alternative which remains, is that of a peaceable separation, or a convulsive rupture. . . . [Great Britain] never asked the great questions, whether nations, like man, have not their principles of growth. . . . They did not inquire . . . whether it were practicable, to give law across the Atlantic, to a people . . . rocked in the cradle of liberty."[74]

• Thus Frederick Douglass in 1852: "Seventy-six years, though a good old age for a man, is but a mere speck in the life of a nation. Three score years and ten is the allotted time for individual men; but nations number their years by thousands. According to this fact, you are, even now, only in the beginning of your national career, still lingering in the period of childhood. . . . There is consolation in the thought that America is young."[75]

• Thus George Fitzhugh in 1867: "Every child and every chicken, that, getting old enough and strong enough to take care of itself, quits its parents and sets up for itself, is quite as singular and admirable a spectacle as that of the thirteen adult States of America solemnly resolving to cut loose from the state of pupilage and dependence, from their parent England, and ever thereafter to enjoy the rights of independent manhood. . . . It had nothing poetic or dramatic about it. A birth, a christening, a circumcision, or the donning of the *'toga virilis,'* in fact, anything that marked an epoch in life, was quite as admirable as this weaning of the American calf from its transatlantic dam."[76]

When a particular motif becomes formulaic in a society's impulse for cultural expression, we may assume that it represents an embodiment of national values and mythical archetypes.[77] Francis Hopkinson, a participant in the Revolution, initiated this particular impulse in American poetry with "The Daughter's Rebellion." It begins,

When fair Columbia was a child,
And Mother Britain on her smil'd
With kind regard, and strok'd her head,
And gave her dolls and gingerbread . . .

and later continues,

But when at puberty arriv'd . . .
And dared to argue with her mother—
Contended pertly, that the nurse,
Should not be keeper of the purse;
But that herself, now older grown,
Would have a pocket of her own.[78]

Thomas Buchanan Read perpetuated this trope in 1861–2 with his massive work, "The Wagoner of the Alleghanies. A Poem of the Days of Seventy-Six." In it, Edgar is a young man who rebels against his father and fights on the patriot side at the Battle of Brandywine. Another young lad is called an eaglet, and he joins Ringbolt, the wild wagoner, with his fierce band of "mountain eagles."[79] In 1875 James Russell Lowell's important commemorative poem, "Under the Old Elm," made this imagery even more explicit for the Centennial reading public.

Never to see a nation born
Hath been given to mortal man,
Unless to those who, on that summer morn,
Gazed silent when the great Virginian
Unsheathed the sword whose fatal flash
Shot union through the incoherent clash. . . .

Out of that scabbard sprang, as from its womb,
Nebulous at first but hardening to a star,

Through mutual share of sunburst and of gloom,
The common faith that made us what we are.

That lifted blade transformed our jangling clans,
Till then provincial, to Americans,
And made a unity of wildering plans;
Here was the doom fixed: here is marked the date
When this New World awoke to man's estate.[80]

It is more difficult in iconography to convey this complex notion of the nation's coming of age; but American artists have found ways to do so nonetheless. The appeal of George Washington crossing the Delaware River late in 1776, I believe, derives in part from the symbolic nature of that crossing. For at that point Washington embarked upon a six-year period of prolonged liminality—seeking small victories, avoiding major defeats, and waiting for the perfect opportunity, which came to him at last in October 1781, at Yorktown.[81] Artists have been equally obsessed with a symbolic event that occurred at the close of the Revolutionary era, an event that in a sense marked its formal ending. I am referring to George Washington's northward journey in the spring of 1789, en route to his inauguration in New York City. His extraordinary reception at Trenton, New Jersey, on April 21 has had especial appeal in Revolutionary iconography.[82] The reasons, once again, have much to do with the theme of national *rite de passage.*

When Washington passed beneath that triumphal arch at Trenton, his period of quiescence at Mount Vernon came fully to an end; and so, too, did the final phase of awkwardness that the nation which was not-quite-yet-a-nation underwent between 1782 and 1789. Cultural anthropologists have suggested that the rituals that accompany puberty—the physiological coming of age—normally do not coincide with the suitable rituals for full social acceptance into the adult community. There are separate symbolic rituals because these are, in fact, sequential stages. Hence the need for rites of separation, followed, often quite a few years later, by rites of incorporation. During the nineteenth century, I believe, many Americans came to regard the years 1776 and 1789 in precisely these terms. First came the initial awakening to manhood, making Independence inevitable and justifiable. Then came the period of further growth necessary to reintegration. As one character remarks in *Drums*: " 'Future historians will divide my life into two epochs: the first devoted to starting a Revolution, the second'—he favored Johnny with an ironical smile—'to stopping it.' "[83]

Van Gennep and many of the social theorists who have taken off, so to speak, from his 1909 classic, *Les Rites de Passage,* emphasize the self-conscious, ceremonial aspect of these rituals for individuals. My concern is with a retrospective process of collective memory and myth-making that is partially inadvertent and partially intentional, societal as well as individual in its application, often implicit rather than explicit in its articulation, and based upon an event regarded as historically unique rather than being capable of repetition at regular intervals. The reasons for these aspects of our pattern are important, because they bring us to the dual question of why our authors have chosen to view the Revolution in this particular way, and what, if anything, is wrong with their vision?

"Men living in democratic societies . . . are forever varying, altering, and restoring secondary matters, but they are very careful not to touch fundamentals. They love change, but they dread revolutions"

THE ANSWER, in a nutshell, is that by and large our authors have been rather conservative in their social outlook; and the net result has been to de-revolutionize the American Revolution. Most of them personally enjoyed the past, which is scarcely surprising; but many were also inclined to yearn for an idealized past that was something of their own concoction. They tended to value social stability above social change, the unanticipated effects of which worried many of them. They were more inclined to interpret the meaning of Independence in terms of achieving political autonomy from Britain, than in terms of altered social relationships among Americans. As early as 1828, for example, James Fenimore Cooper has a character (with whom he is sympathetic) make the assertion that "we have ever been reformers rather than revolutionists. Our own struggle for independence was not in its aspect a revolution."[84]

How could this have come about in little more than one generation? Excesses of the French Revolution played a major part. Ralph Waldo Emerson's father, the Reverend William Emerson, would wag his warning finger at the horrors of the French Revolution and sneer: "See there, ye vaunting innovators, your wild and dreadful desolations!" In 1800 John Quincy Adams found it imperative to "rescue" the American Revolution "from the disgraceful imputation of having proceeded from the same principles as that of France."[85]

David Ramsay, who in 1789 made the first attempt at writing a comprehensive history of the American Revolution, revealed a characteristic ambivalence as his volumes went through several editions during the 1790s. He did not deny our Revolutionary origins, and upheld the right of revolution in principle: "The right of the people to resist their rulers, when invading their liberties, forms the corner stone of the American republics." He had to acknowledge, however, that "to overset an established government, unhinges many of those principles which bind individuals to each other." The troublesome thing about the right of revolution, he conceded, was that "this principle, though just in itself, is not favourable to the tranquillity of present establishments."[86]

After the 1780s we increasingly find expressions of approval for *our* Revolution, but for no other. Marvin Meyers has pointed out that to James Madison, writing as *Publius,* "the founding was a gentle revolution to end all revolutions." In 1857 Rufus Choate distinguished between two types of revolution: destructive and bloody ones filled with terror, which were not good; and those "in which a nation begins," which he approved.[87] By the mid-nineteenth century, as David Potter observed, "the only revolutions with which the American people could feel completely satisfied were the ones that did not succeed. After every revolution that failed, we were free to assume that its success would have fulfilled our ideals and were free to extend our hospitality to the revolutionists who were no longer welcome at home."[88] And by the later 1850s there were not only southerners repudiating Thomas Jefferson as "the inaugurator of anarchy," and the Declaration of Independence as a collection of "powder-cask abstractions," but northerners as well who could scold the new Republican party for basing its platform on "the glittering and sounding generalities of natural rights which make up the Declaration of Independence."[89]

"Natural rights." "The rights of man." How archaic and naïve those phrases had begun to sound; and how soon they came to be repudiated in certain circles. They had been at the epicenter of American ideology in Revolutionary times. Philip Freneau wrote an ode in 1793 entitled "God Save the Rights of Man," and David Ramsay announced America's mission a year later: "To prove the virtues of republicanism, to assert the Rights of Man, and to make society better."[90] In the last letter ever written by Thomas Jefferson, he reaffirmed the "rights of man"; and on occasion in the century and a half since 1826, our imaginative writers have reasserted the centrality of natural rights and the rights of man to the meaning of our Revolutionary experience.[91] More and more often, however, the rights of man were referred to pejoratively—culminating, I suppose, with Irving Babbitt's crack, made in 1924, that America should substitute "the doctrine of the right man for the doctrine of the rights of man."[92]

Perhaps it was inevitable, as property rights in a bourgeois society came to be cherished more than human rights, that the American Revolution would be identified less with the rights of man than with the nation's rite of passage. Perhaps there is an inescapable paradox to the development of national tradition in a society whose origins were Revolutionary, because in order to achieve a sense of tradition it was necessary to minimize the most revolutionary aspects of the Revolution.[93] In other words, as the American people put more and more distance between themselves and their Revolution, and as that Revolution came to be regarded as the determinative event in our evolution as a state, limitations had to be imposed upon what could or could not be justified in the name of Revolution. As S. N. Eisenstadt has explained,

> traditional societies all share in common the acceptance of tradition, the givenness of some actual or symbolic past event, order or figure as the major focus of their collective identity; as the delineator of the scope and nature of their social and cultural order, and as ultimate legitimator of change and of the limits of innovation. Tradition not only serves as a symbol of continuity, it delineates the legitimate limits of creativity and innovation and is the major criterion of their legitimacy.[94]

Quite a literature has been developed in the past two decades about "traditional societies." We have learned how they may gradually be modernized, and even become "post-traditional." What makes the United States somewhat peculiar and certainly different, however, is that it began as a modern society and subsequently needed to acquire or define its traditions; but that proved to be a fairly slow process. One might argue that many traditions did not really begin to take form until our second century as a nation (1876–1976); and still others, such as a constitutional commitment to equality, remained ambiguous until at least 1954. As palpable traditions did begin to emerge, and as the society became somewhat more tradition-oriented, it also seemed more conservative in certain critical respects. One important consequence has been to place us, from time to time, in the awkward position of being—or seeming to be—in conflict with our own inherited value system. We continue at appropriate moments to invoke the principles of 1776, and yet we have tended to oppose anti-colonial rebellions and wars of liberation in the so-called Third World. Although we have certainly become more modern in a technological sense—our capacity to manipulate nature is truly extraordinary—we have also become more traditional in a political sense. Some would say for good cause: that we cherish the stability and viability of our governmental system, and are determined to preserve it.[95]

As Edward Shils has explained, "it takes some time until people become aware of how much they have departed from the previously prevailing tradition."[96] Andrew Dickson White felt no awkwardness in 1890 when he expressed his preference for revolutions "which go backward." No one had a tad of embarrassment about denigrating the Declaration of Independence during those years. And, as Gabriel Kolko has written, "the problem of the emergence of a world Left and revolution was one that transcended the intellectual equipment with which the United States entered the twentieth century and World War One."[97] Not until the 1930s did intellectuals begin to remark upon the contradictions within our quasi-Revolutionary ideology; and only then would they look about for some way to reconcile or reintegrate national tradition with actual practice.[98]

Against this contextual backdrop, then, we can better understand the conservatism of our novelists, and appreciate their use of the *rite de passage* metaphor as a means of replacing revolution with evolution. James Fenimore Cooper loved "the *happy past,*" and has one character in *Satanstoe* declare that "we of New York are content to do as our ancestors have done before us."[99] Cooper wrote that novel, in part, to vindicate claims of the landlord class in New York's rent war of the 1830s and 1840s. As he explained to his British publisher,

> "The Family of Littlepage" will form three complete Tales. . . . I divide the subjects into the "Colony," "Revolution" and "Republic," carrying the same family, the same localities, and same *things* generally through the three different books, but exhibiting the changes produced by time, &c. . . . In the "Republic" we shall have the present aspect of things, with an exhibition of the Anti-Rent commotion that now exists among us, and which certainly threatens the destruction of our system.[100]

Cooper's friend, James Kirke Paulding, was in some respects less conservative. Yet his Revolutionary novels also conveyed a wistful longing for earlier days, warned against the moral perils of modern prosperity, defended the institution of slavery, and expressed a strong preference for the law and order of settled times as against the social confusion of rebellious times.[101] And William Gilmore Simms, as we have already seen, encouraged southerners to utilize their past in order to defend their fragile traditions and protect them from change or destruction.

The novelists of our second phase, 1895–1909, were even less ambiguous in their social conservatism. *A Lover's Revolt,* by John William DeForest, explicitly disapproved of abolitionists and the idea of equality, approved of social deference and the safeguarding of property rights, and yearned for the expansion of an Anglo-Saxon yeoman class: industrious, virtuous, literate, and temperate. When S. Weir Mitchell wrote *The Adventures of François,* in 1896, he described a clever thief who helps an aristocratic family to escape during the French Revolution. Mitchell's sympathies were unmistakably with the beleaguered nobility, for he regarded the French Revolution as a vulgar event. In *Hugh Wynne, Free Quaker,* he makes the point that principles of aristocracy and democracy can co-exist in the same society, that a democracy requires real leadership which only an élite can produce, and that ordinary soldiers can be devoted to an aloof but inspired leader.[102] Mitchell's last historical novel, *The Red City* (1907), is set in Philadelphia during George Washington's second presidential administration, where Hugh Wynne has now become the successful head of a shipping firm.

Who was Dr. S. Weir Mitchell, anyway, and what were his values? During the period 1870–1914 he became Philadelphia's leading citizen, and utterly dominated its social upper crust. The folks at Rittenhouse Square regarded him as a genius—the most versatile American since Benjamin Franklin—and compared *Hugh Wynne* favorably to *Henry Esmond.* A proper Philadelphian, Mitchell went to Newport every summer between 1844 and 1891. Thereafter he went to Bar Harbor in order to avoid the *nouveaux riches* who had begun flocking to Newport. More than proper, he was deeply conservative as well.[103]

In our third phase, 1933–48, there is less of a conservative consensus among the novelists; but no lack of conservatism, nonetheless. Kenneth Roberts inserts a little diatribe against communistic practices among the Indians. He has lovable old "Doc" ridicule egalitarianism and complain that "America's a nation of shopkeepers!" In *Northwest Passage* there is even a recurrent undertone of anti-Semitism.[104]

Frederic Van de Water (1890–1968), a newspaperman from New Jersey, purchased a farm at West Dummerston, Vermont, in 1932, moved his family there in 1934, began to delve into Vermont history, and for a quarter century thereafter became the state's foremost spokesman. After publishing *The Reluctant Republic,* a history, in 1941, he followed with four historical novels set in Vermont during the period 1770–91. Van de Water admired rugged individualism, perceived a special Vermont character in that mold, and sketched an archetypal Vermonter—cut from granite and just as tough.[105]

Francis Van Wyck Mason was born at Boston in 1901, became an importer of embroidered goods, rugs, and antique books after his graduation from Harvard. By the 1930s he had turned his talents to historical fiction, mainly about the Revolutionary era. He soon moved to Southampton, Bermuda, where he became president of the American Society. Mason listed himself in *Who's Who* as a Republican and an Episcopalian.[106]

What so many of these novelists share in common is a strong sense of their own lineage, and therefore of personal as well as cultural and communal involvement in the American Revolution.

Regarding that event as a *rite de passage* helped to make the process of Americanization rather like a fraternity initiation. They allowed the possibility that some persons might join the United States later than others; but older members should make the rules, wield the power, and carefully screen potential new members. William Gilmore Simms's family had been deeply involved on the patriot side in the War for Independence. Harold Frederic proudly observed that "all four of my great-grandfathers had borne arms in the Revolutionary War, and one of them indeed somewhat indefinitely expanded his record by fighting on both sides."[107]

Winston Churchill was descended from several prominent families, and delighted in having illustrious colonial forebears. He admired those fortunate enough to have old-family ties, and married a wealthy and prominent St. Louis woman. Edward A. Uffington Valentine infuriated Churchill by writing an arch review of *Richard Carvel* that contained this condescending compliment: "For a man not to the manner born, and not an inheritor of the spirit and tradition of the old colonial town [i.e., Annapolis] . . . the writer has done remarkably well." Churchill was being stigmatized on account of his birthplace, St. Louis, in the uncultivated (and worse, new) Middle West.[108]

Arthur Guiterman, who wrote *Death and General Putnam and 101 Other Poems* (1935), had great-grandfathers buried in the Ohio Valley and grew up loving Cooper's novels. Inglis Fletcher, the author of half a dozen novels set in Revolutionary Carolina, tells us proudly in her autobiography that "North Carolina had been the home of my mother's people; my grandfather had been born in Tyrrell County, on the opposite side of Albemarle Sound from Edenton. His father and his father's father, all the way back to 1684, had lived on Albemarle Sound near the mouth of the Scuppernong River." Subsequently, she describes a spring meeting of the Society of the Cincinnati, held at her "Bandon Plantation" near Edenton:

> A committee of the D.A.R. came out to supervise the food and see that wineglasses were placed at each sitting. The Cincinnati has a ritual about drink. . . . The guests wandered about the old house and the gardens. They examined ancient documents that some of them had brought. . . . They ate their food with pleasure and they toasted the early members,

those men who fought for the freedom we now enjoy. What interested me most was that these men whose ancestors had fought in the Revolution were men of substance in their own communities. These inheritors who sat at our tables were themselves carrying on the principles that their ancestors had fought for.[109]

Kenneth Roberts may well have been the most conservative and nationalistic of all these novelists in phase III. He could not understand why Prescott and Parkman chose to write about Mexico, Peru, and the French in North America. "I've had a theory for a great many years," he explained to one friend, "that a writer can write more effectively about his own people than he can about people that aren't in his blood. . . . My people have always lived in Maine. All of twenty years ago I started mousing around for something to write that would have my own sort of people in it." Roberts invested a great deal of psychic and physical energy—more than four years—in researching, writing, and rewriting *Northwest Passage.* He had high hopes for its literary and commercial success, hopes that turned out to be justified. But in 1936, soon after the manuscript had gone into production, Walter Edmonds published *Drums Along the Mohawk* to considerable acclaim. Roberts was furious, and consumed by jealousy. Here is a piece of his mind:

I wont discuss Edmonds with you. He gives me a dreadful pain in the neck, and his stuff is about as bogus as it comes. West had a series of new titles that he thought I ought to consider for Northwest Passage. These are: DRUMS, DRUMS ON A RAFT, DRUMS ALONG THE CONNECTICUT, DRUMS BEFORE TICONDEROGA, DRUMS BEFORE BREAKFAST, DRUMS BE DAMNED and DRUMMING WITH ROGERS. His idea is that an historical novel, to be successful, must have the word Drums in its title. Maybe so: I don't know: all I do know is that Edmonds bores me deeply.[110]

One other strand that ties together the conservatism of these novelists is their repeated criticism of so-called freedom-loving patriots who abused the liberties of those who disagreed with them. In *Mellichampe,* by William Gilmore Simms, a Tory relates that

My neighbors came to me at midnight—not as neighbors, but armed, and painted, and howling—at midnight. They broke into my dwelling—a small exercise of their newly-gotten liberty; they tore me from the bed where I was sleeping. . . . Hence it is, that I lift the sword, unsparingly to the last, against the wretches who taught me . . . of what nature was that boon of liberty which they promised, and which it was in the power of such monsters to bestow. (pp. 310–14)

Or in *The Tory Lover:* " 'You are Sons of Liberty, and yet you forbid liberty to others,' said the old gentlewoman" (p. 256). And in *Oliver Wiswell,* Judge Hendon says it loud and clear for Kenneth Roberts:

> We are the people who have land, belongings, position, and we're standing by our guns in opposition to the people who have nothing. We're the conservative people; and what has been true of conservative people in all ages and all lands is true of us. We dissent from extreme and injudicious measures, from violence, from oppression, from revolution, from reckless statements and misrepresentation. We can't stomach liars, bullies or demagogues, or leaders without experience, ability or sound judgment.[111]

What then, in the last analysis, is wrong with such a single-minded presentation of the American Revolution as the national coming of age? We have noted earlier its very real virtues, including the degree to which it anticipates our contemporary belief that a psychological transformation of the American mind was fundamental to the Revolution having occurred when it did, and in the form that it took.[112] What I find objectionable about this dominant motif in our historical fiction is, first of all, that it has been prompted by such conservative motives: by defensive nostalgia, by élitism, by national chauvinism, by a sense of our moral superiority as a people, and by a desire to de-revolutionize the American Revolution. Presenting our Revolution as *the* national rite of passage made it seem historically unique and non-replicable. One comes of age only once. Therefore, having had our revolution then (really a "reform movement," according to Cooper), we need not have another—ever again. Besides, they declared, it was a political revolution, and in no respect a social revolution. Moreover, it provided us with such a beautifully structured society, as well as such an ideal frame of government, that we will never require anything more than minor adjustments—some occasional fine-tuning.

The net effect of these novels has been to trivialize the American Revolution. It was a far more complex event than one ever glimpses in them. It had its conservative side, to be sure;[113] and insofar as the romances call our attention to the very considerable number of reluctant rebels, fiction may be said to have performed a real service. But it had its radical aspects, as well, and they have been slighted by the vast majority of our authors.[114] I object to their denial, or minimization, of the United States's Revolutionary origins. I object to a process of simplification that reduces the significance, grandeur, tragedy, and diversity of a major historical phenomenon to little more than a formulaic cliché.

Ultimately, however, as students of American thought and culture, we would be well advised to recall de Tocqueville's observation that "Revolutions, like love affairs, change your past." What this means in our context, I believe, is that imaginative writers have been perceiving the Revolution as a rite of passage for so long now that that tradition, that perception, has become virtually as important as the original Revolutionary realities. This tradition of the Revolution has been deeply ingrained in our cultural experience, and therefore constitutes a central part of our self-knowledge as a nation. The curious ways in which the Rights of Man came to be seen as the rites of passage have much to do, I think, with a profoundly complex pattern of cultural change that has taken place in the United States between 1776 and the present.[115]

CHAPTER SEVEN

IMAGINATION, TRADITION, AND NATIONAL CHARACTER

THE ESSENTIAL THRUST and implications of my material, hopefully, have now become clear; but perhaps a few summary paragraphs may be helpful at this point. I have suggested that a sense of tradition has been problematic in American culture: partially because of the powerful impetus for change, an enduring desire to break with the "burden of the past"; and partially because the circumstances of our nationality are linked up with a major revolution even though our society has become less and less revolutionary with the passage of time. One result has been a certain ambiguity about our Revolutionary origins. Another result has been the reductive inclination to simplify our past by flattening out the diversities and uncomfortable complexities. Still another has been the penchant for perceiving our Revolution as a "season of youth," and for neglecting those other aspects of our early experience that do not comport well with what we have become in the last century.

It seems significant to me that so many of the difficulties within our elusive sense of tradition derive from the competing pulls of élitism and egalitarianism. The latter is acceptable and admirable, by definition; the former is not. As Henry James put it in 1906, having just revisited the United States after being away for more than two decades: "What was taking place was a perpetual repudiation of the past, so far as there had been a past to repudiate. . . .

It is the huge democratic broom that has made the clearance" (*The American Scene*, pp. 53, 55).

So we have been uncertain how properly to praise the character of our Founding Fathers without enshrining them uncritically as demigods. On the other hand, we do not quite know how to humanize them without either demeaning or stripping them of their exemplary qualities. Similarly, we have not always been comfortable about the suitability of monuments and memorials in a society whose stated ethos, at least, is egalitarian. Likewise our discomfort with the shifting emphasis from Liberty to Prosperity once political security facilitated the full development of commercial tendencies in the United States.

Precisely because of those tendencies and opportunities, there were many who worried about our character in terms of ethics, integrity, and moral fiber. Precisely because of its centrality to American tradition—especially tradition as an instrument of political cohesion—the American Revolution had to be reshaped to suit the social needs and the mentality of later generations. All of which brings us to the purpose of this final chapter: a pulling together of these several strands by means of a series of four postscripts touching as many related issues. First, the problem of dissenting, or alternative, visions of the Revolution's meaning. Second, the state of Revolutionary perception today, during the Bicentennial era. Third, the tension between authentic, romantic, and symbolic impulses in the American imagination as it has confronted and articulated the Revolution. And fourth, the entangled relationship between perceptions of the national character, our sense of tradition, and the consequences of believing that our Revolutionary origins comprised, above all, a national *rite de passage*.

"What a sieve is history; only it lets out the grain, and retains the chaff"

HAS THERE BEEN no alternative reading of the American Revolution, no other imaginative perception of its meaning? Yes, we have in fact had some half a dozen significant authors who tried to offer dissenting versions. They are too few in number, however, too discontinuous in sequence, and too neglected by their contemporary popular cultures to comprise a nay-saying tradition. They are no more than disparate dissenters: writers with a vision of the Revolution's darker side, writers too thoughtful (and sometimes too cynical) simply to reaffirm the mainstream view of the American Revolution as a totally successful, national *rite de passage*.

Although they are few in number and their works (for the most part) had no great impact at the time of initial publication, we would be unwise to ignore them, in part because they provide an antiphonal voice to the tradition we have been examining, and in part because they have elicited somewhat greater interest long after their first appearance; but chiefly because they more nearly approximate historical reality than the dominant novels we have been examining at length. The latter look upon the Revolution through the eyes of Pollyanna. Yet Cassandra, too, must have her turn.

As we saw earlier in Chapter Two, there were occasional voices of criticism, and even satire, aimed at the affirmative Revolutionary tradition. During the later 1840s and 1850s, for example, a few souls dared to burlesque the customary Fourth of July oration.[1] Wendell Phillips rose at a gathering in Faneuil Hall, pointed to portraits of the Revolutionary heroes, and accused anti-abolitionists of being unfaithful to the spirit of 1776. John Greenleaf Whittier would complain in 1847 that Black veterans of the Revolution had been forgotten: "With here and there an exception, they have all passed away, and only some faint traditions linger among their descendants." Thomas Wentworth Higginson of Massachusetts considered himself a residual revolutionary. He declared in 1856 that "a single day in Kansas makes the American Revolution more intelligible than all Sparks and Hildreth can do."[2]

Criticism has also, on occasion, been aimed directly against the mainstream novels. In 1903, for instance, Herbert Croly referred to Winston Churchill's historical fiction as "a kindergarten way of writing history," and blasted *The Conqueror*, Gertrude Atherton's fictionalized biography of Alexander Hamilton, as "a failure."[3] But there has not been very much such criticism, and what little appeared caused about as much notice as a gnat on an elephant's hide. Criticism can, however, take the form of an alternative statement; and that is precisely what Herman Melville, Nathaniel

Hawthorne, Edward Bellamy, William Carlos Williams, Howard Fast, and Gore Vidal all set out to do—in various ways and with varying degrees of success.

Melville's *Israel Potter: His Fifty Years of Exile* began to appear in July 1854 in serialized form in *Putnam's Monthly Magazine.* In March 1855 it was published as a book, contemptuously dedicated to "His Highness the Bunker Hill Monument." Still smarting from the public's three-year neglect of *Moby Dick,* Melville meant his *Israel Potter* to be sarcastic, a parody of patriotism; yet most reviewers did not quite know what to make of this picaresque tale. In essence it is the fable of a young Whig who fights at Bunker Hill, but then undergoes a very long series of misadventures. He spends four decades as a destitute wanderer abroad, woefully out of place in England; and returns to Boston only as a seventy-nine-year-old veteran on July 4, 1826. He comes back at last to his boyhood home in the Housatonic Valley, finds that nothing remains but a bit of the threshold, and promptly expires.[4]

Melville quite obviously wished to comment upon the subversion of Revolutionary ideals and of the putative national character. He sketched Benjamin Franklin, John Paul Jones, and Ethan Allen in strokes that range from snide to nasty. He caused Israel to encounter serious problems of class-consciousness and snobbery. The poor fellow undergoes various forms of identity confusion. When Israel declares that his shipboard station is the maintop, an officer replies: "Belong to the maintop? Why, these men here say you have been trying to belong to the foretop, and the mizzentop, and the forecastle, and the hold, and the waist, and every other part of the ship" (pp. 180–1). When Israel does at last return, after almost half a century of wandering, he submits a petition for a pension based upon his role in the Revolutionary War. His petition is denied, however, and like Melville he learns what it means to be rejected by the people of the United States.

Most important of all, this novel has the makings of a conventional *rite de passage* saga. In about 1768 or 1769, Israel "emancipated himself from his sire."

> He continued in the enjoyment of parental love till the age of eighteen, when, having formed an attachment for a neighbor's daughter—for some reason, not deemed a suitable match by his father—he was severely reprimanded, warned to discontinue his visits, and threatened with some disgraceful punishment in case he persisted.

Israel leaves home in order to escape the tyranny of his father and rejection as a suitor.[5] Once the war ends, however, Israel's phase of "liminality" does not conclude as it ought to. He is regarded as a "vagabond claiming fraternity, and seeking to palm himself off upon decent society." He finds himself an exile rather than the yeoman farmer of his dreams. He becomes impoverished rather than prosperous. He achieves gloom rather than glory, endless misfortune rather than happiness. Instead of going West and growing up with the country, he goes East to England—a reversion instead of the anticipated progression.[6]

Edward Bellamy's *The Duke of Stockbridge. A Romance of Shays Rebellion* was first serialized in a newspaper version in 1879. Its impact was so slight, however, that it did not appear in book form until 1901—and then bowdlerized. Like *Israel Potter,* it is a story of thwarted love; and like Israel, Perez Hamlin, the hero, cannot fulfill his goal of going West to become a yeoman farmer. He cannot because he is killed in the final pitched battle of Shays' Rebellion.[7] Like Melville, Bellamy indicated that the Revolution brought poverty rather than prosperity to many virtuous Whigs. Patriot heroes suffer hardship and languish in prison after the war. Class-consciousness increases and a civil war begins in Massachusetts. Again like Melville, Bellamy wanted us to know that they did not all live happily ever after.[8]

What we have, once more, is an implicit variation on the *rite de passage* motif. When Perez first returns to his Berkshire village in 1786, having been away since early in the War of Independence, his mother immediately "was studying out in the stern face of the man, the lineaments of the boy whose soldier's belt she had buckled round him nine years before." The promise implied in Hamlin's coming of age turns out to be a sham—a hollow promise—for his maturation could *not* be a metaphor for that of the nation as a whole. At least, not the formulaic metaphor with which we have become so familiar.

> The army of the revolution had been for its officers and more intelligent element, a famous school of democratic ideas. Perez was only one of thousands, who came home deeply imbued with principles of social equality; principles, which, despite finely phrased manifestoes and declarations of independence, were destined to work like a slow leaven for generations yet, ere they transformed the oligarchical system of colonial society, into the democracy of our day. . . . The democratic impressions

they had there received, now that they had returned home, served only to exasperate them against the pretensions of the superior class, without availing to eradicate their inbred instincts of servility in the presence of the very men they hated.[9]

In many of the mainstream novels—the yea-saying ones that look upon the Revolution and find it altogether good—this question arises: Will our hero (or heroine) lose hope in the Revolution during its darkest hour? That is so often George Washington's despair at Valley Forge, or Thomas Jefferson's crisis in *The Common Glory*. But Bellamy and Melville have turned the question inside out, so that it becomes: Will the Revolution subsequently betray our hero's faith in its ideals? Will the baser and more selfish tendencies of American society disappoint his altruistic aspirations?

Seven years before *The Duke of Stockbridge* first appeared, Nathaniel Hawthorne's family published a romance he had worked on between 1861 and 1863, a romance that remained unfinished at the time of his death in 1864. *Septimius Felton* unquestionably belongs to our dissenting category. It acknowledges the customary conventions that Cooper's generation had established, yet responds with an alternative vision. The war will make a man out of Robert Hagburn, who matures rapidly in the crisis of 1775–6. But that same war is a bewilderment to Septimius (who seems to have no parents). Robert says to him,

> I never saw such a discontented, unhappy-looking fellow as you are. You have had a harder time in peace than I in war. You have not found what you seek, whatever that may be. Take my advice. . . . [The war] is worth living for, just to have the chance to die so well as a man may in these days. Come, be a soldier. Be a chaplain, since your education lies that way.[10]

Septimius Felton opens in April 1775. The young man whose name provides the title has recently graduated from Harvard College and is aiming at the ministry. He is neither an ideologue nor a fighting man, but rather a scholar who would like to live forever. He detests war because of its tendency to curtail lives. As he says to himself, "What matters a little tyranny in so short a life?" But how is a man of thought supposed to function in a time of intense action? What is he to do when "his manhood felt a call upon it not to skulk in obscurity from an open enemy"? Then Hawthorne gives us, with startling clarity, the finest passage in all these novels on what the Revolution must have been like, especially for someone racked by self-doubt and ambivalence.

Indeed, this war, in which the country was so earnestly and enthusiastically engaged, had perhaps an influence on Septimius's state of mind, for it put everybody into an exaggerated and unnatural state, united enthusiasms of all sorts, heightened everybody either into its own heroism or into the peculiar madness to which each person was inclined; and Septimius walked so much the more wildly on his lonely course, because the people were going enthusiastically on another. In times of revolution and public disturbance all absurdities are more unrestrained; the measure of calm sense, the habits, the orderly decency, are partially lost. More people become insane, I should suppose; offences against public morality, female license, are more numerous; suicides, murders, all ungovernable outbreaks of men's thoughts, embodying themselves in wild acts, take place more frequently, and with less horror to the lookers-on.[11]

In some degree, needless to say, Hawthorne may also have been passing judgment on the psychic consequences of the current Civil War; and his obsession with immortality in this book must have emanated from premonitions of his own impending death. Still, *Septimius Felton* stands as his sole attempt to comment upon the meaning of the American Revolution in a full-length novel. Much earlier, of course, in 1832, the young Hawthorne had published a short story called "My Kinsman, Major Molineux," the piece about which Mrs. Q. D. Leavis made a percipient remark in 1951: "This remarkable tale might have been less commonly overlooked or misunderstood if it had had a sub-title, such as Hawthorne often provided by way of a hint. It could do with some such explanatory subtitle as 'America Comes of Age.' "[12]

There are many mysteries and ambiguities about this story, and in the past generation it has become the touchstone for a minor industry among literary critics. It is not explictly set in any city; it is ostensibly a story of the 1730s. Yet we tend to associate it with Boston just before the Revolution, and that is apparently what Hawthorne intended. It opens with young Robin, age eighteen, as the sole passenger on a ferry crossing to a New England port town. Robin has left his rural village home in order to seek his fortune. In the process he also seeks a kinsman believed to be influential. (Major Molineux and Robin's father are the sons of brothers, one of whom had emigrated to New England, the other having remained in England.)

The search, however, seems only to produce frustration heaped upon rude awakening. Robin is bullied and scorned. He sees his kinsman, at last, but in grave political peril: being tarred and feathered by an angry mob. Robin cannot seem to get guidance. He experiences awkwardness, ignorance, and confusion. "Am I here or there?" he cries out—the desperate plea of one who is buffeted betwixt and between. At the end, a helpful soul offers Robin this comfort: "Some few days hence, if you wish it, I will speed you on your journey. Or, if you prefer to remain with us, perhaps, as you are a shrewd youth, you may rise in the world without the help of your kinsman, Major Molineux." Robin's royalist kinsman would have been a hindrance—like Johnny Tremain's kinsman, Merchant Lyte—rather than a help. But unlike *Johnny Tremain*, in which there is no ambiguity about the forces of good and the forces of evil, Hawthorne's tale explores the painfully divided emotions of obedience and revolt, pity and terror, a mob demanding natural rights yet ritually usurping the authority and rights of others.[13]

In 1925, almost a century after Hawthorne began working on this story, William Carlos Williams wrote an essay and a little book, called *In the American Grain*, which sold poorly, fell out of print, and suffered from neglect for quite a long time. The essay, entitled "The Writers of the American Revolution," was not even published until 1954. Neither important nor unusual, it may be likened to the sketched thoughts of an artist preliminary to doing a much bigger scene.[14] On his large canvas, Williams wanted to show that failure is as much a part of our existence as success. Hence he anticipated Gore Vidal by admiring and devoting an entire chapter to Aaron Burr. He empathized with Burr for personal reasons, too, because he considered Burr (like himself) to be a voluptuary. George Washington and Benjamin Franklin, by contrast, achieved their successes at too high a cost: "the repression of a valuable, anarchic passion within in the case of Washington, the shutting out of the wild spirit of the American continent in the case of Franklin." Williams felt a special concern for episodes from our earlier history that did not fit the tired mold of inexorable success. He most admired those revolutionaries with a strong sense of personal freedom, and those with the courage to disregard public opinion. Above all, he sought freedom from history in order to liberate the imagination. He wanted tradition to inspire imagination rather than impede it.

> If history could be that which annihilated all memory of past things from our minds it would be a useful tyranny.
>
> But since it lives in us practically day by day we should fear it. But if it is, as it may be, a tyranny over the souls of the dead—and so the imaginations of the living—where lies our greatest well of inspiration, our greatest hope of freedom (since the future is totally blank, if not black) we should guard it doubly from the interlopers.
>
> You mean, tradition. Yes, nothing there is metaphysical. It is the better part of all of us.[15]

It is rather ironic that W. E. Woodward has acquired the reputation as our foremost historical "debunker" of the 1920s; for Woodward subsequently declared in his autobiography that he did not like being regarded as a debunker. "I am an admirer of George Washington," he insisted, "and there is not a debunking paragraph in the whole book."[16] William Carlos Williams was the *real* debunker of the 1920s; but he failed to make a dent in the Revolutionary tradition, and for important reasons that have been discussed in a more general context by Edward Shils.

> Much of the reception of beliefs inherited from the past is to be attributed simply to the massive fact of their presence, to their widespread acceptance by other persons to an extent which hampers the imaginative generation of plausible alternative beliefs. In any given particular situation in which long recurrent beliefs are widely accepted, this kind of reception, which we shall call "consensual reception," is probably a major factor in the acceptance of beliefs and norms which have been observed in previous generations and which are recommended traditionally by the elders to their juniors. In other words, this kind of reception reinforces reception on the basis of "pastness."[17]

Later in the same essay, Shils makes an important observation that can help us to understand why the Revolutionary perceptions of Howard Fast and Gore Vidal have enjoyed more commercial success than did those of Melville, Bellamy, Hawthorne, and Williams. Shils is talking about the writer's relationship to traditional forms in his own culture.

> If his creative powers are weak, he will accept what is given and work within it. If they are strong, he will modify the received genre as well as

express his own substantive viewpoint and sensibility. What he accomplishes depends on his capacity to form a coherent whole of what he accepts from what has come down to him as part of the corpus of traditional objectivations and what his own imaginative powers require. An inherited form, if it has had great works accomplished in it, does not simply disappear; it is discriminatingly assimilated and extended.[18]

Whereas *Israel Potter, The Duke of Stockbridge, Septimius Felton,* and *In the American Grain* tried to modify the received genre too vigorously and too soon, Fast and Vidal made larger concessions to tradition, and did so at a more auspicious time.

There can be no doubt about Fast's status as a dissenter. He was an outspoken Communist from the 1930s until his departure from the party in 1957, and he received the Stalin International Peace Prize in 1953. (During World War II he served on the overseas staff of the Office of War Information, then with a signal corps unit, and finally as a war correspondent in Southeast Asia.) In 1950 he openly expressed his contempt for

that group of writers who sell themselves as agents-extraordinary of monopoly capitalism. For them, the sky is the limit, whether they attempt some pretense of literary quality, as does Kenneth Roberts . . . or give up any and all pretensions of either literary quality or historical truth, as does Arthur Schlesinger, becoming, as he does in his latest hastily and badly written tract, *The Vital Center*, a shameless and sniveling tool of the *right*.[19]

Fast's own Revolutionary fiction, however, has always managed to strike a balance between the mainstream tradition, his individual impulse toward social criticism, and political imperatives of the moment. *The Unvanquished* concedes that George Washington "was not a revolutionist" by background, and that many a man who joined him "was neither an intellectual nor a revolutionary, but a man who loved action and excitement and the comradeship that went with a camp."[20] Nonetheless, Fast had total admiration for Washington and the wartime leadership he provided. Moreover, circumstances apparently transformed Washington and his associates, like Alexander Hamilton. "They were in a time between two eras, making the change, but divorced from what had been before them and from what came after them. They were revolutionists."[21]

Throughout this novel Fast adapts the *rite de passage* motif to his own purposes: that so many soldiers in Washington's army were only lads, that Hamilton and Burr were mere "boys" in 1776, and that Nathan Hale was just twenty-one when he died that same year. "He felt large and strong and important, and more a man than he ever had before in his twenty-one years." Ultimately, however, when Washington comes to reflect upon the meaning of his wartime loneliness and privation, he takes pride in something intangible, "which he could think of only as certain rights of man."[22]

In "Journey to Boston," a short story by Fast that is set in 1803, a veteran named Reuben Dover tries to relive his Revolutionary youth but finds that he cannot, and discovers that seeking to do so is a sad form of self-deception: in part because "youth is a land no one ever revisits," but even more because a less-than-Revolutionary nation had chosen to neglect the Revolutionary aspects of its origins. As the disillusioned Reuben writes in his journal: "I must take note of the way this nation has changed, so that the Young are not brought up with honor for those who took the situation as it was and made from it a Revolution."[23]

In *April Morning,* the story of fifteen-year-old Adam Cooper and his father at Lexington in 1775, Fast gives us the *rite de passage* formula in a neatly compressed but unvarnished form. Adam is humiliated because his father treats him as a boy. His mother makes constant reference to his being only a boy; but at Buckman's Tavern, predictably enough, "a boy went to bed and a man awakened." On the symbolic night of April 18, Adam signs the muster roll—a ritual act in which his father acquiesces. Adam has joined the militia, and the patriarchal Moses accepts it with a sense of inevitability. When Moses himself is killed in this first skirmish of independence, the Reverend Solomon Chandler tells Adam: "You've lost your youth and come to manhood, all in a few hours." When Adam responds with self-doubt, "I wish it was true that I have come to manhood," the clergyman consoles him. "Give it time."[24] Only an occasional comment upon the petit-bourgeois character of these minutemen gives one a hint that Fast is less than 100 percent in the mainstream tradition.[25]

The Hessian (1972), set in 1781, seems much more in character for Fast—even for the post-Communist Fast. Essentially an anti-war novel, it emphasizes the bestiality of war, the hypocrisy induced by war, and the psychic disorientation it causes ("I don't know what I believe anymore").[26] What makes the novel especially interesting, however, is the unusual identity of its narrator. Dr. Evan Feversham is a non-practicing Roman Catholic Englishman who came to the colonies in 1769: a total outsider, a man living in Ridgefield, Connecticut, but without any community or sense of community. He heals, and feels compassion. He is a just and cosmopolitan man. But he is also passionless because he lacks an ideology, marginal because he is essentially neutral, cruel because he is cynical.[27] In exploring the painful introspection of an intelligent, perceptive, but rootless man—a man incapable of belonging—Fast has written his most sophisticated novel of the Revolution. *The Hessian* is a provocative inquiry into the behavioral consequences of national character stereotypes; and the implication is clear that a society that could subscribe to myths of Hessian character in 1781 could also fight in Vietnam on the basis of mindless myths about "gooks."[28]

A year after *The Hessian* appeared, Gore Vidal brought out *Burr* (1973); and it remained the number-one national best-seller in fiction for eight months, right through the late summer of 1974. The book sold hotly for many reasons. In addition to being well written and often amusing, it also got a lot of advantageous publicity. But most of all, it seemed to be a Watergate *roman à clef.* Concerned with political duplicity, and deeply cynical in tone, the book declared over and over again that historical reality is not what it superficially seems to be.[29] Hypocrisy among so-called great men is the integrating theme; and the relationship between political morality and national character is *the* problematic issue to be explored. Burr recalls a dialogue he had with Alexander Hamilton in 1797:

> In the green shade we stopped close to the church wall, and Hamilton said something most odd. "I wonder sometimes if this is the right country for me."
>
> "You would prefer to live under the British crown?" I played with him.
>
> "Of course not! But there *is* something wrong here. I sense it everywhere. Don't you?"
>
> I shook my head and said what I believe to be true. "I sense nothing more than the ordinary busy-ness of men wanting to make a place for themselves. Some are simply busier than others, and so will take the higher ground. But it is no different here from what it is in London or what it was in Caesar's Rome."

Hamilton shook his head. "There is more to it than that, Burr. But then I have always thought we might be able to make something unique in this place."

"Our uniqueness is only geographical."

"No, it is moral. That is the secret to all greatness."

"Are great souls *ever* moral?"

"They are nothing else!" So spoke the seducer of Mrs. Reynolds. I should make it plain that I am not one to think such an intrigue of any *moral* importance—rather it was the way in which Hamilton revealed (revelled in?) a sordid seduction in order to cover up what Jefferson and Monroe went to their graves confident was dishonesty at the Treasury. Hamilton demonstrated a perverse—to say the least—morality. But of course his use of the word "moral" was practically theological in its implications; and mine is a secular brain.

Hamilton again thanked me most warmly for my good offices and we left the churchyard together, crossing the exact spot where seven years later I was to place him.[30]

Vidal's counter-traditional novel could be so successful because, for once, the national spirit in 1973–4 coincided with the appearance of this elegant guffaw at Uncle Sam's expense. American society was now in a masochistic mood, and Vidal was more than willing to play the sadist's role. The point, of course, is that he wasn't merely playing.

A more important point involves the timing of Vidal's book; for, in a sense, it inaugurated the Bicentennial in our popular culture. It did much to draw the nation's attention back to the two generations that followed 1776, and in so doing it mediated the distinction between mainstream Revolutionary novels and dissenting ones. By 1973–4, the mainstream had been discredited and the dissenting tradition had somehow become mainstream. This convergence of historical imagination with a national crisis of confidence had turned tradition topsy-turvy![31]

"The comfort of remembrance: a relic of the past to reassure them"

THE SARDONIC INTENT of Gore Vidal's *Burr* was understandably consistent with other neo-historical (or pseudo-historical?) effusions of the Vietnam era: cultural statements that used our Revolutionary tradition as a vehicle for contemporary social criticism. We have already looked at plays by William Gibson and Paul Foster, for example, written in 1967 and 1971.[32] We should also note the volume of twenty-three *George Washington Poems* by Diane Wakoski, filled with bitter whimsy, personal fantasy, and the irony of intentional anachronism. She is sarcastic about conventional patriotism, and mocks Washington's words that "there can only be peace/when we show that we are ready to fight for it." Wakoski seems to reiterate William Carlos Williams with the caustic comment: "George, you did all the right things, but you hardly seemed alive." And she concludes rather poignantly with these lines of cultural self-awareness:

> *How often we ought to rewrite history,*
> *connections often being made at the wrong time,*
> *facts not consistent with the factors.*[33]

At first glance one might assume that cynicism would not sit well with the stuff of national tradition; but actually there is no more effective way to fault a nation than by means of its most familiar icons and cherished clichés. (Thoreau began his countercultural experiment at Walden on the Fourth of July; and the famous industrial strike of shoe workers in Lynn, Massachusetts, began on George Washington's birthday in 1860.) Thus in 1968, the year of the Democratic Convention fiasco in Chicago, Larry Rivers painted his version of *The Boston Massacre,* a massive work in acrylic and oil on canvas that reminds us that when uniformed men kill civilians, justifiable rebellion may result. That same year Rivers also produced *The Paul Revere Event—Four Views,* perhaps to reassert the warning that American freedoms were being menaced by our own rulers. Back in 1953–5 the radical young Rivers had outraged art critics with his *Washington Crossing the Delaware;*[34] and ever since the mid-1960s we have seen a whole series of explicit variations on that theme: by Justin McCarthy, Sante Graziani, J. P. Evans, Charles Santore, and Malcah Zeldis.[35] In 1975 the irreverent Peter Saul produced his own caricature in acrylic on canvas (see figure 32). Washington's boat is sinking amidst the ice blocks, the flushed general rides a startled pink steed into the Delaware River, and a frenzied cast of characters is being tipped overboard. All in all, it is meant to be a rowdy parody of mock heroism.[36]

On July 4, 1976, *Newsweek* published a special Bicentennial issue to which Robert Lowell contributed a new poem at the magazine's invitation. Considered by many to be the leading poet of his generation, Lowell was living in England at the time of his death in 1977; and his poem is entitled "George III." Here is an excerpt:

In '76, George was still King George,
the one authorized tyrant,

not yet the mad, bad old king,

who whimisically picked the pockets of his page
he'd paid to sleep all day outside his door;

who dressed like a Quaker, who danced a minuet
with his appalled apothecary in Kew Gardens;

who did embroidery with the young court ladies,
and criticized them with suspicious bluntness,

who showed aversion for Queen Charlotte, almost
burned her by holding a candle to her face . . .

It was his sickness, not lust for dominion
made him piss purple, and aghast

his retinue by formally bowing to an elm,
as if it were the Chinese emissary.

George—
once a reigning monarch like Nixon,
and more exhausting to dethrone . . .

Could Nixon's court,
could Haldeman, Ehrlichman, or Kissinger

blame their king's behavior
on an insane wetnurse?

Tragic buffoonery
was more colorful once;

yet how modern George is,
wandering vacated chambers of his White House,

addressing imaginary Congresses,
reviewing imaginary combat troops,

thinking himself dead and ordering black clothes:
in memory of George, for he was a good man.[37]

Novels concerning the American Revolution that have appeared since 1974 tend to share this cynicism about personal motives and patriotic commitment. Like Lowell's and Wakoski's poems, the novels are likely to involve some kind of dialogue between our own time and the era when Independence was achieved.[38] Doing so, in one sense, is the ultimate form of intimate historical involvement; in yet another sense, it humanizes the Founding Fathers far more than even W. E. Woodward, D. H. Lawrence, and William Carlos Williams could do back in the 1920s. The "anti-hero" phenomenon has been with us now for several decades, especially in films; but the writers of Revolutionary romances discovered it just in time for the Bicentennial.[39] It is no accident that advocates of Benedict Arnold have been trying for several years to reopen his court-martial and rehabilitate his reputation; for he is the quintessential anti-hero of Revolutionary America.

Recent historical fiction has become intensely (though not very profoundly) existential. Characters simply exist, and barely endure their grim lives. We learn just how fragile our common humanity is, how bestial we can be to one another, how senselessly people behave in wartime—and yet, for all that, we are shown that our survival, if not salvation, hinges upon recovering our humanity. The war's meaning is demonstrated in deeply personal terms, in terms of its impact upon obscure individuals and families. As one remnant of a ravaged family thinks to herself: "Who cares who wins this war? Cassie wanted to tell him. The Bedhams have already lost it." Most of these novels have unhappy endings in which patriotic soldiers and their virtuous women are victimized. Cassie is brutally raped by Banastre Tarleton and his vicious British dragoons, then undergoes the deepest shame, intermittent insanity, and sense of depravity.[40]

Cassandra is a kind of anti-heroine in *Lucifer Land*, a novel set in the "neutral zone" of Westchester County, New York, between 1776 and 1783. The authors comment repeatedly on the senseless brutality of war, on terrified participants who are "caught between principle and practicality," on other souls who ask "why are we fighting this war?" and find neutrality to be an untenable position.[41] Cassie is kidnapped by Gideon, the novel's anti-hero whose parentage is very mysterious. He hopes to change her character by giving her an education in politics and war. She agrees to accompany him on a raiding party, becomes submissive and docile. Gideon gradually replaces her family; and in a sense, with his band, *becomes* her family. Cassie acquires instincts of the pack—accepts their values and defends them. At one point she rescues Gideon by bashing a man's skull with her rifle butt. (Is she a combination of Molly Pitcher and Patty Hearst? Exactly so!) In the spring of 1782, Gideon, who turns out to be her half brother, is killed by Tory marauders; and Cassie finally picks a name for the son she has borne as a result of being gang-raped. Unlike Gideon, unlike most of her kin, however, she has at least survived the war. Cassie has endured, and will now begin her desperate life anew.[42]

Feminism most certainly finds a place in these novels, though often obtrusively or unhistorically. There is more discussion of sex roles in the novels published between 1974 and 1977 than in all previous Revolutionary fiction taken together. We learn of Kate Gifford and Caroline Skinner in *Liberty Tavern* that the topic that *really* absorbed them was "the nature of the Revolution and the future of American women in their new country."[43]

Alongside this attention to feminism and sexuality, of course, we also get another predictable development: explicit sex scenes. Walter Edmonds, Inglis Fletcher, and occasionally Kenneth Roberts infused their novels with a quality of repressed sensuousness that is often handled with consummate skill: Joe Boleo watching Lana Martin suckle her baby; Mrs. McKlennar stripping the wounded Gil Martin in order to wash his grimy body in *Drums Along the Mohawk;* or Oliver Wiswell's temptation in the wilderness with the sultry Julia Bishop.[44] In the newer novels, by contrast, sensuousness is rarely repressed. John Jakes has a special fondness for rape scenes, for example, and in *The Rebels* both of his heroines are viciously abused: Anne Kent by the villainous Malachi Rackham; Peggy McLean in a gang-rape by rebellious slaves and, subsequently, by the tormented Judson Fletcher.[45] By the mid-1970s, in other words, the War for Independence had come to co-feature venery and gunnery with about equal prominence.

In 1970 (at the age of thirty-eight), John Jakes turned from the world of advertising to full-time fiction-writing. Following a fling with science fiction and children's literature, he turned his hand in 1973 to historical novels; and he seems to have sensed just what the mass culture wanted. Ever since 1974 his fast-moving and immensely readable narratives—decked out in Bicentennial red, white, and blue—have been snapped up with cigarettes, lifesavers, and chocolates at check-out counters in every American supermarket. By the fall of 1975 he had three volumes of a projected eight on the racks: *The Bastard* (1974), *The Rebels* (1975), and *The Seekers* (1975). He thereby achieved a remarkable distinction during the Bicentennial year 1975–6, becoming the first American author ever to have three best-sellers in a single year.[46]

Jakes's novels are fundamentally in the mainstream tradition we examined in Chapters Five and Six, with most of the major characters having to undergo a *rite de passage* symbolic of the colonies passing from adolescence to young adulthood. Philip Kent later looks back upon a particular night in 1772 "as a passage of great significance in his life"; and we learn that in 1777 Peggy Ashford McLean "had passed out of girlhood forever."[47]

So, too, with most of the other new Bicentennial novels, even though we get a fresh twist here and there. In *Patriot's Dream,* for instance, we learn about two Virginia cousins born in 1758. The war would be a coming of age for both, of course, but with a paradoxical reversal of the destiny each one presumably should have had. Whereas the radical Jonathan makes an unhappy marriage but prospers, the more conventional Charles runs off to Philadelphia with a slave, marries her, and lives out his life there under an assumed name. The logical endings are turned all topsy-turvy. Charles is true to his love, but gets disinherited. Jonathan tries to be faithful to his ideals, but is eventually poisoned by his resentful, racist, wretched wife.[48]

Hang for Treason, by Robert Newton Peck, did not catch much notice when it was published in 1976; but it is an eminently readable novel, one of the best Revolutionary romances ever written in dialect. The main figure is a seventeen-year-old lad living along the Vermont side of Lake Champlain. "Funny thing," says Able Booker to his younger sister in April 1775, "when it be chore time or plow time or the season for haying, I'm supposed to be a man. But at *politic* time, I'm a boy." Later, Able wonders "when I'll be a man."

> Is there a day, a year, a time in a boy's life when he knows he ain't no longer a kid? I don't see my father as God anymore. Maybe that's a sign we are now man and man. And it sure is certain that Miss Comfort Starr don't see me no more as a boy. Oh, golly, why didn't Comfort and me

have at it tonight instead of just teasing ourselfs to death? I just plumb *know* I won't feel like a man until I get into bed with her.[49]

The problem of intergenerational tension also pervades these novels, as when Jonathan Gifford's stepson, Kemble, informs him early in 1776: "I think you should know, Father—that if you don't join my country's side, I would consider myself free of all obligation—to obey you in any way."[50] But what differentiates the new novels from their predecessors is the point, repeatedly made, that intergenerational tensions and *rites de passage* occurred among Loyalists as well as Whigs.[51] Predicated upon that, but most important of all, is the lesson that neither side had a monopoly of virtue, justice, and truth. The royalist Noah Booker declares in 1775 that "lots of us is a mix of persuasions. No man is any *one* thing"; and as Jonathan Wilde discovers in 1777, "right and wrong are not as clear-cut as they would like to believe."[52]

Ultimately, of course, Vietnam and Watergate cast a kind of double shadow over these Bicentennial tales. "Believe," wonders Cassie, in *Lucifer Land;* "believe all that the generals, the lawyers, the politicians, the ministers tell you. Believe. Aloud she said, 'I do believe that I no longer believe.' "[53] Such skepticism is tempered, however, by wistful yearning for a reaffirmation of faith accompanied by new beginnings. The aged narrator of *Liberty Tavern,* ostensibly writing in 1826, hopes that when his story is read, if ever, it will

> help Americans of that distant era see us not as a set of demigods impossible to emulate, but human like themselves, torn by dissensions without and doubts within, groping toward happiness and repeatedly missing or mistaking it, struggling back from defeat and even from despair, learning painfully to forgive not merely our enemies but our friends and above all, ourselves.[54]

Popular interest in the American Revolution has often tended to peak at times when we were engaged upon a military crusade: in 1846–8 during the Mexican War; in 1898–1900 during the Spanish-American War; and then during World War II when novels about naval aspects of the Revolution were particularly abundant. The ambiguity and guilt that resulted as a residue of Watergate, however, made the customary coming-of-age motif more meaningful than it had been for a very long time in American culture. In 1975–6 the society desperately sought to separate itself from the recent past, and return instead to essential roots, to primordial values, and to a cleansed sense of national self. Commissioned to prepare a poem for Jimmy Carter's inauguration, James Dickey chose to preface "The Strength of Fields" with a line taken directly from Arnold Van Gennep's *Rites de Passage:*

. . . a separation from the world
a penetration to some source of power
and a life-enchanting return . . .

In 1975 James Michener, one of the country's most successful contemporary novelists, felt the urge to explain why he had accepted an appointment to the Bicentennial Advisory Committee. Here is an excerpt from his statement:

> Birth, puberty, acceptance into the adult group, marriage, childbirth, ordination, attaining seventy years, death—these are moments of significance, and a person cheats himself if he fails to observe them ritually. The same rule applies to nations. The great moments of attainment and passage ought to be memorialized, for then history is drawn together and the significance of survival is deepened. The rites of passage become logical times to renew our dedication and to look ahead to challenges no less demanding than those whose passing we celebrate.[55]

Also in 1975, Archibald MacLeish prepared a brilliant but unnoticed verse play for radio performance. Called *The Great American Fourth of July Parade,* it builds upon the extraordinary correspondence that passed between Thomas Jefferson and John Adams during the last fourteen years of their lives. Their spiritual selves engage in an intriguing dialogue—intriguing because they gradually undergo a subtle reversal of roles. At the outset Adams is characteristically pessimistic about the future of the United States, and Jefferson equally optimistic. When Jefferson remarks upon the nation taking the occasion of the Bicentennial to honor its Founding Fathers, Adams lays out their unworthy motives.

More likely for the comfort of remembrance:
a relic of the past to reassure them—
maybe the balm of a familiar word
they hope some orator will button round their souls.
They need the past to bolster their poor present up,
quiet their apprehensions, prove
the great Republic once was *a great Republic . . .*

Jefferson reaffirms the Revolution, but then becomes gloomy because he fears that modern Americans have "forgotten what the revolution was." Adams now must inspirit his comrade, and at the end we hear a cautious reaffirmation of faith: Thomas Jefferson still lives so long as Americans share and perpetuate his ideals.[56]

MacLeish's dialogue between tradition and renewal encapsulates what was best in our Bicentennial ruminations, and what they might have been in better times with more insightful planning. On July 4, 1966, President Lyndon B. Johnson signed into law the American Revolution Bicentennial Bill;[57] but one misadventure followed another, and by 1973–4 there were many different voices raised in protest against so much political mishandling of the national heritage. Some congressmen, many scholars, Native Americans, and the People's Bicentennial Commission all uttered repeated criticism, but to little avail.[58] Commercialism ran rampant. Early American furnishings sold better than ever. The cost of colonial antiques skyrocketed; and one manufacturer offered silver and gold chess sets for $14,000 apiece. One side were British regulars, of course, the other side being Continentals—with Paul Revere astride his steed as the American knight. It had become, perhaps predictably, a Buy-centennial.[59]

Before we grow too melancholy, however, we should recall that most such previous celebrations have also gone awry. In an economy based upon free enterprise and dependent upon vigorous consumer demand, there will always be commercialism. In a pluralistic society of fallible men and women, there will always be partisanship, some degree of politicization, and hence imperfect commemorative occasions. We know a great deal about the fiascos of 1876, for example. Here is an editorial commenting upon the much-anticipated Yorktown Celebration in 1881:

> That the grand celebration of the hundredth anniversary of the surrender of Lord Cornwallis at Yorktown has in so large a measure proved a failure was concisely explained, in homely but forcible language, by a Virginian teamster, who expressed it as his opinion that Colonel Peyton, of the Yorktown Centennial Association, had "bitten off a bigger hunk than he could chaw." That was just it; the Yorktown Centennial Association, like many another, overestimated its powers and while the time was yet far off prepared a programme which it was found impossible to carry out.[60]

What matters most now is that national self-knowledge be candidly achieved, that reaffirmations be accompanied by good intentions, that tradition as well as renewal go forward *pari passu.* The reasons why were expressed most eloquently in 1844 by an obscure radical politician in New York with the wonderful name of Levi Slamm:

> The day now is, when the people of the United States boast of enjoying a greater degree of liberty and happiness than any other nation. But, if there is truth in the remark, that every form of Government that the ingenuity of man can devise, contains within its elements the seeds of dissolution, the day *may* come when the freedom of our Republic will exist only in the history of bygone days. Let us beware then, and by every honest effort, attempt to procrastinate that awful day, and thus preserve and perpetuate the blessings of liberty and independence to the remotest ages of posterity.[61]

"A lingering desire to tell the true story of the Revolution"

NOW THAT WE HAVE LOOKED at all the major forms of cultural expression concerning the Revolution, from Fenimore Cooper's time until our own, we must raise two final questions about the Revolutionary tradition and its place in national culture. First, is there any particular posture (or pattern) to the American imagination when it enters into a historical mood? And second, what relationship exists, if any, between the Revolutionary tradition in particular and the broader self-image that citizens of the United States may have of themselves as a nationality? These issues provide the focus for the last two sections in our inquiry. Let us begin with the American imagination.

The nature of historical imagination has been self-consciously significant to most of the *dramatis personae* in this book, and to the authors of fiction as well as non-fiction. We have reports from William Gilmore Simms right on through Inglis Fletcher, for instance, regarding the inspirational impact of visiting the site of the Battle of King's Mountain. "Something about that lonely grave on the mountainside," wrote Fletcher, "stirred my imagination."[62] Speaking in 1825 at the first dedication of the Bunker Hill Monument, Daniel Webster acknowledged the critical importance of historical imagination in preserving the Revolutionary tradition:

> Our object is, by this edifice, to show our own deep sense of the value and importance of the achievements of our ancestors; and, by presenting this work of gratitude to the eye, to keep alive similar sentiments, and to foster a constant regard for the principles of the Revolution. Human beings are composed not of reason only, but of imagination also, and sentiment.[63]

As we have seen, however, many of our creative writers believed that historians of the Revolution were likely to be deficient in imagination, either by dint of neglect or by an insufficiency of skill. Simms put it this way in his introduction to *The Partisan:* "Imagination, however audacious in her own province, only ventures to embody and model those features of the Past, which the sober History has left indistinct, as not within her notice, or unworthy her regard."[64]

It is possible, to some degree, that one's imaginative perspective upon the Revolution might be contingent upon one's view of its inevitability. To someone like John Adams, for whom the American Revolution seemed historically predestined, there was relatively little place for imagination in writing retrospectively about those remarkable years. To someone like Cooper, by contrast, for whom chance, individual choice, human will, and error all seemed to play a major part in the Revolutionary era, imagination might feast upon the social complexity of that catalytic time.[65]

As we have seen, many of the novelists, poets, dramatists, and painters have indeed been imaginative in their treatment of the Revolution. It is nevertheless curious, if not ironic, that their most dominant impulse can best be described as documentary. John Trumbull approached historical painting with the same archival instinct as his contemporaries Ebenezer Hazard, Jared Sparks, and Peter Force. When Asher B. Durand decided to paint *The Capture of Major André* (1833), he visited the spot in Tarrytown where André had been arrested, and conferred with James Kirke Paulding, a descendant of one of the captors, about matters of costume and other pertinent details.[66] Canova's statue of Washington became so controversial in 1821 because the Founding Father was displayed as a seated Roman general. His costume was symbolic rather than authentic, and therefore unacceptable at the time. Enrico Causici took that lesson to heart, and cast Washington in contemporary dress for the monument erected at Baltimore in 1829. Unlike Canova's, his met with approval.[67]

In Cooper's preface to *Lionel Lincoln* he insisted that "the leading events are true," that he had "stolen no images from the deep, natural poetry of Bryant," and that he had carefully consulted local publications in Boston: "collating with care, and selecting . . . with some of that knowledge of men and things which is necessary to present a faithful picture." Similarly, John Pendleton Kennedy delighted in seeking out Revolutionary records for their precise detail. He coveted historical documents as "the dry timbers of a vast old edifice."[68]

This pattern continues into our own time. Many of the pageants got up for the sesquicentennial in 1926, and for the bicentennial of Washington's birth in 1932, are documentary and remarkable for their sheer factuality. *In the American Grain,* by William Carlos Williams, incorporates lengthy chunks of primary source material; and the John Adams Cantos, by Ezra Pound, have the digestive capacity of a boa constrictor. Pound vastly preferred "significant documents" to "second-rate fiction," regarded the Adams-Jefferson correspondence as a national monument, and wanted Adams to speak for himself in these Cantos.[69] So, too, Inglis Fletcher defended her Revolutionary novels against Carolina critics by pointing out that "they did not realize that my facts were from authentic documents, not from local histories or folk tales."[70]

"Authentic documents" is a very symptomatic phrase here, for it encapsulates a major preoccupation of so many historical painters and supposedly imaginative writers ever since the 1820s. As a critic remarked in 1825 of Matthew Murgatroyd's *The Refugee; a Romance:* "It abounds with petty anachronisms, calculated to impair the verisimilitude of the story."[71] William Gilmore Simms frequently expressed concern about the inaccuracy of local lore and oral traditions. Winston Churchill wanted his Revolutionary novels to be "true"; and the publishing house of J. B. Lippincott was so impressed by Paul Leicester Ford's success during the 1890s with "true" biographies that it subsequently published a whole series of "true" biographies about famous Americans.[72]

Herbert Croly summed up the resulting situation rather well in 1903: "The method of responsible historical fiction has been overstrained, and the result has neither the freedom and the novelty of a story nor the self-restraint and authenticity of a history."[73]

It is fair to say that this self-conscious quest for authenticity has characterized many of the authors we are considering, and continues to do so in the twentieth century: Kenneth Roberts, Gore Vidal, and Thomas Fleming are notable examples in recent decades. They want to set straight the reputations of those who seem to have been abused. They would like to show that *everyone* was not patriotic and honorable in those troubled times. Most simply, as Vidal's aging Aaron Burr declares in 1833: "I still have a lingering desire to tell the true story of the Revolution before it is too late, which is probably now since the legend of those days seems to be cast in lead if the schoolbooks are any guide."[74]

What complicates this clear-cut pattern, however, is the existence of an alternative impulse that we might call the romantic impulse. We find elements of it in Cooper and Simms, in many of the poems and plays discussed earlier in Chapter Four, and especially in novels from the period 1895–1909. Paul Leicester Ford's *Janice Meredith* really is not a very good novel; but it sold so well after 1899, in my opinion, because it appears to combine authentic with romantic criteria. Although it is chock-full of implausible occurrences and ridiculous sentimentality, it is also rich in historical detail: the customs, dress, and rhetoric of Revolutionary times that Ford knew so well. Hence the United States ambassador to Great Britain wrote to Ford in 1900, telling him that "your accurate knowledge of the details of the Revolution is manifest in every page, and makes it a true historical romance."[75]

If nineteenth-century writers with historical imagination felt torn between authentic and romantic imperatives, perhaps their twentieth-century successors more often vacillate between the authentic and the symbolic. As one critic has written of *In the American Grain,* it "grows out of the tension between Williams's reverence for literal, individuating detail and his desire to discover mythic recurrences amid the welter of facts."[76] The same might be said about the better Bicentennial efforts. One co-author of *My Brother Sam Is Dead* (1974) explains their remarkable success in these terms: "It stands alone among Revolutionary juvenile literature as an effort to present a view of the war that incorporates elements of both the Whig and Progressive interpretations, with a strong emphasis on the latter. Few children's books on the subject make any attempt to deal with issues at all. For the most part they are merely stories laid in the period and given verisimilitude by incorporating authentic detail."[77]

Over the entire span, 1776–1976, authors writing about the Revolution have most frequently professed to be in search of *authentic* historical experience. They have often been rather more romantic than authentic, however, and only on occasion have they attempted symbolism in some significant or provocative way. Hawthorne and Melville come to mind immediately for their use of symbolism, of course, but the list is not a very long one. Yet our foremost effusions of historical imagination somehow manage to combine all three.[78] I would say of Trumbull's better scenes, or of Cooper's *Satanstoe*, or of Whittier's poems on the Revolution, that they blend the authentic, the romantic, and the symbolic. In so doing they properly infuse tradition with imagination. Imagination lends vibrancy to tradition; and interacting together, these two qualities have done much to define our understanding of the national character.

"Though obscure and susceptible of contradictory meanings, traditions do not cease to be reverenced. . . . The poet may interpret them, and illustrate and enlarge their influence upon national character"

All of which brings us to the final reprise. There is a persistent refrain throughout these novels—it appears in the non-fiction, art, poetry, and drama as well—persistent, at least, until very recent times. The refrain has been highly symptomatic of our cultural self-awareness, of our quest for self-recognition, and of our desire to explain the United States to those who might misunderstand American actions, origins, or motives. Let us listen to one brief utterance of this refrain from each of the discrete periods that have been delineated.

• Here is James Fenimore Cooper, describing in his introduction to *The Spy* a dialogue he had had with John Jay. "The discourse turned upon the effects which great political excitement produced on character, and the purifying consequences of a love of country, when that sentiment is powerfully and generally awakened in a people."[79]

• Here is a passage from *Alice of Old Vincennes* in which the author insists upon "the dominant element of American character, namely, heroic efficiency. From the first we have had the courage to undertake, the practical common sense which overcomes the lack of technical training, and the vital force which never flags under the stress of adversity."[80]

• And here is a passage about the patriotic Winshore brothers in Carl Sandburg's *Remembrance Rock*. "This would go for their heroes, they agreed. Of Washington Robert would say, 'He sustains the fairest character,' and Locke would say it of Nathanael Greene."[81]

What we are listening to, very clearly, is the explicit articulation in popular fiction of an American obsession that bubbled up during the 1780s just as soon as Independence had been achieved. Some people assumed, as one organization put it in 1787, that "when breaking through the bounds, in which a dependent people have been accustomed to think, and act, we shall properly comprehend the character we have assumed and adopt those maxims of policy, which are suited to our new situation." Others were less assured. As John Fenno asked in 1789, "are we independent in our laws, opinions, manners, and fashions? The fact is, that, in none of those respects, have we yet formed a distinct national character."[82]

During the succeeding generation—what we might approximately call the age of Andrew Jackson—spread-eagle assertions about national character became commonplace.[83] During the later nineteenth century, by contrast, despite the self-confidence of many Americans in those years, some restive questions were raised about the national character. In 1876, for example, one very prominent orator predicted that by 1887, "the time may have come for a full review of our National career and character, and for a complete computation . . . of what a Century of Self-Government has accomplished for ourselves and for mankind."[84]

American exuberance about the national character, especially in the half century from Washington's presidency to Polk's, resulted in part from a reflex action. In response to foreign condescension and partisan domestic criticism, we strutted, puffed, and blew our own horn. John Quincy Adams could privately concede to his mother that the "continued libel upon the character and manners of the American people" contained "too much of truth"; but public orations, journal essays, and historical fiction would play variations on a more aggressive theme. Gouverneur Morris hoped to "assist in cleansing the American character from representations by which it has been sullied." A reviewer heaped praise upon Daniel Webster's historical discourse delivered at Plymouth in 1820. Why? Because Webster provided some measure of vindication against complaints from abroad about our cultural inadequacy; "Americans have been repeatedly charged by those foreign writers, who find it for their interest to hold up our national character to ridicule before the great republic of letters, with being deficient in that patriotic attachment to the land we spring from." And James Kirke Paulding suggested in *The Old Continental* that Hessian misbehavior during the War for Independence resulted from their "being totally ignorant of the grounds of the quarrel, as well as, beyond doubt, stimulated by the most cruel misrepresentations of the motives and character of the people of the United States."[85]

There were a few spokesmen in the early national period who recognized the risks involved in generalizing about American character. But their skepticism and their caveats did not arise from disbelief in the existence of such a chimerical thing as national character. Rather, it arose from a sense of regret that foreign observers had based their generalizations upon an inadequate survey, or simply upon misinformation. Timothy Dwight, for example, an outspoken clergyman and formerly the president of Yale College, criticized the improper attribution of

> actions and characters to all the Americans, which are due to a part only, and that probably very small. This is a very common and very unfortunate practice of your travelers in the United States. They see or hear of something which is done in this country, some local custom, some solitary incident, some good or bad treatment of a foreigner. They find two or three bad inns, make with some sharper a disadvantageous bargain, purchase lands unadvisedly of some jobber and are bitten in the contract, and are otherwise injured, teased, or abused. Immediately the character becomes in their mouths universal; the custom spreads over the whole country; the incidents become a general history; the people have

all turned sharpers and land jobbers; the inns are all dirty, and the innkeepers rude, vulgar, and insolent.[86]

Nevertheless, Dwight most certainly believed in the existence of an American national character; and elsewhere he expressed the belief that, as time passed, it would get better and better.

What, then, did they mean by "character"? Why was the concept so urgently important to them? What special relationship did it have to the American Revolution? And what determinative connection did it have to the society's sense of tradition, or its understanding of the nature and implications of social change in the United States?

It is important to recognize, first of all, that "character" was quite a ubiquitous word in nineteenth-century American discourse. Not surprisingly, then, it has left a slew of false cognates that are likely to mislead the student of American attitudes. Writers would refer to "the character of our New-England people," or to the southern character; to the Virginia "Character"; to faces "full of character"; to "the female character" and to "the character of the [Negro] race."[87] All of these allusions are interesting, and each of them has both roots and results that may be fruitful for historians of American culture. But they are not at the heart of our concern here. They are peripheral.

When people spoke of national character during the decades between the Revolution and the Civil War, they had in mind a particular constellation of *ethical* qualities. "The study of human character," Mercy Otis Warren declared in 1805, "opens at once a beautiful and a deformed picture of the soul." Religion and morality had much to do with character, as did a sense of insistent integrity.[88] When Ann Pamela Cunningham wrote to Benson J. Lossing in 1859 to thank him for his edition of *Mount Vernon and Its Associates,* she expressed the hope that more such books would appear, so that "the rising generation may, in this money-loving age, have constantly brought before them, as worthy of imitation, the Virtue, Courage, and high Nobleness of Soul which marked the men of the Revolution."[89]

That statement, which happens to have been privately expressed, goes very much to the heart of their general intent when referring to the national character. *Virtue*—subordination of self for the common good—was a critical code-word to them. As Catharine Maria Sedgwick wrote of her fictional Lee family in

Revolutionary New England: they embodied a proper republican character, "the foundation of intellect and virtue." Sedgwick subsequently makes her historical point explicit: namely, that the Revolution served as a crucible in which national character could be shaped. "Happy was it for America that, in the beginning of her national existence, she thus tested the virtue of the *people*, and, profiting by her experience, was confirmed in her resolution to confide her destinies to *them!*"[90]

Sedgwick had linked intellect and virtue even-handedly; but two years later, in his famous address "The American Scholar," Emerson elevated one above the other. "Character is higher than intellect," he wrote; and the nation could comfortably resonate with that assertion. Its citizens chose to believe that their governmental institutions were the finest ever achieved; first, because the founders had been men of integrity as well as vision; and second, as Emma Willard declared in her vastly influential United States history textbook (1842), because "the character of America is that of youthful simplicity, of maiden purity; and her future statesman will say, as he reads the story, my country was the most virtuous among the nations."[91]

During the 1830s and 1840s, reformers placed heavy emphasis upon individual perfectibility. They shared an almost religious notion of the individual as a "reservoir" of human possibilities, and believed that by strengthening the country's Christian character, individual perfection would facilitate social improvement generally.[92] So long as the importance of personal integrity and communal character were kept coordinated in this way, the national character could remain a moral concept rather than what it has become in the past century: a constellation of behavioral attributes, values good and bad, plus ethically denatured aspects of social style.

During the later nineteenth century, a series of subtle shifts began to occur. Character continued to be discussed, but more at the level of individuals than in terms of the "national character." Persons were to cultivate character in order to be successful, in order to help in maintaining social stability, and in order to be vocationally reliable. The concept of character increasingly took on status connotations of an élitist nature. A ditch digger or a dirt farmer was not likely to be a person of character; but a clergyman, a doctor, or a philanthropic businessman was. By 1900 "character" had come to be encumbered with occupational and class associations—not to mention athletic prowess—unanticipated a century before.[93]

Which is not to say that the Founding Fathers and Jacksonian generation had been *un*concerned about their personal qualities and the perceptions others had of their character as individuals. They worried a great deal about such matters.[94] But they were equally (if not more) concerned about translating personal character into the kind of political leadership that can transform society. "It is the Part of a great Politician to make the Character of his People," John Adams wrote in 1776, "to extinguish among them the Follies and Vices that he sees, and to create in them the Virtues and Abilities which he sees wanting."[95]

Adams's point of view is crucial, because it would reverberate in American culture for two full generations thereafter. Hence what Parson Weems really wanted to do in writing his biographies (apart from make a lot of money) was to delineate the impact of unusual individuals upon the national character. Hence William Tudor's insistence in 1818 that "we have been exclusively governed by that *regard to character*, which we ever wish to cherish in ourselves, and in the community." But why, ultimately? And why did Tudor choose to italicize those phrases in which he invoked character? "Let us remember," he declared, "that we have nothing more precious than the reputation of our distinguished men, civil or military, living or dead. . . . Let us embrace in all its extent and spirit, that maxim,—full of the soundest wisdom and fit to be urged, again and again, with all possible earnestness,—*character is power.*"[96]

A good reputation elevated the leader in popular esteem, and thereby enhanced his leverage in public affairs. Posthumously, the great leader's qualities served as an index to the national character, and also as a rallying point for ideological principles and political partisanship. Jefferson's character was frequently written about for both of these reasons. In 1859 Abraham Lincoln informed a friend that "the principles of Jefferson are the definitions and axioms of free society." Lincoln's last paragraph was so powerful that Republican newspapers reprinted it and gave it wide circulation:

All honor to Jefferson—to the man who, in the concrete pressure of a struggle for national independence by a single people, had the coolness, forecast, and capacity to introduce into a merely revolutionary document, an abstract truth, applicable to all men and all times, and so to embalm it there, that to-day, and in all coming days, it shall be a rebuke and a stumbling-block to the very harbingers of re-appearing tyrany [sic] and oppression.[97]

Above all others, however, it was the reputation and character of George Washington that dominated the historical imagination in America. Two of the most famous nineteenth-century orations were Webster's "The Character of George Washington" (1832) and Edward Everett's "The Character of Washington," which he delivered 129 times between 1856 and 1860 while touring the country on behalf of the Mount Vernon Ladies' Association. In 1843, when Webster dedicated the Bunker Hill Monument by enumerating national achievements, he grandly volunteered that "America has furnished to the world the character of Washington!"[98] Jared Sparks explained that in writing his biography of Washington (1839) he hoped to illuminate "the character, actions, and opinions of Washington"; and William Gilmore Simms was publicly as well as privately fascinated by Washington's wisdom. That was the quality that set Washington way above Hamilton: "The difference between the two is precisely this, between smartness & wisdom."[99]

Amidst all the changes and cultural discontinuities we have described, concern for the character of Washington held constant. One nationally prominent historian contended in 1865 that copies of George Washington's letters, broadly distributed, "would do more for the formation of our national character . . . than any other source." During the 1890s, such figures as President McKinley and Senator Henry Cabot Lodge carried on the custom of giving orations on February 22 concerning "The Character of Washington." The bicentennial of his birth in 1932 elicited massive memorial volumes that focused upon his "character and service." So did the popular pageants by Percy MacKaye and Paul Green; and also "Washington at Fraunces' Tavern," a poem by Edgar Lee Masters. Here is the very core of that long poem, one of the most eloquent pieces on the character of Washington. It occurs on December 4, 1783, when Washington bid farewell to his officers and staff.

I see him now! His face was grave, but lighted
With noble joy. Somehow he paused a space
After he passed the door, and even after
We officers saluted him. In that moment
I saw fair written in his countenance
The comprehension that this sad, bad world
Is given men unfinished, and left to men
To mold it better, and to write some words
Fit to be spoken and remembered, too;
All is not fate, but part of life is chance;
And what men do, and what they are may alter
Ages to come. In truth he lived life so,
And fought war so, all through his being's roots
And faithful to them. There before us stood
The manifest of his sanity and balance,
The just proportion of his mind and heart,
His will, his judgment which so fairly weighed,
So wisely watched, restrained, discerned and led
Himself, the army, and the Revolution.
Beside these virtues what was eloquence?
What languages? He only spoke his own.
What high accomplishments? So there he stood
A towering, solid man, whose body spoke
His farmer boyhood, and his hunting days,
His tramps across the wilderness, his perils
With Indians, flood, cold, heat—the army, too![100]

What it all comes down to, in the end, is a particular perspective shared by the best among our creative artists who have chosen to infuse the stuff of tradition with imagination. William Gilmore Simms said it many times and in many ways, perhaps most effectively in 1845: "The analysis of the properties, of the constituents and causes of national character, belongs to the first duties of the philosophical poet, and is absolutely essential to the successful labours of any architect who would build his fabric out of the materials of history."[101] Simms sought to demonstrate that formula in writing his series of Revolutionary romances, and there is evidence that a good many of his readers got the message. As one essayist remarked of *Katharine Walton* (1851), its heroine embodied "the best motives and feelings of the times"; consequently, "she seems to affect us as in some sort a representative of what is most distinctively American."[102]

Character that was dramatically bad could be almost as instructive as exemplary character. Simms wrote to a friend in 1853 inquiring about "the private life of [Benedict] Arnold while in Philadelphia? What was the christened name of his wife? Is there any thing in respect to her private history & character?" Kenneth Roberts was equally intrigued by Arnold's character, just as John Esten Cooke used Governor Dunmore as an epitome of bad character in his novels about Revolutionary Virginia.[103]

A quest for the national character in cultural artifacts inspired by the Revolution: we encounter this quest in all forms of imaginative expression—in painting and sculpture,[104] in fiction, essays, plays, and short stories. We encounter it everywhere despite the artists' awareness that they are working with psychological quicksilver. As Howard Fast put it, "there is no precise way of describing the formation and growth of what is sometimes called personality and sometimes character and sometimes other names as foolish."[105]

They continued to do so nonetheless, from James Fenimore Cooper on through Esther Forbes; and, what is noteworthy, though scarcely surprising, found ways to conflate their concern about character with the culture's rhythmic emphasis upon *rite de passage.* In 1829 the very popular Sarah Josepha Hale published a little book called *Sketches of the American Character.* One of the sketches, entitled "Soldier of the Revolution," is narrated retrospectively by an aged veteran; he had been twenty years old when the story took place, and for him the Revolution seemed very much a coming of age. Early on he explains that

> the causes which roused the Americans to take up arms, were most favorable to the development of the virtuous energies of men, and consequently that recklessness of moral character and abandonment of pious principles, which too often fatally distinguishes the mass of that profession, when composed of hired mercenaries, never attached to the soldiers of our armies.[106]

In *The Rebels,* by Lydia Maria Child, the convergence of character analysis with personal and political *rite de passage* becomes even more pronounced. The ways in which character may develop are explicitly discussed, as well as the ways in which character can be demonstrated. What was true of Miss Fitzherbert in

1765–6 was presumably true of the colonies as well: "There is a time, in the lives of most people, when character fearfully fluctuates in the balance; and when circumstances, apparently accidental, may do much to decide it, either to good or evil."[107] Adam Rutledge, the hero of *Raleigh's Eden,* acquires the full stature of manhood in 1774–5 precisely because he then achieves a total moral and political commitment: "His face was stronger—it showed more character." And Carl Sandburg's *Remembrance Rock* is deeply concerned with the impact of war upon character: that of George Washington in the spring of 1776, but also that of ordinary patriots like young Locke Ordway, whose development emerges from "the roots of a growing mind and character."[108]

In sum, our better historical novelists managed to grasp by intuition a connection that social anthropologists have been discussing in various pre-industrial contexts for half a century now: the connection between an individual's life crises and the society's awareness of itself, its traditions, its development, and future prospects. Rituals associated with transitions and life crises transform the individual's "social personality," which A. R. Radcliffe-Brown defined as "the sum of characteristics by which he has an effect upon the social life and therefore on the social sentiments of others."[109] Although most Americans were not very tradition-oriented during the nineteenth century, writers and public figures continued to reiterate the belief that national character could best be discovered in the country's history—most particularly in the story of the American Revolution.[110]

In recent years the American mood with respect to national character has been much less sanguine. Revolutionary fiction occasioned by the Bicentennial, for example, has not entirely ignored the matter; but the new novels have not dwelt upon it at length. When they do discuss the connection between our era of Independence and the development of national character, they do so awkwardly and in a diffident manner.[111] On the infrequent occasion when that important relationship is really explored, we understandably find overtones of Vietnam and Watergate. Kemble Gifford, a character in *Liberty Tavern,* for example, experiences "something Americans cannot endure—failure"; and at the very end, Thomas Fleming's narrator, James Kemble, declares that "it would do us no harm—and perhaps a great deal of good—to remember the dark side of our national character."[112]

As far back as 1775, Edmund Burke declared that "the temper and character which prevail in our Colonies are, I am afraid, unalterable by any human act." It has not been the purpose of this inquiry to ascertain whether or not the American character did, in fact, change during the two centuries since; but certain it is that *perceptions* of the national character have indeed changed. Sixty years after Crèvecoeur first asked his classic question—"What then is the American, this new man?"—James Fenimore Cooper asked it again, and supplied quite a different answer. More recently, a prominent sociologist has suggested that our modern conceptions of character have altered. Our notions have done so for various reasons, but in significant part because we, as a society, have ceased self-consciously to inculcate character in our young people. Santayana's statement that "to be an American is of itself almost a moral condition, an education, and a career," may consequently have lost much of its thrust and force.[113]

One hopes that that tendency is ephemeral and reversible. I see a very encouraging sign in the current obsession with social roots; for our interest in cultural origins has both a moral dimension and an ethical imperative.[114] We are more willing than ever before to confront our mistakes, and we genuinely hope to avoid their recurrence. Our turning to the past may to some extent be a measure of the ways in which we feel the present has failed us—or worse, the ways in which we have failed ourselves. Yet a temporary disillusionment with the present can have a rather salutary effect upon our understanding of the past and our feeling for tradition. We would do well, therefore, to bear in mind this line from Francis Calley Gray's 1818 Fourth of July oration in Boston: "When the legacy of our ancestors is forgotten, there is your liberty destroyed."

Coda: The Civil War, the Revolution, and American Culture

IT HAS BEEN an underlying premise of this book that the American Revolution stands as the single most important source for our national sense of tradition—such as it is, and insofar as we can be said to possess one.[115] That is not an ineluctable premise, however, because the ground I have covered seems eminently worth covering even if the premise could be proven patently untrue. We need to know what difference the Revolution has made to American culture, even though other writers might make strenuous claims for various other events, ideas, and forms of provenience.

The loudest alternative claim, I suspect, could be entered on behalf of the American Civil War. Consequently I feel obliged to say a few words about the relative "merits" of that episode (or of that claim). My purpose is not to proclaim the cultural primacy of 1776 over 1861—which would be a mindless and a fruitless exercise—but simply to explain why I personally feel comfortable with the underlying premise which I have just acknowledged. The Civil War undeniably occupies a central place in our history as well as in our imaginative relationship to the past; as Daniel Aaron has suggested, "the War more than casually touched and engaged a number of writers, and its literary reverberations are felt to this day."[116]

Despite that suggestion, which Aaron more than manages to justify, the dominant contention of his fine book is a negative one: more a wistful concession than a polemical contention. Aaron acknowledges that works written about the Civil War have rarely penetrated its surface; that very few creative writers have had revealing things to say about either the causes or the meaning of the war; and that the "epic character" of the war has not yet been felt or portrayed. Others who have reflected upon this problem seem to agree. Oscar Handlin, for instance, insisted a century after the event that its meaning in American culture remained obscure.[117]

I believe that Professors Aaron and Handlin are correct in their assessment; and that the reasons why are noteworthy. First of all, as Handlin contends, we have not as a people been willing to recognize that

> in our four years of war millions of Americans really hated one another and really wanted to kill one another [,] and that the drama they acted out on the battlefields was less one of gallantry and courage than of hatred. Therefore, the war which settled such incidental questions as the scope of state's rights could not settle the important problems that divided the nation in 1860, neither of the future of Negroes nor of the kind of society that the United States would become. These issues remained to trouble the country for decades to come.[118]

Nationalists and patriots, like Ralph Waldo Emerson, were very disappointed in what the war had wrought. Veterans of the struggle itself became bitterly disillusioned afterwards when they learned of all the wartime profiteering. The writers best equipped to record the war—such as Henry Adams, William Dean Howells, Henry James, and Mark Twain—never got close enough to it to absorb and assess its inner meaning. In sum, most writers during the century since 1865 have either neglected the Civil War, or else treated it superficially (by ignoring the "Negro problem," for example), or else have regarded it as an unmitigated disaster.[119] Whatever else our imaginative artists (and their audiences) may have felt about the American Revolution, on the other hand, they have scarcely regarded it as an unmitigated disaster with pernicious cultural consequences.

Above all, however, there is the issue of character: ethical character and national character. The Civil War came to be regarded as our darkest hour precisely because the basest qualities in our character briefly became ascendant then. The South seceded, and violated the Union, in order to preserve chattel slavery. Northern sympathizers, most especially following Reconstruction, articulated their racism explicitly. In order to hide from the embarrassing materialism of the Gilded Age, social critics in all sections of the country seized upon a nostalgic vision of the Old South. They much preferred a false picture of ante-bellum gentility to the crass realities of their own vulgar, industrial society.[120]

There was precious little about the Civil War era in which we could take pride. Both sides had misbehaved, and many among the northern moralists who helped to destroy slavery acquiesced eventually in its replacement by a caste system in some respects even more dehumanizing. Abraham Lincoln's character became a prominent factor in the "Lincoln legend"; and Robert E. Lee's character was also extolled for generations after Appomattox. But the *national* character was not; and, indeed, the point became awkwardly apparent that Lincoln and Lee were exceptional Americans rather than representative Americans. The rest of us clearly lacked their integrity; and the brilliance of their leadership had neither been sufficient to prevent the tragedy nor adequate to forestall the degradation of national life that occurred under their *epigoni*.[121]

The Civil War divided a nation, whereas the American Revolution created and unified it. The Civil War exposed our vilest flaws, whereas the Revolution shaped our character and (we generally assumed) displayed our courage, principles, and high-mindedness for all the world to see. What happened in 1776 somehow reflected glory upon us, whereas what happened in 1861, when the polity disintegrated, became an object lesson in the perils of extremism and selfishness.

Walt Whitman could call the Civil War "the parturition years (more than 1776–'83) of this henceforth homogeneous Union"; but the vast majority of his contemporaries either sought to repress the hideous events of 1861–5 (and really that meant 1854–65), or else played fast and loose with their memories by transforming them into literally incredible, self-serving myths. The Revolution's image, as we have seen, helped serve to reunite the shattered nation during the quarter century after 1865; but the Civil War Centennial of 1957–65, which took place at a time of domestic tranquility, turned out to be even more of a fiasco than the Bicentennial activity of the 1970s, which took place under far more troubled circumstances.[122]

The American Revolution does not lack its mythological shadows; yet they are neither so distorted, nor do they darken or obscure as much historical reality, as the myths that surround the single greatest aberration in our political, social, and moral history. That is why, in my opinion, the Revolution has remained the foremost provenance of nationality and of tradition in the United States.

SUPPLEMENT

THE DECLARATION OF INDEPENDENCE IN AMERICAN POLITICAL HUMOR

THE DECLARATION OF INDEPENDENCE has reverberated through our culture in many different ways: political, ideological, symbolic, and even (as we have seen) as a negative reference for conservatives, who tend to be embarrassed by it. Precisely because the Declaration is supposed to be an integral part of our value system, it has been used by social critics, from time to time, as a means of demonstrating that our actions are inconsistent with our professed values. The interested reader will find some fascinating examples of such usage, along with an appropriate discussion of their historical context, in Philip S. Foner, ed., *We, the Other People: Alternative Declarations of Independence by Labor Groups, Farmers, Woman's Rights Advocates, Socialists, and Blacks, 1829–1975* (Urbana, Ill., 1976). Satirical versions of the classic Fourth of July oration are mentioned by Barnet Baskerville in "Nineteenth Century Burlesque of Oratory," *American Quarterly*, XX (Winter 1968), 726–43. The Declaration of Independence and Fourth of July oration have also served as prototypes for some of the most charming and whimsical spoofs in all of American political humor and popular culture. So far as I know, these have never been gathered together, despite the fact that the best of them are truly gems. Here, then, are four examples: one from 1833, one from 1859, one from 1921, and the last from 1977.

The first example comes from the story, written by Eliza Leslie, entitled *Russel and Sidney; or, The Young Revolutionists. A Tale of 1777.* First published in *Atlantic Tales: or, Pictures of Youth* (1833), this excerpt is taken from the second edition (Boston, 1835), pp. 170–5. The year is 1777. Russel is a sixteen-year-old boy who has aroused and organized his schoolmates into a committee of protest against their tyrannical schoolmaster, Mr. Peter Puckeridge. Russel declaims *their* Declaration!

When in the course of human events it becomes necessary for the boys of a school to break through the bands that have connected them with the teacher (falsely, meanly, and improperly called their *master*) a decent respect for the opinions of the girls requires them to declare the causes that compel them to a separation.

We hold these truths to be self-evident: that we are in every point of view equal to the man denominated Peter Puckeridge. We can run as fast, we can ride as well: we can shoot much better; and we are no way below him in fishing and trapping. And if any of us are his inferiors in reading, writing and cyphering, (and even this is doubtful) it is only the natural consequence of our youth and inexperience. In all *essential* qualifications we acknowledge no inferiority whatever.

But our causes of complaint are of more serious moment: and after enduring a long train of abuses and vexations, it is our choice, it is our wish, to throw off his government, and declare ourselves independent.

To prove this, let the following facts be submitted to our candid fellow-sufferers.

He has refused to allow the eating of apples in school, even of the sorts least noisy, and best calculated to be managed without paring.

He has refused to permit the windows to be raised in the dog-days; and he has limited our water-drinking to four tin-cups-full a day, the said tin-cup holding but half a pint.

He has refused to mend our pens even when the points were split apart like the prongs of a fork; and he has kept us in pot-hooks when we ought to have been in joining-hand.

He has interdicted us from reading almanacks and other story-books, (even when our lessons were over) preferring that we should sit idle on the benches: and when reduced to this state of idleness, he has barbarously forbidden us the amusement of kicking our heels, or drumming with our fingers. He has particularly waged war against Robinson Crusoe: as if it were not better to employ ourselves with that most useful and entertaining of all books than to sit listless and yawning till school-hours were over.

He obliges us to learn by heart lessons of unusual length and on useless subjects (grammar for instance,) with the wicked and inhuman purpose of making us waste our play-hours in hard study: at the manifest risk of rendering our faces pale, our legs thin, and destroying all our natural smartness.

He has kept us standing long after we should have been seated, listening to tedious explanations of comets, and northern-lights, and milky ways, and other incomprehensible things, which nobody in this world can possibly understand, and least of all Peter Puckeridge.

He has called us in at times unusually early and uncomfortable, obliging us to quit our unfinished plays; and when we naturally refrained from obeying the summons, he has taken from us our kites, our marbles, our balls and our tops, and has deposited them in the gloomy recesses of his own desk: thereby subjecting us to the necessity of picking the lock or cutting holes in the bottom, as the only means of repossessing ourselves of our lawful property.

He is in the frequent practice of inflicting corporal chastisement when we find it necessary to stand opposed to him: with one exception, the writer of this declaration, on whom, as is well-known, he has never yet ventured to lay the finger of violence.

He has plundered our hats: he has ravaged our pockets: he has burnt our playthings: he has ruined our collars by shaking them with his inky hands; excepting always the writer of this declaration.

But our most important and unanswerable reason for rejecting his tyranny is, that we know him to be possessed of high tory principles. We know him to take a childish interest, unbecoming to an American, in the comings and goings, the eatings and sleepings of the men called kings, and the women denominated queens, while he is at no pains whatever to inform himself of the proceedings of Congress. Also he has been heard to insist, most falsely and absurdly, that the red coats of the British regulars have a more military look than the blue coats of our own continental soldiers, and he has presumed to laugh at the militia who have no coats at all. Also, he has dared most treasonably to sneer at the calico gown worn by the brave Colonel Prescott at the battle of Bunker Hill.

Nor have we been wanting in indications of our dissatisfaction. We have tilted his desk by sawing off three inches from one of the legs; we have slipped his handkerchief from his pocket and wiped up ink with it; we have cut sticks with his best pen-knife, and put chinkapin burrs into his hat; and we are taken with unanimous coughs whenever he begins to talk to us. But as no warning has had any effect on him, and as he has not had the grace to retire from office as soon as he knew himself to be unpopular, we therefore absolve ourselves from all allegiance to him and his authority. We throw him off as we would an old coat, and we declare ourselves free and independent of Peter Puckeridge, and that we will never more allow ourselves to be subjected by the frown of his brow, the sharpness of his voice, or the slaps of his ferule. And for the support of this declaration we mutually pledge to each other the heads that can plan, the hearts that can dare, and the hands that can execute.

The second example comes from Charles Farrar Browne (1834–67), a political humorist who wrote under the pen name of "Artemus Ward." Browne left Cleveland for New York City in 1859, and became a contributor to *Vanity Fair.* His so-called goaks and sketches were gathered up in a little volume published in 1862, which turned out to be immensely popular. One of these "goaks," entitled the "Weathersfield Oration," first appeared in *Vanity Fair,* IV (July 13, 1861), 15.

FOURTH OF JULY ORATION.

DELIVERED JULY 4TH,

AT WEATHERSFIELD, CONNECTICUT, 1859.

[*I delivered the follerin, about two years ago, to a large and discriminating awjince. I was 96 minits passin a given pint. I have revised the orashun, and added sum things which makes it approposser to the times than it otherwise would be. I have also corrected the grammers and punktooated it. I do my own punktooatin now days. The printers in* VANITY FAIR *offiss can't punktooate worth a cent.*]

FELLER CITIZENS: I've bin honored with a invite to norate before you today; and when I say that I skurcely feel ekal to the task, I'm sure you will believe me.

Weathersfield is justly celebrated for her onyins and patritism the world over, and to be axed to paws and address you on this, my fust perfeshernal tower threw New Englan, causes me to feel—to feel—I may say it causes me to *feel.* [Grate applaws. They thought this was one of my eccentricities, while the fact is I was stuck. This between you and I.]

I'm a plane man. I don't know nothin about no ded languages and am a little shaky on livin ones. There4, expect no flowry talk from me. What I shall say will be to the pint, right strate out.

I'm not a politician and my other habits air good. I've no enemys to reward, nor friends to sponge. But I'm a Union man. I luv the Union—it is a Big thing—and it makes my hart bleed to see a lot of ornery peple a-movin heaven—no, not heaven, but the other place—and earth, to bust it up. Too much good blud was spilt in courtin and marryin that hily respectable female the Goddess of Liberty, to git a divorce from her now. My own State of Injianny is celebrated for unhitchin marrid peple with neatness and dispatch, but you can't git a divorce from the Goddess up there. Not by no means. The old gal has behaved herself too well to cast her off now. I'm sorry the picters don't give her no shoes or stockins, but the band of stars upon her hed must continner to shine undimd, forever. I'me for the Union as she air, and whithered be the arm of every ornery cuss who attempts to bust her up. That's me. I hav sed! [It was a very sweaty day, and at this pint of the orashun a man fell down with sunstroke. I told the awjince that considerin the large number of putty gals present I was more fraid of a DAWTER STROKE. This was impromptoo, and seemed to amoose them very much.]

Feller Citizens—I hain't got time to notis the growth of Ameriky frum the time when the Mayflowers cum over in the Pilgrim and brawt Plymmuth Rock with them, but every skool boy nose our kareer has bin tremenjis. You will excuse me if I don't prase the erly settlers of the Kolonies. Peple which hung idiotic old wimin for witches, burnt holes in Quakers' tongues and consined their feller critters to the tredmill and pillery on the slitest provocashun may hav bin very nice folks in their way, but I must confess I don't admire their stile, and will pass them by. I spose they ment well, and so, in the novel and techin langwidge of the nusepapers, "peas to their ashis." Thare was no diskount, however, on them brave men who fit, bled and died in the American Revolushun. We needn't be afraid of setting 'em up two steep. Like my show, they will stand any amount of prase. G. Washington was abowt the best man this world ever sot eyes on. He was a clear-heded, warm-harted, and stiddy goin man. He never slopt over! The prevailin weakness of most public men is to SLOP OVER! [Put them words in large letters—A. W.] They git filled up and slop. They Rush Things. They travel too much on the high presher principle. They git on to the fust poplar hobby-hoss whitch trots along, not carin a sent whether the beest is even goin, clear sited and sound or spavined, blind and bawky. Of course they git throwed eventooually, if no sooner. When they see the multitood goin it blind they go Pel Mel with it, instid of exertin theirselves to set it right. They can't see that the crowd which is now bearin them triumfuntly on its shoulders will soon diskiver its error and cast them into the hoss pond of Oblivyun, without the slitest hesitashun. Washington never slopt over. That wasn't George's stile. He luved his country dearly. He wasn't after the spiles. He was a human angil in a 3 kornerd hat and knee britches, and we shan't see his like right away. My frends, we can't all be Washington's, but we kin all be patrits & behave ourselves in a human and a Christian manner. When we see a brother goin down hill to Ruin let us not give him a push, but let us seeze rite hold of his coat-tails and draw him back to Morality.

Imagine G. Washington and P. Henry in the character of seseshers! As well fancy John Bunyan and Dr. Watts in spangled tites, doin the trapeze in a one-horse circus!

I tell you, feller-citizens, it would have bin ten dollars in Jeff Davis's pocket if he'd never bin born!

* * *

Be shure and vote at leest once at all elecshuns. Buckle on yer Armer and go to the Poles. See two it that your naber is there. See that the krip-ples air provided with carriages. Go to the poles and stay all day. Bewair of the infamous lise whitch the Opposishun will be sartin to git up fur perlitical effek on the eve of eleckshun. To the poles! and when you git there vote jest as you darn please. This is a privilege we all persess, and it is 1 of the booties of this grate and free land.

I see mutch to admire in New Englan. Your gals in particklar air abowt as snug bilt peaces of Calliker as I ever saw. They air fully equal to the corn fed gals of Ohio and Injianny, and will make the bestest kind of wives. It sets my Buzzum on fire to look at 'em.

Be still, my sole, be still,
& you, Hart, stop cuttin up!

I like your skool houses, your meetin houses, your enterprise, gump-shun &c., but your favorit Bevridge I disgust. I allude to New England Rum. It is wuss nor the korn whisky of Injianny, which eats threw stone jugs & will turn the stummuck of the most shiftliss Hog. I seldom seek consolashun in the flowin Bole, but tother day I wurrid down some of your Rum. The fust glass indused me to sware like a infooriated trooper. On takin the secund glass I was seezed with a desire to break winders, & arter imbibin the third glass I knocht a small boy down, pickt his pocket of a New York Ledger, and wildly commenced readin Sylvanus Kobb's last Tail. Its drefful stuff—a sort of lickwid litenin, gut up under the per-sonal supervishun of the devil—tears men's inards all to peaces and makes their noses blossum as the Lobster. Shun it as you would a wild hyeny with a fire brand tied to his tale, and while you air abowt it you will do a first rate thing for yourself and everybody abowt you by shun-nin all kinds of intoxicatin lickers. You don't need 'em no more'n a cat needs 2 tales, sayin nothin abowt the trubble and sufferin they cawse. But unless your inards air cast iron, avoid New Englan's favorite Bevrige.

My frends, I'm dun. I tear myself away from you with tears in my eyes & a pleasant oder of Onyins abowt my close. In the langwidge of Mister Catterline to the Rummuns, I go, but perhaps I shall cum back agin. Adoo, peple of Wethersfield. Be virtoous & you'll be happy!

The third example is called "The Declaration of Independence in American," and was written by H. L. Mencken. It first appeared in the Baltimore *Evening Sun* (Nov. 7, 1921) under the title "Essay in American." It is reprinted here from Mencken, *The American Language. An Inquiry into the Development of English in the United States* (3rd ed.: New York, 1929), pp. 398–402.

THE DECLARATION OF INDEPENDENCE IN AMERICAN

When things get so balled up that the people of a country got to cut loose from some other country, and go it on their own hook, without asking no permission from nobody, excepting maybe God Almighty, then they ought to let everybody know why they done it, so that everybody can see they are not trying to put nothing over on nobody.

All we got to say on this proposition is this: first, me and you is as good as anybody else, and maybe a damn sight better; second, nobody ain't got no right to take away none of our rights; third, every man has got a right to live, to come and go as he pleases, and to have a good time whichever way he likes, so long as he don't interfere with nobody else. That any government that don't give a man them rights ain't worth a damn; also, people ought to choose the kind of government they want themselves, and nobody else ought to have no say in the matter. That whenever any government don't do this, then the people have got a right to give it the bum's rush and put in one that will take care of their interests. Of course, that don't mean having a revolution every day like them South American yellow-bellies, or every time some jobholder goes to work and does something he ain't got no business to do. It is better to stand a little graft, etc., than to have revolutions all the time, like them coons, and any man that wasn't a anarchist or one of them I.W.W.'s would say the same. But when things get so bad that a man ain't hardly got no rights at all no more, but you might almost call him a slave, then everybody ought to get together and throw the grafters out, and put in new ones who won't carry on so high and steal so much, and then watch them. This is the proposition the people of these Colonies is up against, and they have got tired of it, and won't stand it no more. The administration of the present King George III, has been rotten from the start, and when anybody kicked about it he always tried to get away with it by strong-arm work. Here is some of the rough stuff he has pulled:

He vetoed bills in the Legislature that everybody was in favor of, and hardly nobody was against.

He wouldn't allow no law to be passed without it was first put up to him, and then he stuck it in his pocket and let on he forgot about it, and didn't pay no attention to no kicks.

When people went to work and gone to him and asked him to put through a law about this or that, he give them their choice: either they had to shut down the Legislature and let him pass it all by himself, or they couldn't have it at all.

He made the Legislature meet at one-horse tank-towns, so that hardly nobody could get there and most of the leaders would stay home and let him go to work and do things like he wanted.

He give the Legislature the air, and sent the members home every time they stood up to him and give him a call-down or bawled him out.

When a Legislature was busted up he wouldn't allow no new one to be elected, so that there wasn't nobody left to run things, but anybody could walk in and do whatever they pleased.

He tried to scare people outen moving into these States, and made it so hard for a wop or one of these here kikes to get his papers that he would rather stay home and not try it, and then, when he come in, he wouldn't let him have no land, and so he either went home again or never come.

He monkeyed with the courts, and didn't hire enough judges to do the work, and so a person had to wait so long for his case to come up that he got sick of waiting, and went home, and so never got what was coming to him.

He got the judges under his thumb by turning them out when they done anything he didn't like, or by holding up their salaries, so that they had to knuckle down or not get no money.

He made a lot of new jobs, and give them to loafers that nobody knowed nothing about, and the poor people had to pay the bill, whether they could or not.

Without no war going on, he kept an army loafing around the country, no matter how much people kicked about it.

He let the army run things to suit theirself and never paid no attention whatsoever to nobody which didn't wear no uniform.

He let grafters run loose, from God knows where, and give them the say in everything, and let them put over such things as the following:

Making poor people board and lodge a lot of soldiers they ain't got no use for, and don't want to see loafing around.

When the soldiers kill a man, framing it up so that they would get off.

Interfering with business.

Making us pay taxes without asking us whether we thought the things we had to pay taxes for was something that was worth paying taxes for or not.

When a man was arrested and asked for a jury trial, not letting him have no jury trial.

Chasing men out of the country, without being guilty of nothing, and trying them somewheres else for what they done here.

In countries that border on us, he put in bum governments, and then tried to spread them out, so that by and by they would take in this country too, or make our own government as bum as they was.

He never paid no attention whatever to the Constitution, but he went to work and repealed laws that everybody was satisfied with and hardly nobody was against, and tried to fix the government so that he could do whatever he pleased.

He busted up the Legislatures and let on he could do all the work better by himself.

Now he washes his hands of us and even goes to work and declares war on us, so we don't owe him nothing, and whatever authority he ever had he ain't got no more.

He has burned down towns, shot down people like dogs, and raised hell against us out on the ocean.

He hired whole regiments of Dutch, etc., to fight us, and told them they could have anything they wanted if they could take it away from us, and sicked these Dutch, etc., on us.

He grabbed our own people when he found them in ships on the ocean, and shoved guns into their hands, and made them fight against us, no matter how much they didn't want to.

He stirred up the Indians, and give them arms and ammunition, and told them to go to it, and they have killed men, women and children, and don't care which.

Every time he has went to work and pulled any of these things, we have went to work and put in a kick, but every time we have went to work and put in a kick he has went to work and did it again. When a man keeps on handing out such rough stuff all the time, all you can say is that he ain't got no class and ain't fitten to have no authority over people who have got any rights, and he ought to be kicked out.

When we complained to the English we didn't get no more satisfaction. Almost every day we give them plenty of warning that the politicians over there was doing things to us that they didn't have no right to do. We kept on reminding them who we was, and what we was doing here, and how we come to come here. We asked them to get us a square deal, and told them that if this thing kept on we'd have to do something about it and maybe they wouldn't like it. But the more we talked, the more they didn't pay no attention to us. Therefore, if they ain't for us they must be agin us, and we are ready to give them the fight of their lives, or to shake hands when it is over.

Therefore be it resolved, That we, the representatives of the people of the United States of America, in Congress assembled, hereby declare as follows: That the United States, which was the United Colonies in former times, is now a free country, and ought to be; that we have throwed out the English King and don't want to have nothing to do with him no more, and are not taking no more English orders no more; and that, being as we are now a free country, we can do anything that free countries can do, especially declare war, make peace, sign treaties, go into business, etc. And we swear on the Bible on this proposition, one and all, and agree to stick to it no matter what happens, whether we win or we lose, and whether we get away with it or get the worst of it, no matter whether we lose all our property by it or even get hung for it.

The fourth and last example is taken from the novel *Lucifer Land* (New York, 1977), pp. 46–7, by Mildred and Katherine Davis. The place is Westchester County, New York; the time is 1776. Gideon MacDonald has been having an argument about the war with Cassie Bedham. Cassie becomes exasperated because she cannot figure out just where Gideon stands. He goes to the center of the room, stops in front of her, spreads his arms, and, in an oratorical voice, proclaims:

When after a course of stewed rabbit, it becomes desirable for our people to dissolve the military obligations which have connected them with some deserted shoreline, and to assume among the powers of the earth their separate and equal paths towards home, to which the laws of greed and nature's precipitation patterns entitle them, a decent respect to the opinions of their womenfolk requires that they should hide the causes which impel them to departure. Namely, laziness, cowardice and homesickness.

The fourth and last example [illegible] taken from the novel [illegible] (New York, 197[illegible]), [illegible] by Mildred [illegible]. The [illegible] Westchester County, New York; the time is 17[illegible]. [illegible] Macdonell has been having an argument about the [illegible] Cassie Beckman [illegible] again [illegible] Gideon stands [illegible] the center of the room [illegible] folded his arms, and [illegible] procedure.

[illegible]

NOTES

INDEX

NOTES

Notes to the Preface

1 Shils, "Tradition," *Comparative Studies in Society and History,* XIII (April 1971), 122–3, 124.

2 For some provocative parallel thoughts, see Samuel P. Huntington, "Paradigms of American Politics: Beyond the One, the Two, and the Many," *Political Science Quarterly,* LXXXIX (March 1974), 19–22.

3 For a sweeping and stimulating start in the right direction, see John Higham, "Hanging Together: Divergent Unities in American History," *The Journal of American History,* LXI (June 1974), 5–28.

4 Hofstadter, "History and the Social Sciences," in Fritz Stern, ed., *The Varieties of History* (New York, 1956), 370.

CHAPTER ONE
Revolution and Tradition in American Culture

1 Tocqueville, *Democracy in America,* edited by J. P. Mayer (Anchor edition: Garden City, N.Y., 1969), 473.

2 *Ibid.,* 376. My italics.

3 *Ibid.,* 507. My italics.

4 *Ibid.,* 32. In his perceptive discussion of Cotton Mather's *Magnalia Christi Americana* (1702), Sacvan Bercovitch has cast new light on the peculiar, ambivalent role of early American writers in defining indigenous traditions—both substantive and fictive. See his *The Puritan Origins of the American Self* (New Haven, Conn., 1975), 57.

5 Margaret E. Hirst, *Life of Friedrich List and Selections from His Writings* (London, 1909), 35. See, generally, William R. Hutchison, *The Modernist Impulse in American Protestantism* (Cambridge, Mass., 1976).

6 Michel Chevalier, *Society, Manners, and Politics in the United States: Letters on North America,* edited by John William Ward (Garden City, N.Y., 1961), 70; Cobden is quoted in H. J. Habakkuk, *American and British Technology in the Nineteenth Century: The Search for Labour-Saving Inventions* (Cambridge, 1962), 60. See also *The American Diaries of Richard Cobden,* edited by Elizabeth Hoon Cawley (Princeton, N.J., 1952).

7 "Thomas's Reminiscences," *The Democratic Review,* VIII (1840), 227; Howells, "The Modern American Mood," *Harper's New Monthly Magazine,* XCV (July 1897), 200. See also the statement made by B. Gratz Brown to his Missouri constituents in 1850: "With the past we have literally nothing to do, save to dream of it. Its lessons are lost and its

tongue is silent. We are ourselves at the head and front of all political experience. Precedents have lost their virtue and all their authority is gone." Quoted in Rush Welter, *The Mind of America, 1820–1860* (New York, 1975), 6.

8 See Jefferson to Madison, Sept. 6, 1789, in *The Papers of Thomas Jefferson,* edited by Julian P. Boyd (Princeton, N.J., 1958), XV, 384–97; Welter, *The Mind of America,* 12–13, 15; Henry George, *Progress and Poverty* (abridged edition: New York, 1970), 157. See also Thomas Paine's insistence, in *The Rights of Man* (1791): "Every age and generation must be as free to act for itself, *in all cases,* as the ages and generation which preceded it. The vanity and presumption of governing beyond the grave, is the most ridiculous and insolent of all tyrannies." *The Life and Works of Thomas Paine,* edited by William M. Van der Weyde (New Rochelle, N.Y., 1925), VI, 92.

9 *The Collected Works of Abraham Lincoln,* edited by Roy P. Basler (New Brunswick, N.J., 1953), V, 537.

10 Michael Paul Rogin, *Fathers and Children: Andrew Jackson and the Subjugation of the American Indian* (New York, 1975), 8.

11 See R. R. Palmer, "The Impact of the American Revolution Abroad," in *The Impact of the American Revolution Abroad. Papers Presented at the Fourth Library of Congress Symposium, May 8 and 9, 1975* (Washington, D.C., 1976), 11–12. "It is the cant of the day," Henry Tuckerman quipped, "to repudiate the past." Tuckerman, "American Society," *North American Review,* LXXXI (July 1855), 30.

12 Emerson to Mary Moody Emerson, Sept. 23, 1826, in *The Letters of Ralph Waldo Emerson,* edited by Ralph L. Rusk (New York, 1939), I, 174; Emerson, "Nature," in *Nature, Addresses, and Lectures* (Boston, 1886), 9. The opening lines of "Nature" were reiterated explicitly in 1838 by Horace Mann in his "Prospectus of the Common-School Journal." See *Life and Works of Horace Mann* (Boston, 1891), II, 4–5.

13 See Perry Miller, "The Romantic Dilemma in American Nationalism and the Concept of Nature," in Miller, *Nature's Nation* (Cambridge, Mass., 1967), 203; *United States Magazine and Democratic Review,* VI (November 1839), 427. Even in George Bancroft's *History of the United States,* Nature dominated tradition as a determinative force in shaping American life. The distinctive character of our people, Bancroft argued, was their individuality, "strengthened by their struggles with Nature in her wildness, by the remoteness from the abodes of ancient institutions" (II, 323).

14 See Karl W. Deutsch, *Nationalism and Social Communication. An Inquiry into the Foundations of Nationality* (New York, 1953), 5–6; David M. Potter, *People of Plenty. Economic Abundance and the American Character* (Chicago, 1954), 50, 61, 69; and Herbert G. Gutman, *Work, Culture, and Society in Industrializing America* (New York, 1976), 69, 75.

15 Potter, *People of Plenty,* 69. See also Conrad Richter, "That Early American Quality," *The Atlantic Monthy,* CLXXXVI (September 1950), 26; James Willard Hurst, *Law and the Conditions of Freedom in the Nineteenth-Century United States* (Madison, Wis., 1956), 24, 27, 36, 70; Erik H. Erikson, *Dimensions of a New Identity. The 1973 Jefferson Lectures in the Humanities* (New York, 1974), 75–83; and Ann Pamela Cunningham to Benson J. Lossing, May 27, 1870: "*Our people* are so fast—so excitable—that nothing seems to be able to long retain *a hold* on remembrance or interest." Lossing Papers, box 2, Huntington Library, San Marino, California.

16 *Democracy and Its Discontents* (New York, 1974), xiii. See also 65, 66, and 69 for variations on this theme; and William Carlos Williams, *Selected Essays* (New York, 1954), 21: "Nothing is good save the new."

17 Lucien Febvre, the great French historian, had completed an unusual book at the time of his death in 1956, but the manuscript has since disappeared. Fernand Braudel tells us that the book "was entitled *Honor and Fatherland.* It explored a field where little has yet been done, that of collective states of mind, being a study of the transition from fidelity to a person—the prince (that is, honor) to fidelity to the nation (patriotism). The history, in short, of the birth of the idea of fatherland." See Braudel, "Personal Testimony," *The Journal of Modern History,* XLIV (December 1972), 466–7.

18 Shils, "Tradition," *Comparative Studies in Society and History,* XIII (April 1971), 126, 130.

19 *Ibid.*, 146, 158. See also S. N. Eisenstadt, "Some Observations on the Dynamics of Traditions," *Comparative Studies in Society and History,* XI (October 1969), 451–75; Eisenstadt, "Post-Traditional Societies and the Continuity and Reconstruction of Tradition," *Daedalus,* CII (Winter 1973), 1–27; Clifford Geertz, "Ideology as a Cultural System," in Geertz, *The Interpretation of Cultures* (New York, 1973), 193–233; T. S. Eliot, "Tradition" (1933) and "Tradition and the Individual Talent" (1917), both in Eliot, *Points of View* (London, 1941), 21–34.

20 See Frances A. Yates, *The Art of Memory* (Chicago, 1966); Albert B. Lord, *The Singer of Tales* (Cambridge, Mass., 1960); and Heinrich Zimmer, *Myths and Symbols in Indian Art and Civilization* (New York, 1946), 11, 73, 169–70.

21 Albert J. Nock once made a perceptive point that is particularly on target in the American case: "Certain traditions have great powers of prepossession, even if they are not followed; indeed much of the usefulness of a tradition is in the fact that it need only be possessed, not followed." Quoted in Merrill D. Peterson, *The Jefferson Image in the American Mind* (New York, 1960), 355.

22 Cf. Daniel Bell, "The End of American Exceptionalism," *The Public Interest,* no. 41 (Fall 1975), 193–224.

23 See Brooks Adams, *The Emancipation of Massachusetts* (Boston, 1887); Charles Francis Adams, *Three Episodes of Massachusetts History* (Boston, 1893), 2 vols.; Ralph and Louise Boas, *Cotton Mather, Keeper of the Puritan Conscience* (New York, 1928); Paul M. Gaston, *The New South Creed: A Study in Southern Mythmaking* (New York, 1970); T. J. Wertenbaker, *Patrician and Plebeian in Virginia* (Princeton, N.J., 1910); Wertenbaker, *The Planters of Colonial Virginia* (Princeton, N.J., 1922); and W. J. Cash, *The Mind of the South* (New York, 1941), especially Book One.

24 When Newburyport, Massachusetts, held its elaborate, carefully planned Tercentenary pageant in 1930, hostility toward Puritanism, the Puritan founders, and the power of church and state became overt and dramatic—most explicitly in some of the parade floats. See W. Lloyd Warner, *The Living and the Dead. A Study of the Symbolic Life of Americans* (New Haven, Conn., 1959), 170–4.

25 See, for example, F. L. Harvey, *History of the Washington Monument and the National Monument Society* (Washington, D.C., 1903); Robert H. Schauffler, ed., *Washington's Birthday* (New York, 1932); Elswyth Thane, *Mount Vernon Is Ours. The Story of Its Preservation* (New York, 1966); Thomas Nelson Page, *Mount Vernon and Its Preservation, 1858–1910* (New York, 1910).

26 Entry for Nov. 8, 1854, *The Diary of George Templeton Strong*, edited by Allan Nevins and Milton Halsey Thomas (New York, 1952), II, 196–7.

27 Frothingham, *History of the Siege of Boston* . . . (Boston, 1849), iii; Frothingham, *The Command in the Battle of Bunker Hill* (Boston, 1850), 4–5.

28 Bancroft to Tyler, Sept. 24, 1887, in *Moses Coit Tyler, 1835–1900: Selections from His Letters and Diaries*, edited by Jessica Tyler Austin (Garden City, N.Y., 1911), 209.

29 See Jared Sparks's review of Jonathan Elliott, ed., *The Debates, Resolutions, and Other Proceedings in Convention on the Adoption of the Federal Constitution*, in *North American Review*, XXV (October 1827), 32.

30 Avery D. Weisman, *The Existential Core of Psychoanalysis: Reality Sense and Responsibility* (Boston, 1965), 94.

31 There has been a pronounced rise in Black concern about genealogy, accompanied by the use of pension records at the National Archives, Freedmen's Bureau records, oral tradition, family Bibles, and plantation records. See *The New York Times*, Oct. 11, 1976, p. 16; Alex Haley, *Roots* (Garden City, N.Y., 1976); and Middleton A. Harris, comp., *The Black Book* (New York, 1974).

32 David Lavender, *California: A Bicentennial History* (New York, 1976), 23.

33 Boas, Introduction to *Traditions of the Thompson River Indians of British Columbia*, collected and annotated by James Teit, *Memoirs of the American Folk-Lore Society*, VI (Boston, 1898), 17–18.

34 Howells's statement appeared in *The Atlantic Monthly*, XX (July 1867), 121. Aaron's book is *The Unwritten War: American Writers and the Civil War* (New York, 1973). Cf. the (to me) surprising statement by James M. Cox that "the American Civil War remains *the* war in the American imagination," in "The Untold Civil War," *The Virginia Quarterly Review*, L (Spring 1974), 310. Much of the thrust of the chapters that follow will attempt to demonstrate the fallacy of Cox's contention; see especially the coda to Chapter Seven, pp. 256–9 below.

35 See Charles Warren, "Why the Battle of New Orleans Was Not Painted," in Warren, *Odd Byways in American History* (Cambridge, Mass., 1942), 190–1.

36 Warner, *The Living and the Dead*, 133–4. See also "The Meaning of July Fourth for the Negro," speech at Rochester, New York, July 5, 1852, in Philip S. Foner, ed., *The Life and Writings of Frederick Douglass* (New York, 1950), II, 187; and Edward F. Hayward, "Some Romances of the Revolution," *The Atlantic Monthly*, LXIV (November 1889), 636. The Associated Press recently conducted a poll to determine "the top 20 stories since 1776." Out of 273 responses from newspaper editors, radio and television news directors, 245 included the American Revolution; an overwhelming majority listed it first. The drafting of the Constitution in 1787 placed second, followed by the Civil War, World War II, the moon landings, and development of the atomic bomb. Reported in the Palo Alto *Times*, Dec. 10, 1976, p. 56.

37 Emerson, "The American Scholar, an Oration Delivered Before the Phi Beta Kappa Society, at Cambridge, August 31, 1837," in Emerson, *Nature, Addresses, and Lectures* (Boston, 1884), 109. See also Rufus Choate's feeling that the Revolution, "of all time past is the period in which we might all wish to have lived." Samuel Gilman Brown, *The Works of Rufus Choate, with a Memoir of His Life* (Boston, 1862), I, 342; and James P. Holcombe, *Sketches of the Political Issues and Controversies of the Revolution: A Discourse Delivered Before the Virginia Historical Society . . . January 17, 1856* (Richmond, Va., 1856), 5, where he asserts that "the period which challenges our consideration by the strongest claims, as first in time, in interest, and in importance, is that which began with the attempt to tax the colonies and closed with the Declaration of Independence."

38 Eisenstadt, "Observations on the Dynamics of Traditions," 454. In a recent essay, Eisenstadt made the same point even more sharply: "In the cultural sphere all 'traditional' societies, however great the differences among them, tend to accept the givenness of some past event, order, or figure (whether real or symbolic) as the major focus of their collective identity. This given sets the scope and nature of their social and cultural order, becoming the ultimate legitimizer of change and the delineator of the limits of innovation." See "Post-Traditional

Societies and the Continuity and Reconstruction of Tradition," *Daedalus*, CII (Winter 1973), 5.

39 See Arthur H. Shaffer, *The Politics of History: Writing the History of the American Revolution, 1783–1815* (Chicago, 1975); Lawrence J. Friedman, *Inventors of the Promised Land* (New York, 1975).

40 "Tradition," 133.

41 *The Monthly Anthology and Boston Review*, I (October 1804), 557.

42 Hezekiah Niles, *Principles and Acts of the Revolution in America* (Baltimore, Md., 1822), preface.

43 Quoted in Daniel J. Boorstin, *The Americans. The National Experience* (New York, 1965), 362.

44 "An Address Delivered at the Laying of the Corner-Stone of the Bunker Hill Monument," June 17, 1825, in Edwin P. Whipple, ed., *The Great Speeches and Orations of Daniel Webster* (Boston, 1879), 135. In 1843, when the same monument was completed and dedicated, Webster was there for a repeat performance: "Heaven has not allotted to this generation an opportunity of rendering high services, and manifesting strong personal devotion, such as they rendered and manifested [in 1775]. . . . But we may praise what we cannot equal, and celebrate actions which we were not born to perform." *Ibid.*, 138.

45 "The First Battles of the Revolutionary War," April 19, 1825, in Everett, *Orations and Speeches on Various Occasions* (2nd ed.: Boston, 1850), I, 78.

46 Quoted in Benjamin T. Spencer, *The Quest for Nationality. An American Literary Campaign* (Syracuse, N.Y., 1957), 43–4.

47 See William Alfred Bryan, *George Washington in American Literature, 1775–1865* (New York, 1952), 19, 65, 67, 93–4.

48 See Peterson, *Jefferson Image in the American Mind*, 12–14.

49 Richard Slotkin, for example, has demonstrated most persuasively that the legend and image of Daniel Boone had taken very distinctive forms, by the 1820s, in New England, the South, and the West. See *Regeneration Through Violence: The Mythology of the American Frontier, 1600–1860* (Middletown, Conn., 1973), ch. 12. "The Fragmented Image: The Boone Myth and Sectional Cultures (1820–1850)."

50 See Peterson, *Jefferson Image in the American Mind*, 37, 49, 63–5. Jefferson's ambiguous positions on the slavery question were variously exploited as well.

51 See Bryan, *George Washington in American Literature*, 18–22, 74–82, 160–8.

52 See Pauline Maier, "Coming to Terms with Samuel Adams," *The American Historical Review*, LXXXI (February 1976), 12–37; John McWilliams, "The Faces of Ethan Allen: 1760–1860," *New England Quarterly*, IL (June 1976), 257–82; Douglass Adair, "The Authorship of the Disputed Federalist Papers," in *Fame and the Founding Fathers.*

Essays by Douglass Adair, edited by Trevor Colbourn (New York, 1974), 27–74; and William R. Taylor, *Cavalier and Yankee: The Old South and American National Character* (New York, 1961), 78–89, for William Wirt's *Patrick Henry.*

53 Adams to Hezekiah Niles, Feb. 13, 1818, in Adrienne Koch, ed., *The American Enlightenment. The Shaping of the American Experiment and a Free Society* (New York, 1965), 228. For the founders' concern about the perspective of Posterity, see also Edmund S. Morgan, *The Meaning of Independence: Adams, Washington and Jefferson* (Charlottesville, Va., 1976).

54 Quoted in Irma B. Jaffe, *John Trumbull: Patriot-Artist of the American Revolution* (Boston, 1975), 236.

55 Quoted in Peter Shaw, *The Character of John Adams* (Chapel Hill, N.C., 1976), 305. In a Fourth of July oration given to the people of Boston in 1876, Robert C. Winthrop reviewed their knowledge of the events of 1776, and then went on to add: "There is quite enough in these traditions and hearsays . . . to show us that the supporters and signers of the Declaration were not blind to the responsibilities and hazards in which they were involving themselves and the country." *Oration Delivered Before the City Council and Citizens of Boston . . .* (Boston, 1876), 56.

56 Both quoted in Shaffer, *The Politics of History,* 32. See also Wesley Frank Craven, *The Legend of the Founding Fathers* (Ithaca, N.Y., 1965), 63, for similar remarks made by George Chalmers at the close of the War for Independence; and John Jay's letter to Jedediah Morse, Feb. 28, 1797, in *The American Revolution: New York as a Case Study,* edited by Larry R. Gerlach (Belmont, Calif., 1972), 181–2.

57 Written in 1784 and quoted in Lawrence Henry Gipson, *The British Empire Before the American Revolution,* XIII (New York, 1967), 316. In the preface to Volume One of his *History of New Hampshire,* and in a letter written to Ebenezer Hazard, Jan. 13, 1784, Belknap displayed extraordinary awareness "that 'tradition,' whatever it might 'pour down,' is always to be suspected and examined"—*ibid.,* p. 317.

58 Jefferson to Barlow, April 16, 1811, *The Writings of Thomas Jefferson,* edited by Andrew A. Lipscomb (Washington, D.C., 1904), XIII, 44. See also Christine M. Lizanich, " 'The March of This Government': Joel Barlow's Unwritten History of the United States," *The William and Mary Quarterly,* XXXIII (April 1976), 315–30.

59 Jefferson to Wirt, Aug. 14, 1814, *Writings of Jefferson,* XIV, 163, 166, 167, 168, 169, 170, 172. After Wirt's *Henry* was eventually published in 1817, Jefferson and his contemporaries were very upset by what they regarded as its inaccuracies and romantic tendencies. John Taylor of Caroline called it "a splendid novel." For the responses of Taylor, Jefferson, and John Adams, see William R. Taylor, *Cavalier and Yankee,* 68–9.

60 See, for example, Jefferson to Dabney Carr, Jan. 19, 1816, and to Joseph C. Cabell, Feb. 2, 1816, *Writings of Jefferson*, XIV, 398–400, 417. See also William Dorsheimer to Benson J. Lossing, May 5, 1863, Lossing Papers, box 2, Huntington Library, in which he talks about "the usual fate of writers who are compelled to rely for their data upon the recollection of individuals."

61 See John C. Fitzpatrick, "Discovery of the Declaration of Independence by the People of the United States," in *The Spirit of the Revolution. New Light from Some of the Original Sources of American History* (Boston, 1924), 13–14.

62 Adams to Francis Adrian Vanderkemp, Feb. 21, 1823, quoted in Shaw, *The Character of John Adams*, 317.

63 Jefferson to Madison, Aug. 30, 1823, *Writings of Thomas Jefferson*, XV, 460. Subsequently in the same letter Jefferson remarks that whether "this dictum also of Mr. Adams be another slip of memory, let history say"; and still later he refers to "this little lapse of memory of Mr. Adams" (pp. 462, 464).

64 Edward W. Emerson and Waldo E. Forbes, eds., *Journals of Ralph Waldo Emerson* (Boston, 1910), III, 516, 534. For a similar episode involving John Pendleton Kennedy and an aged veteran of the Revolution ("Horse-Shoe" Robinson) in 1835, see Kennedy, *Horse-Shoe Robinson* (1852 ed.: New York, 1937), 10.

65 In addition to the two books cited in note 39 above, see William R. Smith, *History as Argument: Three Patriot Historians of the American Revolution* (The Hague, 1966); Cecelia Tichi, "Worried Celebrants of the American Revolution," in Everett Emerson, ed., *American Literature, 1764–1789: The Revolutionary Years* (Madison, Wisc., 1977), 275–91; Bert James Loewenberg, *American History in American Thought: Christopher Columbus to Henry Adams* (New York, 1972), especially chs. 7–10; David D. Van Tassel, *Recording America's Past: An Interpretation of the Development of Historical Studies in America, 1607–1884* (Chicago, 1960), especially part two; Lester J. Cappon, "American Historical Editors Before Jared Sparks," *The William and Mary Quarterly*, XXX (July 1973), 375–400; and Kenneth Silverman, *A Cultural History of the American Revolution* (New York, 1976).

66 See Edmund S. Morgan, ed., *The American Revolution: Two Centuries of Interpretation* (Englewood Cliffs, N.J., 1965); Esmond Wright, ed., *Causes and Consequences of the American Revolution* (Chicago, 1966); Jack P. Greene, ed., *The Reinterpretation of the American Revolution, 1763–1789* (New York, 1968); Lawrence H. Leder, ed., *The Meaning of the American Revolution* (Chicago, 1969); Stephen G. Kurtz and James H. Hutson, eds., *Essays on the American Revolution* (Chapel Hill, N.C., 1973); and "Interdisciplinary Studies of the American Revolution," a special issue of *The Journal of Interdisciplinary History*, VI (Spring 1976).

67 Walzer, "On the Role of Symbolism in Political Thought," *Political Science Quarterly*, LXXXII (June 1967), 194. Later, on p. 196, Walzer also makes the point—quite pertinent to my material and context—that "symbolic systems set (rough) limits to thought, supporting certain ideas, making others almost inconceivable." Sheldon Wolin offers the observation that imagination has an important place in the work of outstanding social theorists (e.g., Plato's portrayal of the ideal political community) because imagination enables the philosopher to transcend the limitations of historical knowledge. See Wolin, *Politics and Vision: Continuity and Innovation in Western Political Thought* (Boston, 1960), 17–21.

68 Goschen, "Uses of Imagination," Nov. 19, 1891, in *Modern Eloquence*, edited by Thomas B. Reed (Philadelphia, 1900), VIII, 559–60. The concept of imagination seems to have been embellished and explicated by intellectuals during the past century; yet it was hardly unknown among the Founding Fathers. Alexander Hamilton wrote of John Adams (in 1800) that "he is a man of an imagination sublimated and eccentric." See Koch, *The American Enlightenment*, 649.

69 Frye, *The Educated Imagination* (Bloomington, Ind., 1964), 96.

70 Trevelyan, *An Autobiography & Other Essays* (London, 1949), 3. For remarkably similar autobiographical statements by two important figures who did much to define the Revolutionary image in American popular culture, see [William Gilmore Simms], "Ellet's Women of the Revolution," in *Southern Quarterly Review*, XVII (1850), 351–2; and Gertrude Atherton, *Adventures of a Novelist* (New York, 1932), in which she describes the inspiration she received from reading a statement about Alexander Hamilton in Lord Bryce's *American Commonwealth*. The effect of that passage was "to excite my imagination as it never had been excited before. Then and there I made up my mind. I would write a life of Hamilton, rescue him from the undeniable obscurity into which he had fallen, give him back his family" (pp. 309–10, 315–16). Her fictionalized biography, published in 1901, became a very popular best-seller.

71 To get some notion of what is happening in this relatively new and still rather suspect field, see Ray B. Browne, ed., *Popular Culture and the Expanding Consciousness* (New York, 1973), especially 1–7, 14–22, 45–59. See also Merrill Lewis, "Language, Literature, Rhetoric and the Shaping of the Historical Imagination of Frederick Jackson Turner," *Pacific Historical Review*, XLV (August 1976), 399–424.

72 Lowell to Hawthorne, April 24, 1851, in J. Donald Crowley, ed., *Hawthorne: The Critical Heritage* (London, 1970), 191.

73 Krieger, "Fiction and Historical Reality: The Hourglass and the Sands of Time," in Ralph Cohen and Murray Krieger, *Literature and History:*

Papers Read at a Clark Library Seminar, March 3, 1973 (Los Angeles, 1974), 68, 75.

74 Simms, *Views and Reviews in American Literature, History and Fiction, First)Series,* edited by C. Hugh Holman (Cambridge, Mass., 1962), 273, 275–6.

75 *Ibid.,* 8, 61–2, 76, 113, 122, 124.

76 *Ibid.,* 124–7, 155. See also Simms to William Bacon Stevens, Dec. 30, 1841; Simms to John C. Calhoun, May 21, 1847; Simms to Benjamin F. Perry, July 15, 1847, in Mary C. Simms Oliphant, *et al.*, eds., *The Letters of William Gilmore Simms* (Columbia, S.C., 1952–6), I, 296; II, 319, 334.

77 "Legends of the Province House," *The Complete Short Stories of Nathaniel Hawthorne* (Garden City, N.Y., 1959), 128–9, 132, 152.

78 *Ibid.,* 129, 146, 149–50, 153.

79 *Ibid.,* 121–2, 128–30.

80 Hawthorne, *Septimius Felton; or, The Elixir of Life* [1863] in *The Complete Writings of Nathaniel Hawthorne,* XIV (Boston, 1904), 168. Hawthorne's fascination with the problem of tradition runs like a bright red thread through this, his last (and unfinished) novel—see also 70, 71, 184, 205, 254, 306–7, 316. At one critical juncture (p. 194), Septimius says: "Nobody can make a tradition; it takes a century to make it."

81 Cooper to Carey and Lea, Dec. 30, 1831, *The Letters and Journals of James Fenimore Cooper,* edited by James F. Beard (Cambridge, Mass., 1960), II, 169–70. See also Horatio G. Jones, Jr., to Benson J. Lossing, Feb. 17, 1853, Lossing Papers, Addenda, box 3, Huntington Library, in which the fervent hope is expressed that Lossing's efforts will "place our country, at no distant day, beside the proud land of Scott and Lockhart, so rich in legendary and poetical interest, as well as historical glory." Cf. Rose Marie Cutting, "America Discovers Its Literary Past: Early American Literature in Nineteenth-Century Anthologies," *Early American Literature,* IX (Winter 1975), 226–51.

82 See Fletcher M. Green, "Listen to the Eagle Scream: One Hundred Years of the Fourth of July in North Carolina (1776–1876)," *North Carolina Historical Review,* XXXI (July 1954), 307; A. V. Huff, Jr., "The Eagle and the Vulture: Changing Attitudes Toward Nationalism in Fourth of July Orations Delivered in Charleston, 1778–1860," *South Atlantic Quarterly,* LXXIII (Winter 1974), 11, 14–15, 22.

83 During the spring of 1839, Jared Sparks gave a course of lectures at Harvard College on the American Revolution—the first such course taught in the United States. He adopted Carlo Botta's *History* as his assigned text "because I can procure no other; all the other histories of the same period being out of print." See Herbert B. Adams, *The*

Life and Writings of Jared Sparks, Comprising Selections from His Journals and Correspondence (Boston, 1893), II, 375.

84 See William Henry Drayton and John Drayton, *Memoirs of the American Revolution, from Its Commencement to the Year 1776 . . .* (Charleston, S.C., 1821), 2 vols.; Alexander Garden, *Anecdotes of the Revolutionary War in America . . .* (Charleston, S.C., 1822); James Thacher, *A Military Journal . . .* (Boston, 1823); and for their use by imaginative writers, see Bryan, *George Washington in American Literature,* 226 n.118.

85 See Van Tassel, *Recording America's Past,* 103–4, 182.

86 *North American Review,* XLVI (April 1838), 477–8.

87 See Lossing, *Biographical Sketches of the Signers of the Declaration of Independence* (New York, 1854), iv.

88 Shils, "Tradition," 144.

89 See Ralph L. Rusk, *The Life of Ralph Waldo Emerson* (New York, 1949), 20, 154; Rusk, *The Letters of Emerson,* VI, 329–32.

90 Rusk, *Life of Emerson,* 221–3, 238, 273–4.

91 See *ibid.,* 433, 489; Michael H. Cowan, *City of the West: Emerson, America, and Urban Metaphor* (New Haven, Conn., 1967), 175–7.

92 "Temperance Address," Feb. 22, 1842, Basler, *Collected Works of Lincoln,* I, 278.

93 "Address Before the Young Men's Lyceum of Springfield, Illinois," Jan. 27, 1838, *ibid.,* 108–9, 112, 115. The italics are Lincoln's.

94 *Ibid.,* II, 370–1 (Sept. 6, 1856); *ibid.,* IV, 433–5 (July 4, 1861). For a compact summary of this problem in American intellectual history, see Merle Curti, "Our Revolutionary Tradition," *The Social Frontier,* I (December 1934), 10–13. Curti reminds us that Lincoln, while a member of Congress in 1848, had declared: "Any people anywhere being inclined and having the power have the right to rise up and shake off the existing government and form a new one that suits them better" (p. 11).

95 Morgan, "Interpreting the American Revolution," in *The American Revolution: Two Centuries of Interpretation,* 4.

96 See pp. 246–56 below.

97 Sullivan, *Thoughts upon the Political Situation of the United States* (Worcester, Mass., 1788), 21; Webster is quoted in Norman Risjord, *Forging the American Republic, 1760–1815* (Reading, Mass., 1973), 245.

98 *North American Review,* XXV (October 1827), 32. On March 6, 1831, James Kirke Paulding informed James Madison that "it has been proposed to me to write the Lives of some few of the most distinguished men of this country, in a manner somewhat different from what has been hitherto attempted by mingling more of their domestic habits and character, & confining the details to such parts only of the History of the United States, as they were more especially connected

with." See Ralph M. Aderman, ed., *The Letters of James Kirke Paulding* (Madison, Wis., 1962), 114–15.

99 Henry Tuckerman, "American Society," *North American Review*, LXXXI (July 1855), 30.

100 One exception was Edward Everett, who engaged Burke directly in *An Oration Delivered at Cambridge on the Fiftieth Anniversary of the Declaration of the Independence of the United States of America* (Boston, 1826), 32–3. Everett insisted that intergenerational relations were not governed by some mythical law of corporations (Burke), but rather by the laws of nature; and Everett queried "that chain of cause and effect, which makes our characters receive impressions from the generations before us, and puts it in our power, by a good or bad precedent, to distil a poison or balm into the characters of posterity?" A second was John Quincy Adams, who wrote to Matthew Clarke on Aug. 17, 1831, in order to congratulate Clarke and Peter Force on undertaking their massive compilation of documents from the Revolutionary era. "The men of the present age are under a sacred obligation, both to that which has past, and that which is to come, to preserve the recorded virtues of their forefathers for the instruction and emulation of their posterity; nor shall they be unremembered who assume upon themselves to perform this duty for their contemporaries." Quoted in Frederick R. Goff, "Peter Force," *The Papers of the Bibliographical Society of America*, XLIV (1st qtr. 1950), 5.

101 *The Works of . . . Edmund Burke* (Bohn's Standard Library: London, 1888), II, 368.

CHAPTER TWO
Revisions of the Revolution in an Un-Revolutionary Culture

1 Pieces of the story, and important insights as well, will be found in Wesley Frank Craven, *The Legend of the Founding Fathers* (New York, 1956); Jack P. Greene, ed., *The Reinterpretation of the American Revolution, 1763–1789* (New York, 1968); and Bernard Bailyn, "Lines of Force in Recent Writings on the American Revolution," in *Reports: XIV International Congress of the Historical Sciences* [San Francisco, August 1975] (New York, 1977), I, 172–219.

2 To the Editors of the Boston *Daily Advertiser*, Jan. 8, 1862, in *Letters of Francis Parkman*, edited by Wilbur R. Jacobs (Norman, Okla., 1960), I, 144–5. Parkman also drew upon the Revolutionary experience in letters he wrote on Sept. 4, 1861, and Oct. 17, 1862 (see *ibid.*, 142–3, 157–8). Robert C. Winthrop echoed Parkman's plaint about the de-

cline of leadership in his widely read Centennial address. See Winthrop, *Oration Delivered Before the City Council and Citizens of Boston . . . July 4, 1876* (Boston, 1876), 93.

3 Webster, *Address, Delivered at Bunker Hill, June 17, 1843, on the Completion of the Monument* (Boston, 1843), 3–4. See also Benson J. Lossing to Ann Pamela Cunningham, March 26, 1870, and Cunningham to Lossing, March 30, 1870, in the Lossing Papers, box 2, Huntington Library. Lossing, the popular historian, believed that "there will be decided disinclination on the part of the public in general to contribute money for relics of Washington." Cunningham, founder and first regent of the Mount Vernon Ladies Association, responded in despair: "I *fear* you are correct, and that if we ever succeed in getting them placed here, it will be only by Herculean labors. Yet, the same public has again and again, in an incredible short period of time in the last four years, raised hundreds of thousands of dollars to present fortunes to public men—or to their widows!! The money seems literally to have been *poured out* for such men, and such purposes; while it took incredible labor, from thousands of patriotic women, during *seven long years,* to *wring* from our people, over our *whole country,* a sum to purchase the home of the *Father* of his country" (her italics).

4 See Robert P. Hay, "Freedom's Jubilee: One Hundred Years of the Fourth of July, 1776–1876," unpublished Ph.D. dissertation (University of Kentucky, 1967), 238.

5 See Robert H. Schauffler, ed., *Washington's Birthday* (New York, 1932); Merrill D. Peterson, *The Jefferson Image in the American Mind* (New York, 1960), 420–2; Frank W. Fetter, "The Revision of the Declaration of Independence in 1941," *The William and Mary Quarterly,* XXXI (January 1974), 133–8; and Kenneth Umbreit, *Founding Fathers. Men Who Shaped Our Tradition* (New York, 1941).

6 Adams to Jefferson, Aug. 24, 1815, in *The Adams-Jefferson Letters,* edited by Lester J. Cappon (Chapel Hill, N.C., 1959), II, 455; Rush, *An Address to the People of the United States* (Philadelphia, 1787), in Hezekiah Niles, *Principles and Acts of the Revolution in America,* edited by Alden T. Vaughan (New York, 1965), 334.

7 See Frederick R. Black, "The American Revolution as 'Yardstick' in the Debates on the Constitution, 1787–1788," *Proceedings of the American Philosophical Society,* CXVII (June 1973), 162–85; Paul C. Nagel, *One Nation Indivisible. The Union in American Thought, 1776–1861* (New York, 1964), 183.

8 See Howard H. Martin, "Orations on the Anniversary of American Independence, 1777–1876," unpublished Ph.D. dissertation (Northwestern University, 1955), 88, 253–7. During the 1790s, just as soon as Thomas Jefferson became marked as having a decided political affiliation, the Federalists also sought to minimize his role in drafting

the Declaration. After 1800, of course, the Republicans mentioned his authorship at every plausible opportunity. See Fletcher M. Green, "Listen to the Eagle Scream: One Hundred Years of the Fourth of July in North Carolina (1776–1876)," *North Carolina Historical Review*, XXXI (July 1954), 301–2, 304.

9 See the remarks made by M. Augustus Jewett on July 4, 1840, in Terre Haute, Indiana: "This immortal declaration is due to circumstances which, in the history of a world, can never occur again . . . we are removed from the yet enduring evils of the old world." Quoted in Rush Welter, *The Mind of America, 1820–1860* (New York, 1975), 21. See also John C. Rainbolt, "Americans' Initial View of their Revolution's Significance for Other Peoples, 1776–1788," *The Historian*, XXXV (May 1973), 418–33.

10 See Webster, *Address, Delivered at Bunker Hill, June 17, 1843*, 22–9; Carolyn Sue Weddington, "The Image of the American Revolution in the United States, 1815–1860," unpublished Ph.D. dissertation (Louisiana State University, 1972), 72; and Peterson, *The Jefferson Image in the American Mind*, 89, 130–1, 449–50.

11 Jefferson to Adams, Sept. 12, 1821, *The Adams-Jefferson Letters*, II, 575. See also Jefferson to Alexander von Humboldt, April 14, 1811, in *The Writings of Thomas Jefferson*, edited by Andrew A. Lipscomb (Washington, D.C., 1904), XIII, 34. Jefferson believed that the newly independent states of Spanish America would "copy our outlines of confederation and elective government [and] abolish distinction of ranks."

12 Advocates of this position would have cheerfully approved the popular slogan in Indonesia during the mid-1960s: "The Revolution is Unfinished." See Clifford Geertz, *The Interpretation of Cultures. Selected Essays* (New York, 1973), 222.

13 Ramsay, *An Oration, Delivered on the Anniversary of American Independence, July 4, 1794* (Charleston, S.C., 1794).

14 See Green, "Listen to the Eagle Scream," *North Carolina Historical Review* (October 1954), 548–9; *The Collected Works of Abraham Lincoln*, edited by Roy P. Basler (New Brunswick, N.J., 1953), I, 112, 278; III, 375–6; IV, 240; Peterson, *The Jefferson Image in the American Mind*, 437.

15 See Charles Warren, "Fourth of July Myths," *The William and Mary Quarterly*, II (July 1945), 261–2, 270–1.

16 See Philip Detweiler, "The Changing Reputation of the Declaration of Independence: The First Fifty Years," *ibid.*, XIX (October 1962), 573.

17 By the later nineteenth century, Paine had become a despised figure for the dominant writers of American history. See, e.g., John Bach McMaster, *A History of the People of the United States from the Revolution to the Civil War* (New York, 1883), I, 150–1. The only sympathetic

treatment came from that curious figure, Moncure Daniel Conway, a former abolitionist who was very much outside the mainstream of American culture during the Gilded Age. Conway chose to live in England from 1863 until 1884, and again from 1892 to 1897. In 1892 he published a two-volume biography of Paine; and subsequently edited *The Writings of Thomas Paine* (1894–6) in four volumes.

18 Edward E. Hale, "Memoir of the Hon. Lorenzo Sabine," *Proceedings of the Massachusetts Historical Society,* XVII (Boston, 1880), 372. It is a routine part of the Lincoln folklore that young Abe was deeply affected by his reading (and rereading) of Weems's *Washington.* The following verses suggest the continued impact of Parson Weems as late as the 1930s.

Let others echo Rupert Hughes
And mix up motes and beams—
The anecdotes that I peruse
Were told by Parson Weems.

Above iconoclastic views
That little hatchet gleams!
"I cannot tell a lie," I choose
The Washington of Weems.

19 At the end of the 1890s, Gertrude Atherton decided to write a fictionalized biography of Hamilton in order to "rescue him from the undeniable obscurity into which he had fallen." *Adventures of a Novelist* (New York, 1932), 310.

In 1902, John Fiske complained that James Madison had been curiously neglected by American historians. "James Madison: The Constructive Statesman," in Fiske, *Essays, Historical and Literary* (New York, 1902), I, ch. 5.

The abilities of John Adams remained remarkably obscure until the third quarter of the twentieth century, when his reputation underwent an amazing renaissance at the hands of Catherine Drinker Bowen (1950), Zoltan Haraszti (1952), George Peek (1954), Clinton Rossiter (1957), Lyman Butterfield (1961), Page Smith (1962), Adrienne Koch (1963), Loren Baritz (1964), Edward Handler (1964), Irving Stone (1965), John Howe (1966), Douglass Adair and John Schutz (1966), Andrew Oliver (1967), Peter Shaw (1976), and "The Adams Chronicles" on PBS (1976).

20 See William R. Smith, *History as Argument: Three Patriot Historians of the American Revolution* (The Hague, 1966); Arthur H. Shaffer, *The Politics of History: Writing the History of the American Revolution, 1783–1815* (Chicago, 1975); and Page Smith, *The Historian and History* (New York, 1964), ch. 12 on David Ramsay. Ramsay began his historical writing

about the Revolution during the mid-1780s, and continued busily until his death in 1815. Mercy Otis Warren had virtually completed her volumes by 1791, but did not publish them until 1805 when the political climate was more congenial to her Jeffersonian outlook. Pitkin's two volumes first appeared in 1828.

21 Abiel Holmes, *The Annals of America* (Cambridge, Mass., 1829), I, preface, 1; Hezekiah Niles, *Principles and Acts of the Revolution in America* (Baltimore, Md., 1822); Jedediah Morse, *Annals of the American Revolution* (Hartford, Conn., 1824).

22 See *The Papers of Daniel Webster: Correspondence,* edited by Charles M. Wiltse (Hanover, N.H., 1974), I, 381. A conceptual framework for the tentative role of tradition in the 1820s, as well as some interesting comparisons, emerge from a contextual reading of two essays by Clifford Geertz, "Ideology as a Cultural System," and, "After the Revolution: The Fate of Nationalism in the New States," in Geertz, *The Interpretation of Cultures. Selected Essays* (New York, 1973), 193–254. See also Charles L. Sanford, ed., *Quest for America, 1810–1824* (Garden City, N.Y., 1964).

23 See Herbert B. Adams, *The Life and Writings of Jared Sparks, Comprising Selections from His Journals and Correspondence* (Boston, 1893), I, 173–5; Peterson, *Jefferson Image in the American Mind,* 20; George Bancroft, "An Incident in the Life of John Adams," *The Century Magazine,* XXXIV (July 1887), 434–40. For the visit made by two young Bostonians in February 1815, see Francis C. Rosenberger, ed., *Jefferson Reader* (New York, 1953), 76–85; and for an interview at Monticello in the summer of 1822 between Jefferson and Daniel Pierce Thompson of Vermont, see "A Talk with Jefferson," *Harper's New Monthly Magazine,* CLVI (May 1863), 833–5. Judge Thompson (1795–1868) would subsequently write a hugely popular novel, *The Green Mountain Boys: A Historical Tale of the Early Settlement of Vermont* (New York, 1839).

24 Everett, *Orations and Speeches on Various Occasions* (2nd ed.: Boston, 1850), I, x. See also John Sanderson, *Biography of the Signers of the Declaration of Independence* (Philadelphia, 1823–7), 9 vols.

25 See Hay, "One Hundred Years of the Fourth of July," 159–65.

26 *Ibid.,* 168–70. See the Trenton, New Jersey, *Emporium and True American,* July 9, 1831. John Fiske, the very popular historian who did so much in the later nineteenth century to shape America's sense of the Revolutionary era, died on the morning of July 4, 1901, with the celebrations of Independence Day echoing through his Brattle Street windows in Cambridge, Massachusetts.

27 Marcus Cunliffe, *The Nation Takes Shape, 1789–1837* (Chicago, 1959), 124.

28 Quoted in Hay, "One Hundred Years of the Fourth of July," 114.

29 See Philip S. Foner, ed., *We,.the Other People: Alternative Declarations of*

Independence by Labor Groups, Farmers, Woman's Rights Advocates, Socialists, and Blacks, 1829–1975 (Urbana, Ill., 1976), 1–2. The quotations are from 1829 and 1830.

30 *Ibid.*, 3–7, 9–10. Strong agitation also occurred in 1836, when working-class people made sharp assertions about their liberty being a sacred inheritance from Revolutionary sires. One labor leader, Seth Luther, referred to the patriots of 1776 as "an immortal band of 'conspirators' who were 'on a strike' " when the Declaration was adopted.

31 Martineau, *Society in America,* edited by Seymour Martin Lipset (Garden City, N.Y., 1962), 98–9; Detweiler, "The Changing Reputation of the Declaration of Independence," 565–6, 570–1.

32 *Ibid.*, 572; Thomas Jefferson to James Madison, Aug. 30, 1823, in Lipscomb, ed., *Writings of Thomas Jefferson,* XV, 460–4; John C. Fitzpatrick, "Discovery of the Declaration of Independence by the People of the United States," in *The Spirit of the Revolution. New Light from Some of the Original Sources of American History* (Boston, 1924), 9, 16–18, 20, 22; Julian P. Boyd, "The Declaration of Independence: The Mystery of the Lost Original," *The Pennsylvania Magazine of History and Biography,* C (October 1976), 438–67.

33 See Weddington, "The Image of the American Revolution in the United States, 1815–1860," 65–72; [Everett], "South America," *North American Review,* XII (April 1821), 434. See also Martin, "Orations on the Anniversary of American Independence," 239–60.

34 During the 1830s and 1840s, Americans became ever more disenchanted on account of the failure of other new nations to adopt governments similar to our own. (Only Texas, which had been settled by citizens from the United States, established a viable republic after winning independence.) Instead of interpreting this non-imitative pattern as a sign of our failure, however, more and more Americans stressed the *uniqueness* of their own Revolution and the superior character of those heroic patriots responsible for it. The net effect, of course, was an increasingly conservative understanding of the Revolution and its proper place in national tradition. As one orator put it: "No intemperate zeal of faction—no lawless spirit of innovation, sweeping in their destructive rage, the decorations of polished life, and the institutions of organized authority, characterized the contest, which eventuated in our freedom." See Weddington, "The Image of the American Revolution in the United States, 1815–1860," 90–2, and the various speeches and contemporary publications she cites in notes 72–4.

35 Sparks to Alexander Everett, Sept. 12, 1826, in Adams, *Life and Writings of Jared Sparks,* I, 509. See also Sparks, "Materials for American History," *North American Review,* XXIII (October 1826), 275–94.

36 Madison to Sparks, Jan. 25, 1828, in Adams, *Life and Writings of Jared Sparks*, II, 219.

37 *The Federalist Papers*, edited by Clinton Rossiter (New York, 1961), 104.

38 Charles Warren, "How Politics Intruded into the Washington Centenary of 1832," *Proceedings of the Massachusetts Historical Society*, LXV (1932), 45–6. Compare Warren's treatment of 1832 with Lyman H. Butterfield, "The Jubilee of Independence, July 4, 1826," *Virginia Magazine of History and Biography*, LXI (1953), 119–40. The year 1832 seems to have been a peculiarly transitional one for men and events that had been *national* symbols of the Revolution. In 1832, for example, while the South Carolina Nullifiers were claiming Thomas Jefferson as a prophet of States' Rights, the Jacksonian Democrats were also recasting him as a strong Unionist to suit their own needs.

39 See Robert P. Hay, "Charles Carroll and the Passing of the Revolutionary Generation," *Maryland Historical Magazine*, LXVII (Winter 1972), 54–62; and Hay, "The Glorious Departure of the American Patriarchs," *The Journal of Southern History*, XXXV (November 1969), 543–55.

40 See Welter, *The Mind of America*, 9; Nagel, *One Nation Indivisible*, 128–67; Paul C. Nagel, *This Sacred Trust: American Nationality, 1798–1898* (New York, 1971), 109, 118. Edward Everett's widely read 1826 *Oration* offered an important harbinger of this theme: "The voice of our fathers' blood begins to cry to us, from beneath the soil which it moistened" (p. 11). One of Benson J. Lossing's admirers broke into verse in the middle of a letter:

'Tis well! I love to see the fire
Our fathers built, return;
I love the memories of the sire,
The ashes *and the* urn!

The correspondent went on to add: "I deem your work peculiarly opportune in these foppish and degenerate days when we appear to be losing sight of our revolutionary landmarks in the fogs of partyism." Josiah Dean Canning to Lossing, April 11, 1853 [from Gill, Mass., in the Connecticut Valley], Lossing Papers, box 1, Huntington Library.

41 Jefferson to John Holmes, April 22, 1820, *The Works of Thomas Jefferson*, edited by Paul Leicester Ford (New York, 1905), XII, 159. For an insightful discussion of this period, see George B. Forgie, "Father Past and Child Nation: The Romantic Imagination and the Origins of the American Civil War," unpublished Ph.D. dissertation (Stanford University, 1971).

42 "The Causes of the American Revolution," *North American Review*,

LXXX (April 1855), 389, 390. See also [William Gilmore Simms], "Ellet's Women of the Revolution," *Southern Quarterly Review*, I (July 1850), 351.

43 See *The Writings and Speeches of Samuel J. Tilden*, edited by John Bigelow (New York, 1885), I, 451-2.

44 See Welter, *The Mind of America*, 4–5, 11–12.

45 *North American Review*, XLVI (April 1838), 486. For Peter Force's political support and subsidy, see George H. Callcott, *History in the United States, 1800–1860* (Baltimore, Md., 1970), 50–1. Force's partnership with Clarke dissolved in 1843, and the entire project terminated in 1855 because Secretary of State Marcy refused to authorize continued governmental support. Nine volumes had appeared in all (1837–53) covering the years 1774 to 1776. See Frederick R. Goff, "Peter Force," *Papers of the Bibliographical Society of America*, XLIV (1st qtr. 1950), 4, 6; and R. Kent Newmyer, "A Nineteenth-Century View of the Historiography of the American Revolution: A Footnote on Plagiarism," *ibid.*, LVIII (2nd qtr. 1964), 165–6.

46 See Alexander Davidson, "How Benson J. Lossing Wrote His Field Books of the Revolution," *Papers of the Bibliographical Society of America*, XXXII (1st qtr. 1938), 57–64; David D. Van Tassel, "Benson J. Lossing: Pen and Pencil Historian," *American Quarterly*, VI (Spring 1954), 32–44; John T. Cunningham, "Historian on the Double," *American Heritage*, XIX (June 1968), 55–64, 78–81.

47 See David D. Van Tassel, *Recording America's Past. An Interpretation of the Development of Historical Studies in America, 1607–1884* (Chicago, 1960), 136–7. Sabine brought out a second, enlarged edition in 1864, *Biographical Sketches of Loyalists of the American Revolution*, in which he complimented William Gilmore Simms generously on his novels of the American Revolution in South Carolina.

48 See Simms, "South Carolina in the Revolution," *Southern Quarterly Review*, XIV (July 1848), 37–77; Simms, "Kennedy's Life of Wirt," *ibid.*, XVII (April 1850), 209–11; Simms, "The Southern Convention," *ibid.*, XVIII (September 1850), 202–3; and Benjamin Blake Minor, "The Impartiality of History," *Southern Literary Messenger*, XIII (July 1847), 448, for a less critical view. Simms insisted that southerners had indeed fought for liberty during the War for Independence; but he also shifted the emphasis, or meaning of liberty, from individual freedom to self-government for the society or community.

49 *The Papers of Daniel Webster: Correspondence*, I, 373. See also John Hope Franklin, "The North, the South, and the American Revolution," *The Journal of American History*, LXII (June 1975), 5–23.

50 Quoted in Tilden G. Edelstein, *Strange Enthusiasm. A Life of Thomas Wentworth Higginson* (New Haven, Conn., 1968), 117–18.

51 See Elizabeth F. L. Ellet, *The Women of the American Revolution* (New

York, 1848–50), 3 vols,; William C. Nell, *The Colored Patriots of the American Revolution* (Boston, 1855); and John Greenleaf Whittier, "The Black Men of the Revolution and War of 1812," in *The National Era,* I (July 19, 1847), 1, reprinted in *The Writings of Whittier* (Boston, 1889), VI, 406–16.

52 For the critical storm that arose in 1851–2 over Jared Sparks's bowdlerization of George Washington's correspondence, see John Spencer Bassett, *The Middle Group of American Historians* (New York, 1917), 101–7. For Hildreth's approach to the American Revolution, see Lawrence H. Gipson, *The British Empire Before the American Revolution* (New York, 1967) XIII, 349–53. For Dawson's critical revisionism, see David D. Van Tassel, "Henry Benton Dawson: A Nineteenth Century Revisionist," *The William and Mary Quarterly,* XIII (July 1956), 319–41. Frothingham's major efforts were his *History of the Siege of Boston* (Boston, 1849), *The Command in the Battle of Bunker Hill* (Boston, 1850), and the *Life and Times of Joseph Warren* (Boston, 1865), a biography he began in 1849.

53 The *Harrison Republican* (Cadiz, Ohio), July 9, 1840. See also Martin, "Orations on the Anniversary of American Independence, 1777–1876," 93, where he points out that by the later 1850s, in large cities such as New York and Brooklyn, the traditional oration became an "entertainment" to which one paid admission. In at least two instances (1859), the oration seems even to have been burlesqued.

54 Quoted in Martin, "Orations," 321–6. See also Rufus Choate, "American Nationality: An Oration Delivered in Boston on the Eighty-Second Anniversary of American Independence, July 5, 1858, in *Addresses and Orations of Rufus Choate* (3rd ed.: Boston, 1879), 481. One factor responsible for this disillusionment was the realization by some—even in a great age of debate and declamatory rhetoric—that eloquence was ephemeral. In a lecture entitled "The Eloquence of Revolutionary Periods," given in 1857, Choate lamented that the spoken words of Revolutionary heroes had perished: "No parchment manuscript, no embalming printed page, no certain traditions of living or dead, have kept them" (*ibid.*, p. 198). That disappointment was responsible, I believe, for the dramatic rise of oral history during the decade following 1844. It took the form, mainly, of interviews with aged survivors of the American Revolution. In addition to Benson Lossing's extensive interviews up and down the seaboard during the later 1840s, see Catherine S. Crary, "Guerrilla Activities of James DeLancey's Cowboys in Westchester County," in *The Loyalist Americans: A Focus on Greater New York,* edited by Robert A. East (Tarrytown, N. Y., 1975), 22; and Samuel Eliot Morison, *John Paul Jones, a Sailor's Biography* (Boston, 1959), 172.

55 See Sylvester Judd, *A Moral Review of the Revolutionary War, or Some of the Evils of That Event Considered. A Discourse Delivered at the Unitarian Church, Augusta, Sabbath Evening, March 13th, 1842* (Hallowell, Me., 1842). See also Herbert G. Gutman, *Work, Culture and Society in Industrializing America* (New York, 1976), 51.

56 Quoted in Thomas J. Wertenbaker, *Norfolk: Historic Southern Port* (Durham, N.C., 1931), 123–4. See also James P. Holcombe, *Sketches of the Political Issues and Controversies of the Revolution: A Discourse Delivered Before the Virginia Historical Society . . . January 17, 1856* (Richmond, Va., 1856), 6, 9–10, 52.

57 See Weddington, "The Image of the American Revolution in the United States, 1815–1860," 164.

58 *Ibid.*, 79–81.

59 "The South and Her Remedies," *DeBow's Review*, X (March 1851), 267. See also [David F. Jamison], "The National Anniversary," *Southern Quarterly Review*, XVIII (September 1850), 190–1; [Simms], "The Southern Convention," 207–8.

60 Keitt's speech first appeared in the *Congressional Globe*, 34th Congress, 1st Session, Appendix, 833–9 (July 16, 1856), and was reprinted in *DeBow's Review*, XXI (November 1856), 491–508, which considerably expanded the speech's visibility and public impact.

61 David M. Potter, *The Impending Crisis, 1848–1861*, edited by Don E. Fehrenbacher (New York, 1976), 421–2. For the text of Lincoln's Cooper Union speech, see Basler, *Collected Works of Lincoln*, III, 522–50.

62 Yancey to James S. Slaughter, June 15, 1858, in John W. DuBose, *The Life and Times of William Lowndes Yancey* (Birmingham, Ala., 1892), I, 376.

63 Quoted in Potter, *The Impending Crisis*, 485.

64 Quoted in Jesse T. Carpenter, *The South as a Conscious Minority, 1789–1861: A Study in Political Thought* (New York, 1930), 195.

65 Quoted in *ibid.*, 197.

66 Quoted in Hay, "One Hundred Years of the Fourth of July," 253–4.

67 *Congressional Globe*, 36th Congress, 2nd Session, 487 (Jan. 21, 1861); "The Southern Confederacy," *DeBow's Review*, XXX (March 1861), 352–3; P. Finley, "The Right of Secession," *ibid.* (April 1861), 398; J. D. B. DeBow, "Editorial," *ibid.* (May and June 1861), 681; J. Randolph Tucker, "The Great Issue: Our Relations to It," *Southern Literary Messenger*, XXII (March 1861), 169; and see David L. Smiley, "Revolutionary Origins of the South's Constitutional Defenses," *North Carolina Historical Review*, XLIV (Summer 1967), 256–69.

68 See *Southern Literary Messenger*, XXXVII (November 1863), 718–26; and *DeBow's Review*, IV (July 1867), 36–47. See also William Gilmore Simms to John J. Bockee, Dec. 12, 1860, in Mary C. Simms Oliphant,

et al., eds., *The Letters of William Gilmore Simms* (Columbia, S.C., 1952–6), IV, 304.

69 See Hay, "One Hundred Years of the Fourth of July," 269–71, 273; and Fletcher M. Green, "The Spirit of '76," *The Emory University Quarterly*, XI (June 1955), 77–8.

70 Bancroft, *History of the United States of America* (New York, 1883), II, 326. See also Myrtle C. Murdock, *Constantino Brumidi. Michelangelo of the U.S. Capitol* (Washington, D.C., 1950), 58.

71 These are handsomely displayed in the Renwick Gallery of the National Collection of Fine Arts (Smithsonian Institution) at 17th Street and Pennsylvania Avenue, Washington, D.C. The Brooklyn Museum has an elegant, glazed porcelain vase, called the "Century Vase," which was exhibited at Philadelphia in 1876. An eagle is perched on the rim, and a bas relief of George Washington on the side is surrounded by such scenes of manufacturing and technological progress as a telephone linesman high on a pole stringing wires (Acc. no. 43.25).

72 See Martin, "Orations on the Anniversary of American Independence, 1777–1876," 75–6; Hay, "One Hundred Years of the Fourth of July," 274, 278–9.

73 There may have been more discontent around than a genteel brahmin like Winthrop could comfortably concede. In 1874 the *National Labor Tribune* had asked whether the Centennial of 1876 would have any meaning for labor because "the dreams have not been realized." In 1875 a Boston labor weekly exploded over injustices being done to the working class: "Our fathers began the Revolution for less cause." On July 1, 1876, the *Workingman's Advocate* pointed to the need for "another revolution," and three days later a group of socialists in Chicago issued their call for a second American Revolution. (See Foner, *We, the Other People*, 18–20.) A serious economic depression occurred between 1873 and 1876. When a still more devastating one struck between 1893 and 1897, radical and labor circles once again expressed their dissatisfaction with Fourth of July celebrations and a Declaration of Independence whose commitment to equality remained unfulfilled (*ibid.*, 24–6). For an essay very sympathetic to labor and equality in its interpretation of the Centennial, see *The New York Times*, March 20, 1876, p. 1.

74 Winthrop, *Oration Delivered Before the City Council and Citizens of Boston . . . July 4, 1876* (Boston, 1876), 74–6.

75 See pp. 49–51 above. See also Sidney Lanier's intentions in writing his *Centennial Cantata:* "The principal matter upon which the citizens of the United States could legitimately felicitate themselves at this time was the fact that after a hundred years of the largest liberty ever

enjoyed by mortals they had still a republic unimpaired." *Sidney Lanier. Centennial Edition* (Baltimore, Md., 1945), II, 271; IX, 352.

76 Winthrop, *Oration*, 72–3, 77, 80–2, 95–6. For the same emphases, see *The New York Times* essays, July 3, 1876, 4; July 5, 1876, 11.

77 Winthrop, *Oration*, 17, 19, 22–3, 83. See also Robert C. Winthrop, *Address at the Unveiling of the Statue of Colonel William Prescott, on Bunker Hill, June 17, 1881* (Cambridge, Mass., 1881), 7; and Winthrop, *Oration on the Hundredth Anniversary of the Surrender of Lord Cornwallis . . . Delivered at Yorktown, 19th October, 1881* (Boston, 1881), 1–3, 73. For similar stress upon states' rights (and de-emphasis of the Declaration of Independence as a liberal document) by a northern writer, see William L. Stone, "The Declaration of Independence in a New Light," *Harper's New Monthly Magazine*, LXVII (July 1883), 211–12.

78 Higginson, "Battle of the Cowpens," May 11, 1881, printed in Thomas B. Reed, ed., *Modern Eloquence: Occasional Addresses* (Philadelphia, 1900), VIII, 618–21. See also Higginson, "The Dawning of Independence," *Harper's New Monthly Magazine*, LXVII (October 1883), 731–44; and P. D. Hay, "Haunts of the 'Swamp Fox,' " *ibid.* (September 1883), 545–57, which heaps lavish praise upon the southern contribution to American Independence.

79 See the pertinent remarks made by Edward Shils in "Tradition," *Comparative Studies in Society and History*, XIII (April 1971), 141: "The continuing transmission of beliefs rests on the need for order, not merely as a stable context for instrumental action but as a transcendent realm of being, centred on the sacred. For many persons what is traditionally transmitted through the recommendation of existing authority meets this need."

80 See Moses Coit Tyler, "The Declaration of Independence in the Light of Modern Criticism," *North American Review*, CLXIII (July 1896), 1; Bliss Perry, "On Keeping the Fourth of July," *The Atlantic Monthly*, XC (July 1902), 3; "Fourth of July," *Harper's Weekly*, XLVIII (July 2, 1902), 1005; and Winston Churchill, *The Crossing* (New York, 1904), 549–51. See also John C. Fitzpatrick, "The Travels of the Declaration of Independence," in Fitzpatrick, *The Spirit of the Revolution* (Boston, 1924), 38; and Milton O. Gustafson, "The Empty Shrine: The Transfer of the Declaration of Independence and the Constitution to the National Archives," *The American Archivist*, XXXIX (July 1976), 272.

81 See Adams, *Life and Writings of Sparks*, I, 494; *North American Review*, XLVI (April 1838), 486–7; and Wendell Phillips, "Public Opinion," *Speeches, Lectures, and Letters* (Boston, 1863), 36.

82 See Milton Berman, *John Fiske: The Evolution of a Popularizer* (Cambridge, Mass., 1961), 148–51, 202, 204, 218.

83 See Donald R. Raichle, "The Image of the Constitution in American History from David Ramsay to John Fiske," unpublished Ph.D. dissertation (Columbia University, 1956), 121–2, 128, 130, 137.

84 *Ibid.*, 2, 51, 252. For other instances of this powerful conservatism in American historical thought, especially during the late 1880s, see Craven, *Legend of the Founding Fathers*, 147–8.

85 See Merrill Jensen, "Historians and the Nature of the American Revolution," in *The Reinterpretation of Early American History. Essays in Honor of John Edwin Pomfret*, edited by Ray Allen Billington (New York, 1968), 118; Bernard Bailyn, "The Losers: Notes on the Historiography of Loyalism," an appendix in *The Ordeal of Thomas Hutchinson* (Cambridge, Mass., 1974), 383–408; and Henry W. Haynes, *Memoir of Mellen Chamberlain* (Cambridge, Mass., 1906).

86 Some of the most notable examples are Parton's *Jefferson* (1874), Bigelow's *Franklin* (1874), Henry Adams's *Gallatin* (1879), McMaster's *Franklin* (1887), Lodge's *Washington* (1889), William Wirt Henry's *Patrick Henry* (1891), Wilson's *Washington* (1896–7), and Buell's *John Paul Jones* (1900). Americans of this generation really received a whole new look at the Founding Fathers, in several instances made possible by the fresh availability of substantial manuscript collections.

87 See Pauline Maier, "Coming to Terms with Samuel Adams," *The American Historical Review*, LXXXI (February 1976), 15; Craven, *Legend of the Founding Fathers*, 171–2.

88 *The New York Times*, July 5, 1876, p. 11; McMaster, *History of the People of the United States*, I, 422; Edward H. O'Neill, *A History of American Biography, 1800–1935* (Philadelphia, 1935), 53, 60, 76.

89 See Peterson, *The Jefferson Image in the American Mind*, 222–3, 225–6, 333–42, 346–7; David A. Wasson, "The Modern Type of Oppression," *North American Review*, CXIX (October 1874), 253–85; Raichle, "The Image of the Constitution in American History," 232; Fiske, "Alexander Hamilton and the Federalist Party," in Fiske, *Essays Historical and Literary* (New York, 1902), I, 99–142.

90 Atherton, *Adventures of a Novelist* (New York, 1932), 49, 309–10, 315–16, 342, 352–3.

91 Tyler, *The Literary History of the American Revolution, 1763–1783* (New York, 1897); Wendell, *A Literary History of America* (New York, 1900), Book Two.

92 See Whitfield J. Bell, Jr., "Everett T. Tomlinson: New Jersey Novelist of the American Revolution," in *New Jersey in the American Revolution—Political and Social Conflict*, edited by William C. Wright (Trenton, N.J., 1974), 76–88.

93 Elbridge S. Brooks, *The Century Book of the American Revolution. The Story of the Pilgrimage of a Party of Young People to the Battlefields of the*

American Revolution (New York, 1897). See also Ernest C. Peixotto, *A Revolutionary Pilgrimage* (New York, 1917).

94 See also Richard Pritchett, "The Day the Liberty Bell Came to Boston" [June 17, 1903], *Yankee* (June 1976), 79–81, 150–3.

95 See Foner, *We, the Other People,* 28–31.

96 Fisher, "The Legendary and Myth-making Process in Histories of the American Revolution," *Proceedings of the American Philosophical Society,* LI (April 1912), 53–75. See also Lawrence H. Gipson, *The British Empire Before the American Revolution* (New York, 1967), XIII, 363–7. There is something both bizarre and ironic in our turn-of-the century obsession with "truth." Elbridge S. Brooks, for example, produced a good many books for young people with such titles as *The True Story of George Washington* (1895), *The True Story of Benjamin Franklin* (1898), and *The True Story of Lafayette* (1899), all of which enjoyed great popularity precisely because they were much more romantic than truthful.

97 My discussion of these authors is intentionally quite cursory here because they have been written about at great length and with considerable insight by other scholars. In addition to works cited in Chapter One, note 66, above, see Bernard Bailyn, "Becker, Andrews, and the Image of Colonial Origins," *New England Quarterly,* XXIX (December 1956), 522–34. Two of the most influential statements by members of this generation are Herbert L. Osgood, "The American Revolution," *Political Science Quarterly,* XIII (March 1898), 41–59; and Charles M. Andrews, "The American Revolution: An Interpretation," *The American Historical Review,* XXXI (January 1926), 219–32.

98 See Thomas C. Kennedy, *Charles A. Beard and American Foreign Policy* (Gainesville, Fla., 1975), 71, 97.

99 *Ibid.,* 111, 114. Beard's two widely read books from his early phase were *An Economic Interpretation of the Constitution of the United States* (1913) and *The Economic Origins of Jeffersonian Democracy* (1915). In 1916 Beard informed students at Amherst College that "there is a vital relation between the forms of state and the distribution of property, revolutions in the state being usually the results of contests over property." Since he had just published two studies of the United States situation in the later eighteenth century, it seems reasonable to assume that Beard had the American Revolution foremost in mind when he made this statement.

100 See Robert E. Brown, *Charles Beard and the Constitution. A Critical Analysis of "An Economic Interpretation of the Constitution"* (Princeton, N.J., 1956), 18.

101 Charles and Mary Beard, *The Rise of American Civilization* (New York, 1927), 201–3, 294, 296. See also Howard K. Beale, "Charles Beard:

Historian," in *Charles A. Beard: An Appraisal,* edited by Beale (Lexington, Ky., 1954), 117–18.

102 See Hacker, "The First American Revolution," *Columbia University Quarterly,* XXVII (September 1935), 259–95; and Hacker, *The Triumph of American Capitalism* (New York, 1940), part 2, which elaborates upon his 1935 argument. For two other widely read books of this period in which the economic emphasis is strong but qualified, see John C. Miller, *The Origins of the American Revolution* (Boston, 1943) and Evarts B. Greene, *The Revolutionary Generation, 1763–1790* (New York, 1943).

103 See Peterson, *The Jefferson Image in the American Mind,* 333–47; and Edward A. Purcell, Jr., *The Crisis of Democratic Theory* (Lexington, Ky., 1973). For reasons not entirely clear to me, there was a surge of popular interest in the Revolution and Founding Fathers during the later 1920s. Gutzon Borglum, for example, began to carve his monumental heads on Mt. Rushmore in 1927. See Douglass Adair, *Fame and the Founding Fathers,* edited by Trevor Colbourn (New York, 1974), 238–9.

104 Van Doren, *Benjamin Franklin* (New York, 1938); *Secret History of the American Revolution* (New York, 1941); *Mutiny in January* (New York, 1943). The last book is very symptomatic of the American outlook during World War II. The story of a crisis in the Continental army—a mutiny by the Pennsylvania line in January 1781—it sought to look at the lives of ordinary soldiers (rather than heroic generals) as real flesh and blood figures. History from "the bottom up" was not discovered *de novo* during the 1960s!

105 It should also come as no surprise that a strong interest in wartime propaganda helped to elicit warm praise for Philip Davidson's *Propaganda and the American Revolution* (Chapel Hill, N.C., 1941). See, e.g., Peter Odegard's generous praise in the *Saturday Review of Literature,* XXV (March 7, 1942), 5–6, 23.

106 For his break with the Soviet Union, see Fast, *The Naked God. The Writer and the Communist Party* (New York, 1957), 194–7; and John P. Diggins, *Up from Communism: Conservative Odysseys in American Intellectual History* (New York, 1975), 433. See also pp. 230–2 below.

107 Diggins, *Up from Communism,* 95–6; and Diggins, "Visions of Chaos and Visions of Order: Dos Passos as Historian," *American Literature,* XLVI (November 1974), 329–46. See Dos Passos, *The Head and Heart of Thomas Jefferson* (New York, 1954); *The Men Who Made the Nation* (New York, 1957); and *The Shackles of Power. Three Jeffersonian Decades* (1966).

108 Arendt, *On Revolution* (New York, 1963), 141. For Arendt's anti-Communist conservatism, see Diggins, *Up from Communism,* 430.

109 Nelson, "The Revolutionary Character of the American Revolution," *The American Historical Review*, LXX (July 1965), 1002; cf. Marian J. Morton, *The Terrors of Ideological Politics: Liberal Historians in a Conservative Mood* (Cleveland, Ohio, 1972), especially chs. 4 and 5; and for my own perspective upon the "schools" of Bernard Bailyn and Merrill Jensen, see Richard M. Jellison, ed., *Society, Freedom, and Conscience. The American Revolution in Virginia, Massachusetts, and New York* (New York, 1976), 126–8, 209–10.

110 Labaree, "The Nature of American Loyalism," *Proceedings of the American Antiquarian Society*, LIV (1945), 15–58; Kenyon, "Where Paine Went Wrong," *The American Political Science Review*, LXV (December 1951), 1086–99. See also Adrienne Koch, *Power, Morals, and the Founding Fathers* (Ithaca, N.Y., 1961), a book begun in 1952 and deeply affected by the attitudinal exigencies of the Cold War. Yet another symptom of the Cold War mentality may be seen in the fact that a remarkable number of military histories of the Revolution were published between 1948 and 1958. See Don Higginbotham, "American Historians and the Military History of the American Revolution," *The American Historical Review*, LXX (October 1964), 29–32.

111 Sydnor, *American Revolutionaries in the Making: Political Practices in Washington's Virginia* (Chapel Hill, N.C., 1952); Roche, "The Founding Fathers: A Reform Caucus in Action," *The American Political Science Review*, LV (December 1961), 799–816; Diamond, "The Revolution of Sober Expectations," in *The American Revolution: Three Views* (American Brands, Inc.: New York, 1975), 57–85. The quotation is from p. 79.

112 See Irving Brant, *James Madison* (Indianapolis, Ind., and New York, 1941–61), 6 vols.; Brant, *Madison* (abridged edition: 1970); Ralph Ketcham, *James Madison* (New York, 1971); Marvin Meyers, ed., *The Mind of the Founder: Sources of the Political Thought of James Madison* (Indianapolis, Ind., 1973); Merrill D. Peterson, ed., *James Madison: A Biography in His Own Words* (New York, 1974); Marvin Meyers, "Founding and Revolution: A Commentary on Publius-Madison," in *The Hofstadter Aegis; A Memorial*, edited by Stanley Elkins and Eric McKitrick (New York, 1974), 3–35; and Paul F. Bourke, "The Pluralist Reading of James Madison's Tenth *Federalist*," in *Perspectives in American History*, IX (1975), 271–95.

113 Gabriel Kolko has made the interesting observation that World War II "made permanent revolutions and the momentum from the Left the central irresistible theme in the history of our times," and that "it also produced a host of new traumas which the United States could confront only as an aspect of its permanent struggle against

the mainstream of history toward the Left which has irresistibly, if elliptically, characterized the history of our generation," *Main Currents in Modern American History* (New York, 1976), 225, 243.

114 See Butterfield, "The Jubilee of Independence," 132; *The Autobiography of Colonel John Trumbull, Patriot-Artist, 1756–1843,* edited by Theodore Sizer (New Haven, Conn., 1953), 172.

115 Greenough to Bryant, May 7, 1851, in *Letters of Horatio Greenough, American Sculptor,* edited by Nathalia Wright (Madison, Wis., 1972), 390. See also "The Meaning of July Fourth for the Negro," speech at Rochester, New York, July 5, 1852, in Philip S. Foner, ed., *The Life and Writings of Frederick Douglass* (New York, 1950), II, 186; and Henry P. Johnston, "Captain Nathan Hale," *Harper's New Monthly Magazine,* LXI (June 1880), 53–60.

116 *The Story of the Revolution* by Henry Cabot Lodge, two hefty volumes published in 1898, begins the story in 1774 (rather than 1763 or 1765) and is dedicated "to the Army and Navy of the United States, Victors of Manila, Santiago and Porto Rico, Worthy Successors of the Soldiers and Sailors Who Under the Lead of George Washington Won American Independence."

117 Wood's essay, part of a much larger book he is writing, appears in *Leadership in the American Revolution: Papers Presented at the Third Symposium, May 9 and 10, 1974* (Library of Congress: Washington, D.C., 1974), 63–88. See also Eric Foner, *Tom Paine and Revolutionary America* (New York, 1976); Alfred F. Young, ed., *The American Revolution. Explorations in the History of American Radicalism* (DeKalb, Ill., 1976); Richard B. Morris, " 'We the People of the United States': The Bicentennial of a People's Revolution," *American Historical Review,* LXXXII (February 1977), 1–19; and "Interdisciplinary Studies of the American Revolution," a special issue of *The Journal of Interdisciplinary History,* VI (Spring 1976), especially 545–677. It is signiffiicant, too, that the 1976 Jefferson Lectures in the Humanities were given from coast to coast by John Hope Franklin on the subject of "Racial Equality in America," and that the most effective Bicentennial series on television was an eight-part adaptation of *Roots* (1976) by Alex Haley—a personalized rendition of Afro-American history.

118 See Jack P. Greene, *All Men Are Created Equal. Some Reflections on the Character of the American Revolution* (Oxford, 1976), 26, 28, 30; Edmund S. Morgan, *The Challenge of the American Revolution* (New York, 1976), 192–5, 212–17.

119 Tocqueville, *Democracy in America,* edited by J. P. Mayer (Anchor edition: Garden City, N. Y., 1969), 636.

120 Andrews, "The American Revolution: An Interpretation," 219; Smith, *The Historian and History* (New York, 1964), 165–6.

CHAPTER THREE
Revolutionary Iconography in National Tradition

1 See Irma B. Jaffe, *John Trumbull. Patriot-Artist of the American Revolution* (Boston, 1975), 243–53; *Compilation of Works of Art and Other Objects in the United States Capitol* (Washington, D.C., 1965), 302–4, 373–5.

2 Huizinga, "My Path to History," in *Dutch Civilisation in the Seventeenth Century and Other Essays* (New York, 1968), 269. This essay was completed in 1943, near the end of Huizinga's life, and first published in 1947. See also the caustic comment by Barbara Novak O'Doherty, "The American 19th Century, Part I: New Found Land," *Art News*, LXVII (September 1968): "No other country seems to have had such a talent for disposing, again and again, of its past. If America seems to have had little art history, it may be because it has a bad memory" (p. 31).

3 Cooper to Charles Kitchel Gardner? [Spring 1823], in James Franklin Beard, ed., *The Letters and Journals of James Fenimore Cooper* (Cambridge, Mass., 1960), I, 95–6, and plate IX following p. 368.

4 Entry for Sept. 14, 1855, in Hawthorne, *The English Notebooks*, edited by Randall Stewart (New York, 1941), 225.

5 Greenough to Cooper, March 7, 1831, in Nathalia Wright, ed., *Letters of Horatio Greenough, American Sculptor* (Madison, Wis., 1972), 73–4. See also Greenough to Cooper, Dec. 20, 1830, in *ibid.*, 66–7.

6 See Brigham, *Paul Revere's Engravings* (2nd ed.: New York, 1969); *An Album of American Battle Art, 1755–1918* (Washington, D.C., 1947), 51–5; Lynn Glaser, *Engraved America: Iconography of America Through 1800* (Philadelphia, 1970), plate 184; *A Bicentennial Treasury: American Masterpieces from the Metropolitan* (New York, 1976), plate 30. Portraits done by folk artists during the 1780s sometimes contained, as part of the background, a Revolutionary battle scene. See, for example, *Captain and Mrs. Samuel Chandler*, by Winthrop Chandler of Woodstock, Connecticut (ca. 1780), National Gallery of Art, Washington, D.C. (reproduced in Jean Lipman and Alice Winchester, *The Flowering of American Folk Art* [New York, 1974], 16).

7 Some of it was at least original, however, in contrast to almost all the nineteenth-century engravings of Revolutionary scenes, which ordinarily were poorly derivative from oil paintings. In that sense, the engravings had the very same relationship to their prototypes as historical dramas to the novels upon which they were based. Cf. Chapter Four, pp. 130–5, below. See also Ian M. G. Quimby, "The Doolittle Engravings of the Battle of Lexington and Concord," *Winterthur Portfolio*, IV (1968), 83–108; and William Loring Andrews, *An Essay on the Portraiture of the American Revolutionary War . . .* (New York, 1896),

an antiquarian account of engraved portraits based upon originals in oil.

8 Sept. 23, 1799, John Trumbull Papers, Yale University Library. In addition to Trumbull's half dozen famous historical scenes, it is interesting to note others he proposed to do or sketched, but never completed: the evacuation of New York, September 1776; the murder of Jane McCrea, Fort Edward, New York, July 26, 1777; the death of General Fraser at Bemis Heights, near Saratoga, October 7, 1777; the siege of Savannah, September–October 1779; the attack on Charleston, South Carolina, May 9–10, 1780; the Battle of Eutaw Springs, South Carolina, September 8, 1781; the preliminary treaty, Paris, November 30, 1782; the arch at Trenton, New Jersey, April 21, 1789; and Washington's inauguration, New York, April 30, 1789.

9 Quoted in Jaffe, *Trumbull*, 260. For a contemporary rejoinder to Randolph, see Horatio Greenough, *The Travels, Observations, and Experience of a Yankee Stonecutter* (New York, 1852), ch. 16.

10 Edgar P. Richardson, *Washington Allston. A Study of the Romantic Artist in America* (Chicago, 1948), 134; George R. Nielsen, "Paintings and Politics in Jacksonian America," *Capitol Studies*, I (Spring 1972), 87–91.

11 See *Works of Art in the United States Capitol*, 116–23.

12 See Rebecca J. Beal, *Jacob Eichholtz, 1776–1842. Portrait Painter of Pennsylvania* (Philadelphia, 1969), 263–4; D. Denise Minault, "Recent Findings Concerning 'The Capture of Major André,' " *Worcester Art Museum Bulletin*, I (November 1971), 2–7.

13 See Wayne Craven, "Asher B. Durand's Career as an Engraver," *American Art Journal*, III (Spring 1971), 39–57; Gordon Hendricks, "Durand, Maverick and the *Declaration*," *ibid.*, 58–71; John Maass, "The Declarations of Independence," *The Magazine Antiques*, CX (July 1976), 106–10; John C. Fitzpatrick, *The Spirit of the Revolution* (Boston, 1924), ch. 2, "Discovery of the Declaration of Independence by the People of the United States," especially 16–18, 20, 22.

14 John Blake White (1781–ca. 1859) painted the best known version of the "sweet potato picture" late in the 1830s, and John Sartain engraved it in 1840. White's canvas hangs in the Senate wing of the Capitol (third floor). George Washington Mark (?–1879) did a charming primitive of the same subject, which is owned by the New-York Historical Society. For negative responses to the Declaration of Independence, see Merrill D. Peterson, *The Jefferson Image in the American Mind* (New York, 1960), 168–9, 201–2.

15 See *Works of Art in the United States Capitol*, 128, 134–7; *An Album of American Battle Art*, 60, 61. The theme of patriotic self-sacrifice also had quite a vogue at mid-century. In 1852 Emanuel Leutze painted *Lady Schuyler Burning Her Wheat Fields on the Approach of the British.*

(Sold in 1976 by the Vose Galleries of Boston to the Los Angeles County Museum of Art.)

16 Ranney's painting (1845) is owned by Mr. Frederick Donhauser, Stony Point, Alaska. Hamilton's (1854) is in the Yale University Art Gallery. And Oertel's (ca. 1859) is at the New-York Historical Society. In 1847 George Peter Alexander Healy (1813–94) painted *Franklin Urging the Claims of the American Colonies Before Louis XVI,* on commission from Louis Philippe, who wanted a historical scene featuring Benjamin Franklin. For a depiction of the Battle of Brandywine done in 1848 by Junius Brutus Stearns (1810–85), see *The Magazine Antiques,* CXI (January 1977), 10.

17 See Ann Hawkes Hutton, *Portrait of Patriotism. "Washington Crossing the Delaware"* (Philadelphia, 1959), ch. 11, for some of the controversy.

18 Sully's picture is in the Museum of Fine Arts, Boston. One version of Hicks's is located in the Mercer Museum of the Bucks County Historical Society, Doylestown, Pennsylvania. Another, done about 1834, belongs to Nina Fletcher Little and is reproduced in Mary Black and Jean Lipman, *American Folk Painting* (New York, 1966), fig. 146. A third, done in 1849 near the end of Hicks's life, is on indefinite loan at the Chrysler Museum in Norfolk, Virginia (reproduced in *The Magazine Antiques,* CIX [May 1976], 866).

19 The sampler is reported by Langdon G. Wright in *New York History,* LVII (April 1976), 240. Public references to "Mary the Mother of Washington" began to be commonplace during the later 1840s and 1850s. See William A. Bryan, *George Washington in American Literature, 1775–1865* (New York, 1952), 73, 118.

20 Hutton, *Portrait of Patriotism,* 33, 39–40, 113–17, 122, 128; De Forest to Andrew De Forest, Aug. 29, 1851, John William De Forest Collection, folder 20, Beinecke Library, Yale University. (I am indebted to James A. Hijiya for this reference.) The painting received some contemporary criticism on account of historical inaccuracies, such as depicting a flag that did not come into existence until mid-1777. See H. W. Mead to Benson J. Lossing, Nov. 28, 1853, Lossing Papers, box 1, Huntington Library.

21 See E. Maurice Bloch, *George Caleb Bingham. The Evolution of an Artist* (Berkeley, Calif., 1967), plate 182. The original painting belongs to a private collector in Seattle.

22 An early copy will be found in the Harry T. Peters Collection at the Museum of the City of New York. See also John Lowell Pratt, ed., *Currier & Ives. Chronicles of America* (Maplewood, N.J., 1968), 28–40.

23 Block, *Bingham,* plate 181; Albert Christ-Janer, *George Caleb Bingham, Frontier Painter of Missouri* (New York, 1975), plate 160.

24 George Harding, a student of Howard Pyle, did a version. J. O. J. Frost did another, ca. 1910, that belongs to Mr. Bertram K. Little of Brookline, Mass. A copy embroidered on silk, ca. 1880, may be found at the New York State Historical Association in Cooperstown.

25 See Bryan, *Washington in American Literature*, 183; Nellie U. Wallington, ed., *American History by American Poets* (New York, 1911), I, 187–8.

26 See Gustavus A. Eisen, *Portraits of Washington* (New York, 1932), 3 vols.; Frances D. Whittemore, *George Washington in Sculpture* (Boston, 1933).

27 See Black and Lipman, *American Folk Painting*, 159–60, and fig. 147; Sotheby Parke Bernet *Newsletter* (January–February 1976), 1; Nicholas B. Wainwright, ed., *Paintings and Miniatures at the Historical Society of Pennsylvania* (Philadelphia, 1974), 255. One of the most popular historical paintings of that era, *Lady Washington's Reception* by Daniel Huntington (1861), hangs in the Brooklyn Museum.

28 William Gilmore Simms to William Porcher Miles, Jan. 18, 1860, in *The Letters of William Gilmore Simms*, edited by Mary C. Simms Oliphant, *et al.* (Columbia, S.C., 1952–6), IV, 185–8, 197n.; Garrett, "The First Score for American Paintings and Sculpture, 1870–1890," *Metropolitan Museum Journal*, III (1970), 326; Clarence W. Bowen, ed., *The History of the Centennial Celebration of the Inauguration of George Washington . . .* (New York, 1892).

29 See Frank B. Mayer's oil on canvas called *The Continentals* (1875), National Collection of Fine Arts, Washington, D.C., in which a drummer and fifer plod valiantly uphill through the snow, while Continental soldiers with fixed bayonets proceed in the background; and Edwin Howland Blashfield's oil on canvas, *Suspense, the Boston People Watch from the Housetops the Firing at Bunker Hill* (ca. 1879–80), owned by the Home Insurance Company in New York and reproduced in Donelson F. Hoopes, *American Narrative Painting* (Los Angeles, 1974), 168–9. See also the engraving of a stout-hearted Continental soldier, simply entitled *'76*, published in *Harper's Weekly* on July 15, 1876, and reproduced as fig. 318 in John Grafton, *The American Revolution. A Picture Sourcebook* (New York, 1975), 133. Also *Dangerous Ground*, fig. 319, from *Harper's Weekly* (May 13, 1876).

30 See Margaret French Cresson, *Journey into Fame. The Life of Daniel Chester French* (Cambridge, Mass., 1947), 71–84, 184–7, 196–7; David B. Little, *America's First Centennial Celebration* (2nd ed.: Boston, 1974).

31 See Thomas H. Pauly, "In Search of 'The Spirit of '76,' " *American Quarterly*, XXVIII (Fall 1976), 444–64.

32 Abigail Adams to Mrs. Shaw, March 4, 1786, *Letters of Mrs. Adams . . . with an Introductory Memoir by Charles Francis Adams* (Boston, 1841), II, 127. See also *The Death of Colonel Owen Roberts*, fig.

158 in Robert G. Stewart, *Henry Benbridge (1743–1812): American Portrait Painter* (Washington, D.C., 1971), 86; Lewis Leary, *Soundings: Some Early American Writers* (Athens, Ga., 1975), 221, for an account of William Dunlap in 1784 experimenting with an oil painting of Washington at the Battle of Princeton beside the fallen body of General Mercer.

33 See Jaffe, *Trumbull*, 93, 151, 236–8, 246. Compare *Washington the Lawgiver* by Antonio Canova (completed in 1821) with *Washington as General* by Hermon A. MacNeil (completed in 1916).

34 See Barbara S. Groseclose, *Emanuel Leutze, 1816–1868: Freedom Is the Only King* (Washington, D.C., 1975), 44, which discusses paintings of battle sites by Peale, Stuart, Trumbull, and Leutze (executed 1781–1853) "in which no battle is seen, only the calm, fixed figure of Washington, whose horse, at times, is more active than he." See also Charles Warren, "Why the Battle of New Orleans Was Not Painted," in *Odd Byways in American History* (Cambridge, Mass., 1942), 185.

35 See William H. Gerdts, *American Neo-Classic Sculpture: The Marble Resurrection* (New York, 1973), 100.

36 Everett, *An Oration Delivered at Cambridge on the Fiftieth Anniversary of the Declaration of Independence* (Boston, 1826), 13–14; Webster, *Address, Delivered at Bunker Hill, June 17, 1843, on the Completion of the Monument* (Boston, 1843), 13, 15–16.

37 See Nina Fletcher Little, *The Abby Aldrich Rockefeller Folk Art Collection. A Descriptive Catalog* (Boston, 1957), 86 and plate 45. In 1919 Daniel Chester French did a major statue called "Disarmament" (for the Victory Arch in New York City). It seems to have symbolically marked the end of this phase of militarism in American historical art.

38 See A. V. Huff, Jr., "The Eagle and the Vulture: Changing Attitudes Toward Nationalism in Fourth of July Orations Delivered in Charleston, 1778–1860," *South Atlantic Quarterly*, LXXIII (Winter 1974), 20–1; Fletcher M. Green, "Listen to the Eagle Scream: One Hundred Years of the Fourth of July in North Carolina (1776–1876)," *North Carolina Historical Review*, XXXI (July 1954), 319–20.

39 See, e.g., Charles J. Peterson, *A History of the Wars of the United States. Containing a History of the Revolution, and of the Wars of 1812 and Mexico . . .* (Philadelphia, 1860). Part One is 487 pages long, entitled "The Military Heroes of the Revolution: With a Narrative of the War of Independence." It is instructive to compare Peterson's tome with Samuel Wilson, *History of the American Revolution, with a Preliminary View of the Character and Principles of the Colonists* (Baltimore, Md., 1834), a book that explicitly sought to de-emphasize the importance of military events. See also William Gilmore Simms to James Chesnut, Jr., March 7, 1856, in *The Letters of William Gilmore Simms*, edited

by Mary C. Simms Oliphant, *et al.* (Columbia, S.C., 1952–6), III, 423, in which Simms expresses the hope that Chesnut will "carry me out to Gum Swamp,—the several battle grounds, and give me some material for a new romance."

40 Milton Berman, *John Fiske. The Evolution of a Popularizer* (Cambridge, Mass., 1961), 150, 217.

41 Gaul's painting was offered for sale in June 1976 by the Coe Kerr Gallery, New York City, for $15,000. Various paintings by Lefferts and Dunsmore were displayed in 1976 at the New-York Historical Society.

42 See Marian Klamkin, *American Patriotic and Political China* (New York, 1973), 37–40.

43 Durand's picture was exhibited in 1843 and promptly engraved. It appears in John Durand, *The Life and Times of Asher B. Durand* (New York, 1894), opposite p. 132; but its location is no longer known. Dunlap's may be found at Fenimore House, the New York State Historical Association, Cooperstown, New York. Tompkins H. Matteson did *George Washington and the Spy—Harvey Birch,* as well as illustrations for biographies of Franklin, Lafayette, and Nathanael Greene published in 1848–9.

44 See Arlene Jacobowitz, *James Hamilton, 1819–1878. American Marine Painter* (Brooklyn, N.Y., 1966), plates 11, 25, and 29; Beal, *Eichholtz,* 267; Susan Fenimore Cooper, comp., *Pages and Pictures from the Writings of James Fenimore Cooper* (New York, 1861); Sinclair Hamilton, *Early American Book Illustrators and Wood Engravers, 1670–1870 . . .* (Princeton, N.J., 1958), I, plate 96.

45 See, for example, the full-page illustrations concerning the Battle of Yorktown by J.·O. Davidson and Rufus F. Zogbaum that accompany J. Esten Cooke, "The Prologue to Yorktown," *Harper's Weekly,* XXV (Oct. 22, 1881), 712–15; the double-page spread from sketches by Davidson entitled *The Yorktown Centennial—The Military and Naval Reviews,* in *ibid.* (Oct. 29, 1881), 728–30; the full-page illustration by Howard Pyle entitled *Washington Taking Leave of His Officers, December 4, 1783,* in *ibid.,* XXVII (Dec. 1, 1883), 769; and *The Minute-Man!,* a drawing by Pyle which appeared on the cover of *Collier's,* XXXVI (Feb. 17, 1906).

46 Works by Ogden (1856–1936) and Yohn (1875–1933) were displayed at the New-York Historical Society in 1976. A picture called *The Battle of Bunker Hill,* by Howard Pyle, was prepared to accompany *The Story of the Revolution* by Henry Cabot Lodge, which was serialized in *Scribner's Magazine* during 1898. For Wyeth, see Douglas Allen, *N. C. Wyeth. The Collected Paintings, Illustrations and Murals* (New York, 1972), 30, 142. See also Howard Pyle, *et al., The Brandywine Heritage* (Chadds Ford, Pa., 1971), 40–1, plates 42 and 45; and *The American*

Historical Scene as Depicted by Stanley Arthurs and Interpreted by Fifty Authors (New York, 1936).

47 It is reproduced in Pyle, *et al.*, *The Brandywine Heritage.*

48 See Park Rinard and Arnold Pyle, *Catalogue of a Loan Exhibition of Drawings and Paintings by Grant Wood with an Evaluation of the Artist and His Work* (Chicago, 1935); James M. Dennis, *Grant Wood. A Study in American Art and Culture* (New York, 1975), 105, 109, 112–13, 132, 177. In 1940 Wood painted a serious portrait of the fictional Oliver Wiswell for Kenneth Roberts's massive novel of the Revolution. It was used on the dust jacket and was elegantly reproduced as a frontispiece to the de luxe edition of that book.

49 Quoted in Frank R. Rossiter, *Charles Ives and His America* (New York, 1975), 230–1.

50 *Ibid.*, 101. For an interesting similarity in Sidney Lanier's intentions in writing his *Centennial Cantata*, see his letter to *The New York Tribune*, May 20, 1876, in *Sidney Lanier. Centennial Edition*, II, edited by Paull F. Baum (Baltimore, Md., 1945), 271–2.

51 See Edward Bruce and Forbes Watson, *Art in Federal Buildings* (Washington, D.C., 1936), I, *Mural Designs, 1934–1936.* The book is mostly unpaginated.

52 For a few vestiges of the genre, see *Paul Revere, 1735–1818: The Events of His Life Painted by A. Lassell Ripley and Some Examples of His Silver and Prints* (Worcester Art Museum, Sept. 14–Oct. 24, 1965), paintings done between 1959 and 1965; James Weeks, *Concord River (North Bridge)*, 1974, in *America 1976. A Bicentennial Exhibition Sponsored by the U.S. Department of the Interior* (Washington, D.C., 1976), 74; and *The War of Independence. A Bicentennial Exhibition of Marine Paintings by Leslie Wilcox* (May 4–29, 1976, at William Blair, Ltd., Bethesda, Md.). Wilcox is an English artist.

53 See Allan Frumkin Gallery *Newsletter*, no. 1 (Spring 1976); and Frumkin Gallery, *A Bicentennial Exhibition. Summer 1976.* Cf. the charming and very thoughtful *Fresh Views of the American Revolution* by Paul Foley and Oscar de Mejo (New York, 1976), which begins by declaring that "the American Revolution was not a war," but rather "a revolutionary idea of what a free nation is and how a free people should govern themselves."

54 See also *The Struggle and the Glory. A Special Bicentennial Exhibition* (Greenfield Village and Henry Ford Museum: Dearborn, Mich., 1976); and *Revolutionary America. An Exhibition* (The Lilly Library: Indiana University, Bloomington, Ind., 1976).

55 See also *Wedgwood Portraits and the American Revolution* (National Portrait Gallery, Smithsonian Institution: Washington, D.C., 1976).

56 See also *Age of the Revolution and Early Republic in Fine and Decorative*

Arts: 1750–1824 (Kennedy Galleries and Israel Sack, Inc.: New York, 1977).

57 See, especially, *A Rising People. The Founding of the United States, 1765 to 1789: A Celebration from the Collections of the American Philosophical Society, the Historical Society of Pennsylvania, the Library Company of Philadelphia* (Philadelphia, 1976), 262–77.

58 See Sidney Kaplan, *The Black Presence in the Era of the American Revolution, 1770–1800* (Washington, D.C., 1973), 22–7, for the draft with Jefferson's passage on the slave trade, subsequently deleted; *To Set a Country Free: An Account Derived from the Exhibition in the Library of Congress Commemorating the 200th Anniversary of American Independence . . .* (Washington, D.C., 1975), 46; and *A Rising People*, 228–9, 261–2.

59 Adams, ed., *The Eye of Thomas Jefferson* (Washington, D.C., 1976), xxxiii.

60 See *Paul Revere's Boston: 1735–1818* (Boston, 1975), 15; *Eye of Thomas Jefferson*, xxxiv, xxxvii; *William Bingham: America—A Good Investment* (Binghamton, N.Y., 1975), iii, 5. Bingham also furnished his Philadelphia home with treasures from Europe.

61 *The New York Times*, Jan. 10, 1975.

62 Kaplan, *Black Presence*, vii.

63 *A Rising People*, ix.

64 *Eye of Thomas Jefferson*, xl.

65 See *American Art: 1750–1800, Towards Independence* (Boston, 1976), 37, 47, 48, 51, 153, 176, 181, 207, 215, 216; Lipman and Black, *Flowering of American Folk Art*, 182–3, 269; *Paul Revere's Boston*, 176, 198; Stephen B. Jareckie, *The Early Republic: Consolidation of Revolutionary Goals* (Worcester, Mass., 1976), 73, 94; and *A Rising People*, 278.

66 See *To Set a Country Free*, 73; *Paul Revere's Boston*, 176. It is altogether possible, of course, that the eagle was added to Cogswell's chest some time after 1782.

67 See also Howard H. Martin, "Orations on the Anniversary of American Independence, 1777–1876," unpublished Ph.D. dissertation (Northwestern University, 1955), 312–13, 321–2, for allusions to the eagle in patriotic orations. On March 11, 1861, one citizen of New York remarked in his diary: "The bird of our country is a debilitated chicken, disguised in eagle feathers. . . . We are a weak, divided, disgraced people, unable to maintain our national existence." *The Diary of George Templeton Strong*, edited by Allan Nevins and Milton H. Thomas (New York, 1952), III, 109.

68 See Elinor Lander Horwitz, *The Bird, the Banner, and Uncle Sam. Images of America in Folk and Popular Art* (Philadelphia, 1976), 83, for a fire engine painting from the nineteenth century with this theme. Miss Liberty is rather wantonly bare-breasted, and the aggressive eagle next

to her seems more interested in her body than in the contents of the chalice she holds. I am aware of the similarities here to Leda and the Swan, a well-established, sensuous motif in European art and mythology.

69 Jareckie, *Consolidation of Revolutionary Goals,* figs. 47, 74. See also *A Rising People,* 215; Joshua C. Taylor, *America as Art* (Washington, D.C., 1976), 11–13, 25, 30, 35; and Boleslaw and Marie-Louise D'Otrange Mastai, *The Stars and the Stripes. The American Flag as Art and as History from the Birth of the Republic to the Present* (New York, 1973), 83–96.

70 Jareckie, *Consolidation of Revolutionary Goals,* fig. 101; Little, *Abby Aldrich Rockefeller Folk Art Collection,* 196. See also Philip M. Isaacson, *The American Eagle* (Boston, 1975), fig. 164; E. McClung Fleming, "From Indian Princess to Greek Goddess. The American Image, 1783–1815," *Winterthur Portfolio,* III (1967), especially 56–66; and Louise Conway Belden, "Liberty and the American Eagle on Spoons by Jacob Kucher," *ibid.,* 102–11. Appropriately, and predictably, the U.S. Bicentennial medal placed Liberty on one side and an eagle on the other.

71 See Klamkin, *Patriotic and Political China,* 13; *Works of Art in the United States Capitol,* 276. See also *Important Frakturs, Embroidered Pictures, Theorem Paintings . . . and Other American Folk Art,* Sotheby Parke Bernet catalogue no. 3692 (Nov. 12, 1974), 59.

72 Bernard Bailyn, *The Ideological Origins of the American Revolution* (Cambridge, Mass., 1967), 55–62.

73 See *American Art: 1750–1800, Towards Independence,* 42, fig. 10; R. J. Dickson, *Ulster Emigration to Colonial America, 1718–1775* (London, 1966), 75; Smith, *Wealth of Nations* (London, 1920), II, 69. See also the mid-eighteenth-century woodcut of the colonial farmer at his plough, in Alfred F. Young, ed., *The American Revolution: Explorations in the History of American Radicalism* (DeKalb, Ill., 1976), 37.

74 Anon., essay-review of Benjamin Trumbull's *History of Connecticut,* in *North American Review,* VIII (December 1818), 72–3. For ideological context, see Harry V. Jaffa, "Agrarian Virtue and Republican Freedom: An Historical Perspective," in Jaffa, *Equality and Liberty: Theory and Practice in American Politics* (New York, 1965), 42–66.

75 Remick's original will be found in the Massachusetts Historical Society. De Woiserie's original is in the Chicago Historical Society; and an aquatint belonging to Mr. and Mrs. J. William Middendorf, II, is reproduced in *American Art: 1750–1800, Towards Independence,* 22–3. De Woiserie's subsequent view of Boston, done ca. 1810, appears in *Paul Revere's Boston,* 149. For other examples of Liberty in colonial iconography during the decade prior to Revolution, see Brigham, *Paul Revere's Engravings,* 49–50, 111, 185, 192–5, 199, 209, 213, and plate 6.

76 See also Brigham, *Paul Revere's Engravings,* 82–3 and plates 75–6.

When Revere engraved shilling notes for the Continental cause in 1775 and early 1776, he included "Magna Charta" in the legend. By November 1776, he had altered the plate so that "Independence" replaced "Magna Charta."

77 Klamkin, *Patriotic and Political China*, 71–2 and fig. 91.

78 *Ibid.*, plate 5 (top) and 73, fig. 94. The Brooklyn Museum has a creamware pitcher made in Liverpool (ca. 1805) for export to the United States (Acc. no. 64.244.25). On one side a design displays the eagle, liberty pole and cap, a basket laden with fruit, and the motto "Independence." On the other side, this poem:

As he tills your rich glebe, the old peasant shall tell
While his bosom with liberty glows
How your Warren expired—how Montgomery fell
And how Washington humbled your foes.

79 In 1794, for example, the Fourth of July was celebrated in Cincinnati to resounding cheers for the "cause of Liberty, triumphant." One year later, however, emphasis was placed upon the soil's fertility and the nation's commerce. Compare the *Centinel of the North-Western Territory* (Cincinnati) for July 12, 1794, and July 18, 1795, both quoted in Robert P. Hay, "Freedom's Jubilee: One Hundred Years of the Fourth of July, 1776–1876," unpublished Ph.D. dissertation (University of Kentucky, 1967), 50–1. From 1793 until 1796, the United States government minted a cent that displayed a liberty pole surmounted by a liberty cap. In 1800, Hugh Henry Brackenridge helped to establish in Pittsburgh a newspaper called *The Tree of Liberty*, which lasted until 1810. See Arthur M. Schlesinger, "Liberty Tree: A Genealogy," *New England Quarterly*, XXV (December 1952), 454 and n.17; and for the theme of "national peace and plenty" in historical fiction of the young republic, see James Kirke Paulding, *The Old Continental; or, The Price of Liberty* (2nd ed.: New York, 1851), I, 129.

80 See the state seals of New Jersey (three ploughs against a shield supported by the figure of Liberty, with "Liberty & Prosperity" on a banner below); Pennsylvania (a plough in the center of a shield surmounted by an eagle); and Maryland (the legend reads: "Industry the Means. Plenty the Result"), reproduced in Grafton, *The American Revolution. A Picture Sourcebook*, 148. New Jersey commissioned Pierre Eugene Du Simitière in 1776 to design a state seal. The motto "Liberty & Prosperity" was not included in his original instructions, however. It later became a part of the seal through common usage, after many printers had begun to incorporate the phrase. Along with Liberty, the other figure supporting the shield is Ceres, the goddess of growing vegetation who symbolizes abundance and prosperity. (Communication to the author from the Department of Education, New Jersey

State Library, Trenton.) See also Sotheby Parke Bernet catalogue no. 3692, p. 6, item 14; James Peale, *Grapes and Apples,* ca. 1810, in Amy LaFollette Jensen, *Paintings in the White House. A Close-up* (n.p., 1965), 30; James Peale, *Still Life,* 1825, in Jareckie, *Consolidation of Revolutionary Goals,* 37; George Inness, *Peace and Plenty,* 1865 and 1868, in LeRoy Ireland, comp., *The Works of George Inness. An Illustrated Catalogue Raisonné* (Austin, Texas, 1965), 78 (plate 311) and 108 (plate 437); and Elihu Vedder, *Peace and Prosperity,* mural in the Library of Congress, Washington, D.C. A coverlet woven in the "Peace & Plenty" pattern, dated 1841, was exhibited during the spring season, 1976, at the Sterling and Francine Clark Art Institute, Williamstown, Massachusetts. (It is owned by John Gerhort.)

81 Both of these are reproduced in *A Rising People,* 208. For other examples, see Donald H. Cresswell, comp., *The American Revolution in Drawings and Prints. A Checklist of 1765–1790 Graphics in the Library of Congress* (Washington, D.C., 1975), figs. 882, 885; and Hay, "One Hundred Years of the Fourth of July," 108. Hay quotes the toast offered in Savannah, Georgia, on July 4, 1807, where patriots drank to the "agriculture and commerce of Georgia—whilst our ships waft the products of the farmers' labor to every quarter of the globe, may *God speed the plough.*" (Italics in the original.) *Republican and Savannah Evening Leader,* July 8, 1807.

82 The peace medal is reproduced in *American Art: 1750–1800, Towards Independence,* 206 (plate 164a).

83 See, for example, John Pendleton Kennedy's extremely popular historical novel, *Horse-Shoe Robinson: A Tale of the Tory Ascendancy* (1835: New York, 1937), 87, 153. For a late-nineteenth-century novelist aware of the peace and prosperity motif following the Revolutionary era, see Sarah Orne Jewett, *The Tory Lover* (Boston, 1901), 399.

84 See Ulysses P. Hedrick, *A History of Agriculture in the State of New York* (Albany, N.Y., 1933), 287–8, 290–2, 318; Arthur Hobson Quinn, ed., *Representative American Plays* (New York, 1917), 45; and Isaac Phillips Roberts, *The Autobiography of a Farm Boy* (Albany, N.Y., 1916).

85 See *American Naïve Painting of the 18th and 19th Centuries. 111 Masterpieces from the Collection of Edgar William and Bernice Chrysler Garbisch* (New York, 1969), plate 77. On April 11, 1853, Josiah Dean Canning concluded a letter to Benson J. Lossing with these words: "Yours at the plough-tail, but with all the pride of glorious '76." Lossing Papers, box 1, Huntington Library.

86 Between 1849 and the early 1860s, Hiram Powers worked intermittently on a sculpture called "Liberty" that he intended for a prominent place in the Capitol. In 1859 Congress balked at the price of "Liberty," however, and voted an appropriation for statues of Franklin and Jefferson instead. Powers completed his figure anyway, and

renamed it "America." Today it belongs to the National Collection of Fine Arts in Washington, D.C.

87 Thoreau, *A Week on the Concord and Merrimack Rivers* (Boston, 1883), 271. The story of Putnam leaving the plough to defend his colony started to circulate as soon as the war began. See *The Pennsylvania Packet*, July 3, 1775. See also James Fenimore Cooper, *Lionel Lincoln; or, The Leaguer of Boston* (Boston, [1825]), 166.

88 Thomas Wyatt, "Life of General Joseph Warren," *Graham's Magazine*, XXXVI (February 1850), 159; *Works of Art in the United States Capitol*, 325. See also Felix O. C. Darley's scenes of minutemen behind the plough, ready to take the field with their rifles at a moment's notice, in Grafton, *The American Revolution. A Picture Sourcebook*, figs. 46 and 52 on pp. 16, 18. For the perpetuation of this theme in American culture right up to our own time, see Howard Fast's short story entitled "Journey to Boston," in *The Howard Fast Reader. A Collection of Stories and Novels* (New York, 1960), 223.

89 Wise, "Oration at Lexington, Virginia, 4th July 1856," *Southern Literary Messenger*, XXIII (1856), 4; Cresson, *Journey into Fame*, 78–9, 84. The great seal of the state of Montana features a plough in the foreground, as does Grant Wood's wonderful rendition of American fertility, *Fall Plowing* (1931), owned by John Deere & Company, East Moline, Illinois.

90 The most delightful and popular object in "The World of Franklin and Jefferson," by the way, was a small flatbed printing press that had been made for Franklin in Paris. Its hardwood and brass gleaming, it remains in good working order and was used at this exhibition to print a most elegant souvenir sheet: the title page of the Treaty of Amity and Commerce made between France and the United States on Feb. 6, 1778.

91 See Dumas Malone, *Jefferson and His Time* (Boston, 1948–74), III, 214–17; V, 18–19. Jefferson wrote in 1787 that "agriculture . . . is our wisest pursuit," a theme he would reiterate on many other occasions. See Merrill Peterson, *Thomas Jefferson and the New Nation* (New York, 1970), 357, 365–6.

92 Quoted in Edwin M. Betts, ed., *Thomas Jefferson's Farm Book . . .* (Princeton, N.J., 1953), 47. See also Jefferson's "description of a Mould-board of the least resistance," March 23, 1798, in American Philosophical Society *Transactions*, IV, no. xxxviii (1799), 313–22.

93 The Fogg Art Museum at Harvard University devoted the first of its three Bicentennial exhibitions to Franklin. See Louise Todd Ambler, *Benjamin Franklin. A Perspective* (Boston, 1975). The second concerned Lafayette, and the third was called "Harvard Divided," its focus upon Loyalism.

94 Franklin to Washington, March 5, 1780, in Adrienne Koch, ed., *The*

American Enlightenment (New York, 1965), 92; Charles S. Sydnor, *American Revolutionaries in the Making. Political Practices in Washington's Virginia* (2nd ed.: New York, 1965), 19. On June 2, 1785, Jeremy Belknap delivered an election sermon entitled "The True Interest of the State and How Best to Promote Its Prosperity."

95 Koch, *American Enlightenment*, 404, 406–7.

96 Jefferson to Adams, Jan. 21, 1812, *ibid.*, 353. On March 27, 1804, Jefferson's postmaster, Gideon Granger, wrote to DeWitt Clinton that before the Louisiana Purchase Americans in the West most wanted security, but "now it is prosperity." Quoted in Richard E. Ellis, *The Jeffersonian Crisis: Courts and Politics in the Young Republic* (New York, 1971), 90. See also the statements by Nicholas Collins (in 1789) and by Jefferson (in 1816) quoted by Daniel J. Boorstin, *The Lost World of Thomas Jefferson* (Boston, 1948), 227, 234.

97 See *America—A Good Investment*, 6.

98 Theodore Sizer, ed., *The Autobiography of Colonel John Trumbull, Patriot-Artist, 1756–1843* (1841: New Haven, Conn., 1953), 92–3; Jaffe, *John Trumbull*, 104.

99 See Walter Muir Whitehill's introduction to *Paul Revere's Boston*, 15.

100 See Willis F. Woods, *et al.*, *Lewis and Clark's America. A Voyage of Discovery* (Seattle, 1976), 2 vols.

101 Saint-Mémin's marvelous profiles pervade several of these shows. See *Eye of Thomas Jefferson*, xxv, 74–7, 268; Jareckie, *Consolidation of Revolutionary Goals*, 29, 30; and Hugh Honour, *The European Vision of America* (Cleveland, 1975), fig. 289.

102 I might add two points about the logistical and mechanical aspects of these shows. First, they required an incredible amount of cooperation, national and international, between public and private institutions, and between both sorts of institutions and private individuals. (The French government, the National Endowments for the Arts and the Humanities, Exxon, and IBM seem to have been especially generous.) Second, at least three of the major catalogues were printed by the Meriden Gravure Company, which deserves a standing ovation for the quality of its work.

103 See Gerdts, *American Neo-Classic Sculpture*, 124–5.

104 The Wilmington, North Carolina, *Daily Herald*, Nov. 9, 1860, reprinted in *Southern Editorials on Secession* (New York, 1931), 227. See also Julian P. Boyd, "Thomas Jefferson's 'Empire of Liberty,'" *Virginia Quarterly Review*, XXIV (Autumn 1948), 538–54.

105 Lodge, *The Story of the Revolution* (New York, 1898), II, ch. 10, "The Meaning of the American Revolution." See also the immensely popular historical novel by Maurice Thompson, *Alice of Old Vincennes* (Indianapolis, Ind., 1900), 360, for an emphasis upon "the guns of freedom" in 1778–9.

106 Oliver Wendell Holmes to John Lothrop Motley, July 18, 1869, in John T. Morse, Jr., *Life and Letters of Oliver Wendell Holmes* (London, 1896), II, 181–2. In this letter Holmes refers bemusedly to a controversial public letter written nine years before, in January 1860, by Caleb Cushing of Massachusetts. Cushing had perceived sectional separation as the only practical solution to the national controversy and prophesied the American Civil War: "Cruel war, *war at home;* and, in the perspective distance, a man on horseback with a drawn sword in his hand, some Atlantic Caesar, or Cromwell, or Napoleon, to secure to the weary world a respite from the dissonant din of the raving ideologies of the hour, and the fratricidal rage they engender; the reason of force to replace the impotent force of reason; and a line of epauletted Emperors to close up the truncated series of the honored Presidents of the United States." Quoted in Claude M. Fuess, *The Life of Caleb Cushing* (New York, 1923), II, 243.

107 The Trego painting is in the Valley Forge Historical Society. Pickett's is in the Newark Museum. On the equestrian statue by Daniel Chester French, Washington's right arm is raised and he triumphantly holds a drawn sword straight up—just as Caleb Cushing had envisioned. For a modern equestrian example, see *George Washington with Lafayette,* by Sandor Bodo, advertised in *The Magazine Antiques,* CX (December 1976), 1156.

108 Cooper to Greenough, Sept. 15, 1829, Beard, *Letters and Journals of Cooper,* I, 390.

109 See *The American Flag in the Art of Our Country* (Allentown Art Museum, Pa.: June 14 through Nov. 14, 1976), 11, 32; *The Magazine Antiques,* CXI (January 1977), 62.

110 July 6, 1852, *Journals of Ralph Waldo Emerson,* edited by Edward W. Emerson and W. E. Forbes (Boston 1909–14), VIII, 300.

111 Greenough, *The Travels, Observations, and Experience of a Yankee Stonecutter* (New York, 1852), 192. See Chapter Two, p. 73, above. In a biographical sketch of the painter Robert W. Weir, Henry Tuckerman explained (in 1867) that "these curious encounters with the past through family or local association, are among the singular experiences of artist-life. One occurred while on a sketching excursion at Tappan. In crossing a field, Weir saw a very old man hoeing; entering into conversation with him, he remarked, 'You must remember well incidents of the Revolutionary war?' 'Oh! yes,' replied he, scraping his hoe on an adjacent rock, and pointing across the river, 'I stood on that stone and saw Major André hung, over there.' " Henry T. Tuckerman, *Book of the Artists. American Artist Life . . .* (New York, 1867), 211.

112 See Beal, *Jacob Eichholtz, 1776–1842,* 259 and plate 891; Edward Biddle and Mantle Fielding, *The Life and Works of Thomas Sully,*

1783–1872 (Philadelphia, 1921), 335; William P. Cumming and Hugh Rankin, *The Fate of a Nation: The American Revolution Through Contemporary Eyes* (London, 1975), fig. 181. For the broad distribution of the André episode in nineteenth- and twentieth-century Anglo-American culture, see Grafton, *The American Revolution. A Picture Sourcebook*, 89–94, and *1776. The British Story of the American Revolution* (National Maritime Museum, Greenwich, London: April 14 to Oct. 2, 1976), 143–5.

113 *Notions of the Americans: Picked Up by a Travelling Bachelor* (Philadelphia, 1833), I, 217–18, 220, 222. See also William Gilmore Simms, "The Case of Major André," in Simms, *Views and Reviews in American Literature, History and Fiction*, second series (New York, 1845), 101–22.

114 See, e.g., *North American Review*, n.s., VI (July 1822), 22; *The Columbian Centinel* [Boston, Mass.], May 28, June 14, 15, and 18, 1825.

115 See Albert Ten Eyck Gardner, *Yankee Stonecutters: The First American School of Sculpture, 1800–1850* (New York, 1945), 4. In 1818 Trumbull undertook a public subscription in order to raise $7,000 to commission an English artist to make an engraving of his painting, *The Declaration of Independence.* He encountered broad public apathy and suffered great disappointment.

116 *Ibid.*, 5. For another example of the public concern over commissioning European artists to portray American Revolutionary events, see Hendricks, "Durand, Maverick and the *Declaration*," 62.

117 Gerdts, *American Neo-Classic Sculpture*, 98.

118 Quoted in Carl Bode, *The Anatomy of American Popular Culture, 1840–1861* (Berkeley, Calif., 1959), 94.

119 Greenough, *Travels and Experience of a Yankee Stonecutter*, 38–9. Herman Melville's disillusioned novel about the American Revolution, *Israel Potter* (New York, 1855), is contemptuously dedicated to "His Highness the Bunker Hill Monument."

120 Nevins and Thomas, eds., *Diary of Strong*, I, 18–19. For pictures of the site and monument, see *A Memorial of the American Patriots Who Fell at the Battle of Bunker Hill . . . with an Account of the Dedication of the Memorial Tablets on Winthrop Square, Charlestown, June 17, 1889* (4th ed.: Boston, 1896), 11, 166, 185.

121 James P. Holcombe, *Sketches of the Political Issues and Controversies of the Revolution: A Discourse Delivered Before the Virginia Historical Society . . . January 17, 1856* (Richmond, Va., 1856), 4–5.

122 *The Monthly Anthology*, I (October 1804), 557. See also pp. 246–56 below.

CHAPTER FOUR
Reshaping the Past to Persuade the Present

1 Simms, *Views and Reviews in American Literature, History and Fiction,* first series, edited by C. Hugh Holman (Cambridge, Mass., 1962), 54.

2 See, for example, Clinton Scollard, "The Eve of Bunker Hill," in Nellie Urner Wallington, ed., *American History by American Poets* (New York, 1911), I, 160–1; Edward Everett Hale, "The Marching Song of Stark's Men," *ibid.*, I, 201–2; and *The Poetical Works of Thomas Buchanan Read* (Philadelphia, 1903), III, 91, 126–7, 135–7.

3 "The Battle of King's Mountain," written for the centennial celebration of the battle on Oct. 7, 1880, in *Poems of Paul Hamilton Hayne* (Boston, 1882), 274.

4 Tocqueville, *Democracy in America,* edited by J. P. Mayer (Anchor edition: Garden City, N.Y., 1969), 487. Note the explicit echoes in these words of Emerson's "Nature," written just a few years earlier in 1836, and quoted above in Chapter One, p. 6.

5 See Samuel T. Pickard, *Life and Letters of John Greenleaf Whittier* (Boston, 1895), I, 100–1.

6 Pound to Ransom, Oct. 15, 1938, *The Letters of Ezra Pound, 1907–1941,* edited by D. D. Paige (New York, 1950), 319. The 1951 English edition of the same volume strangely omits this letter.

7 Pound, "The Jefferson-Adams Letters as a Shrine and a Monument," in *Impact: Essays on Ignorance and the Decline of American Civilization,* edited by Noel Stock (Chicago, 1960), 167, 174, 181.

8 See *Poems by George P. Morris: With a Memoir of the Author* (New York, 1860), 67, 82–3, 102, 172, 212, 360.

9 Believing "that spread-eagleism would be ungraceful and unworthy," Lanier hoped to transcend the customary nationalistic banalities. He explained to Dudley Buck, who wrote the music for Lanier's cantata, that "I have tried to make it . . . full of fire and of large and artless simplicity befitting a young but already colossal land." It is significant and symptomatic of the national mood in 1875–6 that Lanier was a southerner, his collaborator a northerner. As Lanier observed in a subsequent letter to Buck, "*then* everyone will be in a temper to receive a poem of reconciliation." Lanier to Bayard Taylor, Jan. 9 and April 8, 1876; Lanier to Buck, Jan. 15 and 29, 1876; *Sidney Lanier. Centennial Edition,* edited by Charles R. Anderson (Baltimore, Md., 1945), IX, 295, 299, 310, 353, 357. See also Edwin Mims, *Sidney Lanier* (Boston, 1905), 176–7, 181.

10 Roosevelt, "History as Literature" (1912), in *History as Literature and Other Essays* (New York, 1913), 10. This is Volume 26 in *The Works of Theodore Roosevelt* (Elkhorn edition).

11 See, for example, Fred Lewis Pattee, ed., *The Poems of Philip Freneau. Poet of the American Revolution* (Princeton, N.J., 1902–7), 3 vols.; Frank Landon Humphreys, *Life and Times of David Humphreys. Soldier—Statesman—Poet* (New York, 1917), 2 vols.; Leon Howard, *The Connecticut Wits* (Chicago, 1943); Kenneth Silverman, *A Cultural History of the American Revolution* (New York, 1976); John Griffith, "*The Columbiad* and *Greenfield Hill:* History, Poetry, and Ideology in the Late Eighteenth Century," *Early American Literature,* X (Winter 1975/6), 235–50; Gillian B. Anderson, "'The Temple of Minerva' and Francis Hopkinson: A Reappraisal of America's First Poet-Composer," *Proceedings of the American Philosophical Society,* CXX (June 15, 1976), 166–77. *The Temple of Minerva,* an oratorio and the first American attempt at grand opera, was performed at Philadelphia in December 1781, for George and Martha Washington. It celebrated the Franco-American alliance.

12 [John Knapp?], "National Poetry," *North American Review,* VIII (December 1818), 171.

13 Wallington, *American History by American Poets,* I, 153–5. See also Seymour W. Whiting, "Alamance," and Clinton Scollard, "Montgomery at Quebec" in *ibid.,* 141–2, 168–70; John Greenleaf Whittier, "Lexington," in Burton Egbert Stevenson, ed., *Poems of American History* (Boston, 1908), 153 ("Swift as their summons came they left/The plough mid-furrow standing still"); Hiram Rich, "Morgan Stanwood," *ibid.,* 151–2; and Thomas Buchanan Read, "The Wagoner of the Alleghanies," in *Poetical Works of Read,* III, 126.

14 Wallington, *American History by American Poets,* I, 190–3, 208–13, 261–5; *ibid.,* 180–1; *ibid.,* 173–5, 197–9, 202–3; *ibid.,* 181–4, 243–4.

15 *Ibid.,* 230–1.

16 See Stevenson, *Poems of American History,* 214.

17 *Ibid.,* 186–7.

18 Brander Matthews, ed., *Poems of American Patriotism* (New York, 1922), 40–2.

19 See *Poems by George P. Morris,* 83–4; Stevenson, *Poems of American History,* 231–2. There are constant echoes of *The Spy,* by James Fenimore Cooper, in this recurrent use of the Neutral Ground. See, e.g., Clinton Scollard's poem, "The Way to the Neutral Ground," in Wallington, *American History by American Poets,* I, 193–5.

20 "National Poetry," *North American Review,* 173. See Howard Fast's novel, *The Unvanquished* (New York, 1942), 143–7, in which twenty-one-year-old Nathan Hale repeatedly spurns the advances of an eighteen-year-old harlot (in Manhattan) who offers the patriot free sex.

21 Lewis Leary, ed., *The Last Poems of Philip Freneau* (New Brunswick, N.J., 1945), 57.

22 *The Complete Poetical Works of Oliver Wendell Holmes* (New York, 1890),

23. See also George Morris, "A Hero of the Revolution," in *Poems by George P. Morris,* 102–3; and Guy Humphreys McMaster, "Carmen Bellicosum," in Wallington, *American History by American Poets,* I, 228–30.

23 Stevenson, *Poems of American History,* 138.

24 *The Poetical Works of James Russell Lowell* (Boston, 1882), 415–16. See also Francis M. Finch, *The Blue and the Gray and Other Verses* (New York, 1909).

25 Wallington, *American History by American Poets,* I, 297–8; Pickard, *Life and Letters of Whittier,* II, 740.

26 It is the lead poem in Guiterman, *Death and General Putnam and 101 Other Poems* (New York, 1935). The Benét poems about Washington, Abigail and John Adams, Jefferson, Franklin, Hamilton, Burr, John Paul Jones, and Benedict Arnold are delightful as limericks but poor as poetry. Yet the Benéts very clearly had done some biographical burrowing into the lives of their subjects.

27 See, for example, Freneau, "On the Memorable Victory of John Paul Jones" (1781) in Pattee, *Poems of Freneau,* II, 75–80; Wallace Rice, "John Paul's First Victory," in Wallington, *American History by American Poets,* I, 223–5; and Walt Whitman, "An Old-Time Sea-Fight," parts 35 and 36 in "Song of Myself," in *The Complete Poetry and Prose of Walt Whitman,* introduction by Malcolm Cowley (New York, 1948), 96–8.

28 For sentimental poems that emphasize the difficult war years and loneliness of responsibility without full power, see Margaret J. Preston, "The Boys' Redoubt," and Ernest L. Valentine, "The Tears of Washington," in Wallington, *American History by American Poets,* I, 165–8, 186–7; and Read, "The Wagoner of the Alleghanies," *Poetical Works of Read,* III, 165–6.

29 See George Morris, "Land of Washington," in *Poems by George P. Morris,* 67: Walt Whitman, "Washington's Monument, February, 1885," in *Complete Poetry of Walt Whitman,* 441; and S. Weir Mitchell, "The Birthday of Washington," in Wallington, *American History by American Poets,* I, 113–16.

30 *Poetical Works of James Russell Lowell,* 410.

31 Wallington, *American History by American Poets,* I, 213. Arnold has inevitably and repeatedly been likened to Judas Iscariot. See the Benéts' *Book of Americans,* 38:

> *While this is a fellow whom few can admire,*
> *For he sold his own country for money and ire.*

32 Charlotte Fiske Bates, "André," in Stevenson, *Poems of American History,* 239. See also Nathaniel Parker Willis, "André's Request to Washington," *ibid.,* 238–9. For another expression of ambivalence about Washington, see John Greenleaf Whittier to Edward Everett,

Feb. 20, 1836, an open letter that was printed in *The Liberator:* "George Washington was another signer of the Constitution. I know that he was a slaveholder . . . the only blot on the otherwise bright and spotless character of the Father of his Country." Pickard, *Life and Letters of Whittier,* I, 197.

33 Samuel Longfellow, ed., *Life of Henry Wadsworth Longfellow. With Extracts from His Journals and Correspondence* (Boston, 1893), III, 17–18, 23–4, 28. See also John Van Schaick, Jr., *Characters in Tales of a Wayside Inn* (New York, 1974).

34 Wallington, *American History by American Poets,* I, 159–60. See also Read, "The Wagoner of the Alleghanies," *Poetical Works of Read,* III, 184–8; and Lawrence Lee, *A Hawk from Cuckoo Tavern* (Gaylordsville, Va., 1930), 5–7, in which a Kinsman of Thomas Jefferson rides long and hard to Charlottesville to warn him that Tarleton intends to capture him, whereupon Jefferson escapes.

35 "What's in a Name?" Wallington, *American History by American Poets,* I, 150–1.

36 *Ibid.,* 175–7; Stevenson, *Poems of American History,* 194. Ezra Pound was quite familiar with Longfellow's *Tales of a Wayside Inn.* See his letter to Hubert Creekmore of February 1939, in Paige, *Letters of Ezra Pound,* 322.

37 Cincinnatus Hiner ("Joaquin") Miller (1839–1913), "Washington on the Delaware," in Wallington, *American History by American Poets,* I, 187–8; and Will Carleton (1845–1912), "Across the Delaware," Stevenson, *Poems of American History,* 188.

38 During ante-bellum times, William Gilmore Simms admired and enjoyed the friendship of George Bancroft. The Civil War, however, turned that relationship exceedingly sour. Paul Hamilton Hayne worked for quite some time on a biography of Simms, his good friend and fellow southerner. It appeared in essay form in 1870, and as a long poem seven years later. Margaret J. Preston, a conventional poetess with ties both North and South, wrote the biographical introduction to *Poems of Paul Hamilton Hayne* (1882). During the 1920s and 1930s, a cluster of literary types began gathering as a winter colony near Rollins College in Winter Park, Florida. Quite a number of them were popular writers—including Clinton Scollard, Arthur Guiterman, Winston Churchill, and Irving Bacheller—who occasionally chose the American Revolution as their subject. See Arthur Guiterman, *Brave Laughter,* introduction by Eleanor Graham (New York, 1943), 53.

39 Mary C. Simms Oliphant, *et al.,* eds., *The Letters of William Gilmore Simms* (Columbia, S.C., 1952–6), I, 349. For Simms's poem, "Battle of Eutaw Springs," see Wallington, *American History by American Poets,* I, 272–4; and see Bryant to Charles Folsom, March 9, 1827, in *The Letters*

of William Cullen Bryant, edited by W. C. Bryant, II, and Thomas G. Voss (New York, 1975), I, 231.

40 See Parke Godwin, *A Biography of William Cullen Bryant, with Extracts from His Private Correspondence* (New York, 1883), II, 330.

41 See "The Last Leaf" in *Complete Poetical Works of Holmes*, 1; *The Poetical Works of Fitz-Greene Halleck* (New York, 1848), 53–9; and James Grant Wilson, *The Life and Letters of Fitz-Greene Halleck* (New York, 1869), 350–1.

42 See Wallington, *American History by American Poets*, I, 228–30, 274–6.

43 See *The Poetical Works of Thomas Buchanan Read* (Philadelphia, 1903), III, 7–262. It was first published in 1862, and is one of the few poems among this genre that explicitly emphasizes the attractiveness of preserving tradition. See, e.g., p. 19 (as well as pp. 25, 31):

And old traditions, dimmed by years,
Breathed from invisible lips there came,
And lingered in my credulous ears,
And night and day disturbed my soul,
Until, perforce, I wrote the whole:
That is the picture,—this the scroll.

44 *Poetical Works of James Russell Lowell*, 407–10.

45 See Ida Gertrude Everson, *George Henry Calvert. American Literary Pioneer* (New York, 1944); and *Sidney Lanier. Centennial Edition*, edited by Charles R. Anderson (Baltimore, Md., 1945), I, 60–82.

46 *Poems of Paul Hamilton Hayne*, 274–7. This poem is presented as having been narrated by an aged volunteer who had taken part in the fight, "to certain of his friends and neighbors, upon the fiftieth anniversary of the conflict, viz. Oct. 7, 1830." Two lines near the close are especially symptomatic and resonant with themes I have touched upon earlier.

Would ye be worthy of your sires who on King's Mountain side
Welcomed dark death for freedom's sake as bridegrooms clasp a bride?

47 The service was actually held in Faneuil Hall. At the special request of Boston's Black citizens, O'Reilly (1844–90) read his poem for them on Dec. 18, 1888, at a Negro church on Charles Street, prefacing the poem with a short speech. See James J. Roche, *Life of John Boyle O'Reilly Together with His Complete Poems and Speeches* (New York, 1891), 325–6, and 408–14, for the complete text of his poem.

48 See Pickard, *Life and Letters of Whittier*, I, 100–1.

49 See *Poetical Works of William Cullen Bryant* (New York, 1879), 134, 166, 178; Godwin, *A Biography of Bryant*, I, 354.

50 Matthews, *Poems of American Patriotism*, 14; Newton Arvin, *Longfellow. His Life and Work* (Boston, 1963), 141, 216. See also William Collins's

poem, "Molly Maguire at Monmouth," in *Poems of American Patriotism,* 43–6. The poem is ostensibly about Molly Pitcher in June 1778; but the title alludes to a secret organization that was highly problematic in American politics during the period 1865–77. For allusions to the Civil War in "The Wagoner of the Alleghanies," see *Poetical Works of Thomas Buchanan Read,* III, 82, 84, 86, 89–92, 125.

51 Wallington, *American History by American Poets,* I, 274–6. See also Whittier, "The Black Men of the Revolution and War of 1812," in *The National Era,* I (July 19, 1847), p. 1, reprinted in *The Writings of Whittier* (Boston, 1889), VI, 406–16. And see Edward Everett Hale, "New England's Chevy Chase" (dated April 19, 1882), in Stevenson, *Poems of American History,* 148–50.

52 *Ibid.,* 153–4. On May 1, 1875, Whittier commented on this poem in a letter to James R. Osgood: "I stretched my Quakerism to the full strength of its drab in writing about the Lexington folks who were shot and did not shoot back. I cannot say anything about those who *did* shoot to some purpose on Bunker Hill. These occasional poems are fatal to any poet save Dr. Holmes. He always manages to come off safely." Pickard, *Life and Letters of Whittier,* II, 602. The closing remark presumably refers to "Grandmother's Story of Bunker-Hill Battle, as She Saw It from the Belfry," and "A Ballad of the Boston Tea-Party," in which Holmes even includes a humorous Darwinian allusion (*Complete Poetical Works of Holmes,* 195, 233–6):

Since Father Noah squeezed the grape
And took to such behaving
As would have shamed our grandsire ape
Before the days of shaving,—

53 Wallington, *American History by American Poets,* II, 152–5. *The New York Times* reprinted this poem on Jan. 21, 1876, p. 2.

54 *Poems of Paul Hamilton Hayne,* 280.

55 *Ibid.,* 283.

56 "National Poetry," 173–4. "The Wagoner of the Alleghanies," by Thomas Buchanan Read, ostensibly concerns the Battle of Brandywine and the severe winter at Valley Forge. But much of its 255 pages actually comprise a romantic pastoral and almost gothic tale. Allusions to the American Revolution do not begin to appear until p. 82.

57 Wallington, *American History by American Poets,* I, 250.

58 *Ibid.,* 155. See also Mary A. P. Stansbury, "The Surprise at Ticonderoga," *ibid.,* 156–9; and *Sidney Lanier. Centennial Edition,* edited by Charles R. Anderson (Baltimore, Md., 1945), I, lviii.

59 *The Poetical Works of Lowell,* 408.

60 *Ibid.,* 420.

61 *Ibid.,* 97.

62 "An Ode for the Fourth of July, 1876," *ibid.*, 417–18. For Winthrop's *Oration*, see Chapter Two, pp. 60–1, above.

63 Wallington, *American History by American Poets*, II, 301–2.

64 Barrett Eastman's "The Baptism of the Flag," which is about John Paul Jones, will be found in *ibid.*, I, 216–19, as will Minna Irving's "Betsy's Battle Flag," 172–3. Clinton Scollard and Wallace Rice published *Ballads of Valor and Victory, Being Stories in Song from the Annals of America* in 1903, gathering together poems they had written since 1897. *Let the Flag Wave. With Other Verses Written in War-Time* (New York, 1917) is by Scollard also. An interesting sketch of Scollard, written by his second wife, will be found in *The Singing Heart. Selected Lyrics and Other Poems of Clinton Scollard* (New York, 1934), vii–xlvii. *Poems of American Patriotism*, chosen by Brander Matthews, was first published in 1882 and then in an attractive edition illustrated by N. C. Wyeth in 1922.

65 James Grant Wilson, *The Life and Letters of Fitz-Greene Halleck* (New York, 1869), 169, 172, 350–1, 514–15.

66 "The Death of Warren," Stevenson, *Poems of American History*, 166–7; Finch, *The Blue and the Gray*, 13–15.

67 Park Benjamin, "A Paean for Independence," *Graham's Magazine*, XLVII (July 1855), 45; Holcombe, *Sketches of the Political Issues and Controversies of the Revolution: A Discourse Delivered Before the Virginia Historical Society . . . January 17, 1856* (Richmond, Va., 1856), 63. See also *Revolutionary Memorials, Embracing Poems by the Rev. Wheeler Case, published in 1778*, edited by Rev. Stephen Dodd (New York, 1852). On p. iv he expresses the hope that "this precious relic of that fearful period when men's principles were tested, will be acceptable to the patriotic community."

68 See John Fanning Watson to Lossing, ca. 1851, Lossing Papers, Addenda, box 2, Huntington Library; Thomas Balch to Lossing, June 8, 1855, *ibid.*, Addenda, box 3; Joseph B. Wakeley to Lossing, Feb. 1, 1861, *ibid.*, box 1; Lossing to Ann Pamela Cunningham, March 26 and April 2, 1870, *ibid.*, box 2.

69 *The Poetical Works of Thomas Buchanan Read* (Philadelphia, 1903), III, 13–262, especially 86–7, called "The Brave at Home," 91–2, "The Patriot's Cry," and 109 ff., "The Young Patriot"; Hale, "The Marching Song of Stark's Men," in Wallington, *American History by American Poets*, I, 201–2.

70 After 1882 the old favorites were as likely to be reprinted as new ones written. I visited "La Cuesta Encantada," the so-called Hearst Castle at San Simeon, California, on Jan. 14, 1977. Prominently displayed in William Randolph Hearst's third-floor "study" (or boardroom) was an oversized, lavishly illustrated, single-volume edition of "The Last Leaf" by Oliver Wendell Holmes, published in 1885.

71 See Francis C. Rosenberger, *XII Poems* (New York, 1946), poems V–VIII; Edgar Lee Masters, "Jefferson," in *Poems of People* (New York, 1936), 21–2; Lawrence Lee, *Monticello and Other Poems* (New York, 1937), 3–4; Allen Tate, "On the Father of Liberty," *The Sewanee Review Quarterly,* XXXVIII (January 1930), 60. In Cantos XXXI to XXXIII, composed during the mid-1930s, Ezra Pound became deeply engaged with Jeffersonian thought, especially the idea that freedom involves the exercise of liberty which does not encroach upon the freedom of others. It saddened Pound that Jeffersonian democracy had decayed and become transmuted into capitalist democracy, a phenomenon Jefferson would have despised.

72 Karl Shapiro, "Jefferson," in Shapiro, *V-Letter and Other Poems* (New York, 1944), 19. "Jefferson" is a brilliant poem—both well informed and rich with emotion.

73 It should be pointed out, however, that *The Testament of Freedom,* by Randall Thompson (1943), a composition for orchestra and chorus, is organized around passages declaring America's Revolutionary birth. Following World War II, Ezra Pound used his long-standing interest in Jefferson and John Adams to support his conviction that he had really acted as an American patriot in broadcasting from Rome. See Donald Davie, *Ezra Pound: Poet as Sculptor* (New York, 1964), 166.

74 This statement occurred in Burckhardt's lectures at Basel in 1868–71 and appeared posthumously in his *Force and Freedom. Reflections on History,* edited by James Hastings Nichols (New York, 1943), 153.

75 Interview with Benjamin DeMott, *The New York Times Book Review,* Jan. 9, 1977, 22. See also L. Hugh Moore, Jr., *Robert Penn Warren and History* (The Hague, 1970).

76 See, for example, Edmund S. Morgan, "Slavery and Freedom: The American Paradox," *The Journal of American History,* LIX (June 1972), 5–29; Morgan, "The Puritan Ethic and the American Revolution," *The William and Mary Quarterly,* XXIV (January 1967), 3–43; Bernard Bailyn, *The Ordeal of Thomas Hutchinson* (Cambridge, Mass., 1974), especially ch. 3; Jack P. Greene, *All Men Are Created Equal. Some Reflections on the Character of the American Revolution* (Oxford, 1976); and Gordon S. Wood, "Revolution and the Political Integration of the Enslaved and Disenfranchised," in *America's Continuing Revolution,* introduction by Stephen J. Tonsor (Anchor edition: Garden City, N.Y., 1976), 95–113.

77 But see *The Cantos of Ezra Pound* (New York, 1970), 167–8. See also the line in Canto LXII: "the ethics, so called, of Franklin / If moral analysis / be not the purpose of historical writing . . ." (*ibid.,* p. 346).

78 See Davie, *Ezra Pound: Poet as Sculptor,* 163–5; Noel Stock, *Poet in Exile: Ezra Pound* (Manchester, Eng., 1964), ch. 13, "Pound as Historian." Cf. Frederick K. Sanders, *John Adams Speaking: Pound's Sources for the Adams Cantos* (Orono, Me., 1975).

79 It is certainly true, however, that some of Pound's perceptions of the Revolution were less insightful than others. In 1944, for example, he wrote that "the central fact of the American Revolution of 1776 was the suppression, in 1750, of the paper money issue in Pennsylvania and other colonies." Pound, *Impact: Essays on Ignorance and the Decline of American Civilization,* 185.

80 "National Poetry," *North American Review,* 175.

81 Montrose J. Moses, *The American Dramatist* (Boston, 1925), 109. See also 13, 106–7.

82 Grimsted, "Melodrama as Echo of the Historically Voiceless," in *Anonymous Americans: Explorations in Nineteenth-Century Social History,* edited by Tamara Hareven (Englewood Cliffs, N.J., 1971), 81. In 1798, when William Dunlap's *André* was performed for the first time, he had to alter one scene that did not appear to be sufficiently patriotic. The audience hissed because it felt that Dunlap might have inadvertently insulted the United States. See Montrose J. Moses, ed., *Representative Plays by American Dramatists, 1765–1819* (New York, 1918), 505, which quotes from Dunlap's own account of that first performance. For an extraordinarily similar repetition of this incident in 1898, involving Clyde Fitch's *Nathan Hale,* see Arthur Hobson Quinn, *A History of the American Drama, from the Civil War to the Present Day* (New York, 1936), 273.

83 Rosamund Gilder, review of *Valley Forge* in *Theatre Arts Monthly,* XIX (February 1935), 96. For the very same sentiments in the nineteenth century, see Quinn, *History of the American Drama, from the Civil War to the Present Day,* 136. See also Murray H. Nelligan, "American Nationalism on the Stage: The Plays of George Washington Parke Custis (1781–1857)," *Virginia Magazine of History and Biography,* LVIII (July 1950), 299–325.

84 Gassner, in *Current History,* n.s., IV (March 1943), 88. See also Samuel Blaine Shirk, *The Characterization of George Washington in American Plays Since 1875* (Philadelphia, 1949), 26–7.

85 *Ibid.,* 28–9, 36–7, 69; Paul Z. DuBois, *Paul Leicester Ford: An American Man of Letters, 1865–1902* (New York, 1977), 55, 77–78, 83–85, 125, 148.

86 R. Fellow, "American History on the Stage," *The Atlantic Monthly,* L (September 1882), 310. See also Jeannette L. Gilder, "The American Historical Novelists," *The Independent,* LIII (Sept. 5, 1901), 2098–2100.

87 See William A. Bryan, *George Washington in American Literature, 1775–1865* (New York, 1952), 180, 183–4; Edward Fitz-Ball, *The Pilot: A Nautical Burletta, in Three Acts* (London, 1825); Burnett, *Blanche of Brandywine* (New York, 1858); and George P. Morris, *Briar Cliff; or, Scenes of the Revolution* (1826), adapted from a novel called *Whig and Tory.* The play was reprinted in *The Magazine of History with Notes and*

Queries, XLIX (New York, 1935), extra no. 194. Here is one example of the dialogue, taken from the end of Scene VI (Miss Polly is the mistress of Briar Cliff):

POLLY: Oh miserable woman that I am—Is there no redress—I shall go mad!
DR. MEREDITH: Don't, Madam. I've not a strait-jacket at hand.
POLLY: I shall faint.
DR. MEREDITH: Bless me, don't, Madam! I'll take it as a personal favor, for I've not my instrument about me.
POLLY: Oh me—their cruelty will send me to an early grave!
DR. MEREDITH: An early grave—umph! Oh I see how it is—bless my soul, her blood is in a state of orgasm, and the indication is depletion under the form of *venesection*—Madame—
POLLY: Stand off, you monster, you gallipot—you murderer of monkeys!
DR. MEREDITH: Nay, Madam, only allow me to feel your purse—*pulse I mean*
POLLY: Away, you lump of opium—you bundle of drugs!
[Exit, in a huff.]
DR. MEREDITH (angrily): Whew, whew, whew! No, I never swear, but that old woman is enough to provoke a saint. To treat a man of science and learning in this manner—and accuse me of killing her monkey.
D—n her monkey.

88 See Chapter Three, pp. 84 and 105, above.

89 Norman Philbrick, ed., *Trumpets Sounding: Propaganda Plays of the American Revolution* (New York, 1972), 2–3. The seven patriot and Loyalist plays in this anthology were written between 1774 and 1779. See also Moses, ed., *Representative Plays by American Dramatists, 1765–1819,* for Mercy Otis Warren, *The Group* (1775), Hugh Henry Brackenridge, *The Battle of Bunkers-Hill* (1776), John Leacock, *The Fall of British Tyranny* (1776), and Samuel Low, *The Politician Out-witted* (1789); and see Edmund M. Hayes, ed., "Mercy Otis Warren: *The Defeat,*" *New England Quarterly,* XLIX (September 1976), 440–58.

90 See Pattee, ed., *The Poems of Freneau,* II, 39–72. For the most detailed treatment of American plays written in the period 1774–97, see George O. Seilhamer, *History of the American Theatre* (Philadelphia, 1888–91), Vols. II and III.

91 Quoted in Moses, *American Dramatist,* 64. Although it is one of Dunlap's best plays, *André* failed because the hero was a British spy and because the actors muffed several key lines on opening night. Gate receipts were $800 the first night, a pathetic $271 the second night, $329 on the third and final night. *The Glory of Columbia—Her Yeomanry* (1803) is one of Dunlap's worst plays: the parts are haphazardly arranged, the humor is stilted and scarcely related to the story, and the whole drama disjointed. Nevertheless, the play proved to be very popular and enjoyed many productions—even though it, too, concerns the Arnold-André conspiracy. Why? Because its collec-

tive hero was the common folk of Revolutionary America. It appealed overtly to egalitarianism and national chauvinism. See Oral Sumner Coad, *William Dunlap. A Study of His Life and Works and of His Place in Contemporary Culture* (New York, 1917), 62, 171.

92 See, especially, George Lippard, *Washington and His Generals, or Legends of the American Revolution* (Philadelphia, 1847); Joel T. Headley, *Washington and His Generals* (New York, 1847); and [Rufus W. Griswold], *Washington and the Generals of the American Revolution* . . . (Philadelphia, 1847), 2 vols.

93 See Bryan, *Washington in American Literature,* 182–3, 231, 236.

94 Bannister, *Putnam, the Iron Son of '76. A National Military Drama* (New York, n.d.), 5. In addition to Putnam and George Washington, the cast includes people named Cabbageall, Renegade, and Oneactah. In other melodramas about the Revolution we find Queerfish, a British soldier; Welcome Sobersides, a Yankee sergeant; Krout, a Pennsylvania German; and Fulmenifer, a symbolic characterization of Benjamin Franklin.

95 MS in the Library of Congress. For a plot summary, see Shirk, *George Washington in American Plays Since 1875,* 46–7.

96 William Dunlap's *André* (1798) seems to have been the finest of the batch, and it became Dunlap's best known play. In 1887 Brander Matthews edited a modern edition for the Dunlap Society; and in January 1917 a scene from the last act was produced at an American Drama matinée under the auspices of The Drama League of America. See also Joseph Breck, *West Point, or, A Tale of Treason* (Baltimore, 1840); Horatio Hubbell, *Arnold, or, the Treason of West Point* (Philadelphia, 1847); J. R. Orton, *Arnold* (New York, 1854); W. W. Lord, *André* (New York, 1856); and Clyde Fitch, *Major André* (New York, 1904). Fitch did a fair amount of reading about the Revolution in preparing his *André*, and worked on the script from time to time between 1895 and its first production in November 1903. See Montrose J. Moses, *Clyde Fitch and His Letters* (Boston, 1924), 98, 252–3.

97 See David Trumbull, *The Death of Capt. Nathan Hale* (Hartford, Conn., 1845); Edward C. Rossi, "Nathan Hale" (1896, MS in the Library of Congress); and Clyde Fitch, *Nathan Hale* (New York, 1899).

98 See Hofstadter, *The Paranoid Style in American Politics and Other Essays* (New York, 1965), 3–40; Davis, ed., *The Fear of Conspiracy: Images of Un-American Subversion from the Revolution to the Present* (Ithaca, N.Y., 1971), xiii–xxiv.

99 "Benedict Arnold as a Subject for Fictitious Story," in Simms, *Views and Reviews in American Literature, History and Fiction,* 67. See also Simms to Evert A. Duyckinck, Feb. 20, 1846; Simms to Henry C. Baird, March 4, 1853, Dec. 17, 1853, and Oct. 14, 1855, in *Letters of William Gilmore Simms,* II, 146–7; III, 266, 267, 406.

100 Various versions of the following conversation commonly appeared in American schoolbooks of the nineteenth century: " 'What treatment,' inquired Arnold from a British officer, 'am I to expect, should the rebels make me their prisoner?'—'They will cut off,' replied the officer, 'the leg that was wounded at Saratoga, and bury it, with all the honours of war; but, having no respect for the rest of your body, they will hang it on a gibbet.' " William Grimshaw, *History of the United States . . .* (rev. ed., Philadelphia, 1826), 168–9. See also the dialogue in Sarah Orne Jewett's novel of the Revolution, *The Tory Lover* (Boston, 1901), 354–5.

101 Holland, *The Highland Treason,* in *Essays: And a Drama in Five Acts* (Boston, 1852), 243–4. Holland meant this morality play to be read as a long poem. His introductory "Remarks" begin: "I wish it distinctly understood that the following Drama, in the form I have given it is not at all designed for the stage, but solely for perusal."

102 See also *The Widow's Son, or Which Is the Traitor?* (1825) by Samuel Woodworth, and such tales as "The Female Spy" by Woodworth, written ca. 1846 and printed at the back of Robert F. Greeley, *Arthur Woodleigh; A Romance of the Battle Field in Mexico* (New York, 1847), 77–94; Emerson Bennett, *The Female Spy; or, Treason in the Camp* (Cincinnati, 1851), about Arnold and André; and Bennett, *Rosalie DuPont; or, Treason in the Camp* (Cincinnati, 1851). *Letters of the British Spy* (1803), by William Wirt, was extremely popular during the first third of the nineteenth century. By 1832 it had gone through ten editions.

103 *The Diary of George Templeton Strong,* edited by Allan Nevins and M. H. Thomas (New York, 1952), 1, 202. Paul Leicester Ford spent a good portion of 1890 in London looking for new documents pertaining to the Revolution, particularly at the Public Record Office. One of his most interesting discoveries was Benedict Arnold's treasonable assessment of American strengths, which Arnold had sent to Lord George Germain. Ford published it as *The Present State of the American Rebel Army, Navy, and Finances. Transmitted to the British Government in October 1780, by Benedict Arnold* (Brooklyn, N.Y., 1891). The document shed new light on the events of 1780, and suggested additional reasons for Arnold's defection.

104 Fellow, "American History on the Stage," 313–14.

105 *Ibid.*, 316.

106 *The Early Plays of James A. Herne,* edited by Arthur Hobson Quinn (Princeton, N.J., 1940), viii.

107 The Dunlap Society printed only 190 copies of *Bunker-Hill.* The play, by the way, is dedicated to Aaron Burr.

108 Fellow, "American History on the Stage," 310.

109 See Moses and Gerson, *Clyde Fitch and His Letters,* 104, 127–8, 136.

Fitch (1865–1909), the flamboyant, aesthete son of a Union army officer, is considered the most successful playwright active in the United States at the turn of the century.

110 There are many editions. One of the most accessible is Bernard Shaw, *Nine Plays* (New York, 1946), 271–354, with eight pages of "Notes" at the end by Shaw. The play opened in Britain on April 17, 1897; in Albany, New York, on Oct. 1, 1897; and the following week in New York City.

111 See Walter Kerr, "A 'Devil's Disciple' Unencumbered by Shaw," *The New York Times*, Aug. 18, 1974, 1 and 5. "We are also now able to see the play past Shaw. Shaw, decent fellow, has at last removed himself; we are not listening for him to say anything new; we are not fearful of being scolded tomorrow for having missed the point."

112 See *History of the George Washington Bicentennial Celebration* (Washington, D.C., 1932), I, 557–716; and *George Washington Play and Pageant Costume Book* (Washington, D.C., 1931).

113 See Shirk, *George Washington in American Plays Since 1875*, 39 n., 42–3.

114 *The Nation*, CXXXIX (Dec. 26, 1934), 750. For the text, see Anderson, *Valley Forge. A Play in Three Acts* (Washington, D.C., 1934). NBC presented a television adaptation for the Bicentennial on Dec. 3, 1975.

115 Published as *The Patriots. A Play in a Prologue and Three Acts* (New York, 1943). Theater in America presented a new performance for television on May 26, 1976.

116 *The Congressional Record*, 78th Congress, 1st Session, LXXXIX, part 3, p. 3336. See also Margaret Mayorga, ed., *Plays of Democracy* (New York, 1945), which includes "The Ballad of Valley Forge" by Alfred Kreymborg (1943), 1–12; and "Haym Salomon" by Marcus Bach (1940), 55–75. The editor explains in her preface that some months before Pearl Harbor she and the publisher decided that it would be a good idea to publish a book of plays about modern democracy—"not historical baggage, with which schools were already burdened; not propaganda; but plays showing the various points of view of our democratic way of life in dramatic contrast."

117 Nathan, "The Best Play of the Season," *The American Mercury*, LVI (April 1943), 486. See also the interesting review by John Gassner in *Current History*, n.s., IV (March 1943), 88–91, in which Gassner praised Kingsley for his scrupulous interpretations of historical facts: "Human motives still require imaginative insight into the cold array of documents with which the historian is usually confronted."

118 See especially his essay entitled "American Theme—The Common Glory," in Green, *Dramatic Heritage* (New York, 1953), 67–74, where he declares: "I believe in the American way" (p. 69).

119 See "Symphonic Outdoor Drama: A Search for New Theatre Forms," in Green, *Drama and the Weather. Some Notes and Papers on*

Life and the Theatre (New York, 1958), 1–44; and "Symphonic Drama," in *Dramatic Heritage*, 14–26. See also Vincent S. Kenny, *Paul Green* (New York, 1971), 77, 91; and Agatha Boyd Adams, *Paul Green of Chapel Hill*, edited by Richard Walser (Chapel Hill, N.C., 1951), 72.

120 MacKaye lived in Shirley Centre, Massachusetts. His theme, he explained, involved "the relation of the will of Washington to the world's will" (preface, p. x).

121 See Shirk, *Washington in American Plays Since 1875*, 82–3, 90–1.

122 See Green, *Dramatic Heritage*, 68 and *passim*. See also Green, *Franklin and the King. Historical Play in One Act* (New York, 1939), which was written for *America in Action. A Series of One-Act Plays for Young People, Dealing with Freedom and Democracy*. The short play takes place in London on a winter evening in 1774. And see Green, *The Highland Call. A Symphonic Play of American History in Two Acts* (Chapel Hill, N.C., 1941), which was prepared in 1939 for the Fayetteville Historical Celebration in the Cape Fear Valley of North Carolina. The story involves Flora Macdonald, the Scottish heroine. Its thrust is a reaffirmation of democracy and the American heritage.

123 Green, *Dramatic Heritage*, 49–51.

124 *Ibid.*, 24.

125 Green, *Drama and the Weather*, 81–2.

126 *The Common Glory. A Symphonic Drama of American History: With Music, Commentary, English Folksong and Dance* (Chapel Hill, N.C., 1948), vii.

127 "Virginia's Glory," *The New York Times*, July 27, 1947, section II, 2.

128 Green, *Drama and the Weather*, 35–6.

129 It had six performances in November 1975, for example, at the Grand Valley State Colleges, near Grand Rapids, Michigan. The Theatre Department's handbill promised "a most unusual evening's entertainment because of its experimental theatricality, its uncompromising political incisiveness, and its very un-traditional portrait of the American Revolution. The play was written . . . at the height of the Vietnamese war and the civil rights protest actions in the United States; and it reflects the stormy, riotous activities of those years in its focus upon the nature of political revolution and radical thinking."

130 That flurry included revivals of *The Patriots* (1776) by Robert Munford, and *The Old Glory* (1964) by Robert Lowell. Only one part of Lowell's trilogy relates to the Revolution at all: "My Kinsman, Major Molineux." Noteworthy among original productions written for the Bicentennial are *The American Revolution* (1973) by Paul Sills; *Drums at Yale* (1974) by Walter A. Fairservis, a play within a play about Nathan Hale; *The Godmother* (1975) by J. Elizabeth Jeffries,

about an English indentured servant sent to America; *The Estate* (1976) by Ray Aranha, about Jefferson's inner torment over slavery; *The Decision* (1976), about the Continental army in crisis during the winter of 1776–7; and *Beau Johnny* (1976) by Tim Kelly, about the confrontation between Generals Gates and Burgoyne at Saratoga in 1777.

131 Sherman Edwards and Peter Stone, *1776. A Musical Play* (New York, 1970), 153.

132 See Herbert Lindenberger, *Historical Drama: The Relation of Literature and Reality* (Chicago, 1975). In an author's note to his short play, *The Critical Year,* Paul Green declares that he has "been more interested in depicting something of the spirit of the times than in following the actual facts of history" (Mayorga, ed., *Plays of Democracy,* p. 80). It seems a bit sad that Green should consider the two incompatible.

133 See Lily B. Campbell, *Shakespeare's "Histories": Mirrors of Elizabethan Policy* (San Marino, Calif., 1947), especially part I; "The Use of Historical Patterns in the Reign of Elizabeth," in *Collected Papers of Lily B. Campbell . . . 1907–1952,* edited by Louis B. Wright (New York, 1968), 323–55; E. M. W. Tillyard, *Shakespeare's History Plays* (New York, 1946), 7–10, 54–8; and M. M. Reese, "Origins of the History Play," in *Shakespeare, the Histories: A Collection of Critical Essays,* edited by Eugene M. Waith (Englewood Cliffs, N.J., 1965), 42–54. Reese puts the matter most succinctly: "Playwright and historian were equally conscious of their duty as moralists to hold up a mirror to the times, and in this *genre* the didactic functions of history and drama were congenially allied" (p. 46).

134 It seems significant to me that William Dunlap—as good at historical drama as any playwright we have produced—knew, admired, and understood Elizabethan drama. As an appendix to his *André* (1798), Dunlap printed a number of documents designed to illustrate the tragedy's relationship to Revolutionary history. See Coad, *William Dunlap,* 165–7. See also Arthur Schlesinger, Jr., "The Historical Mind and the Literary Imagination," *The Atlantic Monthly,* CCXXXIII (June 1974), 54–9, a brilliant review of Gore Vidal's novel *Burr;* and John Updike's play, *Buchanan Dying.*

CHAPTER FIVE
A Responsive Revolution in Historical Romance

1 Morison, *Vistas of History* (New York, 1964), 23.

2 Neither literary critics nor the authors themselves have been very consistent in their application of these terms. William Gilmore

Simms, for example, liked to distinguish between his Revolutionary romances, his historical novels of the borderlands, and his contemporary fiction; yet he often used the labels loosely and interchangeably. See Mary C. Simms Oliphant, *et al.*, eds., *The Letters of William Gilmore Simms* (Columbia, S.C., 1952–6), II, 230; III, 19; IV, 624–5; and the 1850 foreword to *The Old Continental* by James Kirke Paulding.

3 See Cooper, *Lionel Lincoln; or, The Leaguer of Boston* (1825), 136, 284, 320; Child, *The Rebels; or, Boston Before the Revolution* (1825: Boston, 1850), 106, 150.

4 See Simms, *Joscelyn, a Tale of the Revolution* (1867: Columbia, S.C., 1975), xii, 1, 6; *Letters of Simms,* V, index entry under "Shakespeare." Herman Melville much admired Shakespeare; and see Sidney Lanier, *Shakspere and His Forerunners: Studies in Elizabethan Poetry and Its Development from Early English* (New York, 1902), 2 vols., being two sets of lectures that Lanier gave at Baltimore in 1879–80 but that were not published until twenty-one years after his death.

5 Simms, *Katharine Walton* (1851: New York, 1854), 2–3.

6 Paulding, *The Old Continental; or, The Price of Liberty* (1846: New York, 1851), II, 37–8, 41. See also Simms, *The Partisan* (1835: New York, 1882), vii; Robert Montgomery Bird, *The Hawks of Hawk-Hollow: A Tradition of Pennsylvania* (Philadelphia, 1835), II, 255.

7 "The Soldier of the Revolution," in Hale, *Sketches of American Character* (Boston, 1829), 35, 48. See Chapter Two, pp. 44 and 49–51, above.

8 *Joscelyn: A Tale of the Revolution,* 4; see also Simms's fascinating letter to the Charleston *Mercury,* Sept. 15, 1855, in which he reported the seventy-fifth anniversary celebration of the Battle of King's Mountain. "It is estimated that ten or fifteen thousand people will be upon the ground—a grand and noble sight, calculated to stir the blood, and elevate the imagination." *Letters of Simms,* III, 394–8.

9 *Horse-Shoe Robinson* (1835: New York, 1937), 11. See also the intriguing remark made by John F. Watson of Philadelphia in 1830: "I have chiefly aimed to furnish *the material,* by which better, or more ambitious writers, could elaborate more formal History,—and from which as a Repository, our future Poets, Painters, and Imaginative Authors could deduce their themes for their own and their country's glory. Scanty, therefore, as these crude materials may prove,—*Fiction,* may some day lend its charms to amplify and consecrate *facts.*" Quoted in David D. Van Tassel, *Recording America's Past. An Interpretation of the Development of Historical Studies in America, 1607–1884* (Chicago, 1960), 56 n. 32.

10 Belknap, *History of New Hampshire* (Boston, 1784–92), I, 1.

11 Randolph to Josiah Quincy, May 23, 1813, in Edmund Quincy, *Life of Josiah Quincy of Massachusetts* (Boston, 1868), 331.

12 Adams to Jefferson and Thomas McKean, July 30, 1815, in Lester J.

Cappon, ed., *The Adams-Jefferson Letters* (Chapel Hill, N.C., 1959), II, 451.

13 See Steven Marcus, "Historical Novels," *Harper's Magazine*, CCXLVIII (March 1974), 85–90; A. D. Hook, "Jane Porter, Sir Walter Scott, and the Historical Novel," *Clio*, V (Winter 1976), 181–92.

14 See, for example, John Jay to Jedediah Morse, Feb. 28, 1797, in Larry R. Gerlach, ed., *The American Revolution: New York as a Case Study* (Belmont, Calif., 1972), 181–2; John Adams to William Tudor [1818?], in John P. Kennedy, *Memoirs of the Life of William Wirt* (Philadelphia, 1850), II, 51.

15 Sparks, "Materials for American History," *North American Review*, XXIII (October 1826), 276. In 1837 he could still make this assertion: "The Revolutionary period, like the Colonial, has hitherto been but imperfectly elucidated . . . the voluminous materials, printed and unprinted, widely scattered . . . some obvious and well known, many unexplored." Sparks, "American History," in *The Boston Book. Being Specimens of Metropolitan Literature*, edited by B. B. Thatcher (Boston, 1837), 131.

16 DeForest, "The Great American Novel," *The Nation*, VI (Jan. 9, 1868), 27.

17 See William Gilmore Simms, *Views and Reviews in American Literature, History and Fiction*, first series, edited by C. Hugh Holman (Cambridge, Mass., 1962), 258–92; Anna Robeson Burr, *Weir Mitchell: His Life and Letters* (New York, 1929), 234; Austin Briggs, Jr., *The Novels of Harold Frederic* (Ithaca, N.Y., 1969), 65; Kenneth Roberts to Chilson Leonard, Dec. 26, 1935, Roberts Papers, the Phillips Exeter Academy Library. In creating the character of Natty Potter in *Northwest Passage* (1937), Roberts must have been making a private joke at Cooper's expense; for Natty Potter is the exact obverse of Natty Bumppo.

18 See Paul Z. DuBois, *Paul Leicester Ford: An American Man of Letters, 1865–1902* (New York, 1977), 145. For the impact of *The Spy* upon American historical drama, see Arthur Hobson Quinn, *A History of the American Drama from the Beginning to the Civil War* (2nd ed.: New York, 1943), 279; and Samuel Blaine Shirk, *The Characterization of George Washington in American Plays Since 1875* (Philadelphia, 1949), 54, 130.

19 Burgess, *The Novel Now* (New York, 1967), 133; Allen, "History and the Novel," *The Atlantic Monthly*, CLXXIII (February 1944), 119–20. See also Jay Williams, "History and Historical Novels," *The American Scholar*, XXVI (Winter 1956–7), 67–74; and Ralph Ellison, *et al.*, "The Uses of History in Fiction," *The Southern Literary Journal*, I (Spring 1969), 57–90.

20 Cooper, *The Pilot: A Tale of the Sea* (New York, 1823), I, v. For William Gilmore Simms's view of historical writing in the United States, see

Letters of Simms, I, xliii–iv; III, 435; IV, 9; Simms, *Views and Reviews in American Literature, History and Fiction*, 36, 42–3, 49, 55, 84. For John Pendleton Kennedy's view, see *Horse-Shoe Robinson*, xxv.

21 William E. Griffis, *The Pathfinders of the Revolution* (Boston, 1900), 5. See also William O. Stoddard, *The Fight for the Valley* (New York, 1904), v–vi. In 1855 Walt Whitman had remarked in his preface to *Leaves of Grass*: "Great genius and the people of these states must never be demeaned to romances. As soon as histories are properly told, there is no more need of romances."

22 Chambers, *The Maid-at-Arms. A Novel* (New York, 1902), vii; see also Chambers, *The Reckoning* (New York, 1905), viii.

23 Roberts to Chilson Leonard, Nov. 27, 1935, Roberts Papers, Phillips Exeter Academy Library. Back in 1912, Sydney George Fisher had blamed the low level of extant historical fiction and drama on the poor quality of available historical narratives and interpretations. "There has recently been some discussion in the newspapers on the hopelessness of all efforts to make good plays or even good novels out of the scenes of our struggle for independence. Why should our Revolution, it is asked, be so totally barren in dramatic incident and dramatic use and some other revolutions so rich in that use? May it not be because our Revolution has been so steadily and persistently written away from the actual occurrences, that novelists and play writers when they search for material find a scholastic, academic revolution that never happened and that is barren of all the traits of human nature." Fisher, "The Legendary and Myth-making Process in Histories of the American Revolution," *Proceedings of the American Philosophical Society*, LI (April 1912), 75.

24 Allen, "History and the Novel," 120. See also the autobiographical comments of Inglis Fletcher, a very popular historical novelist of the 1940s and 1950s. "The historian deals with events, and the novelist deals with the people who make the events. . . . It is much harder to make truth sound like fiction than it is to make fiction sound like truth. . . . Our history should be taught, not by events, but through the people who make them. That is the function of the historical novelist." Quoted in Richard Walser, *Inglis Fletcher of Bandon Plantation* (Chapel Hill, N.C., 1952), 68, 74. For John Dos Passos, see his remarks (made in 1929) quoted in John Diggins, "Visions of Chaos and Visions of Order: Dos Passos as Historian," *American Literature*, XLVI (November 1974), 330; and for Howard Fast's contempt toward historians, see *The Unvanquished* (New York, 1942), 315–16.

25 *The American Historical Review*, X (June 1905), 444. We tend to forget how different the criteria of historical veracity were as recently as the nineteenth century. Carlo Botta explained in the preface to his *History of the War of the Independence of the United States of America* (1821) that "I

have sometimes made a single orator say what has been said in substance by others of the same party. Sometimes, also, but rarely, using the liberty granted in all times to historians, I have ventured to add a small number of phrases, which appeared to me to coincide perfectly with the sense of the orator, and proper to enforce his opinion." Referring to the 1870s, the following comment appears in *The Education of Henry Adams* (1907: Modern Library edition, New York, p. 301): "History [as a discipline] had lost even the sense of shame. It was a hundred years behind the experimental sciences. For all serious purposes, it was less instructive than Walter Scott and Alexandre Dumas."

26 Roberts to Chilson Leonard, Dec. 11, 1937, and undated note; and Roberts to Clara Claasen, Dec. 16, 1937, Roberts Papers, Phillips Exeter Academy Library. See also Commager, "Our Beginnings: A Lesson for Today," *The New York Times Magazine*, Jan. 26, 1941, reprinted in Lawrence H. Leder, ed., *The Meaning of the American Revolution* (Chicago, 1969), 187.

27 "Historical Fiction," in Allen, *Essays and Monographs: Memorial Volume* (Boston, 1890), 118. Allen was one of Frederick Jackson Turner's beloved mentors at the University of Wisconsin.

28 "History as a Literary Art," in Morison, *By Land and by Sea* (New York, 1953), 297.

29 "The Historical Mind and the Literary Imagination," *The Atlantic Monthly*, CCXXXIII (June 1974), 59. See also George Dangerfield's review of *Burr* by Gore Vidal, *The New York Times Book Review*, Oct. 28, 1973, 2.

30 Murray Krieger, "Fiction and Historical Reality: The Hourglass and the Sands of Time," in *Literature and History: Papers Read at a Clark Library Seminar, March 3, 1973* (Los Angeles, 1974), 49, 68.

31 See "Recent American Novels," *North American Review*, XXI (July 1825), 78–104; Rufus Choate, "The Importance of Illustrating New England History by a Series of Romances like the Waverley Novels" (1833), in *Addresses and Orations of Rufus Choate* (Boston, 1879), 1–39; Paul Leicester Ford, "The American Historical Novel," *The Atlantic Monthly*, LXXX (December 1897), 721–8; Brander Matthews, *The Historical Novel and Other Essays* (New York, 1901), ch. 1; Walter D. Edmonds, "How You Begin a Novel," *The Atlantic Monthly*, CLVIII (August 1936), 189–92; and Hervey Allen, "History and the Novel," *ibid.*, CLXXIII (February 1944), 119–21.

32 See G. H. Maynadier, "*Ivanhoe* and It's Literary Consequences," in *Essays in Memory of Barrett Wendell* (Cambridge, Mass., 1926), 221–33.

33 Tucker to Cabell, Jan. 1, 1825, Cabell Papers, University of Virginia. See also William Wirt to Dabney Carr, Aug. 27, 1824, Wirt Papers, Virginia State Library, Richmond.

34 Lyle H. Wright, "A Statistical Survey of American Fiction, 1774–1850," *Huntington Library Quarterly,* II (April 1939), 309–18. See also James D. Hart, *The Popular Book. A History of America's Literary Taste* (New York, 1950), 80.

35 Quoted in Harry B. Henderson, III, *Versions of the Past. The Historical Imagination in American Fiction* (New York, 1974), 114.

36 See George H. Callcott, *History in the United States, 1800–1860: Its Practice and Purpose* (Baltimore, Md., 1970), 33.

37 See Irma B. Jaffe, *John Trumbull: Patriot-Artist of the American Revolution* (New York, 1975), 154; James Franklin Beard, "Cooper and the Revolutionary Mythos," *Early American Literature,* XI (Spring 1976), 98. Such massive and ambitious schemes seem destined for inevitable failure. In the later 1930s Neil Swanson conceived and contracted to do a series of thirty or more historical novels, biographies, and narratives—all set during the Revolutionary era and period immediately following. He fell far short of his goal, of course, but did produce *The First Rebel* (New York, 1937), about the Scots-Irish in Pennsylvania, 1763–7; *The Silent Drum* (New York, 1940), set in Maryland and Pennsylvania during the Stamp Act crisis; and *Unconquered. A Novel of the Pontiac Conspiracy* (Garden City, N.Y., 1947).

38 Simms to James Henry Hammond, Dec. 15, 1852, *Letters of Simms,* III, 222–3. Late in the autumn of 1856 Simms undertook a lecture tour in the North. His topic, "South Carolina in the Revolution," thinly disguised his purpose as a sectional apologist. See *ibid.,* III, 521–49.

39 Simms to Hammond, *ibid.,* IV, 17. See also John Higham, "The Changing Loyalties of William Gilmore Simms," *The Journal of Southern History,* IX (May 1943), 210–23; C. Hugh Holman, "William Gilmore Simms' Picture of the Revolution as a Civil Conflict," *ibid.,* XV (November 1949), 441–62.

40 See Ellis Paxson Oberholtzer, *The Literary History of Philadelphia* (Philadelphia, 1906), 251–62; Roger Butterfield, "George Lippard and His Secret Brotherhood," *Pennsylvania Magazine of History and Biography,* LXXIX (July 1955), 285–309.

41 Simms to Henry Carey Baird, Oct. 14, 1855, *Letters of Simms,* III, 407.

42 In addition to a count of titles published, which I have made, there is also literary evidence that shows authors and potential authors declining to write Revolutionary romances. See, e.g., Neville B. Craig to Benson J. Lossing, Nov. 29, 1855, Lossing Papers, Addenda, box 3, Huntington Library.

43 For other titles, information about their authors and circumstances of publication, see Albert Johannsen, *The House of Beadle and Adams and Its Dime and Nickel Novels. The Story of a Vanished Literature* (Norman, Okla., 1950), especially I, 83, 86; II, 429.

44 N. C. Iron, *The Maid of Esopus,* 57, 66, 74.

45 *Ibid.*, 123, 126.

46 See Fredson Bowers, ed., *The Works of Stephen Crane,* IX (Charlottesville, Va., 1971), 303–12.

47 *Ibid.*, X (1975), 158–9. Crane's family had been located in and around Newark, New Jersey, ever since the seventeenth century. In 1896 he informed the editor of the Newark *Sunday Call* that "during the Revolution the Cranes were pretty hot people. The old man Stephen served in the Continental Congress (for New Jersey) while all four sons were in the army. William Crane was Colonel of the Sixth Regiment of New Jersey Infantry. The Essex Militia also contained one of the sons." See R. W. Stallman and Lillian Gilkes, eds., *Stephen Crane: Letters* (New York, 1960), 94, 124.

48 *Stephen Crane: Letters,* 224–5.

49 *Works of Crane,* X, 159–60.

50. As with the iconography discussed in Chapter Three above (pp. 84–8), we can see the shift occurring quite palpably as the Civil War approached during the later 1850s. Here is John Esten Cooke, for example, a popular historical novelist from Virginia, writing in 1858. Come back with me, he invited, and "the past will live again; the former day will lie before you like a stately landscape . . . the stormy glories of the Revolution will burst into bloom, like bloody flowers." Cooke, "A Nest of Cavaliers," *Harper's Magazine,* XVII (June 1858), 80.

51 See, for example, Walter D. Edmonds, *Drums Along the Mohawk* (Boston, 1936), 196, 198, 281, 427–8; Kenneth Roberts, *Oliver Wiswell* (New York, 1940), 209, 291. Esther Forbes, the author of *Johnny Tremain,* worked for two years (during the 1930s) on a novel about a man who sought to remain neutral during the Revolution.

52 See Richard Crowder, *Carl Sandburg* (New York, 1964), 8, 140–1, 148, 150. Professional historians who specialize in the colonial period may see some irony in the years 1933–48 being a fertile period for historical fiction, because that was decidedly *not* a propitious time for early American historiography. See Lester J. Cappon, "The Colonial Period Re-examined," in *Research Opportunities in American Cultural History,* edited by John Francis McDermott (Lexington, Ky., 1961), especially 10–12.

53 For the most recent vintage, see pp. 232–9 below. Some of the principal authors are John Jakes, MacKinlay Kantor, Harriette Simpson Arnow, Thomas Fleming, Richard F. Snow, James Lincoln Collier, and Christopher Collier.

54 Quoted in Merle Curti, *The Growth of American Thought* (3rd ed.: New York, 1964), 237–8.

55 Cooper to Samuel Carter Hall, May 21, 1831, in James F. Beard, ed., *The Letters and Journals of James Fenimore Cooper* (Cambridge, Mass.,

1960), II, 83–4. It is reasonable to hear Cooper's voice in this line from *Lionel Lincoln* (1825): the American Revolution "established a new era in political liberty, as well as a mighty empire" (p. 57).

56 Paulding to Thomas W. White, March 7, 1834, printed in Paulding, *The Dutchman's Fireside* (2nd ed.: New York, 1868), ix. See also Paulding, "National Literature" (1820), reprinted in Kendall B. Taft, ed., *Minor Knickerbockers* (New York, 1947), 15–19.

57 Catharine Maria Sedgwick, *The Linwoods; or, "Sixty Years Since" in America* (New York, 1835), I, 206.

58 Simms to P. C. Pendleton, Dec. 1, 1840, *Letters of Simms*, I, 201.

59 See Cooper, *The Spy. A Tale of the Neutral Ground* (Dolphin paperback edition: Garden City, N.Y., n.d.), 8, 40, 64, 79, 142, 183, 243–4, 305, 315–16, 353, 426; and Cooper, *Lionel Lincoln*, 48. The remark to Harvey Birch is from p. 426.

60 Winston Churchill, *Richard Carvel* (New York, 1899), foreword; S. Weir Mitchell, *Hugh Wynne, Free Quaker* (Philadelphia, 1899), I, 2; Frederick A. Ray, *Maid of the Mohawk* (Boston, 1906), 1–2. See also *The Son of a Tory; A Narrative of the Experiences of Wilton Aubrey in the Mohawk Valley and Elsewhere During the Summer of 1777*, now for the first time edited by Clinton Scollard (Boston, 1901); and Winston Churchill, *The Crossing* (New York, 1904), which is presented as the autobiography of David Ritchie, a young North Carolinian on the Revolutionary frontier.

61 See also Robert and Elizabeth Shackleton, *The Quest of the Colonial* (New York, 1908); and Ezra Cornell to Rebecca Chase, Nov. 25, 1855, in *The Autobiography of Mary Emily Cornell* (Ithaca, N.Y., 1929), 16. A fierce fight developed in 1895–6 between the Daughters and Sons of the American Revolution over the ultimate control, physical restoration, and use of Independence Hall in Philadelphia. It was formally open as a historic shrine on July 4, 1898. For sardonic comments upon this tendency at an early stage, see R. Fellow, "American History on the Stage," *The Atlantic Monthly*, L (September 1882), 309.

62 See Francis Otto Matthiessen, *Sarah Orne Jewett* (Boston, 1929), 116–17; Richard and Beatrice Hofstadter, "Winston Churchill: A Study in the Popular Novel," *American Quarterly*, II (Spring 1950), 17.

63 Maurice Thompson, *Alice of Old Vincennes* (Indianapolis, Ind., 1900), 9. Sales figures for most of these books are difficult to get. *Janice Meredith* sold more than 275,000 within two years of its publication in 1899, and sales did not decline significantly until years later. It went through many editions. *Richard Carvel* had sold 736,000 copies by 1945; and *The Crossing* more than 500,000.

64 Thompson, *Alice*, 59. Back in the period 1821–46, at least some of the romances had been rather egalitarian in tone. See, for example, Sedgwick, *The Linwoods*, especially the marriage between Isabella

Linwood, a wealthy socialite, and Eliot Lee, the portionless younger son of a New England farmer (II, 285–6).

65 See, for instance, the case of Charles Fownes (alias John Brereton) in *Janice Meredith* (1899: Airmont paperback edition, New York, 1967), 119, 156, 351, 418, 421, who turns out to be the great-grandson of the Stuart king; and the case of Alice Tarleton, foster daughter of Gaspard Roussillon, in *Alice of Old Vincennes,* 130.

66 Paul Leicester Ford, the author of *Janice Meredith,* had been deeply disturbed by the slums, riots, strikes, and general social unrest of the 1890s. See DuBois, *Ford,* ch. 5.

67 See *Carvel,* 292–3, 334, 389, 391; *Meredith,* 38–9.

68 *The Crossing,* 549. See also Henry James, *The American Scene* (1907: New York, 1967), 265–66.

69 For the theme of leadership in Roberts, see *Rabble in Arms* (New York, 1933), 284, 309–10, 322, 428–9, 450, 518, 541; *Northwest Passage* (New York, 1937), 61, 85, 87–8, 96–7, 105, 107, 110, 113, 115, 117, 120, 122, 124, 128, 136, 159, 198, 253, 259, 261, 284–5, 302, 315. Howard Fast's *The Unvanquished* (New York, 1942) is a novel about the growth of George Washington as a leader in wartime. See especially 67, 187, 313–14. Washington provides an ideal prototype because a democracy wants "leaders who serve a people but do not rule them."

70 See Edmonds, *Drums Along the Mohawk,* 364, 404–5, 496; Fletcher, *Raleigh's Eden* (1940: Bantam paperback edition, New York, 1970), ix, 65, 425–6, 439; and Robert Graves, *Proceed Sergeant Lamb* (New York, 1941), 134. See also Inglis Fletcher, *Pay, Pack, and Follow. The Story of My Life* (New York, 1959), 277.

71 James Boyd, *Drums* (1925: New York, 1968), 26, 28, 383–4. See also Edward Stanley, *Thomas Forty* (New York, 1947), 242, 276; and F. Van Wyck Mason, ed., *The Fighting American* (Garden City, N.Y., 1943), xii.

72 Sandburg, *Remembrance Rock* (New York, 1948), 446, 575. See also Edmonds, *Drums Along the Mohawk,* 209, 281; and Edmonds, "How You Begin a Novel," 189.

73 Lancaster (1896–1963) is quoted in his obituary, *The New York Times,* June 21, 1963, 29. See also Conrad Richter, *The Free Man* (New York, 1943), the story of an indentured servant from Germany who arrives in Philadelphia just before the Revolution; Roberts, *Northwest Passage,* 704; and Fletcher, *Raleigh's Eden,* 95, 439.

74 Boyd, *Drums,* 290–1, 323, 427.

75 See Roberts, *Oliver Wiswell* (New York, 1940), 202, 258, 381. The implicit argument of these novelists is not at all unlike the explicit argument of their contemporary historian, Charles S. Sydnor, in *Gentlemen Freeholders: Political Practices in Washington's Virginia* (Chapel Hill, N.C., 1952), especially chs. 1, 8, and 9.

76 *Raleigh's Eden,* 16–17, 94–5, 199, 201, 323, 334, 337, 339, 343, 368, 420;

Fletcher, *Pay, Pack, and Follow,* 243. A recurrent theme in many of these novels is whether one can only become a gentleman (or a lady) by breeding, or whether a person of humble birth can *learn* to be properly cultivated. "I thought a gentleman was born, not made," says Adam Rutledge in *Raleigh's Eden* (p. 170). See also Paulding, *The Old Continental,* I, 124; Elswyth Thane, *Dawn's Early Light* (1943: Popular Library paperback edition, New York), 98, 101, and *passim.* The heroine, young Tibby Mawes, is the illegitimate daughter of two indentured servants, and eventually marries well above her station.

77 See also *Rabble in Arms,* 232, 427–9, 439, 457, 579.

78 See also *Oliver Wiswell,* 112, 209, 291, 313, 432, 433, 493, 531, 547–8.

79 See also *Remembrance Rock,* 550, 601, 606, 607.

80 *Raleigh's Eden,* 153, 218, 219, 383, 419, and finally, on pp. 449–50, the explicit denunciation of isolationism. "Ann's face flushed. Her voice trembled with emotion. 'Why should our men fight outside our own Province?' she asked passionately. 'Let the other Colonies fight their own battles as we have fought ours.' "

81 *Remembrance Rock,* 575, 602. See also Thane, *Dawn's Early Light,* 127.

82 See, e.g., *Drums Along the Mohawk,* 33, 56–7, 82, and especially 86.

83 See David M. Potter, *People of Plenty. Economic Abundance and the American Character* (Chicago, 1954), 26–8.

84 See Chapter Seven below, especially pp. 236 and 255.

85 See John P. McWilliams, Jr., *Political Justice in a Republic. James Fenimore Cooper's America* (Berkeley, Calif., 1972), 63, 129.

86 "The Song of Marion's Men," by William Cullen Bryant, appeared in his *Poems* in 1832. Washington Irving then got the volume published in London, but displeased Bryant by altering a line: from "The British foeman trembles" to "The foeman trembles in his camp." See also Robert E. Spiller, *The American in England During the First Half Century of Independence* (New York, 1926), 133–4.

87 For the context of these feelings, see Rush Welter, *The Mind of America, 1820–1860* (New York, 1975), 32–3; and Bradford Perkins, *Castlereagh and Adams. England and the United States, 1812–1823* (Berkeley, Calif., 1964), especially chs. 16 and 17.

88 Morris, *Briar Cliff; or, Scenes of the Revolution* (1826), reprinted in *The Magazine of History with Notes and Queries,* XLIX (New York, 1935), extra no. 194, p. 45.

89 See William A. Bryan, *George Washington in American Literature, 1775–1865* (New York, 1952), 99, 225–30; Frank W. Thistlethwaite, *The Anglo-American Connection in the Early Nineteenth Century* (Philadelphia, 1959), 173–4; and Charles Dickens, *American Notes for General Circulation,* edited by John S. Whitley (1842: Penguin paperback edition, 1972), 323.

90 See Jon L. Wakelyn, *The Politics of a Literary Man: William Gilmore*

Simms (Westport, Conn., 1973), 171–2, 198; Hawthorne, *The English Notebooks,* edited by Randall Stewart (New York, 1941), 213. Reciprocity came slowly, but in 1884 a bust of Longfellow was placed in Westminster Abbey "by the English admirers of an American poet."

91 Robert P. Hay, " 'Thank God We Are Americans': Yankees Abroad on the Fourth of July," *Indiana Magazine of History,* LXIII (June 1967), 119–20.

92 Whittier to James R. Osgood, March 20, 1875, in Samuel T. Pickard, *Life and Letters of John Greenleaf Whittier* (Boston, 1895), II, 602.

93 *The New York Times,* July 3, 1876, 2, and July 5, 1876, 1 and 2; Winthrop, *Oration Delivered Before the City Council and Citizens of Boston . . . July 4, 1876* (Boston, 1876), 48–9.

94 See Edward P. Crapol, *America for Americans: Economic Nationalism and Anglophobia in the Late Nineteenth Century* (Westport, Conn., 1973); Charles S. Campbell, "Edward J. Phelps and Anglo-American Relations," in H. C. Allen and Roger Thompson, eds., *Contrast and Connection. Bicentennial Essays in Anglo-American History* (Athens, Ohio, 1976), 210–11.

95 See Frederic, *In the Valley* (New York, 1890), 280, 424–7; Briggs, *Novels of Harold Frederic,* 65, 68–9.

96 Morison, *One Boy's Boston, 1887–1901* (Boston, 1962), 66–7. See also S. Weir Mitchell to Amelia G. Mason, Aug. 27, 1912, in Anna Robeson Burr, *Weir Mitchell: His Life and Letters* (New York, 1929), 281.

97 See Donald F. Warner, *The Idea of Continental Union: Agitation for the Annexation of Canada to the United States, 1849–1893* (Lexington, Ky., 1960); Bradford Perkins, *The Great Rapprochement: England and the United States, 1895–1914* (New York, 1968); and Gabriel Kolko, *Main Currents in Modern American History* (New York, 1976), 41.

98 Churchill, *Carvel,* 534. See also *ibid.,* 282, 298, 447; Ford, *Janice Meredith,* 432, 448, 536; Henry Cabot Lodge, *The Story of the Revolution* (New York, 1898), II, 232–3, 239; and James K. Hosmer, "The American Evolution: Dependence, Independence, Interdependence," *The Atlantic Monthly,* LXXXII (July 1898), especially pp. 34–5: "The work of our fathers, then, was to sever the English-speaking world,—a work one hundred years ago most noble and necessary to be done, for only so, in that day, could freedom be saved. At the present time, however, may it not be the case that the work to be done is not of severence, but of union?"

99 Sarah Orne Jewett, *The Tory Lover* (Boston, 1901), 319; Mitchell, *Hugh Wynne,* II, 38–9.

100 See DuBois, *Ford,* 82.

101 Shirk, *The Characterization of Washington in American Plays,* 59–60, 129. Sir George Otto Trevelyan published his six-volume history of *The American Revolution* between 1897 and 1907. It had a great deal of

impact at that time, and provided an additional aid to renewed Anglo-American understanding. Sydney George Fisher's *The Struggle for American Independence* (Philadelphia, 1908) stressed Britain's mildness and "spirit of conciliation" in the Revolutionary crisis, and explicitly sought to correct the anti-British prejudices of his predecessors.

102 See Charles Grant Miller, *The Poisoned Loving-Cup. United States School Histories Falsified Through Pro-British Propaganda in Sweet Name of Amity* (Chicago, 1928); Bessie L. Pierce, *Civic Attutudes in American School Textbooks* (Chicago, 1930); Ray A. Billington, *et al.*, *The Historian's Contribution to Anglo-American Misunderstanding: Report of a Committee on National Bias in Anglo-American History Textbooks* (New York and London, 1966), 29–66; and Arthur Walworth, *School Histories at War* (Cambridge, Mass., 1938), ch. 1. For a manifestation in historical fiction of this ambivalence of the 1920s, see Boyd, *Drums* (1925), 303, 306, 320, 337, 427.

103 See Zechariah Chafee, Jr., *Free Speech in the United States* (Cambridge, Mass., 1941), 10, 55, 487, 522.

104 Felix Frankfurter subsequently related a marvelous conversation derived from a social incident in 1940 (when Secretary Stimson announced that the American fleet would protect allied shipping against German submarines). Justice Frankfurter attended a dinner at the Norwegian Embassy in Washington, and recalled:

> There was present that night Senator Gerry of Rhode Island, a direct descendent of Elbridge P. Gerry. He was very nice but not profoundly intellectual, the generous donor to the Supreme Court of one of the finest, perhaps the finest law collection in private hands, coming down from all the Gerrys, a beautiful collection. He was one of the guests, and as the speech of Stimson's went on about why we were giving this help to England—the menace to freedom—I could see Gerry's face. He was an isolationist, and I could see great disapproval on his face. I'd had pleasant relations with him because he was a friend of Justice Roberts, and I'd seen him at Justice Roberts' so that it was a perfectly easy, pleasant, non-intimate relation. When the speech was over, and as we started to go in to join the ladies I said, "Senator Gerry, one of these days I'd like to ask you a question."
>
> He said, "Why don't you ask it now?"
>
> I said, "It's likely to lead to some discussion. There isn't time, but if I can put it to you quickly, it was plain enough that you didn't approve of this speech of the Secretary of War. You don't like it, and so that leads me to put to you this question: How is it that I who, as far as I know, haven't remotely a drop of English blood in me, who never heard the English language spoken, certainly never spoke a word of it until I was twelve, who never saw England until I was past thirty, have such a deep feeling about the essential importance of the maintenance of England, have such a sense of kinship professionally speaking with English institutions and feel that ours are so deeply

related to their history and therefore am profoundly engaged in this cause with Englishmen, wheras you who I believe have nothing but English ancestry would on the whole view with equanimity the destruction of England?"

He said, "The difference is that I have something you haven't got."

I said laughingly—he was a very rich man—"I suspect that you have a great many things I haven't got." I wanted to say how I envied his wine cellar. He had a famous wine cellar, "but what in particular is there that bears on the question that I put to you?"

"You see, you haven't got what I have—a memory of the red coats."

Felix Frankfurter Reminisces. Recorded in Talks with Dr. Harlan B. Phillips (New York, 1960), 275–6.

105 See Fast, *The Unvanquished* (1942), 24–5, 41, 89–90, 93, 107–9, 215, 298, 304; Thane, *Dawn's Early Light* (1943), 125–7, 131, 134; Robert Graves, *Sergeant Lamb's America* (New York, 1940), 261–2, 318; and Graves, *Proceed, Sergeant Lamb* (New York, 1941), 302, 304.

106 Fletcher, *Raleigh's Eden* (1940), 218, 346, 360, 592; Thane, *Dawn's Early Light*, 24, 47, 159. See also Allen Guttmann, *The Wound in the Heart. America and the Spanish Civil War* (New York, 1962), 145, 147.

107 Fletcher, *Raleigh's Eden*, 413, 595; Thane, *Dawn's Early Light*, 26–8, 254. The latter novel became the first in a series of six that are very much Anglo-American in setting and sentiment.

108 *Remembrance Rock*, 368; Fletcher, *Raleigh's Eden*, 346, 404; Fletcher, *Pay, Pack, and Follow*, 240.

109 It is also significant that in 1940, for the first time, a major novel about the Revolution appeared in which the Loyalist position is portrayed with great sympathy: Kenneth Roberts's *Oliver Wiswell*. A few years earlier Honoré Willsie Morrow had written *Let the King Beware* (New York, 1936), in which the hero is a Massachusetts Tory who returns to England. A few years later, Robert Gessner sought to make Benedict Arnold's defection understandable in *Treason* (New York, 1944); and Kenneth Roberts treated Arnold with great sympathy on several occasions.

110 *Lamb's America*, 374–6; *Proceed, Sergeant Lamb*, 49–50, 72, 141, 148, 165–6, 168, 174, 242–4, 314–15. Lamb's last thoughts were supposedly written in 1814.

111 See Swiggett (1891–1957): *War Out of Niagara. Walter Butler and the Tory Rangers* (1933); *The Extraordinary Mr. [Gouverneur] Morris* (1952); *The Forgotten Leaders of the Revolution* (1955); and others. Swiggett begins the introduction to *War Out of Niagara* as follows: "In my childhood, which began intellectually with the Spanish War, I delighted in the American historical novels of the Revolution and Civil War of which there were so many. . . . Shortly after the beginning of the century I read *The Maid at Arms*, by Robert W. Chambers,

and there encountered the villainous Walter Butler. I have been trying to find out all about him ever since."

112 For an obituary biography of Swiggett, see *The New York Times*, March 8, 1957, 25. James Boyd died in 1944 at Princeton, New Jersey, where he had gone to participate in a special course given for members of the armed services of the British Commonwealth. Every summer between 1928 and 1939 Elswyth Thane did historical research at the British Museum, and *The Light Heart* (1947) is dedicated "To My Friends in England."

113 See Chapter Seven, pp. 232–9, below. See also the symptomatic book by Charles B. Flood, *Rise, and Fight Again. Perilous Times Along the Road to Independence* (New York, 1976), which describes four catastrophic American defeats during the Revolution. "It is easy to be proud of these earlier Americans in their victories," Flood writes, "but where you get to know them is suffering in the snow at Quebec, or starving aboard the British prison ships in New York. . . . When they were through, they had worn down the best army in the world." The wonderful thing about the patriots from the perspective of 1976, apparently, was their stunning similarity to the tenacity of Viet Cong guerrillas and North Vietnamese.

114 During the 1930s, Valley Forge became a common metaphorical device for describing (hopefully) our capacity to survive the bleak winter and privation of economic depression. In addition to works cited earlier, such as Maxwell Anderson's *Valley Forge* (1934), see, e.g., Howard Fast, *Conceived in Liberty: A Novel of Valley Forge* (New York, 1939); Rupert Sargent Holland, *Steadfast at Valley Forge* (Philadelphia, 1939); and also Guttmann, *America and the Spanish Civil War*, 144.

115 Thompson, *Alice of Old Vincennes* (1900), 417, 418–19. This idiotic notion of happy, singing, contented slaves persisted right up to the 1940s. See also Thane, *Dawn's Early Light*, 60; and Fletcher, *Raleigh's Eden*, 28, 117, 446.

116 See especially Roberts, *Oliver Wiswell*, 13, 30, 107, 115, 563; and compare *Oliver Wiswell*, 274, 296, 298, 424, 564–5, 576, 648, with Mary Beth Norton, *The British-Americans. The Loyalist Exiles in England, 1774–1789* (Boston, 1972), especially chs. 2–4.

117 I have found at least one striking instance where a distinguished historian's understanding of colonial ideology at the time of the Stamp Act crisis was decidedly inferior to that of a contemporary novelist. Referring to the Glorious Revolution of 1688–9, George Bancroft remarked that "the day for shouting Liberty and equality had not come; the cry was, Liberty and property." *History of the United States* (Boston, 1844), III, 8. Lydia Maria Child, on the other hand, correctly recognized that "Liberty and property" rather than "Liberty and

equality" was the patriot rallying cry in 1765. See *The Rebels; or, Boston Before the Revolution* (1850), 10.

118 Carl L. Becker, *The History of Political Parties in the Province of New York, 1760–1776* (Madison, Wis., 1909), 22.

119 See Kennedy, *Horse-Shoe Robinson*, 216–17, 545–6; Frederic, *In the Valley*, 148–9, 189–90. In James Fenimore Cooper's *Satanstoe* (1845: Lincoln, Nebr., 1962), there is a pre-Revolutionary dialogue (p. 26) that explicitly anticipates the dialogue in Carl Becker's classic little essay called "The Spirit of '76," first printed in *The Spirit of '76 and Other Essays* (Washington, D.C., 1927), 9–58.

120 See Bailyn, *The ideological Origins of the American Revolution* (Cambridge, Mass., 1967), especially 85–93, 130–8, 301–19; and Bailyn, *The Ordeal of Thomas Hutchinson* (Cambridge, Mass., 1974). Cf. Cooper, *Satanstoe*, 42, 75, 78, 80, 92–3, 118, 122, which anticipates much of Bailyn's argument.

121 See also 327, 379.

122 See also 110, 364, 368, 517. In so many respects, Richard Carvel undergoes the very same psychological transformation that Cornelius Littlepage does in Cooper's *Satanstoe* (1845). See also DeForest, *A Lover's Revolt*, 140, 149, 174, 365.

123 See Alice P. Kenney, "The Albany Dutch: Loyalists and Patriots," *New York History*, XLII (October 1961), 331–50, especially 343–4.

124 Compare Paulding, *The Old Continental*, II, 21, 79, with Catherine Crary, "The Tory and the Spy: The Double Life of James Rivington," *The William and Mary Quarterly*, XVI (January 1959), 61–72. See also Frederick C. Ray, *Maid of the Mohawk* (New York, 1906), 199; and Edward Stanley, *Thomas Forty* (New York, 1947), ch. 14, and 250–1.

125 Compare Joseph Schiffman, ed., *The Duke of Stockbridge* (Cambridge, Mass., 1962), 68, 168, with Kenneth Lockridge, "Land, Population and the Evolution of New England Society, 1630–1790," *Past & Present*, no. 39 (April 1968), 62–80. On the declining status of clergymen, compare *Duke of Stockbridge*, 197, with Edmund S. Morgan, *The Challenge of the American Revolution* (New York, 1976), ch. 3, "The Revolution Considered as an Intellectual Movement" (first published in 1963).

126 See Sandburg, *Remembrance Rock*, 611–13; Fletcher, *Raleigh's Eden*, 435, 446. See also John Jakes, *The Rebels* (New York, 1975), 88, 148–9.

127 See also Paulding, *The Old Continental*, I, 13, 28. Neither John, the young hero, nor Jane, his heroine, has a living mother.

128 See Matthew C. O'Brien, "John Esten Cooke, George Washington, and the Virginia Cavaliers," *Virginia Magazine of History and Biography*, LXXXIV (July 1976), 259–65. One of the favorite lesser characters who reappears in quite a number of the novels is Colonel

Alexander Scammell (1747-81), who served throughout the war from the siege of Boston in 1775 until his much lamented death in the final assault at Yorktown in 1781. Scammell's father, a prominent and wealthy doctor who came to Massachusetts from England in 1737, died when the boy was only six years old. See, e.g., S. Weir Mitchell, *Hugh Wynne, Free Quaker* (Philadelphia, 1898), II, 185; Howard Fast, *The Unvanquished* (New York, 1942), 58, 258.

129 *In the Valley,* 401–2. See also 163, 326–7.

130 Paulding, *The Old Continental,* I, 8. *The Spy,* of course, is set in the neutral ground, as is Frank O. Hough's *The Neutral Ground* (Philadelphia, 1941); Edward Stanley's *Thomas Forty* (New York, 1947); Mildred and Katherine Davis's, *Lucifer Land* (New York, 1977).

131 Kennedy, *Horse-Shoe Robinson,* 281–2; Fletcher, *Raleigh's Eden,* 500, 516, 522, 542.

132 There are important captivity episodes, for example, in *Hugh Wynne* (1898), *The Tory Lover* (1901), *Sergeant Lamb's America* (1940 and 1941), and *Thomas Forty* (1947).

133 See Paulding, *The Old Continental,* I, 100–1, 190–1; II, 36; and Roberts, *Oliver Wiswell,* ch. 38.

134 Sedgwick, *The Linwoods,* II, 97, 233. See also Paulding, *The Old Continental,* II, 6, 13–14; Mitchell, *Hugh Wynne,* II, 12; Roberts, *Oliver Wiswell,* 124, 127–8, 312, 323; and Oscar Brand, *Songs of '76: A Folksinger's History of the Revolution* (New York, 1972), 79.

135 Cooper, *Lionel Lincoln,* ch. 30; Kennedy, *Horse-Shoe Robinson,* 387, 480–1; James Lincoln Collier and Christopher Collier, *My Brother Sam Is Dead* (New York, 1974), 227–8.

136 In Mitchell, *Hugh Wynne,* it is Jack Warder who does. In Graves, *Proceed, Sergeant Lamb,* it is Colonel Mackenzie (see II, 192, 313). In Roberts, *Oliver Wiswell,* it is Oliver himself who plans to write a history of the war when it is over, and therefore takes notes throughout (see 3, 35–6, 55, 59, 118–19, 121, 551–2). And in Gore Vidal's *Burr* (New York, 1973), the author uses twenty-one installments of the "Memoirs of Aaron Burr."

137 See Krieger, "Fiction and Historical Reality," 48–9.

138 I have not mentioned Rafael Sabatini (1875–1950) in this study because he was born in central Italy and lived for most of his adult life in Herefordshire, England. His novel, *The Carolinian* (Boston, 1925), was influential, however, and Esther Forbes began her career as a literary editor at Houghton Mifflin by doing a superb editorial job on an unwieldy manuscript from Sabatini. Published in 1921 as *Scaramouche,* it was an instantaneous success. The author of *Johnny Tremain* would surely have known *The Carolinian.* See the pamphlet by Margaret Erskine, *Esther Forbes* (Worcester, Mass., 1976), 15.

139 Compare Sandburg, *Remembrance Rock,* 418, with *The Complete Short*

Stories of Nathaniel Hawthorne (Garden City, N.Y., 1959), 519, 528. Sandburg's characters "saw this procession pass with its pounding shuddering music, its arms and uniforms of authority." Hawthorne's character responds to Robin, "Let go my garment, fellow! I tell you, I know not the man you speak of. What! I have authority, I have—hem, hem—authority."

140 See Shils, "Tradition," in *Comparative Studies in Society and History,* XIII (April 1971), 143–4. Inglis Fletcher and Robert Graves seem to have looked over their shoulders at Roberts in the way that so many novelists in the periods 1821–46 and 1895–1909 were self-conscious about Cooper.

141 Bird, *Hawks of Hawk-Hollow,* II, 255; Conrad Richter, "That Early American Quality," *The Atlantic Monthly,* CLXXXVI (September 1950), 26. See Chapter One, p. 7, above.

142 William Cullen Bryant, II, and Thomas G. Voss, eds., *The Letters of William Cullen Bryant* (New York, 1975), I, 231.

143 See Thane, *Dawn's Early Light,* 207–8; and Chapter Three, p. 81, above.

144 Betsy James Wyeth, *The Wyeths. The Letters of N. C. Wyeth, 1901–1945* (Boston, 1971), 740–1. Andrew Wyeth would do illustrations for Kenneth Roberts in 1940 and after. It should also be pointed out that a number of the writers I have discussed were themselves artists, including Benson J. Lossing, Harold Frederic, and Robert W. Chambers.

CHAPTER SIX
The American Revolution as National Rite de Passage

1 John Pendleton Kennedy, *Horse-Shoe Robinson: A Tale of the Tory Ascendancy* (1835: New York, 1937), 387, 480–1, 507. For an earlier form of the captivity narrative in American literature, and its cultural meaning, see Richard Van Der Beets, "The Indian Captivity Narrative as Ritual," *American Literature,* XLIII (January 1972), 548–62. For a Revolutionary novel in which capture by Indians figures significantly, see Kenneth Roberts, *Rabble in Arms* (New York, 1933), ch. 4 and *passim.* Peter Merrill, along with a party of four patriots, is captured along the edge of Lake Champlain by seven Sac Indians. They spend the winter of 1776–7 as prisoners of the western Indians, are adopted by the Sac tribe, and have the white blood ritually purged from their veins (365, 367, 382).

2 *Dutchman's Fireside* (New Haven, Conn., 1966), 115–16. For other aspects of Sybrandt's coming of age, see 108–9, 118, 120, 199. For simi-

lar examples from this first phase, see Paulding, *The Old Continental; or, The Price of Liberty* (1846: New York, 1851), I, 13, 30, 78–9, 82; II, 154–7; James Fenimore Cooper, *The Pilot; A Tale of the Sea* (1823: New York, n.d.), 185, 218, 261, 269, 280, 282–3; Cooper, *Satanstoe* (1845: Lincoln, Nebr., 1962), 75, 78, 92–3; and Kennedy, *Horse-Shoe Robinson*, 125–6, 246, 251, 466, 532.

3 *Hugh Wynne, Free Quaker* (Philadelphia, 1898), I, 162. For other manifestations of Wynne's coming of age, see I, 5, 7, 17, 68, 85, 87, 181, 223, 241, 245–6; II, 80–1, 173, 179, 188, 189, 190, 259, 261. For similar examples from this second phase, see Harold Frederic, *In the Valley* (New York, 1890), ch. 7, "Through Happy Youth to Man's Estate," set in 1772, and 99, 132–5, 281–2, 384, 415; John William DeForest, *A Lover's Revolt* (New York, 1898), 167, 169, 175–88, 273; Winston Churchill, *Richard Carvel* (New York, 1899), 77–8, 81, 89–90, 101, 128, 144, 422, 436; Paul Leicester Ford, *Janice Meredith* (1899: Airmont paperback edition, New York, 1967), 156, 382–3; Sarah Orne Jewett, *The Tory Lover* (Boston, 1901), 19, 57–8, 82, 89, 96; and H. A. Stanley, *The Backwoodsman. The Autobiography of a Continental on the New York Frontier During the Revolution* (New York, 1901), ch. 1.

4 Sandburg, *Remembrance Rock* (New York, 1948), 569–73, 629–30, 633–4. We are told that Locke "died for a future America." His shroud is sewn on July 4, 1776, and he is buried the next day. When Robert dies in 1777, his last words are: "I hope the people to come after will understand what it costs to win a war." Although this book did not fulfill the author's (or the publisher's) commercial expectations, it is written in beautiful prose. Chapter 22, "I Must Forget You," may be the finest piece of lyrical writing in all of these novels. It is certainly the most moving. None of the novel seems hackneyed, and for the most part it comes across as being both realistic and idealistic.

5 *Ibid.*, 373–4. For similar examples from this third phase, see James Boyd, *Drums* (1925: New York, 1968), 19, 29–30, 35, 44, 73, 164, 171, 197, 219, 262, 267; Walter D. Edmonds, *Drums Along the Mohawk* (Boston, 1936), 478–9; Inglis Fletcher, *Raleigh's Eden* (1940: Bantam paperback edition, New York, 1970), 170–1, 183, 393, 485, 512, 517, 530, 537.

6 *My Brother Sam Is Dead* (New York, 1974), 154–5. For other mentions of the Meeker brothers verging on manhood and seeking autonomy, see 10, 25, 38, 102, 182, 185, 188–9. For similar examples from this most recent phase, see John Jakes, *The Bastard* (New York, 1974), 123, 176, 236, 288, 296, 310, 313–14, 318, 433; Jakes, *The Rebels* (New York, 1975), 196; MacKinlay Kantor, *Valley Forge* (New York, 1975), 30, 73; and Richard F. Snow, *Freelon Starbird* (Boston, 1976), 39.

7 See Alfred M. Tozzer, *Social Origins and Social Continuities* (New York,

1925), 88–9 ff. Van Gennep's classic was published in English translation by the University of Chicago Press (1960).

8 Victor W. Turner, *The Ritual Process. Structure and Anti-Structure* (Chicago, 1969), 94–5. Turner adapts this passage almost verbatim from an essay he first published in 1965.

9 See Turner, *Dramas, Fields, and Metaphors: Symbolic Action in Human Society* (Ithaca, N.Y., 1974), especially 65, 182, 196–7, 231–2, 240, 258–60, 273; and David Hatch Barlow, "American Literature," *Graham's Magazine*, XXXVIII (June 1851), 409.

10 Tocqueville, *Democracy in America*, edited by J. P. Mayer (Anchor edition, Garden City, N.Y., 1969), I, 407; *Southern Literary Messenger*, XV (January 1849), 10.

11 *The Spy; A Tale of the Neutral Ground* (Dolphin Books, Garden City, N.Y., n.d.), 183.

12 Cooper, *Satanstoe*, 368. See also Catharine Maria Sedgwick, *The Linwoods; or, "Sixty Years Since" in America* (New York, 1835), I, 67: "It ought not to have been expected, that when the young country came to the muscle and vigour of manhood, it should continue to wear the leading-strings of its childhood, or remain in the bondage and apprenticeship of its youth." (Said in the context of 1778.)

13 Uttered by a woman disguised as a troubador in order to help her brother escape from prison, in N. C. Iron's *The Maid of Esopus; or, The Trials and Triumphs of the Revolution* (New York, 1861), 13.

14 Benjamin Franklin is speaking to John Paul Jones and Lt. Wallingford, the young hero who was moving slowly from neutrality to a patriot position in Jewett, *The Tory Lover*, 197–8. For comparable statements, see Mitchell, *Hugh Wynne*, I, 53, 100. In Churchill, *Richard Carvel*, 456, the hero declares the winter of 1774–5 to be "the darkest of my life," for his own personal crisis exactly parallels that of the colonies.

15 Boyd, *Drums*, 410–11.

16 Jakes, *The Bastard*, 550. See also 400, and *The Rebels*, 506.

17 See Claude Lévi-Strauss, "The Structural Study of Myth," in *Structural Anthropology* (New York, 1963), 229. See also John G. Cawelti, *Adventure, Mystery, and Romance: Formula Stories as Art and Popular Culture* (Chicago, 1976), chs. 1 and 2.

18 DeForest, *A Lover's Revolt*, 277. Edmund Wilson, by the way, called this book "DeForest's most genuinely searching novel." See *Patriotic Gore. Studies in the Literature of the American Civil War* (New York, 1962), 736.

19 *Richard Carvel*, 16, 74. See also Sedgwick, *The Linwoods*, I, 32–3, 55, 156.

20 Mitchell, *Hugh Wynne*, I, 278; Boyd, *Drums*, 350–1, 371–2, 410–11, 413; Elswyth Thane, *Dawn's Early Light* (1943: Popular Library paperback

edition, New York), 30, 82, 84, 152, 157. Although Hugh Wynne and Richard Carvel are both threatened by villainous Loyalist relatives—Wynne by his scheming cousin Arthur, and Carvel by his treacherous uncle Grafton—each one remains fairly unconcerned about whether he will ever get his due inheritance. Their basic commitments are to higher principles.

21 See J. S. LaFontaine, ed., *The Interpretation of Ritual. Essays in Honour of A. I. Richards* (London, 1972), 54–5.

22 Mitchell, *Hugh Wynne,* I, 284; James Otis Kaler, *Lafayette at Yorktown* (New York, 1895), 6–7; Hale, "The Soldier of the Revolution," in *Sketches of American Character* (Boston, 1829), 30–1, 37, 39, 47. Hale points out that the knowing glances that passed between the veteran's young auditors "recalled forcibly to his mind some passages in his early life" (p. 30).

23 *Oliver Wiswell* (New York, 1940), 301. The dominance and persistence of this frame of reference goes a long way, in my view, toward suggesting the cultural resonance of materials treated by Edwin G. Burrows and Michael Wallace in "The American Revolution: The Ideology and Psychology of National Liberation," *Perspectives in American History,* VI (1972), 167–306.

24 "Camden: A Tale of the South," *Casket,* VI (1831), 10–11; Mitchell, *Hugh Wynne,* I, 270. See also anon., *Ambrose and Eleanor; or The Disinherited Pair. A Tale of the Revolution* (New York, 1834), 2 vols.; John R. Willis, *Carleton; or Patriotism, Love, and Duty. A Tale of 1776* (Philadelphia, 1841), 2 vols.; anon., *Ernest Harcourt; or The Loyalist's Son. A Romance of the Revolution* (Philadelphia, 1843); Frank Hough, *If Not Victory* (New York, 1939).

25 See James Ewell Heath, *Edge-Hill, or The Family of the Fitzroyals* (Richmond, Va., 1828), I, 65; Paulding, *The Old Continental,* I, 70; Sedgwick, *The Linwoods,* I, 32; Jakes, *The Rebels,* 122, 160.

26 Jewett, *Tory Lover,* 297. There comes an interesting point in Cooper's *Lionel Lincoln* when an elderly farmer is called a Father of Liberty because he seems too old to be a Son of Liberty. "Yes, yes," he responds, "I am father and son, too! I have four boys in camp, and seven grand'uns in the bargain; and that would be eleven good triggers in one family" (p. 407). Cf. Chapter Seven, note 51, below.

27 *Russel and Sidney; or, The Young Revolutionists. A Tale of 1777* (1833: Boston, 1835), 159, 301–2.

28 Maurice Thompson, *Alice of Old Vincennes* (Indianapolis, Ind., 1900), 78, 105, 286, 378, 410. See also Charles R. Talbot, *A Romance of the Revolution* (Boston, 1884); Charles C. Coffin, *Daughters of the Revolution and Their Times, 1769–1776. A Historical Romance* (Boston, 1895); Amy E. Blanchard, *A Girl of '76* (Boston, 1898); Blanchard, *A Revolutionary*

Maid. A Story of the Middle Period of the War for Independence (Boston, 1899); Blanchard, *A Daughter of Freedom* (Boston, 1900).

29 Jakes, *The Rebels*, 258, 525. At the close of *Thomas Forty*, Tom and Faith are married the very night that peace is declared with Great Britain. How fortuitous for them to have ships along the Hudson River firing celebration rockets all through their wedding night!

30 Eliza Leslie, *Russel and Sidney*, 164, 182, 254–5, 257, 301–2, 312. In *Horse-Shoe Robinson*, it is fair to say, Mildred Lindsay's character is fully developed. (In fact, Kennedy seriously considered using her name as the novel's title.) By the eve of Independence, as "war rumbled in the distance, and, at length, broke out in thunder," Mildred "had, in the meantime, grown up to the verge of womanhood" (p. 84).

31 Churchill, *Richard Carvel*, 37–8, 78, 93; Frederic, *In the Valley*, 356, 376; DeForest, *A Lover's Revolt*, 137, 273, 277, 287; Thompson, *Alice of Old Vincennes*, 304.

32 C. R. H. Jackson, "The Moral Value of Physical Activities," in *Reaching the Boys of an Entire Community*, edited by C. B. Horton (New York, 1909), 53. I am indebted to Jeffrey P. Hantover, professor of sociology at Vanderbilt University, for permitting me to read his unpublished paper on "Manliness and American Citizenship" (1976), which concerns the period 1880–1914.

33 Kaler, *Lafayette at Yorktown*, 1–3; W. Bert Foster, *With Washington at Valley Forge* (Philadelphia, 1902; reprinted 1923), 351–2, 369. See also Wayne Whipple, *The Story of Young George Washington* (Philadelphia, 1915). Chapter 7 is entitled "A Boy No Longer," and on p. 113, when young George gets his surveyor's license at the age of seventeen, we are told that it was "a kind of ticket of admission from boyhood to young manhood."

34 See Whitfield J. Bell, Jr., "Everett T. Tomlinson: New Jersey Novelist of the American Revolution," in *New Jersey in the American Revolution: Political and Social Conflict*, edited by William C. Wright (1970: Trenton, N.J., 1974), 84.

35 Churchill, *Richard Carvel*, 81–2, 127, 367.

36 Thompson, *Alice of Old Vincennes*, 60, 128, 130.

37 Thane, *Dawn's Early Light*, 7–8, 18, 51, 256–7. Henner Frey, the hero of Conrad Richter's *The Free Man* (1943), is a young indentured servant from the Palatinate who arrives in Philadelphia on the eve of the American Revolution. Both of his parents die during the trans-Atlantic voyage.

38 "England and America in the Schoolbooks of the Republic, 1783–1861," *University of Birmingham Historical Journal*, IX (1963), 93.

39 Michael Walzer, "On the Role of Symbolism in Political Thought," *Political Science Quarterly*, LXXXII (June 1967), 203.

40 See Mitchell, *Hugh Wynne*, I, 114; Jewett, *The Tory Lover*, 57–8, 82, 89,

96, 402, and especially ch. 42, "The Passage Inn"; Thane, *Dawn's Early Light*, 8–9, 286–7; Jakes, *The Bastard*, 302, 314.

41 See Norman Pettit, "The Puritan Legacy," *New England Quarterly*, XLVIII (June 1975), 287–8. See also Sacvan Bercovitch, *The Puritan Origins of the American Self* (New Haven, Conn., 1975), 108.

42 Seabury, *Letters of a Westchester Farmer*, in Henry Steele Commager and Richard B. Morris, eds., *The Spirit of 'Seventy-Six* (New York, 1958), 329. See also Kenneth S. Lynn, "Adulthood in American Literature," *Daedalus*, CV (Fall 1976), 54.

43 Quoted in George Louis Beer, *British Colonial Policy, 1754–1765* (New York, 1907), 167 n.2. Hunter was commenting on the Navigation Acts, especially the friction that occurred wherever local and imperial authorities came into contact.

44 See Ernest C. Mossner, *The Life of David Hume* (Edinburgh, 1954), 554; Noel Perrin, ed., *The Adventures of Jonathan Corncob, Loyal American Refugee* (London, 1787; Boston, 1976); Lydia Maria Child, *The Rebels; or, Boston Before the Revolution* (Boston, 1850), 29: "With high ideas of English power, and with very gross ignorance of the colonial character, Somerville regarded the resistance of America as the discontented murmuring of a wayward child [1765]."

45 E.g., Marinus Willett, *A Narrative of the Military Actions of Colonel Marinus Willett* (New York, 1831); John P. Becker, *The Sexagenary, or Reminiscences of the American Revolution* (Albany, N.Y., 1833); K. M. Hutchinson, *A Memoir of Abijah Hutchinson, a Soldier of the Revolution* (Rochester, N.Y., 1843); and Charles I. Bushnell, ed., *Memoirs of Samuel Smith, a Soldier of the Revolution, 1776–1783* (New York, 1860).

46 Death, as anthropologists have shown, "means a passage into the final stage of existence, just as the adolescent rites mark progress from childhood to manhood" (Tozzer, *Social Origins and Social Continuities*, p. 118). If initiation ceremonies are "rites of transition," so death and funerals require "rites of separation" (see Max Gluckman, "Les Rites de Passage," in *Essays on the Ritual of Social Relations*, edited by Gluckman [Manchester, Eng., 1962], 3). I believe that the deaths of Dr. Warren and General Montgomery in 1775 came to have such vast symbolic impact upon American society because they signified a coinciding of the two linked processes of social change. (See, e.g., Charles F. Montgomery, ed., *American Art: 1750–1800, Towards Independence* [New Haven, Conn., 1976], 83, 87, 89, 98–9, 124.) In order to be regenerated, a society's former identity must die and be replaced. Hence the period from April 1775 until July 1776 came to be regarded as critically "liminal"—a threshold between two distinct stages of American development. For symbolic deaths (set in 1775) in the historical novels, see Cooper, *Lionel Lincoln*, 290–1; Esther Forbes, *Johnny*

Tremain (1943: Dell paperback edition, New York, 1970), 249–56; Howard Fast, *April Morning* (New York, 1961), 158.

47 *The Quintessence, Being a selection from the American and Foreign Annuals* (Sandbornton, N.H., 1830), a chapter of which, entitled "The Young Provincial," was reprinted in *Yankee* (June 1975), 81–5, 92–6. The quotations are from 83, 85, 95, 96. See also the important but strangely neglected collection edited by Richard M. Dorson, *America Rebels: Narratives of the Patriots* (New York, 1953). Quite a number of these nineteen narratives come from reminiscent veterans during the period 1820–40.

48 *The Adventures of Ebenezer Fox, in the Revolutionary War* (Boston, 1847), 15–18. For an important and pertinent theoretical statement in the framework of symbolic anthropology, see Turner, *The Ritual Process,* 103, 128–9, 166–7.

49 *Adventures of Ebenezer Fox,* 18, 37, 40–1, 44, 49, 56–8, 96–149, 227, 229, 232. In some respects this charming little book is reminiscent of Benjamin Franklin's rather more famous autobiography.

50 Cooper, *Satanstoe,* 19, 34, 42, 49. See also *The Spy,* ch. 35.

51 See also DeForest, *A Lover's Revolt,* 167, 169, and 175–88; Thompson, *Alice of Old Vincennes,* 128.

52 See Daniel Scott Smith, "Parental Power and Marriage Patterns: An Analysis of Historical Trends in Hingham, Massachusetts," *Journal of Marriage and the Family,* XXXV (August 1973), 419–28; Robert A. Gross, *The Minutemen and Their World* [Concord, Mass., during the Revolution] (New York, 1976), 75–6, 88–9, 100.

53 First asserted by Burrows and Wallace in "The Ideology and Psychology of National Liberation," 168, and developed by Michael Paul Rogin in *Fathers and Children: Andrew Jackson and the Subjugation of the American Indian* (New York, 1975), 19.

54 Cooper, *Lionel Lincoln,* 23, 43, 59, 71, 383.

55 Quoted in Murray Krieger, "Fiction and Historical Reality: The Hourglass and the Sands of Time," in *Literature and History. Papers Read at a Clark Library Seminar, March 3, 1973* (Los Angeles, 1974), 50–1.

56 See Rogin, *Fathers and Children,* 188, 205.

57 See Charles H. Bohner, *John Pendleton Kennedy. Gentleman from Baltimore* (Baltimore, Md., 1961), 99.

58 See the perceptive and influential essay by Stanley Elkins and Eric McKitrick, "The Founding Fathers: Young Men of the Revolution," *Political Science Quarterly,* LXXVI (June 1961), 181–216.

59 See Wendell E. Tripp, "Robert Troup: A Quest for Security in a Turbulent New Nation, 1775–1832," unpublished Ph.D. dissertation (Columbia University, 1973), 9–10, 30, 32. Troup appears in Gore Vidal's *Burr. A Novel* (New York, 1973), 83, 141.

60 See Frederic, *In the Valley*, 133–5, 279, 281–2; Mitchell, *Hugh Wynne*, II, 80–1, 173.

61 See Andrew Sherburne, *Memoirs* (2nd ed.: Providence, R.I., 1831), 18–21; John O. Sands, ed., "Christopher Vail, Soldier and Seaman in the American Revolution," *Winterthur Portfolio*, XI (1976), 53–73. Vail enlisted in 1775 at the age of seventeen. In 1777 he assisted Colonel Return Jonathan Meigs, and twice became a prisoner of war. He witnessed Cornwallis's surrender in 1781, and got married in November 1782. This document covers the period 1775–82, with a gap in 1777–9. It is based upon a journal kept by Vail during the war, but considerable portions were written afterwards.

62 Rogin, *Fathers and Children*, 39. See especially Winston Churchill, *The Crossing* (New York, 1904), 550.

63 See especially Peter Freese, *Die Initiationsreise: Studien zum jugendlichen Helden im modernen amerikanischen Roman; mit einer exemplarischen, Analyse von J. D. Salinger's "The Catcher in the Rye"* (Neumünster, 1971); and Marjorie Garber, "Coming of Age in Shakespeare," *The Yale Review*, LXVI (June 1977), 517–33.

64 See Peter G. Jones, *War and the Novelist. Appraising the American War Novel* (Columbia, Mo., 1976), especially 6, 7, 12, 19, 32, 44, 63, 65, 113; Joseph J. Waldmeir, *American Novels of the Second World War* (The Hague, 1969); Chester E. Eisinger, "The American War Novel: An Affirmative Flame," *Pacific Spectator*, IX (Summer 1955), 272–87.

65 Letter from Houghton Mifflin Company to the author, Oct. 1, 1975.

66 *Johnny Tremain. A Novel for Old & Young*, 148–9. Johnny's father, who was French and Roman Catholic, died in 1758, before Johnny's birth at a convent in southern France (164, 233).

67 165.

68 See 17, 26, 45, 112–13, 137, 165, 173, 180–1, 200–1, 233–4, 237, 249, 253, 256.

69 Hugh Wynne serves an apprenticeship to a blacksmith. Thomas Forty serves an apprenticeship to James Rivington, the New York printer. Philip Kent, hero of *The Bastard* and *The Rebels*, serves an apprenticeship to William Edes, the Boston printer.

70 Woodward, "The Graying of America," *The New York Times*, Dec. 29, 1976, 27; Woodward, "The Aging of America," *The American Historical Review*, LXXXII (June 1977), 583–94; and see the extraordinary statement made by Bernard DeVoto in 1920, quoted in Wallace Stegner, *The Uneasy Chair. A Biography of Bernard DeVoto* (Garden City, N.Y., 1973), 34.

71 See Merle Curti, "Young America," *The American Historical Review*, XXXII (October 1926), 34–55. In 1845, twenty-one-year-old Thomas Wentworth Higginson decorated his dormitory room at Harvard with

a bust of Hebe. See Tilden G. Edelstein, *Strange Enthusiasm. A Life of Thomas Wentworth Higginson* (New Haven, Conn., 1968), 1.

72 J. T. Trowbridge, "We Are a Nation," *The Atlantic Monthly*, XIV (December 1864), 773. On May 25, 1859, William Gilmore Simms sent to James Gardner an ode that Simms had written in 1825 on the occasion of Lafayette's visit to Charleston. Simms explained that the ode "may show you in what way the visit of the veteran impressed the new generation that was then on its march to manhood, whatever may be the sort of manhood to which the present may lay claim." See Mary C. Simms Oliphant, *et al.*, eds., *The Letters of William Gilmore Simms* (Columbia, S.C., 1952–6), IV, 156. (The editors incorrectly use the date 1823; the visit occurred in 1825.)

73 "The Structural Study of Myth," 229.

74 *An Oration Delivered at Cambridge on the Fiftieth Anniversary of the Declaration of Independence* (Boston, 1826), 5–6.

75 "The Meaning of July Fourth for the Negro," speech at Rochester, New York, July 5, 1852, in Philp S. Foner, ed., *The Life and Writings of Frederick Douglass* (New York, 1950), II, 182–3.

76 "Revolutions of '76 and '61 Contrasted," *DeBow's Review*, IV (July 1867), 36–7.

77 See John G. Cawelti, "The Concept of Formula in the Study of Popular Literature," in Ray B. Browne, ed., *Popular Culture and the Expanding Consciousness* (New York, 1973), 115, 117–19; and also Cawelti's new book, cited in note 17 above.

78 Burton E. Stevenson, ed., *Poems of American History* (Boston, 1908), 140. See also Will Carleton's "The Prize of the Margaretta," in *ibid.*, 155–6.

79 See *The Poetical Works of Thomas Buchanan Read* (Philadelphia, 1903), III, especially 43–5, 109–15, 119. See also George Henry Calvert's "Bunker Hill," in Nellie Urner Wallington, ed., *American History by American Poets* (New York, 1911), I, 162–3.

80 "Under the Old Elm: Poem Read at Cambridge on the Hundredth Anniversary of Washington's Taking Command of the American Army, 3d July 1775," *The Poetical Works of James Russell Lowell* (Boston, 1882), 415. See also two commemorative poems by Paul Hamilton Hayne, called "MacDonald's Raid" and "King's Mountain," in *Poems of Paul Hamilton Hayne* (Boston, 1882), 273–4.

81 Occasionally the authors of Revolutionary romances will refer to the "voyage of life." See, e.g., Cooper, *The Pilot*, 382, 393.

82 See *A Rising People. The Founding of the United States, 1765 to 1789. A Celebration from the Collections of the American Philosophical Society, the Historical Society of Pennsylvania, the Library Company of Philadelphia* (Philadelphia, 1976), 291; Hugh Honour, *The European Vision of America* (Cleveland, 1975), plate 223; the engravings of Washington at Tren-

ton that promptly appeared in the *Columbian Magazine* for May 1789; and Catherine L. Albanese, *Sons of the Fathers. The Civil Religion of the American Revolution* (Philadelphia, 1976), 151–2.

83 Tozzer, *Social Origins and Social Continuities,* 99–100; Boyd, *Drums,* 286.

84 Cooper, *Notions of the Americans: Picked Up by a Travelling Bachelor* (2nd ed.: Philadelphia, 1833), I, 269. On Sept. 24, 1830, Cooper recorded in his journal (in Paris) that "one of the chief merits of all our innovations, is, that they have been gradual, and that they have rather followed, than preceded opinion." James F. Beard, ed., *The Letters and Journals of James Fenimore Cooper* (Cambridge, Mass., 1960), II, 33.

85 Ralph L. Rusk, *The Life of Ralph Waldo Emerson* (New York, 1949), 11; Edmund S. Morgan, ed., *The American Revolution: Two Centuries of Interpretation* (Englewood Cliffs, N.J., 1965), 21. See also Benjamin F. Butler, *Representative Democracy in the United States* (Albany, N.Y., 1841), 30–1.

86 Ramsay, *The History of the American Revolution* (2nd ed.: London, 1793), II, 323. See also Robert P. Hay, "Freedom's Jubilee: One Hundred Years of the Fouth of July, 1776–1876," unpublished Ph.D. dissertation (University of Kentucky, 1967), 43–4.

87 Meyers, "Founding and Revolution: A Commentary on Publius-Madison," in Stanley Elkins and Eric McKitrick, eds., *The Hofstadter Aegis: A Memorial* (New York, 1974), 35; *Addresses and Orations of Rufus Choate* (3rd ed.: Boston, 1879), 171–2.

88 Potter, *People of Plenty: Economic Abundance and the American Character* (Chicago, 1954), 130. See also 131, 134–5. For a superb piece of evidence in support of Potter, see "American Biography," *American Quarterly Review,* I (March 1827), 35.

89 See Merrill D. Peterson, *The Jefferson Image in the American Mind* (New York, 1960), 168–9, 201–2.

90 Freneau in the *National Gazette,* II, no. 63 (June 5, 1793), 4; Ramsay is quoted in Russell B. Nye, *The Cultural Life of the New Nation, 1776–1830* (New York, 1960), 47.

91 See, e.g., Sidney Lanier, "Psalm of the West" (1876), in Charles R. Anderson, ed., *The Works of Sidney Lanier* (Baltimore, Md., 1945), I, 77; Sandburg, *Remembrance Rock,* 362.

92 Morgan, ed., *The American Revolution: Two Centuries of Interpretation,* 20; Babbitt is quoted in John P. Diggins, *Up from Communism: Conservative Odysseys in American Intellectual History* (New York, 1975), 395.

93 See Edward Shils, "Tradition," *Comparative Studies in Society and History,* XIII (April 1971), 137.

94 "Some Observations on the Dynamics of Traditions," *ibid.,* XI (October 1969), 453.

95 See *ibid.,* 468. See also Stanley Hoffmann, "The American Style: Our Past and Our Principles," *Foreign Affairs,* XLVI (January 1968), 362–76;

Cole Blasier, *The Hovering Giant: U.S. Responses to Revolutionary Change in Latin America* (Pittsburgh, 1976); David V. J. Bell and Allan E. Goodman, "Vietnam and the American Revolution," *The Yale Review*, LXI (October 1971), 26–34; and cf. Thomas J. Osborne, "1776 and the New Radicalism," *Thought*, XLVIII (Spring 1973), 19–32, for a conservative counter-argument.

96 "Tradition," 155.

97 White, "The Government of American Cities," *The Forum*, X (December 1890), 357–72; Isabel Barrows, ed., *First Lake Mohonk Conference on the Negro Question* (Boston, 1890), 117–21; Peterson, *Jefferson Image in the American Mind*, 269; Kolko, *Main Currents in Modern American History* (New York, 1976), 57.

98 See Merle Curti, "Our Revolutionary Tradition," *Social Frontier*, I (December 1934), 10–13; Stuart W. Chapman, "The Right of Revolution and the Rights of Man," *Yale Review*, XLIII (Summer 1954), 576–88.

99 *Satanstoe*, 266, 419. See also 5–7, 74 n., 150 n., 165, 369.

100 *Ibid.*, 280–1, 297–8, 333; Cooper to Richard Bentley, Jan. 22, 1845, *Letters and Journals of Cooper*, V, 7. In 1838 Cooper had written Horatio Greenough to express his fear of impending social revolution in the United States. See *ibid.*, III, 331; and see Mike Ewart, "Cooper and the American Revolution: The Non-Fiction," *Journal of American Studies*, XI (April 1977), 61–79.

101 Paulding, *The Dutchman's Fireside*, 48–9, 79–80; *The Old Continental*, I, 114. For John Trumbull's detestation of the French Revolution, see Theodore Sizer, ed., *The Autobiography of Colonel John Trumbull, Patriot-Artist, 1756–1843* (New Haven, Conn., 1953), 164–5.

102 DeForest, *Lover's Revolt*, 170–2; Mitchell, *The Adventures of François* (New York, 1898); *Hugh Wynne*, II, 55; Jewett, *Tory Lover*, 259.

103 See E. Digby Baltzell, *Philadelphia Gentlemen. The Making of a National Upper Class* (Glencoe, Ill., 1958), 152, 154–5, 221.

104 Roberts, *Rabble in Arms*, 369, 383; *Northwest Passage*, 523, 586–7, 673. See also this remark in *Oliver Wiswell*: "If all the property in the world were distributed, and an equal share given to everyone, the bulk of mankind would soon be destitute, and a few would have everything" (p. 202).

105 See the biographical introduction by H. Nicholas Muller, III, to the reprint of Van de Water's *Reluctant Republic* (Taftsville, Vt., 1974).

106 See also the paragraph on Mason in Inglis Fletcher, *Pay, Pack, and Follow. The Story of My Life* (New York, 1959), 298; and F. Van Wyck Mason, ed., *The Fighting American* (Garden City, N.Y., 1943), xii, xiv, xix.

107 See *Letters of Simms*, I, 159–60; V, 359; Austin Briggs, Jr., *The Novels of Harold Frederic* (Ithaca, N.Y., 1969), 63. William E. Griffis, who wrote

The Pathfinders of the Revolution (1900), was descended from participants in the war, and many of the characters in the novel were based upon his Revolutionary ancestors. (Letter to the author from Hughes Griffis, Feb. 25, 1975.) Paul Leicester Ford was a descendant of Noah Webster.

108 See Richard and Beatrice Hofstadter, "Winston Churchill: A Study in the Popular Novel," *American Quarterly*, II (Spring 1950), 12–28; "Concerning *Richard Carvel*," *The Bookman*, IX (July 1899), 403–5. Judging from various casual allusions, there is more than a touch of anti-Semitism in *Richard Carvel*; see, e.g., 292–3, 334, 389, 391.

109 Fletcher, *Pay, Pack, and Follow*, 4, 22–3; see also 296, 301. Conrad Richter was writing about his own ancestors in *The Free Man* (New York, 1943). See his foreword to that patriotic novella about eastern Pennsylvania on the eve of Revolution. For his nostalgia about an earlier way of life in America, see Richter, "This Once Ideal Village," *Saturday Evening Post*, CCXIX (Oct. 12, 1946), 4.

110 Roberts to Chilson Leonard, Nov. 27, 1935, Aug. 21, 1936, Roberts Papers, Phillips Exeter Academy Library. In a subsequent (undated) note to Leonard, Roberts remarked: "They gave *Crumbs Along the Mohawk* Page I a couple of months ago, & mebbe you can imagine how that burned me up." There has, in fact, been an obsession with drums in the titles of Revolutionary novels. In addition to those by Edmonds and James Boyd, see Emma G. Sterne, *Drums of Monmouth* (New York, 1935) and Harvey Chalmers, *Drums Against Frontenac* (New York, 1949).

111 Page 258; see also 182, 196, and especially 381.

112 Cf. Bernard Bailyn, "The Central Themes of the American Revolution: An Interpretation," in Stephen G. Kurtz and James H. Hutson, eds., *Essays on the American Revolution* (New York, 1973), especially 11–15.

113 There were, indeed, some Whigs like Gouverneur Morris who would say, as late as 1774, that "government should be founded on stationary and not revolutionary principles." See Jared Sparks, *The Life of Gouverneur Morris, with Selections from His Correspondence . . .* (Boston, 1832), I, 27.

114 For a remarkably well-balanced recent assessment by a distinguished political scientist, see Alpheus T. Mason, "America's Political Heritage: Revolution and Free Government—A Bicentennial Tribute," *Political Science Quarterly*, XCI (Summer 1976), 197–217, especially 197; and see Harvey C. Mansfield, Jr., "The Right of Revolution," *Daedalus*, CV (Fall 1976), 151–2.

115 Cf. Daniel W. Bjork, "The American Revolution as a 'Screen Memory,' " *South Atlantic Quarterly*, LXXV (Summer 1976), 279; and for

contextual understanding, see Joseph F. Kett, *Rites of Passage: Adolescence in America, 1790 to the Present* (New York, 1977).

CHAPTER SEVEN
Imagination, Tradition, and National Character

1 See pp. 54–6 above, and the Supplement, pp. 260–5, below.
2 Whittier, "The Black Men in the Revolution and War of 1812," *The Writings of John Greenleaf Whittier* (Boston, 1889) VI, 406; Tilden G. Edelstein, *Strange Enthusiasm. A Life of Thomas Wentworth Higginson* (New Haven, Conn., 1968), 162, 189, 215–16.
3 Croly, "Some Really Historical Novels," *The Lamp*, XXVI (July 1903), 511–12.
4 There are two brief studies by literary critics: Arnold Rampersad, *Melville's Israel Potter. A Pilgrimage and Progress* (Bowling Green, Ohio, 1969); and Alexander Keyssar, *Melville's Israel Potter. Reflections on the American Dream* (Cambridge, Mass., 1969). The contemporary impact of *Israel Potter* was negligible. See Hugh W. Hetherington, *Melville's Reviewers: British and American, 1846–1891* (Chapel Hill, N.C., 1961), 239–46.
5 Melville, *Israel Potter: His Fifty Years of Exile* (Warner Books edition: New York, 1974), 22, 23, 29.
6 *Ibid.*, 180, 205, 207, 209–10, 215, 219. For an earlier but obscure domestic counterpart of Israel Potter, see Asa Greene, *The Debtors' Prison: A Tale of a Revolutionary Soldier* (New York, 1834).
7 In the mainstream novels it is not unusual for secondary characters, even patriots, to be killed during the war—their *rite de passage* thereby going uncompleted. But it never happens to a principal figure. See, e.g., John Pendleton Kennedy, *Horse-Shoe Robinson* (1835: New York, 1937), 432–3, 438–9, 450–1, 543.
8 Bellamy, *The Duke of Stockbridge. A Romance of Shays' Rebellion*, edited by Joseph Schiffman (Cambridge, Mass., 1962), 10, 12, 14, 24, 27, 31, 36, 42, 49, 117, 207, 264, 276.
9 *Ibid.*, 51, 140. For the *rite de passage* theme in non-fiction by another, contemporary nay-sayer, see Frederick Douglass, "The Meaning of July Fourth for the Negro," speech at Rochester, New York, July 5, 1852, in Philip S. Foner, ed., *The Life and Writings of Frederick Douglass* (New York, 1950), II, 182–3, 186.
10 *Septimius Felton* (1863) in *The Complete Writings of Nathaniel Hawthorne*, Old Manse edition, XIV (Boston, 1904), 277–8.
11 *Ibid.*, 88, 90, 99–101, 143. The long quotation will be found on pp. 158–9.
12 Q. D. Leavis, "Hawthorne as Poet," *The Sewanee Review*, LIX (Spring

1951), 199. See also Julian Smith, "Coming of Age in America: Young Ben Franklin and Robin Molineux," *American Quarterly*, XVII (Fall 1965), 550–8. The story was composed in 1828–9, published in *The Token* (1832), and then reprinted in *Snow-Image* (1852).

13 *The Complete Short Stories of Nathaniel Hawthorne* (Garden City, N.Y., 1959), 517–30. The most thoughtful commentary from my perspective is by Peter Shaw, "Fathers, Sons, and the Ambiguities of Revolution in 'My Kinsman, Major Molineux,'" *New England Quarterly*, XLIX (December 1976), 559–76, which cites the pertinent literature that appeared during 1951–76 following Q. D. Leavis's seminal essay. I find some of Shaw's points unclear or questionable; but I am in absolute agreement with his conclusion: "By making ritual connections between coming of age and revolution he provides a clear insight into the essential ambiguities of both." Hawthorne "appears to suggest that as the emotions of the actors who overthrew authority were divided, so must be our evaluation of their/our Revolution" (p. 576).

14 In *Selected Essays of William Carlos Williams* (New York, 1954), 38–54. "A great many causes, mainly economic in nature, served to foment the American Revolution" (p. 39).

15 Williams, *In the American Grain* (1925: New York, 1956), 189. See also Alan Holder, "In the American Grain: William Carlos Williams on the American Past," *American Quarterly*, XIX (Fall 1967), 499–515.

16 Woodward, *The Gift of Life. An Autobiography* (New York, 1947), 245, 295–6. He refers to his *George Washington, the Image and the Man* (New York, 1926).

17 Shils, "Tradition," *Comparative Studies in Society and History*, XIII (April 1971), 130.

18 *Ibid.*, 148.

19 Fast, *Literature and Reality* (New York, 1950), 13–14; see also 86.

20 Fast, *The Unvanquished* (New York, 1942), 18, 121, 128.

21 *Ibid.*, 67, 187, 313–15.

22 *Ibid.*, 35, 38–9, 42–3, 46, 48, 53, 61, 69, 70, 73–5, 89, 92, 94–6, 99, 117, 122, 134, 140–1, 155, 157, 260, 266, 300. The quotations appear on 146 and 234.

23 "Old Sam Adams (Three Tales)," in *The Howard Fast Reader. A Collection of Stories and Novels* (New York, 1960), 216, 225–6. For an essay that is critical of Fast's Revolutionary fiction, see Stanley Meisler, "The Lost Dreams of Howard Fast," *The Nation*, CLXXXVIII (May 30, 1959), 498–500.

24 *April Morning* (New York, 1961), 19–20, 26, 40, 46, 56, and 68–9, 71–4, 119, 166, 173–4, 184. The quotations appear on pp. 66 and 107.

25 See *ibid.*, 121, 138.

26 *The Hessian* (New York, 1972), 138, 177, 181, 187, 190, 192. The quo-

tation occurs on pp. 50–1. It is noteworthy that *The Hessian* achieved none of the commercial success enjoyed by *April Morning.*

27 *Ibid.*, 80, 88, 91, 105, 192.

28 *Ibid.*, 27, 34, 38, 138.

29 *Burr, A Novel* (New York, 1973), 6–7, 20, 37, 51, 137–8, 156, 198. We learn that "Burr is not a Burrite," and that Charlie Schuyler is not a "real" Schuyler (131, 136, 378, 389, 392, 417).

30 *Ibid.*, 210. See also 321–2, 405; and the title essay in Gore Vidal, *Homage to Daniel Shays. Collected Essays, 1952–1972* (New York, 1972), 435–7, 443.

31 For a very pertinent comment upon this phenomenon in general, see Shils, "Tradition," pp. 153–4: "The outcome is a compromise between the culture of the centre and the culture of the periphery. The compromise takes the form of modifications of the peripheral traditional beliefs in the direction of the central traditional beliefs. This indeed is what is involved in the cultural aspect, by the incorporation of the periphery into the centre. But in the course of time, the culture of the centre begins to yield in the opposite directions. . . . A few pockets of the 'pure culture' of traditional beliefs—i.e. less modified culture of traditional beliefs—survive. Each pocket or rather its circle of traditionalist spokesmen becomes a *laudator temporis acti.*" (The Latin is from Horace's *Ars Poetica,* line 173. It refers to an old man who is "given to praising the days he spent as a boy," and now reproves the young people several generations removed from his own youth.)

32 See p. 141, above.

33 Wakoski, *The George Washington Poems* (New York, 1967), 31, 42, 54, 56. The cover of this book uses a photograph of a whimsical sculpture (1961–2) by Marisol entitled "The Generals," in which George Washington and Simon Bolívar ride astride the same stolid steed. The original work is in the Albright-Knox Art Gallery in Buffalo, New York.

34 See Sam Hunter, *Rivers* (New York, [1971]), 9, 11, 18, and plates 8, 9, 49, 50. The 1968 paintings belong to the New England Merchants National Bank of Boston. *Crossing the Delaware* is in the Museum of Modern Art, New York.

35 See Elinor Lander Horwitz, *The Bird, the Banner, and Uncle Sam. Images of America in Folk and Popular Art* (Philadelphia, 1976), 72, 161; *The American Flag in the Art of Our Country, June 14–November 14, 1976* (Allentown Art Museum, Pennsylvania, 1976), 68, 71.

36 It was exhibited at the Allan Frumkin Gallery, New York City, in 1975, and at the Chicago Art Institute in 1976. On Christmas night, 1972, 58 men wearing uniforms of the Continental army reenacted the event right at Washington Crossing, Pennsylvania, in front of

14,000 spectators. On Christmas night, 1976, 160 men did so once again upon command from St. John Terrell, a theatrical producer: "Gentlemen, to the boats." *The New York Times*, Dec. 26, 1972; Dec. 26, 1976.

37 *Newsweek* (July 4, 1976), 20–1. In 1964 Lowell prepared a stage version of "My Kinsman, Major Molineux," which was revived in New York for the Bicentennial in 1976. The play's message is a bit more obscure even than Hawthorne's story; but at one point a man in periwig proclaims, "I'm on the side of youth," and subsequently a clergyman declares that eighteen-year-old Robin "is just a boy." See Lowell, *The Old Glory* (New York, 1965), 65, 73, 108.

38 For an interaction between then and now that verges upon parapsychology, see Barbara Michaels, *Patriot's Dream* (New York, 1976). For an earlier exploration of the Revolution in science fiction, see Avram Davidson, "I Do Not Hear You, Sir," in Daniel Roselle, ed., *Transformations II. Understanding American History Through Science Fiction* (Fawcett Crest Book: Greenwich, Conn., 1974), 36–47. And for a mystical new trilogy with space-time warps, see Jean Anne Bartlett, *Aaron Burr Gothic* (1977: Popular Library edition, New York), a trilogy.

39 See especially MacKinlay Kantor, *Valley Forge* (New York, 1975), 110, 125, 134, 144, 265; Richard F. Snow, *Freelon Starbird* (Boston, 1976), 2, 207–9; William Eastlake, *The Long Naked Descent into Boston* (New York, 1977).

40 Mildred and Katherine Davis, *Lucifer Land* (New York, 1977), 278–9, 281, 289, 298, 300. See also Harriette Simpson Arnow, *The Kentucky Trace. A Novel of the American Revolution* (New York, 1974), 8, 71, 174.

41 Davis, *Lucifer Land*, 34–5, 42, 63–4, 73, 96, 120, 145–6, 221, 224.

42 *Ibid.*, 127, 168, 175–6, 178, 187, 196–7, 203, 206, 208, 295, 307, 315, 320, 323, 326. The complicated dénouement in *Lucifer Land* (304–8) is startlingly similar to that of Cooper's *Lionel Lincoln; or, The Leaguer of Boston* (Boston, n.d.), especially 402–3, 417.

43 See Davis, *Lucifer Land*, 77, 196; Thomas Fleming, *Liberty Tavern* (Garden City, N.Y., 1976), 74–5, 330, 332–4, 362–3, 374–5, 377–8; and John Jakes, *The Bastard* (New York, 1974), 387–8; Arnow, *The Kentucky Trace*, 149.

44 See Edmonds, *Drums Along the Mohawk* (Boston, 1936), 489, 503, 516–17, 520–1, 523, 590–1; Roberts, *Oliver Wiswell* (New York, 1940), chs. 67–74.

45 Jakes, *The Rebels* (New York, 1975), 112–16, 258–65, 398–407.

46 "Paper Back Talk," *The New York Times Book Review*, Sept. 7, 1975, and Jan. 25, 1976; letter from John Jakes to the author, May 21, 1976.

47 *The Bastard*, 331, 400, 433, 550, 628; *The Rebels*, 258.

48 Michaels, *Patriot's Dream*, 100–1, and chs. 22–3.

49 Peck, *Hang for Treason* (Garden City, N.Y., 1976), 17, 159. For the *rite*

de passage theme throughout this novel, see 12, 50, 55, 66–70, 78, 108, 110–12, 124, 132–4, 142, 195, 200. See also Kantor, *Valley Forge*, 30, 73. Peck's newest Revolutionary novel is *The King's Iron* (Boston, 1977), which takes place in 1776 between Fort Ticonderoga and Boston.

50 Fleming, *Liberty Tavern*, 81. See also 76, 83, 129, 137, 148–9, 170–1, 218, 385; and see Michaels, *Patriot's Dream*, 198–9, 238–9, 247, 339; Snow, *Freelon Starbird*, 10; Peck, *Hang for Treason*, 26, 61, 65, 112, 200; and Wakoski, *George Washington Poems*, 11, 36–7.

51 See Fleming, *Liberty Tavern*, 269–70, 349, 480–1, 486. This novel is unusual and creative, by the way, in having as its main character a middle-aged man (Jonathan Gifford is forty-seven in 1778) who undergoes both a political and an emotional transformation during the course of the Revolutionary War. Cf. Chapter Six, p. 194, above.

52 Peck, *Hang for Treason*, 23; Michaels, *Patriot's Dream*, 145. Peck makes the point throughout his novel that Whigs and royalists could be equally brutal. Peck also provides the most accurate and realistic rendering of Ethan Allen's character to be found in any of the novels in which Allen figures; see especially 112.

53 Davis, *Lucifer Land*, 269. See also Archibald MacLeish, *The Great American Fourth of July Parade. A Verse Play for Radio* (Pittsburgh, 1975), 13, 16, 33, 45.

54 Fleming, *Liberty Tavern*, 13. For fresh attempts at historical candor in current children's literature, see Judith Sloan Hoberman, "Recycling the Red, White, and Blue: The Bicentennial and Books for Children," *Harvard Educational Review*, XLVI (August 1976), 473–6; Elizabeth M. Graves, "Children's Books for the Bicentennial," *Commonweal*, CIII (Nov. 19, 1976), 758–9.

55 Michener, "A Slice of Cake in Every Hamlet," *The New York Times*, April 5, 1975. Dickey's poem was published in *ibid.*, Jan. 21, 1977.

56 MacLeish, *Fourth of July Parade*, 3, 11, 27–8, 50. The quotations are on pp. 20–1, 36. For an earlier poem about Jefferson by MacLeish, entitled "Brave New World," see Francis C. Rosenberger, ed., *Jefferson Reader* (New York, 1953), 228–30.

57 Public Law 89–491, 89th Congress, Joint Resolution 162. For its legislative history, see House Report No. 1672 accompanying H. J. Res. 903; Senate Report No. 1317; and *Congressional Record*, CXII, June 28–29, 1966.

58 See *The New York Times*, Feb. 9 and July 4, 1973; April 13 and June 16, 1974; Jan. 31 and July 20, 1975.

59 See the Ithaca, New York, *Journal*, Jan. 13, 1973; *The New York Times*, Nov. 4, 1973, and Jan. 4, 1974; New York *Amsterdam News*, Summer 1976 Special Bicentennial Edition ["Black Bicentennial"]; and Jesse Lemisch, "Bicentennial Schlock," *The New Republic*, CLXXV (Nov. 6, 1976), 21–3.

60 *Harper's Weekly*, XXV (Oct. 29, 1881), 730.

61 [Levi D. Slamm], *The Injustice of the Tariff on Protective Principles. The Plebeian Tracts, No. 2* (New York, 1844), 6.

62 See Simms's letter to the Charleston *Mercury*, Sept. 15, 1855, in Mary C. Simms Oliphant, *et al.*, eds., *The Letters of William Gilmore Simms* (Columbia, S.C., 1952–6), III, 394–8; Fletcher, *Pay, Pack, and Follow. The Story of My Life* (New York, 1959), 238, 279. See also Michaels, *Patriot's Dream*, 171.

63 Webster, "An Address Delivered at the Laying of the Corner-Stone of the Bunker Hill Monument, June 17th, 1825," in *A Memorial of the American Patriots Who Fell at the Battle of Bunker Hill, June 17, 1775 . . .* (4th ed.: Boston, 1896), 200.

64 Simms, *The Partisan* (1835: New York, 1882), vii. Oliver Wiswell keeps a journal throughout the war because he plans to write a history of the Revolution eventually. Throughout the novel, consequently, Kenneth Roberts keeps up a running commentary on the lessons of history and writing history properly. See *Oliver Wiswell* (New York, 1940), 3, 35–6, 55, 59, 118–19, 121, 391, 431, 473, 655.

65 See Adams to Jefferson, May 29, 1818, in Charles Francis Adams, ed., *The Works of John Adams* (Boston, 1856), X, 313.

66 John Durand, *The Life and Times of A. B. Durand* (New York, 1894), 120–1. One of the contemporary criticisms that most irritated Trumbull involved the question of literal accuracy: whether figures appeared in a picture who should not have been there, or whether others were missing who had been present historically. See Gordon Hendricks, "Durand, Maverick and the *Declaration*," *The American Art Journal*, III (Spring 1971), 61.

67 William H. Gerdts, *American Neo-Classic Sculpture: The Marble Resurrection* (New York, 1973), 101. When Houdon came to America in 1785 to prepare a life statue, Jefferson and others agreed that "an Exact *Copy*" of Washington's figure and features should be the major objective. See J. Meredith Neil, *Toward a National Taste. America's Quest for Aesthetic Independence* (Honolulu, 1975), 100.

68 Cooper, *Lionel Lincoln*, vii, viii, xi; Charles H. Bohner, *John Pendleton Kennedy: Gentleman from Baltimore* (Baltimore, Md., 1961), 90–1. The reasons why Cooper's quest for authenticity made *Lionel Lincoln* an inferior novel are explained by Jeffrey Steinbrink in "Cooper's Romance of the Revolution: *Lionel Lincoln* and the Lessons of Failure," *Early American Literature*, XI (Winter 1976–7), 340.

69 See Samuel Blaine Shirk, *The Characterization of George Washington in American Plays Since 1875* (Philadelphia, 1949), 86, 90, 94; Williams, *In the American Grain* (1925: New York, 1956), especially 144–53, 158–73; William Vasse, "American History and the Cantos," *The Pound News-*

letter, no. 5 (January 1955), 13–19; Frederick K. Sanders, *John Adams Speaking: Pound's Sources for the Adams Cantos* (Orono, Me., [1975]); and "The Jefferson-Adams Letters as a Shrine and a Monument" (1937), in Pound, *Impact: Essays on Ignorance and the Decline of American Civilization*, edited by Noel Stock (Chicago, 1960), 167, 174.

70 Fletcher, *Pay, Pack, and Follow*, 207, 277. See also F. Van Wyck Mason, ed., *The Fighting American* (Garden City, N.Y., 1943), xx; the Washington, D.C., *Star-News*, Sept. 27, 1973, C-4; and Henry James, *The American Scene* (1907: New York, 1967), 33, 51, 69, 246–7, 453.

71 "Recent American Novels," *North American Review*, XXI (July 1825), 84–5. See also the review of William A. Caruthers, *The Cavaliers of Virginia* in *Southern Literary Messenger*, I (March 1835), 385–6; and Donald A. Ringe, "The American Revolution in American Romance," *American Literature*, XLIX (November 1977), 354–55.

72 See *Letters of Simms*, IV, 148–50; V, 324; C. Hugh Holman, "William Gilmore Simms' Picture of the Revolution as a Civil Conflict," *The Journal of Southern History*, XV (November 1949), 441–2, 444, 461; Churchill, *The Crossing* (New York, 1904), 550; and see Chapter Two above, note 96.

73 Croly, "Some Really Historical Novels," *The Lamp*, XXVI (July 1903), 512. Examples of the quest for authenticity in historical restoration projects (during the later nineteenth century) pertaining to the Revolution may be found in Charles B. Hosmer, Jr., *Presence of the Past. A History of the Preservation Movement in the United States Before Williamsburg* (New York, 1965), 78–85.

74 Vidal, *Burr*, 6–7, and 20, 37, 51, 137–8, 156, 198. See also Roberts, *Rabble in Arms* (New York, 1933), 1; Roberts, *Oliver Wiswell*, 3, 483, 486; Roberts to Chilson Leonard, April 20, 1937, Roberts Papers, the Phillips Exeter Academy Library; Arthur B. Tourtellot, "History and the Historical Novel: Where Fact and Fancy Meet and Part," *Saturday Review of Literature*, XXII (Aug. 24, 1940), 3–4, 16; Fleming, *Liberty Tavern*, pp. 13 and 286, where the narrator declares in 1826: "I have promised to tell the whole truth about our supposed Golden Age."

75 Joseph H. Choate to Ford, March 28, 1900, Paul Leicester Ford Papers, Collection of American Literature, The Beinecke Rare Book and Manuscript Library, Yale University.

76 James E. Breslin, *William Carlos Williams. An American Artist* (New York, 1970), 89. On p. 118 Breslin refers to Williams's "descent to particulars for renewal."

77 Christopher Collier, "Johnny and Sam: Old and New Approaches to the American Revolution," *The Horn Book Magazine*, LII (April 1976), 135–6.

78 The earliest review of Melville's *Israel Potter* (March 12, 1855) referred to it as "this veritable history, which is a mixture of fun, gravity, ro-

mance and reality." Quoted in Hetherington, *Melville's Reviewers*, 241. The reviewer was most likely William Ellery Channing, Jr.

79 Cooper, *The Spy. A Tale of the Neutral Ground* (1821: Dolphin Books edition, Garden City, N.Y., n.d.), 5. For other statements of concern about national character in this period, and particularly the Revolution's impact upon character, see also Cooper, *Lionel Lincoln*, 121–2, 136, 152, 161, 386, 402; Bohner, *John Pendleton Kennedy*, 94; Catharine Maria Sedgwick, *The Linwoods; or, "Sixty Years Since" in America* (New York, 1835), I, 65, 95–6, 101–2, 217; II, 68, 82; and Lydia Maria Child, *The Rebels; or, Boston Before the Revolution* (1825: Boston, 1850), 139, 142–5, 281, 283.

80 Thompson, *Alice of Old Vincennes* (Indianapolis, Ind., 1900), 303. See also Sarah Orne Jewett, *The Tory Lover* (Boston, 1901), 165, 175, 192, 194, 356, 374, 399, and especially ch. 25, "A Man's Character." One of the primary points of *The Conqueror* (New York, 1902), by Gertrude Atherton, is that Alexander Hamilton epitomized much that was best in the national character.

81 Sandburg, *Remembrance Rock* (New York, 1948), 551. See also 337, 373–4, 518; and Inglis Fletcher, *Raleigh's Eden* (1940: Bantam paperback edition, New York, 1970), 371, 380.

82 *Rules and Regulations of the Society for Political Inquiries* (Philadelphia, 1787), 1; Fenno, "National Character," *American Museum*, VI (November 1789), 392 (the page is misnumbered, and is actually 391).

83 See the quotations from 1812 in Michael Paul Rogin, *Fathers and Children: Andrew Jackson and the Subjugation of the American Indian* (New York, 1975), 140, 147; and from 1828 in Charles Warren, *Odd Byways in American History* (Cambridge, Mass., 1942), 183.

84 Robert C. Winthrop, *Oration Delivered Before the City Council and Citizens of Boston . . . July 4, 1876* (Boston, 1876), 74.

85 John Quincy Adams to Abigail Adams, May 7, 1799, in Worthington C. Ford, ed., *Writings of John Quincy Adams* (New York, 1913), II, 418; Morris, *An Oration Delivered July 5th, 1813, Before the Washington Benevolent Society of the City of New-York . . .* (New York, 1813), 5; [William Tudor?] in *North American Review*, series 2, VI (July 1822), 21–2; Paulding, *The Old Continental; or, The Price of Liberty* (1846: New York, 1851), I, 10 (see also 34, 62, 77, 152, 189–90).

86 Dwight, *Travels in New England and New York*, edited by Barbara M. Solomon (Cambridge, Mass., 1969), IV, 184–5; see also 186, 211. For de Tocqueville's explanation of American national character resulting from regional interpenetration, see J. P. Mayer, ed., *Democracy in America* (Anchor edition: Garden City, N.Y., 1969), I, 385, 404.

87 The two most useful modern authorities are William R. Taylor, *Cavalier and Yankee: The Old South and American National Character* (New York, 1961); and Burton J. Bledstein, *The Culture of Professionalism. The*

Middle Class and the Development of Higher Education in America (New York, 1976), ch. 4, "Character."

88 Warren, *History of the Rise, Progress and Termination of the American Revolution* (Boston, 1805), I, 2; III, 400; Henry W. Warner, *Inquiry into the Moral and Religious Character of the American Government* (New York, 1838); and Martin Duberman, *James Russell Lowell* (Boston, 1966), xx–i.

89 Cunningham to Lossing, Nov. 17, 1859, Lossing Papers, box 1, Huntington Library.

90 Sedgwick, *The Linwoods,* I, 52–3; II, 261. See also Cooper, *The Spy,* ch. 35; and "American Biography," in *American Quarterly Review,* I (March 1827), 35: "Our revolution shines in contrast with all others of modern times, not only in the dignity and value of its tenor and results, but in the purity and simplicity of the lives and characters of its leading, or most conspicuous agents."

91 Emerson, *Nature, Addresses, and Lectures* (Boston, 1884), 99; Willard is quoted in Carl Bode, *The Anatomy of American Popular Culture, 1840–1861* (Berkeley, Calif., 1959), 237. See also Edward Everett, *An Oration Delivered at Cambridge on the Fiftieth Anniversary of the Declaration of Independence* (Boston, 1826), 30.

92 See John L. Thomas, "Romantic Reform in America, 1815–1865," *American Quarterly,* XVII (Winter 1965), 656–7, 660. Cf. Kathryn Kish Sklar, *Catharine Beecher, A Study in American Domesticity* (New Haven, Conn., 1973), 79, 93, 95, 101, 129.

93 See Theodore Roosevelt, "Character and Success," *The Outlook,* LXIV (March 31, 1900), 725–7; Henry James, *The American Scene,* 12; and Bledstein, *The Culture of Professionalism,* ch. 4.

94 See Peter Shaw, *The Character of John Adams* (Chapel Hill, N.C., 1976), 279; George Bancroft, "An Incident in the Life of John Adams," *The Century Magazine,* XXXIV (July 1887), 434; Lewis Leary, *Soundings: Some Early American Writers* (Athens, Ga., 1975), 271, 276.

95 Adams to Mercy Otis Warren, Jan. 8, 1776, in *Warren-Adams Letters,* I (1743–1777), Massachusetts Historical Society *Collections,* LXXII (Boston, 1917), 202.

96 [William Tudor], "Battle of Bunker Hill," *North American Review,* VII (July 1818), 258. See also *American Military Biography; Containing the Lives and Characters of the Officers of the Revolution, Who Were Most Distinguished in Achieving Our National Independence* (Cincinnati, Ohio, 1834).

97 See John Adams to Thomas Jefferson, July [3], 1813, in Lester J. Cappon, ed., *The Adams-Jefferson Letters* (Chapel Hill, N.C., 1959), II, 349–50; Merrill D. Peterson, *The Jefferson Image in the American Mind* (New York, 1960), 130–9, 158, 413–14, 416–17, 478–9; and Lincoln to Henry L. Pierce, April 6, 1859, in Roy P. Basler, ed., *The Collected Works of Abraham Lincoln* (New Brunswick, N.J., 1953), III, 375–6.

98 Webster, *Address Delivered at Bunker Hill, June 17, 1843 . . .* (Boston, 1843), 35–7; William A. Bryan, *George Washington in American Literature, 1775–1865* (New York, 1952), 18, 25, 29–31, 38, 42–3, 45, 49–50, 56, 62–3, 67, 69, 73, 77 n., 78, 113, 191, 201, 233; Edgar P. Richardson, "A Penetrating Characterization of Washington by John Trumbull," *Winterthur Portfolio,* III (1967), 1–23.

99 Simms to George Bancroft, Jan. 15, 1858, *The Letters of Simms,* IV, 5; Simms, *Views and Reviews in American Literature, History and Fiction,* first series, edited by C. Hugh Holman (Cambridge, Mass., 1962), 72.

100 See George Washington Greene, *Historical View of the American Revolution* (5th ed.: Boston, 1876), vii; Robert H. Schauffler, ed., *Washington's Birthday* (New York, 1932), 143–5, 217, 239–46; *History of the George Washington Bicentennial Celebration* (Washington, D.C., 1932), I, part 2, 32–6; MacKaye, *Washington. The Man Who Made Us* (New York, 1919); Green, *Dramatic Heritage* (New York, 1953), 62; and Masters, *Poems of People* (New York, 1936), 18–19.

101 Simms, *Views and Reviews in American Literature, History and Fiction,* 81; see also *ibid.,* 58, and Simms, "Works of Imagination," *The Magnolia,* n.s., I (July 1842), 51–2.

102 Edward F. Hayward, "Some Romances of the Revolution," *The Atlantic Monthly,* LXIV (November 1889), 629. See also William F. Allen, "Historical Fiction," in David B. Frankenburger, *et al.,* eds., *Essays and Monographs* (Boston, 1890), 120.

103 Simms to Henry Carey Baird, March 4 [1853], Dec. 17, 1853, Oct. 14, 1855, *Letters of Simms,* III, 226, 267, 406; Roberts, *Rabble in Arms* (New York, 1933), 118, 126, 178–80; Matthew C. O'Brien, "John Esten Cooke, George Washington, and the Virginia Cavaliers," *Virginia Magazine of History and Biography,* LXXXIV (July 1976), 261.

104 See Lillian B. Miller, "Paintings, Sculpture, and the National Character," *The Journal of American History,* LIII (March 1967), 696–707; Lucille W. Grindhammer, *Art and the Public: The Democratization of the Fine Arts in the United States, 1830–1860* (Stuttgart, 1975), 25.

105 See, e.g., John Pendleton Kennedy, *Horse-Shoe Robinson* (1835: New York, 1937), 8–9, 11, 340–1; Williams, *In the American Grain,* 130–57, 188–207; Sidney Kingsley, *The Patriots* (New York, 1943), 176; Fast, "Old Sam Adams," 238.

106 Hale, *Sketches of American Character* (Boston, 1829), 27–8.

107 Child, *The Rebels,* 139, 142–3.

108 Fletcher, *Raleigh's Eden,* 371, 380; Sandburg, *Remembrance Rock,* 337, 374, 518, 551.

109 Radcliffe-Brown, *The Andaman Islanders* (Cambridge, 1933), 284–5.

110 See James P. Holcombe, *Sketches of the Political Issues and Controversies of the Revolution: A Discourse Delivered Before the Virginia Historical So-*

ciety . . . January 17, 1856 (Richmond, Va., 1856), 4–5; *The Monthly Anthology and Boston Review*, I (October 1804), 554; Josiah Royce, *California . . . A Study of American Character* (1886: Santa Barbara, Calif., 1970), 3–4, 393–4.

111 See Jakes, *The Bastard*, 224; Jakes, *The Rebels*, 187, 196, 328–9, 339; Kantor, *Valley Forge*, 43; Peck, *Hang for Treason*, 64.

112 Fleming, *Liberty Tavern*, 382, 501. See also 338, 341–2, 488.

113 Cooper, *Satanstoe* (1845: Lincoln, Nebr., 1962), 55; E. Digby Baltzell, "The Protestant Establishment Revisited," *The American Scholar*, XLV (Autumn 1976), 511.

114 In addition to Alex Haley's *Roots* (New York, 1976), see also Irving Howe, *World of Our Fathers* (New York, 1976); William A. Owens, *A Fair and Happy Land* (New York, 1975); Nicholas P. Hardeman, *Wilderness Calling: The Hardeman Family in the American Westward Movement, 1750–1900* (Knoxville, Tenn., 1976); Dorothy Gallagher, *Hannah's Daughters: Six Generations of an American Family* (New York, 1977); Willard Espy, *Oysterville: Roads to Grandpa's Village* (New York, 1977); and *The New York Times Book Review*, Dec. 26, 1976, 21.

NOTES TO THE CODA

The Civil War, the Revolution, and American Culture

115 For affirmations of this point of view from the diverse perspectives of Edmund S. Morgan, Sidney E. Mead, Martin E. Marty, and Catherine L. Albanese, see Morgan, *The Challenge of the American Revolution* (New York, 1976), xi; and Albanese, *Sons of the Fathers. The Civil Religion of the American Revolution* (Philadelphia, 1976), viii–ix. See also Henry James, *The American Scene*, 288, where the point is made that nowhere in the United States, except for Mount Vernon and Independence Hall, "does our historic past so enjoy the felicity of an 'important' concrete illustration."

116 Aaron, *The Unwritten War. American Writers and the Civil War* (New York, 1973), xix.

117 *Ibid.*, xv–vii, xviii, 309, 334, 339; Handlin, "The Civil War as Symbol and as Actuality," *The Massachusetts Review*, III (Autumn 1961), 133–43.

118 Handlin, "The Civil War as Symbol and as Actuality," 143.

119 Aaron, *The Unwritten War*, 91–2, 330, 332. See also Edmund Wilson, *Patriotic Gore. Studies in the Literature of the American Civil War* (New York, 1962); Robert A. Lively, *Fiction Fights the Civil War. An Unfinished Chapter in the Literary History of the American People* (Chapel Hill, N.C., 1957).

120 See Cruce Stark, "Brothers at/in War: One Phase of Post-Civil War

Reconciliation," *The Canadian Review of American Studies,* VI (Fall 1975), 178–80.

121 See Roy P. Basler, *The Lincoln Legend. A Study in Changing Conceptions* (Boston, 1935); Thomas L. Connelly, *The Marble Man. Robert E. Lee and His Image in American Society* (New York, 1977); and Frank E. Vandiver, "Jefferson Davis—Leader Without Legend," *The Journal of Southern History,* XLIII (February 1977), 3–18.

122 See Robert G. Hartje, *Bicentennial USA. Pathways to Celebration* (Nashville, Tenn., 1973), ch. 4, "The Civil War Centennial."

INDEX